Predictive Modeling Applications in Actuarial Science

Volume II: Case Studies in Insurance

Predictive modeling uses data to forecast future events. It exploits relationships between explanatory variables and the predicted variables from past occurrences to predict future outcomes. Forecasting financial events is a core skill that actuaries routinely apply in insurance and other risk-management applications. *Predictive Modeling Applications in Actuarial Science* emphasizes lifelong learning by developing tools in an insurance context, providing the relevant actuarial applications, and introducing advanced statistical techniques that can be used to gain a competitive advantage in situations with complex data.

Volume II examines applications of predictive modeling. Where Volume I developed the foundations of predictive modeling, Volume II explores practical uses for techniques, focusing especially on property and casualty insurance. Readers are exposed to a variety of techniques in concrete, real-life contexts that demonstrate their value, and the overall value of predictive modeling, for seasoned practicing analysts as well as those just starting out.

Edward W. (Jed) Frees is the Hickman-Larson Chair of Actuarial Science at the University of Wisconsin–Madison. He received his PhD in mathematical statistics in 1983 from the University of North Carolina at Chapel Hill and is a Fellow of both the Society of Actuaries (SoA) and the American Statistical Association (the only Fellow of both organizations). Regarding his research, Professor Frees has won several awards for the quality of his work, including the Halmstad Prize for best paper published in the actuarial literature (four times).

Glenn Meyers, PhD, FCAS, MAAA, CERA, retired from ISO at the end of 2011 after a 37-year career as an actuary. He holds a BS in mathematics and physics from Alma College, an MA in mathematics from Oakland University, and a PhD in mathematics from SUNY at Albany. A frequent speaker at Casualty Actuarial Society (CAS) meetings, he has served, and continues to serve, the CAS and the International Actuarial Association on various research and education committees. He has also served on the CAS Board of Directors. He has several published articles in the *Proceedings of the Casualty Actuarial Society*, *Variance*, and *Actuarial Review*. His research contributions have been recognized by the CAS through his being a three-time winner of the Woodward-Fondiller Prize; a two-time winner of the Dorweiler Prize; and a winner of the DFA Prize, the Reserves Prize, the Matthew Rodermund Service Award, and the Michelbacher Significant Achievement Award. In retirement, he still spends some of his time on his continuing passion for actuarial research.

Richard A. Derrig is founder and principal of OPAL Consulting LLC, which is a firm that provides research and regulatory support to property casualty insurance clients. Primary areas of expertise include financial pricing models, database and data-mining design, fraud detection planning and implementation, and expert testimony for regulation and litigation purposes.

INTERNATIONAL SERIES ON ACTUARIAL SCIENCE

The *International Series on Actuarial Science*, published by Cambridge University Press in conjunction with the Institute and Faculty of Actuaries, contains textbooks for students taking courses in or related to actuarial science, as well as more advanced works designed for continuing professional development or for describing and synthesizing research. The series is a vehicle for publishing books that reflect changes and developments in the curriculum, that encourage the introduction of courses on actuarial science in universities, and that show how actuarial science can be used in all areas where there is long-term financial risk.

A complete list of books in the series can be found at www.cambridge.org/statistics. Recent titles include the following:

PREDICTIVE MODELING APPLICATIONS IN ACTUARIAL SCIENCE

Volume II: Case Studies in Insurance

EDWARD W. FREES

University of Wisconsin–Madison

GLENN MEYERS

RICHARD A. DERRIG

OPAL Consulting LLC

CAMBRIDGE
UNIVERSITY PRESS

CAMBRIDGE
UNIVERSITY PRESS

32 Avenue of the Americas, New York, NY 10013

Cambridge University Press is part of the University of Cambridge.

It furthers the University's mission by disseminating knowledge in the pursuit of education, learning, and research at the highest international levels of excellence.

www.cambridge.org
Information on this title: www.cambridge.org/9781107029880

© Cambridge University Press 2016

First published 2016

Printed in the United States of America by Sheridan Books, Inc.

A catalogue record for this publication is available from the British Library.

ISBN 978-1-107-02988-0 Hardback

Contents

Contributors

Ernesto Schirmacher is Latin America's regional actuary for Liberty International, part of Liberty Mutual Insurance. He is a Fellow of the Society of Actuaries, an affiliate member of the Casualty Actuarial Society, and a member of the American Academy of Actuaries. He has worked in both direct and reinsurance companies in a variety of projects, such as asbestos reserving, economic capital modeling, and ratemaking using generalized linear models and other statistical techniques.

Dan Tevet is a director of data science at Liberty Mutual Insurance in Boston, where he leads a team of actuarial analysts and data scientists on the construction and implementation of predictive modeling and engineering solutions for the Distribution organization. Previously, he worked on product analytics for the personal property department at Liberty Mutual, and before that, he was at ISO in Jersey City, New Jersey, in the predictive modeling and specialty commercial lines divisions. He is a Fellow of the Casualty Actuarial Society and an active volunteer for the CAS.

Greg Taylor holds an honorary professorial position in risk and actuarial studies at the University of New South Wales. He previously spent 44 years in commercial actuarial practice and 8 years as an actuarial academic. He has published two books on loss reserving and numerous other articles in mathematics, statistics, and actuarial science. He is an officer of the Order of Australia and holds a Gold Medal from the Australian Actuaries Institute and a Silver Medal from the United Kingdom Institute and Faculty of Actuaries.

James Sullivan is a commercial pricing actuary specialising in long tailed lines. He is a Fellow of the Institute of Actuaries Australia and was a co-op scholar at the University of New South Wales. His research interests are focused on using generalized linear modeling and gradient boosting algorithms for pricing alternative investments opportunities.

Peng Shi is an assistant professor of actuarial science, risk management, and insurance at the University of Wisconsin–Madison. He is an associate of the Society of Actuaries. His research interests are predictive modeling, multivariate regression and dependence models, longitudinal data, and asymmetric information in insurance.

James Guszcza is the U.S. predictive analytics lead for Deloitte Consulting's Actuarial, Risk, and Advanced Analytics practice. He is a Fellow of the Casualty Actuarial Society and a past faculty member in the Department of Actuarial Science, Risk Management, and Insurance at the University of Wisconsin–Madison.

Mona Salah Ahmed Hammad, ASA, PhD, is assistant professor of the Mathematics and Insurance department, Faculty of Commerce, Cairo University, Egypt. Her current research includes ratemaking, health insurance, and multilevel linear modeling. She has acted as an actuarial advisor to the Egyptian Financial Supervisory Authority (EFSA) and was recently awarded second place for best paper in the nonlife track in the 30th International Congress of Actuaries (ICA2014).

Galal Abdel Haleim Harby, PhD, is currently vice-president of Al Ahram Canadian University in Egypt, where he has also acted as dean of the School of Business Administration since 2008. His permanent affiliation is as a professor of insurance in the Math and Insurance department, Faculty of Commerce, Cairo University, Egypt. He has published several books and papers, has served as an insurance advisor to the Egyptian Financial Supervisory Authority (EFSA), and is a winner of Cairo University's encouraging prize for scientific research in property insurance.

Ji Yao, FIA, CERA, is a lecturer in actuarial science at the University of Kent and an actuarial consultant. He has more than 10 years of experience in general insurance market on pricing, reserving, and capital modeling. His research interests include predictive modeling, stochastic claim reserving, data mining, and, more recently, Big Data.

Louise Francis, FCAS, MAAA, is the consulting principal and founder of Francis Analytics and Actuarial Data Mining Inc., where she leads reserving, pricing, predictive modeling, simulation, and related actuarial projects and engagements. Ms. Francis is a former VP research for the Casualty Actuarial Society (CAS) and has been involved in a number of CAS initiatives, including estimating reserve variability, improving data quality, and reviewing papers for the CAS journal *Variance*. She presents frequently on data mining-related topics and is a five-time winner of the CAS's Data Management and Information call paper program.

Glenn Meyers, FCAS, MAAA, CERA, PhD, recently retired after a 37-year actuarial career that spanned both industry and academic employment. For his last 23 years of working, he was employed by ISO as a research actuary. He has received numerous awards for his publications from the Casualty Actuarial Society that include being the first recipient of the Michaelbacher Significant Achievement Award, which "recognizes a person or persons who have significantly and fundamentally advanced casualty actuarial science."

Luyang Fu, PhD, FCAS, is the department head of Predictive Analytics at Cincinnati Insurance Companies, where he leads the development of predictive models to support all business units, including personal line, commercial line, claims, and marketing. Prior to joining Cincinnati Insurance, he led the development of personal line pricing models, commercial line underwriting models, and enterprise risk models at State Auto Insurance Companies. He holds a master's degree in finance and a doctorate in agricultural and consumer economics from the University of Illinois at Urbana-Champaign.

Xianfang Liu, PhD, FCAS, is an actuary in the Predictive Analytics department at Cincinnati Insurance Companies, leading the development of commercial property and workers' compensation underwriting and pricing models. He has a PhD in mathematics from East China Normal University and a master's degree in computer science from Johns Hopkins University.

Claudine Modlin is a Fellow of the Casualty Actuarial Society and the leader of Willis Towers Watson's property/casualty pricing and product management team in the Americas. Her primary areas of expertise are predictive analytics and insurance pricing. Claudine has a bachelor's degree in mathematics from Bradley University, and prior to joining Willis Towers Watson in 2002, she was employed as an actuary at Allstate Insurance Company and AIG.

Mohamad A. Hindawi is currently a vice president of quantitative research and analytics at Allstate Insurance Company. Prior to that, he was a senior consultant with Towers Watson. His areas of expertise include predictive modeling and product management. He is a Fellow of the Casualty Actuarial Society and received his PhD in mathematics from the University of Pennsylvania.

Jim Weiss is the director of analytic solutions at ISO, a Verisk Analytics company. He is coauthor of "Beginner's Roadmap to Working with Driving Behavior Data," which was awarded the 2012 Casualty Actuarial Society (CAS) Management Data and Information Prize. He is a Fellow of CAS, a member of the American Academy of Actuaries, and a Chartered Property Casualty Underwriter.

Udi Makov is the head of actuarial research for Telematics at Verisk Insurance Solutions. He's also the director of the actuarial research center at the University of Haifa, where he specializes in statistical methods in insurance, Bayesian statistics, and mixture models. Dr. Makov holds a PhD in mathematical statistics from the University of London.

Preface

In January 1983, the North American actuarial education societies (the Society of Actuaries and the Casualty Actuarial Society) announced that a course based on regression and time series would be part of their basic educational requirements. Since that announcement, a generation of actuaries has been trained in these fundamental applied statistical tools. This two-set volume builds on this training by developing the fundamentals of predictive modeling and providing corresponding applications in actuarial science, risk management, and insurance.

The series is written for practicing actuaries who wish to get a refresher on modern-day data-mining techniques and predictive modeling. Almost all of the international actuarial organizations now require continuing education of their members. Thus, in addition to responding to competitive pressures, actuaries will need materials like these books for their own continuing education. Moreover, it is anticipated that these books could be used for seminars that are held for practicing actuaries who wish to get professional accreditation (known as VEE, or validated by educational experience).

Volume I lays out the foundations of predictive modeling. Beginning with reviews of regression and time series methods, this book provides step-by-step introductions to advanced predictive modeling techniques that are particularly useful in actuarial practice. Readers will gain expertise in several statistical topics, including generalized linear modeling and the analysis of longitudinal, two-part (frequency/severity) and fat-tailed data. Thus, although the audience is primarily professional actuaries, the book exhibits a "textbook" approach, and so this volume will also be useful for continuing professional development.

An international author team (seven countries, three continents) developed Volume I, published in 2014. You can more learn more about Volume I at

http://research.bus.wisc.edu/PredModelActuaries

Volume II examines applications of predictive models, focusing on property and casualty insurance, primarily through the use of case studies. Case studies provide a learning experience that is closer to real-world actuarial work than can be provided by traditional self-study or lecture/work settings. They can integrate several analysis techniques or, alternatively, can demonstrate that a technique normally used in one practice area could have value in another area. Readers can learn that there is no unique correct answer. Practicing actuaries can be exposed to a variety of techniques in contexts that demonstrates their value. Academic actuaries and students see that there are valid applications for the theoretical material presented in Volume I. As with Volume I, we have extensive sample data and statistical code on the series website so that readers can learn by doing.

The first three chapters of Volume II focus on applications of the generalized linear model (GLM), arguably the workhorse of predictive modeling in actuarial applications. Chapter 1, by Ernesto Schirmacher, gives an overview of the use of GLMs in pricing strategy, focusing on private passenger automobile. Dan Tevet's Chapter 2 reinforces this discussion by examining insurance for motorcycles, emphasizing the comparison between frequency-severity and pure premium models. In Chapter 3, Greg Taylor and James Sullivan demonstrate how to use GLM techniques in loss reserving. Although the two books in the series are written independently, readers with access to the first book will appreciate these three chapters more deeply after reviewing the foundations in Chapters 2–6 of Volume I.

Chapters 4 and 5 provide extensions of the generalized linear model. Like Chapter 1, in Chapter 4, Peng Shi and James Guszcza also examine pricing strategies for personal automobile insurance. However, they show how to price insurance when more than one type of coverage, such as third-party liability and personal injury protection, is available in the database; by taking advantage of the multivariate nature of claims, they are able to incorporate dependencies among coverages in their pricing structure. For another approach to incorporating dependencies, in Chapter 5, Mona S. A. Hammad and Galal A. H. Harby use multilevel models. They provide a unique and interesting case study of group health insurance in the Egyptian market. Chapters 8 and 16 of Volume I provide an introduction to mixed and multilevel modeling.

Chapters 6 and 7 describe applications of unsupervised predictive modeling methods. Most predictive modeling tools require that one or more variables be identified as "dependent variables" or the "outcome of interest," and other variables are used to explain or predict them; this is known as a supervised predictive model. In contrast, unsupervised models treat all variables alike and do not require this identification. Chapter 12 of Volume I, by Louise Frances, introduced unsupervised learning with a focus on common methods of dimension reduction, principal components/factor analysis, and clustering. Chapter 6 of this volume, by Ji Yao, builds on this introduction with an application in insurance ratemaking. Louise A. Frances, the author of Chapter 7 of this volume, also follows up with two advanced unsupervised learning techniques, a variation of principal components known as PRIDIT, and a (unsupervised) variation of random forests, a tree-based data-mining method. She applies these techniques to help identify predictors of claims that are fraudulent or questionable.

Chapters 8 through 11 show how to use predictive modeling techniques in problems that are currently receiving substantial attention in actuarial science and insurance risk modeling. In Chapter 8, Glenn Meyers shows how to take the output of a Bayesian Monte Carlo Markov chain (MCMC) stochastic loss reserve model and calculate the predictive distribution of the estimates of the expected loss over a finite time horizon. Luyang Fu and Xianfang (Frank) Liu, in Chapter 9, compare GLM modeling to finite mixture models to study claims triaging and high-deductible pricing using workers, compensation data.

Chapter 10, by Mohamad A. Hindawi and Claudine H. Modlin, provides a framework for managing claim escalation. This chapter also discusses claims triaging and text mining, using penalized regression techniques, such as elastic net, to help with variable selection. In Chapter 11, Udi Makov and Jim Weiss describe how to analyze data collected from policyholders' vehicles via telematics to help determine motor vehicle premium rates. Data collected via telematics are volatile and voluminous, and actuaries and data scientists must take particular care when applying predictive modeling techniques.

Acknowledgments

Funding for this project was provided by the Casualty Actuarial Society and the Canadian Institute of Actuaries. The authors also thank the Wisconsin School of Business for hosting the book's website.

1

Pure Premium Modeling Using Generalized Linear Models

Ernesto Schirmacher

Chapter Preview. Pricing insurance products is a complex endeavor that requires blending many different perspectives. Historical data must be properly analyzed, socioeconomic trends must be identified, and competitor actions and the company's own underwriting and claims strategy must be taken into account. Actuaries are well trained to contribute in all these areas and to provide the insights and recommendations necessary for the successful development and implementation of a pricing strategy. In this chapter, we illustrate the creation of one of the fundamental building blocks of a pricing project, namely, pure premiums. We base these pure premiums on generalized linear models of frequency and severity. We illustrate the model building cycle by going through all the phases: data characteristics, exploratory data analysis, one-way and multiway analyses, the fusion of frequency and severity into pure premiums, and validation of the models. The techniques that we illustrate are widely applicable, and we encourage the reader to actively participate via the exercises that are sprinkled throughout the text; after all, *data science is not a spectator sport*!

1.1 Introduction

The pricing of insurance products is a complex undertaking and a key determinant of the long-term success of a company. Today's actuaries play a pivotal role in analyzing historical data and interpreting socioeconomic trends to determine actuarially fair price indications.

These price indications form the backbone of the final prices that a company will charge its customers. Final pricing cannot be done by any one group. The final decision must blend many considerations, such as competitor actions, growth strategy, and consumer satisfaction. Therefore, actuaries, underwriters, marketers, distributors, claims adjusters, and company management must come together and collaborate on setting prices. This diverse audience must clearly understand price indications and the implications of various pricing decisions. Actuaries are well positioned to explain and

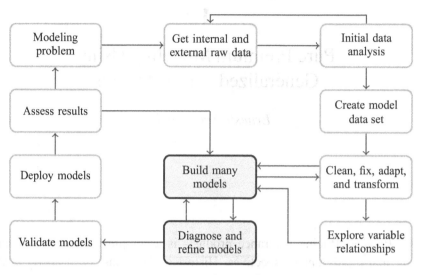

Fig. 1.1. Overall project cycle.

provide the insight necessary for the successful development and implementation of a pricing strategy.

Figure 1.1 shows one possible representation of an overall pricing project. Any one box in the diagram represents a significant portion of the overall project. In the following sections, we concentrate on the lower middle two boxes: "Build many models" and "Diagnose and refine models."

We concentrate on the first phase of the price indications that will form the key building block for later discussions, namely, the creation of pure premiums based on two generalized linear models. One model will address frequency, and the other one will target severity. These pure premiums are rooted in historical data.

Because our pure premiums only reflect historical data, they are unsuitable for use as price indications for a future exposure period. They lack the necessary trends (socioeconomic and company) to bring them up to date for the appropriate exposure period, and they also lack the necessary risk loadings, expense, and profit provisions to make them viable in the marketplace.

In Section 1.2, we describe the key overall characteristics of the dataset we have available, and in Section 1.3, we start exploring the variables. This dataset is an artificial private passenger automobile dataset that has many features that you will encounter with real datasets. It is imperative that you thoroughly familiarize yourself with the available data. The insights you gain as you explore the individual variables and their interrelationships will serve you well during the model construction phase.

In Sections 1.4 and 1.5, we start building models: frequency and severity, respectively. We illustrate several techniques that are widely applicable. We start with one-way analyses and move on to multiway analyses. The models we build are not necessarily the best ones, and we encourage the reader to explore and try to create better models. Data analysis is not a spectator sport. *The reader must actively participate!* To this end, we have sprinkled many exercises throughout the text. Most exercises require calculations that are best done in an environment that provides a rich set of data manipulation and statistical functions.

Exercise 1.1. Prepare your computing environment. Download the comma-delimited dataset `sim-modeling-dataset.csv` and load it into your environment.

All the exercises come with solutions (we have used the open-source R environment to illustrate the necessary calculations), but the reader will benefit most by looking at the solutions only after an honest attempt at their solution.

Section 1.6 combines the frequency and severity models to create pure premiums, and Section 1.7 shows some simple validation techniques on a portion of the data that our models have never seen. It is important that our modeling efforts do not overstate the accuracy or performance of the models we create. With today's available computing power and sophisticated algorithms, it is easy to overfit some models to the data. An overfit model tends to look very good, but when confronted with new data, its predictions are much worse.

Finally, Section 1.8 has some concluding remarks.

1.2 Data Characteristics

The modeling dataset `sim-modeling-dataset.csv` has been compiled for the actuarial department of a fictitious insurance company. The data set consists of private passenger automobile policy and claims information. It is an observational cross section of all in-force policies during the calendar years 2010 to 2013. There are a total of 40,760 rows and 23 variables[1] (see Table 1.1). The variables can be grouped into five classes: control variables, driver characteristics, geographic variables, vehicle characteristics, and response variables.

It is important to note that one record in our dataset can represent multiple claims from one insured. The variable `clm.count` measures the number of claims, and the variable `clm.incurred` has the sum of the individual claim payments and any provision for future payments; that is, it represents the ultimate settlement amount.

---

[1] The dataset actually contains 27 columns. One column identifies the rows (`row.id`). Driver age, years licensed, and vehicle age are represented by two columns each; one column is a string, and the other one is an integer.

Table 1.1. *Available Variables in Our Dataset*

Control	Driver	Vehicle	Geographic	Response
year	age	body.code	region	clm.count
exposure	driver.gender	driver.age		clm.incurred
row.id	marital.status	vehicle.value		
	yrs.licensed	seats		
	ncd.level	ccm		
	nb.rb	hp		
	prior.claims	length		
		width		
		height		
		fuel.type		

The variable year identifies the calendar year, and exposure measures the time a car was exposed to risk during the calendar year. We have one geographical variable, region, that tells us the garaging location of the vehicle. Unfortunately, the variable region has been coded as a positive integer, and we do not have any information about how these regions are spatially related. This is a significant drawback for our dataset and highlights that good data preparation is crucial. We want to retain as much information as possible.

The driver characteristic variables measure the age and gender of the principal operator of the vehicle, the marital status, the number of years that the operator has been licensed, the no claim discount level (higher level reflects a greater discount for not having any claims), and the number of prior claims. The variable nb.rb tells us whether this policy is new business (nb) or renewal business (rb).

The vehicle characteristic variables measure various attributes such as the body style (body.code); the age and value of the vehicle; the number of seats; and the vehicle's weight, length, width, and height. The variables ccm, hp, and fuel.type measure the size of the engine in cubic centimeters, the horsepower, and the type of fuel (gasoline, diesel, or liquefied petroleum gas), respectively.

We have two response variables, clm.count and clm.incurred, which measure the number of claims and the ultimate cost of those claims. All the variables in our dataset can be categorized as either continuous or categorical. Table 1.2 shows some summary statistics for the 14 continuous variables, and Table 1.3 has some information on the 12 categorical variables.

Overall frequency and severity statistics by calendar year across the entire dataset are given in Table 1.4. Note that the volume of business increased by about 78% from 2010 to 2012 and then decreased by 17% in 2013. Frequency for the first two years is at approximately 11% and then jumps up significantly to approximately 20%.

Table 1.2. *Summary Statistics for Continuous Variables*

Variable	Mean	Standard Deviation	Min.	Median	Max.
exposure	0.51	0.27	0.08	0.50	1.00
driver.age	44.55	10.78	18.00	44.00	93.00
yrs.licensed	3.21	1.89	1.00	3.00	10.00
vehicle.age	3.26	2.59	0.00	3.00	18.00
vehicle.value	23.50	8.89	4.50	22.10	132.60
ccm	1,670.69	390.12	970.00	1,560.00	3,198.00
hp	86.38	19.62	42.00	75.00	200.00
weight	1,364.22	222.01	860.00	1,320.00	2,275.00
length	4.32	0.36	1.80	4.28	6.95
width	1.78	0.10	1.48	1.74	2.12
height	1.81	0.09	1.42	1.82	2.52
prior.claims	0.83	1.33	0.00	0.00	21.00
clm.count	0.08	0.30	0.00	0.00	5.00
clm.incurred	66.52	406.23	0.00	0.00	11,683.58

Table 1.3. *Summary Statistics for Categorical Variables*

Variable	No. of Levels	Base Level	Most Common	Sample Levels
year	4	2013	2012	2010, 2011, 2012, 2013
nb.rb	2	NB	NB	NB, RB
drv.age	74	38	38	18, 19, 20, 21, 22, 23, 24, 25, and others
driver.gender	2	Male	Male	Female, Male
marital.status	4	Married	Married	Divorced, Married, Single, Widow
yrs.lic	8	1	2	1, 2, 3, 4, 5, 6, 7, 8+
ncd.level	6	1	1	1, 2, 3, 4, 5, 6
region	38	17	17	1, 10, 11, 12, 13, 14, 15, 16, and others
body.code	8	A	A	A, B, C, D, E, F, G, H
veh.age	15	1	1	0, 1, 10, 11, 12, 13, 14+, 2, and others
seats	5	5	5	2, 3, 4, 5, 6+
fuel.type	3	Diesel	Diesel	Diesel, Gasoline, LPG

Table 1.4. *Exposure, Claim Counts, Claim Amounts, Frequency, and Severity by Calendar Year for the Entire Dataset*

Year	Exposure	Claim Count	Claim Amount	Frequency	Severity
2010	3,661.9	422	287,869	0.115	682.2
2011	5,221.7	551	314,431	0.106	570.7
2012	6,527.2	1,278	1,021,152	0.196	799.0
2013	5,386.2	1,180	1,087,735	0.219	921.8
Total	20,797.1	3,431	2,711,187	0.165	790.2

The mean severity across all calendar years is at 790, but there are sharp increases over time, except for 2011, when we saw a decrease.

It is customary to split your data into three sets: training, testing, and validation. The training set is used to formulate your models. You do all the preliminary testing of your models against the testing set. The training and testing sets are used extensively to guide the development of your models and to try as best as possible to avoid both underfitting and overfitting. The validation set is used *only once* to determine how your final model will perform when presented with new data.

This three-way split of your data (train, test, validate) is only feasible when you have a large amount of data. In our case, we only have about 41,000 observations across four calendar years. This is a small dataset, so we will use a different testing and validation strategy, namely, cross-validation.

Rather than split our data into three sets, we will only split it into two sets: a training set and a validation set. We will use the training dataset to both develop and test our models. Because we only have one set of data for both training and testing, we cannot use standard testing techniques, so we will use k-fold cross-validation. We will set aside approximately 60% of our data as the training set.[2] The remainder will go in the validation set.

In k-fold cross-validation, we use all the training data to develop the structure of our models. Then, to test them, we split our training data into, say, five subsets called *folds*, and we label them 1 through 5. We set aside fold 1, combine folds 2 to 5, and estimate the parameters of our model on these data. Then we calculate our goodness-of-fit measure on fold 1 and set it aside. We repeat this procedure by setting aside fold 2, then fold 3, and so forth. At the end, we will have calculated five goodness-of-fit measures. We average them out, and that is our final goodness-of-fit estimate.

1.3 Exploratory Data Analysis

In this section, we start by exploring individual variables to gain a better understanding of the information we have available in our dataset. During exploratory data analysis, you want to concentrate on understanding how well each variable is populated, what kinds of values each variable takes, how missing values are coded, and the interrelationships between variables.

1.3.1 EDA for Frequency

From the previous section (see Table 1.4), we know that the overall frequency for the entire dataset is equal to 16.5%. For the training dataset, it is equal to 16.1%–very close to the overall frequency.

---

[2] We assigned a uniform random number, $u \in (0, 1)$, to each record. The training dataset consists of all records with $u < 0.6$, and the validation set consists of all those records with $u \geq 0.6$.

Table 1.5. *Frequency by Calendar Year and New/Renewal Business Indicator for the Training Dataset*

	Exposure		Claim Count		Frequency (%)	
Year	NB	RB	NB	RB	NB	RB
2010	1,504.5	684.6	193	67	12.8	9.8
2011	2,105.9	1,042.4	271	69	12.9	6.6
2012	2,643.5	1,278.5	551	189	20.8	14.8
2013	2,248.6	964.9	526	137	23.4	14.2
Total	8,502.5	3,970.4	1,541	462	18.1	11.6

Exercise 1.2. Add a random number u_i between 0 and 1 to each record. Calculate the frequency for all records with $u_i < 0.6$. How close is your estimate to the overall frequency of 16.5%? How variable is the frequency estimate as we resample the random numbers u_i?

We would like to understand how this frequency depends on the variables that we have at our disposal. Let's start by looking at the variable nb.rb. This variable is an indicator letting us know if the policy is new business (NB) or renewal business (RB). The frequency in our training dataset by this new/renewal business indicator is in Table 1.5. Notice that over the training data, the frequency for new business is equal to 18.1%, and for renewal business, it is equal to 11.6%. This looks like a significant difference; thus this variable is a good candidate to include in our models. Also note that on a year-by-year basis, there is a gap between the new and renewal business frequency. The gap for the last three years is quite large.

Exercise 1.3. What is the frequency of each region on the entire dataset? Has it been stable over time?

Next we can look at driver.age. This variable tells us the age of the principal operator of the vehicle. In the training data, we have ages 18 to 87, 89 to 90, and 93, for a total of 73 unique ages.[3]

Exercise 1.4. Verify that age 88 is not in the training dataset but that it is in the validation dataset. How should our modeling deal with such situations?

We should be suspicious of some of these very advanced ages and check that our data are accurate. Also, we should check how much exposure we have for all ages. A

---

[3] For the entire dataset, we have 74 unique ages. Age 88 is not represented in the training dataset but is in the validation dataset.

Pure Premium Modeling

six-point summary over the training dataset for the frequency of claims by driver age[4] is

Min.	Q1	Q2	Mean	Q3	Max.
0%	9.2%	14.5%	16.8%	18.5%	184.6%

where Qn stands for the nth quartile. Note that the maximum frequency is equal to 184.6%, and upon looking into our data, we know it comes from four policies:

Row ID	Driver Age	Exposure	Claim Count
2885	19	1.000	1
2886	19	0.083	0
14896	19	0.167	0
14897	19	0.917	3

Also, the next highest frequency value is equal to 92.3%, and it comes from the two policies with drivers aged 89 years old that are in our training dataset. These two policies have a total exposure of 1.083 car-years and one claim.

Exercise 1.5. Check the exposure and number of claims for all the drivers aged 76 years old in the training dataset.

Figure 1.2 shows the driver age frequencies together with the amount of exposure. Clearly there is an overall decreasing frequency trend as driver age increases. The bulk of the exposure (approximately 98%) is concentrated in the age range from 25 to 70. Note that even though the frequency trend is decreasing, there is significant volatility in the individual driver age frequencies. For example, in the age range from 30 to 34 there is a zigzag pattern:

Driver age	30	31	32	33	34
Frequency	20.0%	18.2%	20.3%	22.4%	19.5%

Similar zigzag patterns occur between the ages of 50 to 70. Also there seems to be a spike in frequency around 47 years old. This could be due to young drivers using their parents' cars.

We have been looking at the frequencies in our training dataset for the calendar years 2010, 2011, 2012, and 2013 combined. We must also check that these patterns are consistent from one calendar year to the next. Each calendar year has less exposure

---

[4] First we calculated the frequency for each individual age, and then took the six-point summary across the 73 frequencies.

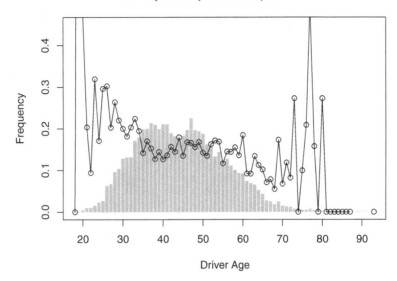

Fig. 1.2. Frequency and exposure by the driver age variable and for all three years of the training data. The *y*-axis has been restricted to the range [0, 0.45] to enhance the information shown. Four points have been omitted from the graph: (19, 184.6%), (20, 48.5%), (77, 50.3%), and (89, 92.3%).

than all three years combined, and so we expect that the individual calendar year frequency patterns will be more volatile.

Exercise 1.6. Create a graph similar to Figure 1.2, but add one frequency path for every calendar year.

Just as we have explored the frequency of claims by new or renewal business or by driver age, we should explore it across all other variables we have available in our dataset. We can mechanically create all sorts of tables and graphs for all variables at our disposal, but it would be better to concentrate our efforts on variables that we know from past experience have been important.

Exercise 1.7. Explore frequency by size of engine (variable `ccm`) for the entire dataset.

Exercise 1.8. Investigate the frequency of claims by the variables `driver.gender` and `marital.status`.

Exercise 1.9. From Exercise 1.8, we know that the frequency for married policyholders is about 15.8% and for widowers is about 27.3%. Is this difference significant? Is the difference in frequency between single and married policyholders significant?

Now let us shift attention to the variable `hp`. This variable represents the horsepower of the insured vehicle. In our training dataset, there are 63 unique values for horsepower ranging from a low of 42 to a high value of 200 but not all values between

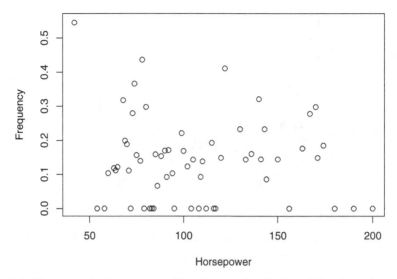

Fig. 1.3. Frequency by horsepower. To enhance the display of the data, the graph omits two frequency values: 0.585 and 0.923. The corresponding horsepower values are 48 and 125, respectively.

these two extremes are equally represented. The six largest frequencies by horsepower are 0.366, 0.411, 0.436, 0.545, 0.585, and 0.923. These six frequencies come from vehicles with horsepower equal to 74, 122, 78, 42, 48, and 125, respectively. It looks like the largest value might be an outlier. Also note that the exposure is concentrated in the following five values:

Horsepower	65	105	90	70	75
Exposure	848	1,442	1,631	2,486	2,628

These five values account for about 72% of the total exposure in the training dataset. Figure 1.3 does not show any systematic relationship between horsepower and frequency, so this variable is not a strong candidate for inclusion into the model for frequency that we develop in Section 1.4.

Another variable that is probably not a good predictor of frequency might be length; that is the length of the vehicle. In our dataset the unit of measurement for the variables length, width, and height is the meter. This unit is a bit awkward, so we transform these variables to use decimeters as the unit of measurement.

Exercise 1.10. Would we get different models if we use the variable length in units of meters or in units of decimeters?

Exercise 1.11. Explore the length of the vehicle variable. Start by describing the key characteristics of the lengths we have in our dataset. How many different lengths do we have? Are they uniformly distributed?

Exercise 1.12. Is the frequency of accidents related to the length of the vehicle? Make a scatter plot of vehicle length against frequency. Do you see any trends?

So far we have looked at the frequency of claims by one variable at a time; that is, we have performed one-way explorations. We should also conduct two-way explorations. For example, how does frequency vary by driver age and driver gender? Do we see different frequencies for males and females across different ages?

Exercise 1.13. Explore how frequency varies by driver age and driver gender. For driver age, create three groups: young (34 or less), middle (35 to 64), and old (65 and over).

Exercise 1.14. Explore the frequency of each variable. You should do one-way explorations to get an impression of the range of outcomes for each variable. Also you should explore how frequency behaves from one calendar year to the next. Pay attention to how much exposure you have and the empirical frequency estimates you get. Also do two-way explorations for those pairs of variables you think would be related (such as age and gender).

1.3.2 EDA for Severity

So far we have explored the frequency side of our dataset. Let's turn our attention to the severity side. Here the questions are very similar to the ones we have been asking for severity: how does severity behave in relation to the predictors we have available?

The amount of data we have available to estimate severity is much smaller. Our entire dataset consists of 40,760 records, but only 3,169 of them have a claim. The total number of claims in our dataset is equal to 3,431 (some records have more than one claim), and the distribution of claim counts is given in Table 1.6. The average severity across our training dataset is equal to

$$\frac{\text{Total claim cost}}{\text{Total number of claims}} = \frac{1,578,258}{2,003} = 787.95$$

and now we want to see how severity depends on other predictor variables.

Exercise 1.15. Check that across the training dataset, the total incurred claims is 1,578,258 and the claim counts are 2,003.

Table 1.6. *Number of Records by Number of Claims for the Entire Dataset*

Number of claims	0	1	2	3	4	5	6+
Number of records	37,591	2,927	225	15	1	1	0

Table 1.7. *Severity for New/Renewal Business for the Training Dataset*

	New/Renewal Business	
	NB	RB
Claims Incurred	1,251,473	326,785
Claim Counts	1,541	462
Severity	812	707

Let's take a look at our new/renewal business indicator variable (nb.rb). In Table 1.7 we have the claims incurred, claim counts, and severity split by new and renewal business. As expected, new business tends to have a higher severity than renewal business: 812 versus 707. This variable might be a good candidate to include in our severity model.

Exercise 1.16. Use a similar approach to Exercise 1.9 to see if the difference in severity between new and renewal business is significant.

Another variable to investigate would be fuel.type. This is a categorical variable with three levels, Diesel, Gasoline, and LPG (liquefied petroleum gas), and from Exercise 1.14 we know that the amount of exposure in these levels is uneven. Similarly, the number of claims are uneven: diesel vehicles have 1,972, gasoline vehicles have 24, and LPG vehicles have 7. With only 31 claims in the gasoline and LPG categories, it will be very difficult to get good severity parameter estimates.

Exercise 1.17. Estimate the mean severity on the training dataset for the variable fuel.type and provide a measure of variability for your estimate.

Owing to space constraints, we do not show our exploration of the remaining variables. The reader should continue to explore how severity depends on the rest of the variables. Use the techniques illustrated in this and the frequency sections, and when you see a pattern, try to understand what the plausible drivers might be.

Exercise 1.18. For each variable in our dataset, explore severity. Do one-way analyses to understand the range of severities for each variable. Also do two-way analyses where one variable is year to see how stable severity estimates are across calendar years. Pay close attention to the number of claims you have in each category.

1.4 Frequency Modeling

From Section 1.3 we know that the overall frequency for our training dataset is equal to 16.1%, and we have some variables that might be good candidates for inclusion in a frequency model, such as driver age and new/renewal indicator.

Table 1.8. *The Number of Records by Claim Counts*

Number of claims	0	1	2	3	4	5	6+
Number of records	37,591	2,927	225	15	1	1	0

We will start building our frequency model by doing one-way analyses. Then we will move into multiway analyses by adding additional variables.

At this point we need to make two choices: link function and response distribution. For most insurance pricing applications we would like to have a multiplicative rating plan and so we'll be using a logarithmic link function. As for the distribution of the response variable we are modeling claim counts; hence we can choose between Poisson, negative binomial, or binomial distributions. Keep in mind that our goal is to estimate the *mean frequency*, and while distributional assumptions are important, they are not nearly as critical as finding the correct variables to include in your model.

For the entire dataset the distribution of claim counts is given in Table 1.8, and as we have seen in Table 1.4, the mean frequency is equal to 16.5%. If the distribution of these claim counts is Poisson, then the variance should be equal to the mean. In most insurance datasets, the variance of the frequency is not equal to the mean. Typically the variance is larger than the mean. This phenomenon is known as overdispersion.

Exercise 1.19. Make a table showing the distribution of exposures by claim counts and compute the mean frequency and its variance. Is the variance equal, smaller, or larger than the mean?

1.4.1 One-Way Frequency Models

The simplest generalized linear model we can fit to our frequency data is usually called the *null model*, and it consists of just estimating an intercept term. This null model should replicate the overall mean frequency. Let us fit a Poisson model with a log-link function and just an intercept parameter. The estimated coefficient is

```
Call:
glm(formula = clm.count ~ 1,
    family = poisson(link = "log"), data = dta,
    subset = train, offset = log(exposure))


Coefficients:
            Estimate Std. Error z value Pr(>|z|)
(Intercept) -1.82891    0.02234  -81.85   <2e-16 ***
```

Note that the estimated value of the intercept term, -1.82891, is on the scale of the linear predictor, and by taking the inverse of the link function, we can put that estimate

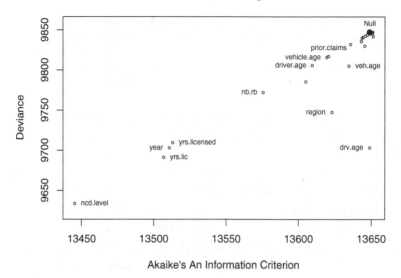

Fig. 1.4. AIC and deviance for single-variable models.

on the scale of the response variable; that is, the estimated frequency for the null model is

$$\exp(-1.82891) = 0.1605879;$$

which matches the estimate from the raw training data (as it should[5]).

At this point we are going to assume that the Poisson distribution is an adequate model for our data and we would like to understand which single-variable model provides the best fit to our training dataset. So we'll fit a series of models and use Akaike's An Information Criterion[6] (AIC) and the deviance[7] as two measures of model quality.

Figure 1.4 shows AIC on the *x*-axis and deviance on the *y*-axis. The best variables would appear in the lower left-hand corner of the display, where both the deviance and the AIC have low values. Here we see the variable `ncd.level`, `year`, and `yrs.lic`. In the opposite corner of the display we have the null model, that is, the frequency model that only has an intercept term. This is the simplest model we can fit to our data and usually the worst performing one. From Figure 1.4 we can see that there are several variables that are clustered very close to our null model.

The reader probably noticed that there is a pair of variables that look nearly identical, namely, `years.licensed` and `yrs.lic`.[8] These variables are almost the same.

---

[5] You should always check the output of a simple model against independent calculations. One of the most common errors is to mis-specify the weights or offset terms.

[6] Akaike's An Information Criterion is calculated as minus twice the maximized log-likelihood plus twice the number of parameters.

[7] The deviance in a generalized linear model plays the same role as the sum of squared errors in the standard linear regression model.

[8] There is another pair of variables: `driver.age` and `drv.age`.

The abbreviated name (`yrs.lic`) is a categorical version of the integer valued full named variable. So when we are fitting our generalized linear models, the full name variable is considered continuous, and only one parameter is estimated. When the abbreviated name is fitted, then for each level of the variable, we fit one parameter. In the case of `drv.age`, there are 73 unique ages in our training dataset.

In Figure 1.4 `driver.age` is located near the coordinates (13610, 9806), and the variable `drv.age` is in the lower right-hand corner at coordinates (13648, 9703). From the perspective of deviance, the categorical version (`drv.age`) has a much better fit to the data. But from the perspective of Akaike's AIC, the continuous version (`driver.age`) has a much lower score. Deviance does not take model complexity into account. The model for `driver.age` has only two parameters (the intercept and the coefficient for `driver.age`), but the model for `drv.age` has 73 parameters! Clearly, with 73 parameters, we would be able to achieve a much closer fit to our training data than with just 2 of them. Of course, we have not looked to see if all 73 parameters are really needed, and I would suspect that a judicious consolidation of the parameters would lower the AIC and increase the deviance but overall have a performance similar (if not better) to `driver.age`.

Fitting a frequency generalized linear model on the categorical variable `drv.age` yields 73 parameters: one intercept and 72 age parameters. The base level for this variable is age 38. Because we only have one variable in our model, each parameter of the model represents the frequency for that age group (the intercept represents the frequency for the base level, namely, the age 38 group). For example, the 29-year-old drivers have a total number of claims equal to 47 and a total exposure of 213.6 in the training dataset; so the empirical frequency for this group is

$$\frac{47}{213.6} = 0.22$$

The parameter estimates from the generalized linear model are as follows:

intercept	−2.05993
drv.age 29	0.54605

therefore, the estimated frequency is equal to $\exp(-2.05993 + 0.54605) = 0.22005$; the same estimate as the empirical calculation.

Exercise 1.20. Verify that the frequency for the twenty nine year old drivers (in the training dataset) is indeed equal to 22.00% and check that you get the same answer from a generalized linear model. Also, what is the estimated frequency for drivers aged 38?

Now Figure 1.5 shows the parameter estimates for the variable `drv.age`. The 13 ages 18, 74, 79, 81–88, 90, and 93 have zero reported claims and so their estimated

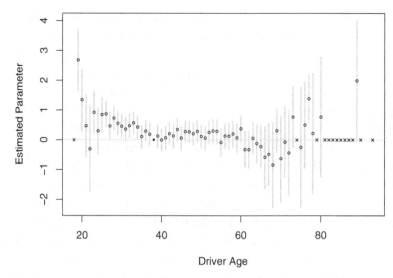

Fig. 1.5. Estimated parameters for `drv.age` in a log-link Poisson frequency model. Thirteen age categories have no reported claims, and the parameters for these levels should be equal to negative infinity. We have displayed them with a cross symbol and at a value of zero. The base level for this variable is at age = 38, and it is shown as a solid black dot with a value of zero. The gray lines represent 95% confidence intervals for each parameter.

parameters should be equal to negative infinity. In Figure 1.5 we have displayed these estimates with a cross symbol at a value equal to zero. The base level for this variable is age = 38, and it is displayed with a solid black dot. We have also displayed 95% confidence intervals. Note that the vast majority of these confidence intervals cross the horizontal line at zero.

Note that the variables `yrs.licensed` and `yrs.lic` are very close to each other. These two variables are nearly identical. The abbreviated version is a categorical variable with 8 levels: 1, 2, ..., 8+. Fitting a frequency log-link Poisson generalized linear model with only this variable[9] yields the parameter estimates in Table 1.9.

Note that the parameter estimates for `yrs.lic` decrease from about -1.5 to -2.5 as the number of years licensed increases (there are a few reversals). This trend makes sense as we would expect drivers who have been licensed for many years to be less accident prone compared to inexperienced drivers.

Exercise 1.21. The parameter estimates in Table 1.9 look quite smooth. Could we, instead of estimating one parameter for each level of the variable `yrs.lic`, use the continuous variable `yrs.licensed` and estimate a single parameter? How different would the parameter estimates be?

---

[9] We are estimating a model with no intercept term, namely, `clm.count ~ yrs.lic − 1`, and with an offset term for exposures.

Table 1.9. *Estimated Frequency Coefficients and*
Standard Errors for the Variable yrs.lic

yrs.lic	Estimate	Std. Error	Exposure
1	−1.48491	0.03965	2807.7
2	−1.73770	0.04527	2773.9
3	−1.95056	0.05689	2173.1
4	−1.87459	0.06178	1707.7
5	−2.15342	0.07931	1369.7
6	−2.48761	0.11396	926.5
7	−2.32516	0.14142	511.4
8+	−2.22175	0.21320	202.9

Note: The last column has the amount of exposure in car-years. The estimated model is based on the training dataset and has no intercept term.

Note that all the standard errors are small compared to the size of the parameter estimate. For the last two levels (7 and 8+), the estimates increase. This reversal in the trend probably does not make sense from a business perspective. We may decide to set the last three parameters to a value of −2.50. That would be a frequency of approximately $\exp(-2.50) = 8.2\%$.

As noted, the standard errors in Table 1.9 are small compared to the estimated parameters. But we should be cautious about their size. They are probably too optimistic (small) and we should not place too much trust in them. Our dataset is overdispersed, and so the true size of the standard errors is larger.

Exercise 1.22. Recompute the parameter estimates for yrs.lic, but adjust the standard errors to account for overdispersion in our dataset.

From Figure 1.4 it looks like the top six predictive variables for frequency are: ncd.level, year, region, yrs.lic, drv.age, and prior.claims. The variable year is not a predictive variable as it does not describe an attribute or characteristic of a customer or the vehicle. It is best to think of it as a *control variable*. This variable would control for the effects of time in our dataset and we should include it in all of our models.

Exercise 1.23. Redo Figure 1.4, but include year with the null model. Are the most predictive variables similar to our previous list?

The variable ncd.level has six levels, region has 38 levels, yrs.lic has nine levels, and we will use the continuous version of driver age, namely, driver.age. The variable prior.claims is also continuous.

1.4.2 Multiway Frequency Models

Now that we have a better idea about which single-variable models fit our data better, we can move on to build multiway models, that is, models that incorporate more than one predictor variable. We can look at all two variable models and select the best one. We can then look at all three variable models and again select the best one, and so forth. This strategy is not feasible. Usually we have too many variables to look at.

Another strategy would be to sequentially build a bigger and bigger model. While this strategy is computationally less burdensome, its main drawback is that it is dependent on the order in which we add predictors to our model. A greedy algorithm where we add the next best single variable to our current model does not guarantee that our final model will be optimal.

A better strategy would be to use our domain knowledge to select an initial subset of variables and then sequentially add or remove predictors. We illustrate some multiway models but leave the selection of an "optimal" subset of variables as a challenge to our readers.

Region has many levels, and unfortunately for this dataset, we do not know how these regions are related geographically. In practice, we would have a map and know which regions are adjacent to each other. This would help us tremendously to consolidate the parameters in a rational way. Given this limitation, we approach this problem from a purely mechanical point of view. This is not the recommended approach, but it illustrates the technique of consolidating levels of a variable and making our models more parsimonious. So let's take a look at the estimated parameters on a one-way basis and on a multiway basis; that is, let's fit a frequency model with `region` as the only variable, and also let's create a frequency model with the five variables: `region`, `ncd.level`, `yrs.lic`, `driver.age`, and `prior.claims`. In Figure 1.6 we have the estimated parameters for `region` based on both a one-way and a multiway model. In the one-way panel (Figure 1.6b) the first four regions – 7, 2, 20, and 27 – have parameter estimates that are well separated from each other. After these regions we have a string of parameter estimates that are all close to each other. The last two regions – 26 and 8 – are a bit further to the right.

On the multiway panel (Figure 1.6b) the first *three* regions – 7, 2, and 20 – look the same as in the one-way analysis. Region 27 is now part of the large cluster of regions. And finally, region 26, which was together with region 8, is now also part of the middle cluster.

We can code a new categorical variable, `region.g1`, with the assignments of regions to levels, as shown in Table 1.10.

Exercise 1.24. Refit our frequency model with the variable `region.g1` instead of the variable `region`.

Table 1.10. *New Assignments*
of Regions to Levels of the
Variable `region.g1`

Level	Regions
R0	17, 21, 26
R1	27, 28, 34, 37
R2	6, 29, 30
R3	3, 4, 5, 11, 12, 13, 35
R4	9, 10, 15, 16, 38
R5	1, 22, 25, 31
R6	14, 18, 19, 23, 24, 32, 34
R7	7, 2, 20
R8	8

Note: The assignments are based on Figure 1.6b.

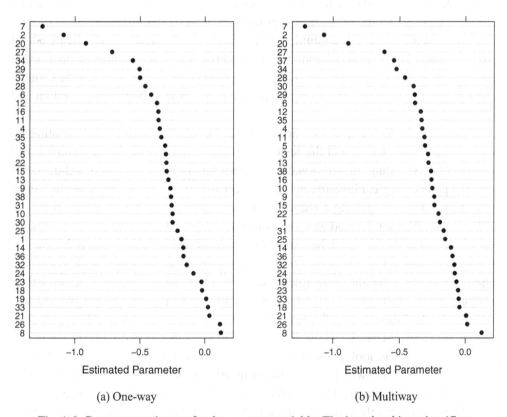

(a) One-way　　　　　　　　(b) Multiway

Fig. 1.6. Parameter estimates for the `region` variable. The base level is region 17 on both plots, and it is not shown. In the left-hand panel, we have the one-way estimates, and on the right-hand side, we have multiway estimates, where our model includes `ncd.level`, `yrs.lic`, `driver.age`, and `prior.claims`. Note that the ordering of the regions (on the *y*-axis) is not the same for both plots! In both plots, we have included the control variable `year`.

Pure Premium Modeling

Table 1.11. *Analysis of Deviance Table*

Variable	Df	Deviance	Resid. Df	Resid. Dev	Pr(>Chi)
NULL			24,494	9,847.2	
year	3	144.188	24,491	9,703.0	0
region.g1	8	92.187	24,483	9,610.8	0
ncd.level	5	213.604	24,478	9,397.2	0
driver.age	1	8.921	24,477	9,388.3	0.003
yrs.lic	7	16.068	24,470	9,372.2	0.025
prior.claims	1	69.871	24,469	9,302.3	0

Note: Variables are added sequentially to the model.

Based on the answer to Exercise 1.24, almost all of the parameter estimates for the new region variable are statistically different from zero. Table 1.11 is an analysis of deviance. This table shows how the deviance changes as we *sequentially* add terms to our frequency model. The starting point is the null model, that is, the model with an intercept only. The first column gives the name of the variable that is being added to the model. The second column gives the contribution to the number of parameters estimated by adding this variable. The third column gives the deviance for the variable being added. The fourth and fifth columns give the residual degrees of freedom and the residual deviance.

For example, as we add the variable ncd.level, we would be estimating an additional 5 parameters, and the residual deviance would drop by an amount equal to 213.604. Spending an additional five parameters to reduce the residual deviance by 214 points is a great investment. For the variable yrs.lic we are investing seven parameters but only getting a reduction in the residual deviance of about 16 points. This trade-off is not as good as for the other variables. The last column shows that it is significant at the 5% level, but not at the 1% level (the *p*-value is about 2.5%).

We still have a lot of variables to look at. For example, we could look at seats, hei.dm (vehicle height in decimeters), or ccm (engine size in cubic centimeters) among others. In Figure 1.7 we have a plot similar to Figure 1.4, but our starting model has the following five[10] variables: region.g1, ncd.level, driver.age, yrs.lic, and prior.claims. From this scatterplot the variables body.code and marital.status look particularly promising. Notice that for marital.status the drop in deviance will be equal to about 10 points. For body.code it will be about 20 deviance points. The variable marital.status has four levels, and we would be estimating three new parameters. So getting a drop of 10 deviance points by spending three parameters seems like a reasonable return. The variable body.code is

---

[10] We are also including the control variable year.

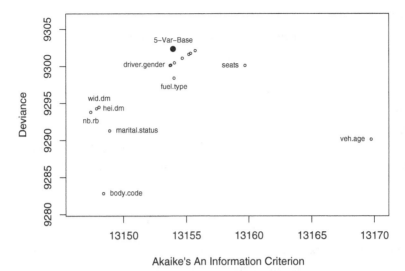

Fig. 1.7. The base model, labeled "5-Var-Base," is our starting frequency model with variables `region.g1`, `ncd.level`, `driver.age`, `yrs.lic`, and `prior.claims`. To this model we are adding one variable at a time and plotting the resulting AIC against the deviance. The coordinates of the base model are (13,153; 9,302). Nine points far away from the base model have been labeled.

a categorical with eight levels. Hence adding this variable into our base model requires the estimation of seven additional parameters, and we would be getting a drop of about 20 deviance points – perhaps still a good return. Also the new/renewal business indicator (`nb.rb`) looks promising.

Let's add these three variables and see if this expanded model is superior to our previous model. Just as we did an analysis of deviance on a single model, we can take a look at the difference in deviance from two *nested* models, as we have here. Table 1.12 shows that the difference in deviance between these two models is about 39,

Table 1.12. *Analysis of Deviance Table Between Two Nested Models*

Model	Resid. Df	Resid. Dev	Df	Deviance	Pr(>Chi)
1	24,469	9,302.3			
2	24,458	9,263.8	11	38.580	0

Note: Model 1's variables are `year`, `region.g1`, `ncd.level`, `driver.age`, `yrs.lic`, and `prior.claims`. Model 2 has all the variables from Model 1 plus `marital.status`, `body.code`, and `nb.rb`. These additional variables make Model 2 significantly different than Model 1.

and we had to estimate an additional 11 parameters; this is an excellent trade-off. The expanded model is significantly different from the base model.

Exercise 1.25. For the variables that Model 1 and Model 2 have in common, are the parameter estimates very different?

Exercise 1.26. From Figure 1.7, the variable `seats` might be a good explanatory variable (in terms of deviance, but not in terms of AIC). Add this variable to Model 2 and do an analysis of deviance just as we did between Model 1 and Model 2. Do we get a new frequency model that is significantly different from Model 2?

1.4.3 Cross-Validation for Frequency

Now that we have looked at several variables (both in isolation and along others), we should spend some time testing some potential models. It is clear that as we add more and more variables to a model, we should be able to create a better and better fit to the training data. But creating a model that fits the training data is not our goal. In fact, if we spend a lot of energy fitting our models to the training dataset, it is very likely that our model will be useless. To illustrate this point, let's fit a sequence of models where we keep adding variables and track the average error. Figure 1.8 shows

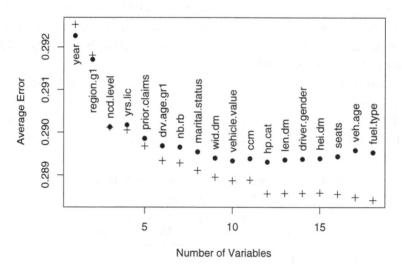

Fig. 1.8. Cross-validation results as we increase the number of variables in the model. The variable label shown represents a model that includes the current variable and all prior (to the left) variables. The point labeled "ncd.level" corresponds to the frequency model that includes the variables `year`, `region.g1`, and `ncd.level`. The data points with the plus symbol represent the average error on the training dataset. The filled circles are the mean error of a 10-fold cross-validation on the training dataset.

how the average error monotonically drops as we add additional variables (see the points labeled with a plus). The filled circles show the mean value of a 10-fold cross-validation. Note how the cross-validated models decrease up to the variable `vehi-cle.value` and then increase from there on.

Figure 1.8 shows the typical pattern that we see in most modeling exercises as we increase the complexity of the models we are working on. There is a point where adding additional predictors results in overfitting to the data we are using. Overfitted models generalize very poorly on data they have never seen.

Exercise 1.27. How would you create Figure 1.8?

1.5 Severity Modeling

Severity modeling is more challenging than frequency. We have less data to work with and the observations are usually much more volatile. It is not uncommon for the range of severities to span three or four orders of magnitude. Usually the bulk of the policies with claims have small severities and a small number of policies have very large severities. This typically results in a very right skewed distribution, as shown on the histogram in Figure 1.9. Note that nearly all of the observations are concentrated in the left side of the display. There are very few observations above 6,000; in fact, only 17 records out of 3,169!

Exercise 1.28. What is the incurred cost for each of the 17 records with the largest severities?

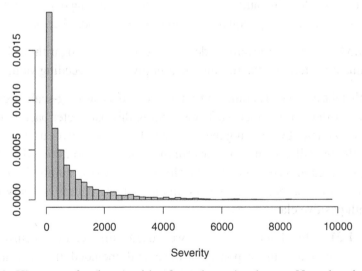

Fig. 1.9. Histogram for the severities from the entire dataset. Note that the range of claim severities goes from, essentially, zero to 10,000, that is, four orders of magnitude!

From Table 1.4 we know that the average severity across the entire dataset is equal to

$$\text{Severity} = \frac{\text{Incurred Cost}}{\text{Number of Claims}} = \frac{2,711,187}{3,431} = 790.20$$

and restricting ourselves to the training dataset (CYs 2010–2012), we get

$$\text{Severity} = \frac{1,578,258}{2,003} = 787.95$$

With our training dataset we have only 2,003 claims to work with. A six-point summary for severity is as shown in the following table

Min.	1st Qu.	Median	Mean	3rd Qu.	Max.
10.0	86.1	364.4	785.6	995.8	8,354.0

Note that the third quartile is only about 995 but the largest observation is close to 8,350. The median is a about half of the mean. The distribution of severities is heavily skewed toward the right-hand side.

Exercise 1.29. It seems that we have two different means. One says that the mean severity for our training dataset is equal to 787.95, and the other one says that it is equal to 785.56. The difference is not very large, but we should understand why they are not equal! Which one is right?

Fitting a gamma log-link null severity model to the training dataset yields a parameter estimate for the intercept equal to 6.66943 with a standard error of 0.03199.

Exercise 1.30. Verify that the null model for severity using a logarithmic link function and a gamma error term on the training dataset gives the preceding values.

Notice that the estimated parameter for the intercept is on a log-scale because we are using the logarithmic link function. Transforming this parameter back to the scale of the response variable (by applying the inverse link function) gives us $\exp(6.66943) = 787.9471$: the overall severity for our training dataset. Also notice that the number of degrees of freedom is equal to 1,855. This is equal to the number of observations less the number of estimated parameters. In our training dataset we only have 1,856 records with positive claim counts.

Exercise 1.31. In Exercise 1.30 we used the claim incurred amount (clm.incurred) as our response variable and included the logarithm of the claim counts as an offset term. Fit a model without the offset term by using a severity response variable and verify that you get the same parameter estimates.

The variable `year` controls for the effects of time and from this point on we will include this variable in all of our models. Claim costs are subject to inflation, and another approach would be to deflate our data using an approximate measure of claims inflation. We should still include the variable `year` to capture any other temporal effects that are not captured by inflation.

Exercise 1.32. Should we also include the control variable `year` in our frequency models?

As with our frequency model, we now need to search for explanatory variables that will help us predict the severity of claims. The process is the same as what we did for frequency modeling; therefore, we will keep this section short and ask the reader to work through more exercises.

1.5.1 One-Way Severity Models

We can start by fitting each individual variable and looking for those that provide the best fit. In Figure 1.10 we have a scatterplot of AIC versus deviance for all single variable models (including the control variable `year`) for severity.

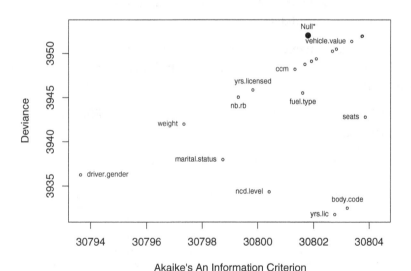

Fig. 1.10. Scatterplot of AIC versus deviance for single-variable models for severity. The null (`intercept + year`) model is depicted with a solid circle and labeled "Null*." Three variables, `drv.age`, `region`, and `veh.age`, which have very large AICs, have been omitted to enhance the display. Their coordinates are (30,850; 3,842), (30,829; 3,880), and (30,819; 3,936), respectively. Twelve points have been labeled with the corresponding variable name.

Note that all models have lower deviance than the null model, but not all models have a lower AIC that the null model. In fact, three variables have an AIC that is much bigger than that of the null model. The three variables are drv.age, region, and veh.age. These variables are all categorical with a large number of levels. Akaike's AIC penalizes[11] a model based on the number of fitted parameters. Perhaps, instead of using the variables drv.age and region, we should use the grouped versions that we found with our frequency model. The groupings for frequency might not be the best groupings for severity, but they are a good starting point.

Exercise 1.33. What is the AIC and deviance for the model that includes region.g1 and the control variable year? Repeat for the variable drv.age.gr1.

Exercise 1.34. Which models are farthest away from the null model?

Exercise 1.35. To Figure 1.10, add a set of circles centered at the null model and passing through various points in the graph. Verify that ncd.level and driver.gender are equally far apart from the null model.

From Figure 1.10 it looks like two potentially good variables to consider next might be ncd.level and driver.gender.

Exercise 1.36. Fit a log-link gamma severity model to the training dataset on the variables year and ncd.level. What information do you see for the estimated coefficients? Is this a good candidate to include in our severity model?

From the answer to Exercise 1.36 the variable ncd.level has a poor review. One level is significant, but the others are not. An analysis of deviance table (see Table 1.13) also tells us that this is not statistically significant.

Exercise 1.37. Does the variable driver.gender help us differentiate the severities of our policyholders?

Table 1.13. *Analysis of Deviance for a Single Model*

Variable	Df	Deviance	Resid. Df	Resid. Dev	Pr(>Chi)
NULL			1,855	3,997.8	
year	3	45.789	1,852	3,952.0	0
ncd.level	5	17.692	1,847	3,934.3	0.1096

Note: The variables are added sequentially. For the no claim discount variable we are estimating an additional 5 parameters but getting a reduction in deviance of only 18 points – not a significant improvement.

---

[11] In R the AIC is calculated as minus twice the maximized log-likelihood plus twice the number of parameters.

Even though the variables `ncd.level` and `driver.gender` are furthest away from the null model (in the AIC vs. deviance plane), only one of them seems to be a strong explanatory variable.

Exercise 1.38. Would `marital.status` be a good variable to help explain severities?

The variable `vehicle.value` is very close to the null model (see Figure 1.10) and so it does not seem to be a good candidate. But upon reflection, this does not seem to be right. Luxury vehicles are likely to be more expensive to repair, and so the value of the vehicle should be informative.

Exercise 1.39. Fit a severity log-link model with a gamma error to the variables `year` and `vehicle.value`. What is the coefficient for the variable `vehicle.value`? What is its standard error?

From Exercise 1.39 we know that the parameter estimate for `vehicle.value` has a negative sign. That does not make sense, and we should more carefully look at the data. Figure 1.11 shows a scatterplot of `vehicle.value` against `severity`, that is, a one-way summary of our data.

The assumption that a straight line adequately models the logarithm of the expected severity is probably not a good choice. From Figure 1.11 we see that the relationship between severity and vehicle value is nonlinear.

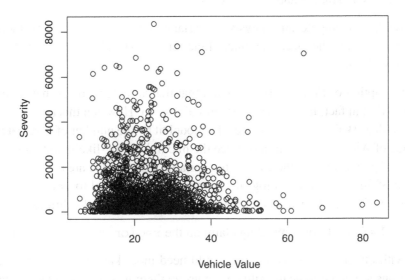

Fig. 1.11. Vehicle value versus severity. Note that we have very few observations with a vehicle value greater than 60, and all of them (except one) have a very small severity. These observations are partly responsible for the negative sign in our parameter estimate.

Exercise 1.40. Print Figure 1.11 on a piece of blank paper and, by hand, draw a smooth curve that captures the overall shape of the points. Set it aside.

Now use your computer to add a scatterplot smooth to the same figure. Compare your hand-drawn curve with the one drawn with the help of your computer. Are the two curves close to each other?

Based on the answer to Exercise 1.40, a single slope parameter for the variable `vehicle.value` might not be the best choice for parameterization. A simple approximation to the smooth might be to have a straight line decreasing in the range [0, 15), then a horizontal segment in the range [15, 35), and again a straight line segment from [35, 85); that is, we would like a piecewise linear function with three segments. Exercise 1.41 shows us how to create a piecewise linear function.

Exercise 1.41. How can you define a piecewise linear function with three segments over the intervals [0, 15], (15, 35], and (35, 85]?

Exercise 1.42. What are the coefficients α_i of the basis functions (defined in Exercise 1.41) $p_0(x)$, $p_1(x)$, $q_1(x)$, and $q_2(x)$ so that we have a piecewise linear function

$$f(x) = \alpha_0 p_0(x) + \alpha_1 p_1(x) + \alpha_2 q_1(x) + \alpha_3 q_2(x)$$

passing through the points (0, 45), (15, 15), (35, 15), and (85, 5)?

Exercise 1.43. Fit a piecewise linear function to `vehicle.age`. What are the parameter estimates and their standard errors?

Exercise 1.44. Compute an analysis of variance table for the severity model that includes `year` and the piecewise linear function of `vehicle.value` that we fitted in Exercise 1.43.

In the caption of Figure 1.10 we noted that the variable `region` has a very high value of AIC; in fact, it is higher than our null model. How can this be?

Recall that Akaike's AIC penalizes the model fit by the number of parameters. In R the value of AIC is equal to minus twice the maximized log-likelihood plus twice the number of parameters. In the case of the variable `region` we are estimating parameters for 38 regions. Fitting a log-link gamma severity model to `year` and `region` yields a set of parameter values that (nearly all) are not statistically different from zero.

Exercise 1.45. Verify the preceding claim on the `region` parameter estimates.

As with our frequency model, we would need more knowledge of how the various regions are geographically situated to group them in a sensible manner. From an implementation perspective we would consult with our underwriters to understand how the various regions stack up in terms of their severity and perhaps choose a few representative parameter estimates. The current estimates suggest that `region` is not a variable that we would like to include in our model. From a business perspective we might want to include it in our model. We can initially set all the parameters equal to zero. Later, if we wanted to differentiate our rates by region, we would have the flexibility to do so.

Exercise 1.46. Investigate all remaining variables and determine which ones would be good candidates to include in our severity model.

1.5.2 Multiway Severity Models

Let's move on to considering several variables at the same time. Perhaps driver age together with marital status might provide a good model. The variable drv.age provides a very big reduction in deviance (see caption of Figure 1.10), but given the large number of levels for this categorical variable, its AIC is even bigger than that of the null model. Perhaps a sensible grouping of driver ages can result in a powerful variable.

Before fitting a model to the variable drv.age, let's check how the residuals from our null+marital.status model behave against this out-of-model variable. In Figure 1.12 you can clearly see that the residuals are not centered on the line $y = 0$. In the early ages (18–25) where the residuals are positive, our current model underpredicts. In the middle portion, there are many ups and downs for the median residuals. Based on these residuals, there is signal in the driver age variable that our current model has not taken into account.

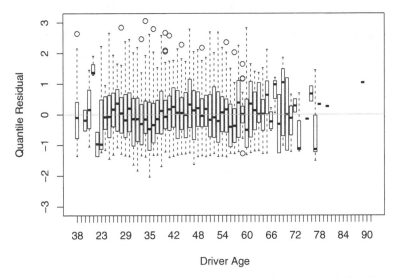

Fig. 1.12. Out-of-model variable drv.age against quantile residuals for the model that includes year and marital.status. The first box-and-whisker diagram corresponds to our base level age of 38. All remaining ages are in ascending order.

Exercise 1.47. Fit a model to `year`, `marital.status`, and `drv.age`. Does it make sense to group various ages into single parameter values? Which driver age parameters are statistically significant at the 5% level?

Exercise 1.48. Plot `drv.age` against quantile residuals when `drv.age` considered as an in-model-variable (include `year` and `marital.status`). Based on this graph, what grouping of ages would you recommend?

We still have many other variables to evaluate, such as `driver.gender`, `ccm`, `veh.age`, `body.code`, `seats`, and `hei.dm`. The three most promising variables are `body.code`, `weight`, and `driver.gender`.

Exercise 1.49. Based on Figure 1.10, the gender of the principal driver seems to be a good candidate. Fit a gamma log-link severity model to the training dataset with the variables `year` and `driver.gender`. Do the estimated parameter values make sense to you?

Exercise 1.50. Continue investigating the remaining variables for inclusion in the severity model, in particular, `body.code` and `weight`.

1.6 Pure Premium

In this section we combine our frequency and severity models into a pure premium. The formula is simple:

$$\text{Pure Premium} = \text{Frequency} \times \text{Severity}$$

For discussion purposes we use frequency and severity models with the variables listed in Table 1.14. These models are not necessarily the best models we could construct, and we challenge our readers to build better ones.

Exercise 1.51. Build better frequency and severity models than those specified in Table 1.14.

Table 1.14. *Variables Used in the Component Models for Pure Premium*

Frequency	Severity
year	year
ncd.level	marital.status
drv.age.gr2	driver.gender
yrs.lic	weight
region.g1	body.code
prior.claims	

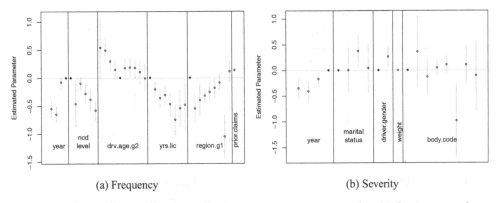

(a) Frequency   (b) Severity

Fig. 1.13. Parameter estimates and 95% confidence intervals for the frequency and severity models used for the pure premium calculation. The intercepts are not shown, but the base levels for categorical variables are shown as solid circles. The estimated value of the intercept for the frequency and severity models is -1.21777 and 6.26338 with standard errors equal to 0.08411 and 0.23612, respectively.

Figure 1.13 shows the parameter estimates for the models we have chosen (intercept terms are not shown). These parameter estimates should be considered our best indications given the training data we are using. Note that for the frequency model, there are some estimates that are counterintuitive. For example, with the no claim discount variable, we would expect to have strictly decreasing estimates as the discount level increases. Yet level 2 (the first one shown in the graph) is well below the next three levels and thus not conforming to the expected pattern. You can also see some reversals for the variable `yrs.lic`.

Exercise 1.52. Verify the parameter estimates shown in Figure 1.13 by fitting a frequency and a severity model to the variables listed in Table 1.14.

To compute the indicated pure premium, we need to calculate expected frequency and expected severity and then multiply them togeher. For a generalized linear model with a log-link function the general formula is

$$E[Y] = \exp(\beta_0 + \beta_1 x_1 + \beta_2 x_2 + \cdots + \beta_n x_n + \text{offset})$$

where Y represents our response variable (usually claim counts or claim amounts), β_0 is the intercept term, β_i with $i > 0$ are the estimated coefficients, and the x_i are the values of the corresponding explanatory variables (some of them are indicator variables and others are numeric variables) and the offset term (if included).

Exercise 1.53. How would you calculate the pure premium for `row.id` 3764 in our dataset?

Doing these calculations for the training dataset yields the summary statistics for frequency, severity, and pure premium shown in Table 1.15.

Table 1.15. *Summary Statistics for Expected Frequency, Severity,*
and Pure Premiums across the Training Dataset

	Min	Q1	Q2	Mean	Q3	Max
Frequency (%)	0.1	3.2	6.4	8.2	11.1	97.1
Severity ($)	199.5	614.8	741.9	758.7	873.0	2,171.0
Pure Premium ($)	0.6	22.4	46.1	64.7	84.4	1,242.0

The indicated pure premiums range from a minimum of 60 cents to a maximum of 1,242. We should investigate these very low and very high pure premiums. What profile do these customers have?

Exercise 1.54. Identify the records with very low and very high pure premiums. Do the low (high) pure premium records have any characteristics in common?

It is clear from Table 1.15 and Figure 1.13 that our indicated pure premiums are not yet viable as the foundation for a set of rates we would like to charge our customers. We have some counterintuitive parameter estimates, and some of our pure premiums are clearly extremely low or extremely high. Nonetheless, we should check how close (in aggregate) are our indicated pure premiums to our incurred claims. For the training dataset, the total pure premium is equal to 1,585,725, and the total incurred claims is 1,578,258; that is a ratio equal to 1.0047.

Exercise 1.55. Verify that over the training dataset the total of pure premiums based on the indicated parameters are within 0.5% of the total incurred claims.

To partially address these issues, we will modify our indicated parameter estimates to remove reversals and counterintuitive values. We will then use these revised parameters to calculate expected frequency, expected severity, and pure premiums. Figure 1.14 is the same as Figure 1.13 but shows the modified parameter estimates as an a cross symbol. We have only modified seven frequency parameters (one for `ncd.level`, two for `drv.age.gr2`, and four for `yrs.lic`). No severity parameters were modified.

With these changes to our indicated parameters we can compute the expected frequency, severity, and pure premiums across the entire dataset. Table 1.16 shows the six-point summary statistics for expected frequency, severity, and pure premium across the training dataset.

Also summing the expected pure premium and the claim incurred across the training dataset yields 1,654,799 and 1,578,258, respectively. Our pure premium is no longer in balance with the total incurred claims. Pure premiums, in total, are almost 5% larger than the incurred claims. This is a consequence of modifying our indicated

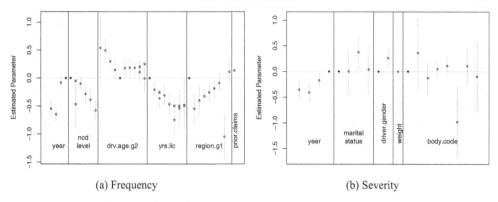

(a) Frequency   (b) Severity

Fig. 1.14. Indicated and modified parameter estimates for our frequency and severity models. Modified parameters are shown with a cross symbol. We have only modified seven frequency parameters. No parameters were modified for severity.

parameter estimates. For the parameters that we modified, we increased all of them except one. To compensate for these adjustments, we could modify the intercept terms in our frequency or severity models. This is an easy adjustment, and we illustrate it in what follows, but it is not optimal. What we should do is reestimate our model with the variables that we modified as offsets. This would allow the intercept and nonmodified variables to adjust their coefficients to compensate for the modified variables.

We only made adjustments to the frequency model, so we'll adjust that intercept term. We are using a logarithmic link function for frequency, and so the adjustment is equal to[12]

$$-\log\left(\frac{2{,}092.4}{2{,}003}\right) = -0.043664$$

The new frequency intercept term should be equal to

$$-1.217769 - 0.043664 = -1.261433$$

Table 1.16. *Summary Statistics on the Training Dataset for Expected Frequency, Severity, and Pure Premium Based on the Modified Parameter Estimates Shown in Figure 1.14*

	Min	Q1	Q2	Mean	Q3	Max
Frequency (%)	0.2	3.5	6.7	8.5	11.5	97.1
Severity ($)	199.5	614.8	741.9	758.8	873.0	2,171.0
Pure premium ($)	0.8	24.3	48.6	67.6	88.6	1,312.0

[12] The value of the numerator is the sum of the expected frequency across all the training records with the modified parameters as shown in Figure 1.14a.

With this change the total pure premium is equal to 1,584,098, and the total incurred claims equal 1,578,258: a ratio equal to 1.0037.

Exercise 1.56. Estimate a Poisson log-link frequency model on the training dataset with the variables `year`, `ncd.level`, and `driver.gender`. In conjunction with our business partners we would like to restrict the no claim discount for levels 1 to 6 to the following percentages: 0%, 10%, 20%, 25%, 30%, and 35%. How do the parameter estimates change given this restriction?

1.7 Validation

In the prior sections we explored our dataset and created some frequency and severity models on the training data. We transformed some predictors, grouped levels of a predictor, and created piecewise linear transforms of variables to enhance our models. We have also done cross-validation to ensure that our models have not overfitted the training dataset and that they will perform well on new data.

This is the "moment of truth" section. Our fitted frequency and severity models will see for the very first (and only) time our validation dataset. If we fine-tuned our models appropriately during construction, then we should see good performance. The performance should be similar to what we see on the training dataset. If performance degrades significantly on the validation dataset, that is a clear sign of overfitting. An overfitted model will perform poorly on new data.

During training we scored our entire dataset with three new variables: `efq`, `esv`, and `epp`. These three variables represent expected frequency, expected severity, and the pure premium, respectively. They are based on the models we created in Section 1.6.

Table 1.17 shows aggregate actual claim counts and incurred claims together with expected claims and pure premium for both the training and the validation datasets. Note that the ratio of predicted to actual over the training dataset is very close to unity, but over the validation dataset we are underpredicting by about 6.5 percentage points.

We have a performance gap between the training and validation datasets. This is expected. We calibrated our parameters with the training data, and so we expect our model to fit well on this dataset. On the validation dataset we know we are not going to perform as well. How big the gap between the training and validation data is before we get worried depends on the application domain we are working in.

We also need to assess how this gap is spread by both in-model variables and out-of-model variables. Another key consideration is to determine if key segments of our book of business have a large or small performance gap.

Table 1.17. *Actual and Predicted Claim Counts and Claims Incurred across the Training and Validation Datasets*

Variable		Training	Validation
Claim counts	Predicted	2,003	1,335
	Actual	2,003	1,428
	Ratio	1.0000	0.9351
Claims incurred	Predicted	1,584,098	1,060,082
	Actual	1,578,258	1,132,929
	Ratio	1.0037	0.9357

Exercise 1.57. Do an actual versus expected table for `driver.gender` similar to Table 1.17.

As shown in Table 1.17, over the entire training dataset the ratio of predicted to actual claims incurred is equal to 1.0037, and across the validation dataset it is equal to 0.9357. From Exercise 1.57 we can see that over the training dataset for male drivers, the ratio of predicted over actual claims incurred is equal to 1.014, and for females it is 0.947. We are slightly overpredicting the male experience and to a greater degree underpredicting the females.

Exercise 1.58. Repeat Exercise 1.57 with the no claim discount variable (`ncd.level`). Also investigate all other in-model variables.

Figure 1.15 shows mean claims incurred and expected pure premium segmented into 20 equally large bins ordered from smallest to largest pure premium. For example, the 19th bin (second to last on the right) corresponds to records having pure premiums between the 90th and 95th percentiles, namely, all records with pure premiums in the interval (142, 186]. Note that average actual claims incurred across the training dataset for this bin is equal to about 140 (solid circle). Using the validation dataset yields an average claims incurred close to 195 (plus symbol). The pure premium over the validation dataset is approximately 160 (cross symbol).

For many of the bins in Figure 1.15 all three points are close to each other. There are some bins where there are larger discrepancies, such as bins 12, 13, 18, and 19. This is valuable information that a pricing committee would take into account when taking these pure premium indications and transforming them into market rates.

Another tool we can use to assess the adequacy of our model is the Lorenz curve and the Gini index. The Lorenz curve is a way of visualizing a distribution function. A standard way of visualizing a distribution function would be to plot $(x, F(x))$. On the horizontal axis we have the quantiles, x, and on the vertical axis we have the probability $F(x)$ of quantiles being smaller than or equal to x.

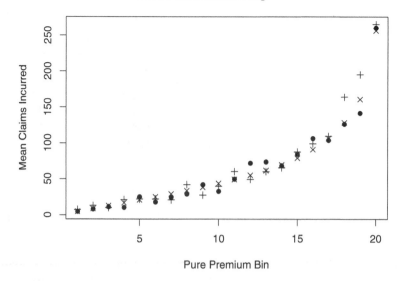

Fig. 1.15. Mean claims incurred by pure premium bin. The solid circle represents the average claims incurred over the training dataset. The plus-shaped data points are the average actual claims incurred over the validation data set, and the cross-shaped data points represent the average pure premium over the validation dataset. The average pure premiums over the training dataset are nearly identical to the ones over the validation dataset and so have been omitted from the plot.

For the Lorenz curve we use the horizontal axis to plot the proportion of observations, and on the vertical axis we plot not the quantiles but rather the cumulative proportion of quantiles. The Gini index is equal to twice the area trapped between the line $y = x$ and the Lorenz curve.

This is a measure of the distance between this distribution and the uniform distribution, where all the points have equal probability. The 45° line is known as the line of equality. The further away we are from the line of equality, the more skewed our distribution tends to be.

Exercise 1.59. Given a sample $x_1 \leq \cdots \leq x_n$, how should we construct the Lorenz curve and calculate the Gini index?

Ideally our pure premium model should help us differentiate the risks in our portfolio. In insurance pricing a typical application of the Lorenz curve would plot on the horizontal axis the proportion of cumulative exposures and on the vertical axis the proportion of cumulative pure premiums. Figure 1.16 shows the Lorenz curve for the pure premiums over the training dataset. The Gini index is equal to 0.2898. On the validation data the Gini index is equal to 0.2939: essentially the same as on the training dataset.

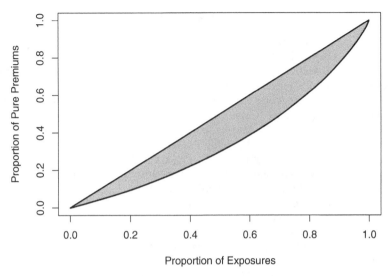

Fig. 1.16. The Lorenz curve for the pure premium distribution on the training data. The Gini index is equal to 0.2898 (twice the shaded area).

1.8 Conclusions

Over the last sections we have discussed some of the key areas necessary to develop a pure premium model. We have done some exploratory data analysis to familiarize ourselves with the data and gain some insights that would prove useful during the modeling phase. We then embarked on the creation of some frequency and severity models. We used both continuous and discrete variables. We transformed some of our variables to help us extract more of the signal that is embedded in our dataset. We put our two submodels together to from our pure premium. We also adjusted some of our estimated coefficients to better align with our business practices. Finally, we validated our proposed model against new data to assess the performance that we should observe once we put it into production.

We have accomplished a lot! Yet there is more work to do. Having a pure premium model is just one component of an overall pricing exercise. At a minimum you will need to do a rate level indication and project your proposed gross premiums to the appropriate future exposure period. You will also need to consider expenses and profit levels and incorporate them into your final premiums. Also implementation and monitoring of your new rates are of critical importance.

We hope the reader has also taken the time to be an active participant (rather than a passive spectator) and attempted to solve all the exercises. You are now in an excellent position to continue learning and refining these techniques. The bibliography has some entries that we have found very useful, and we hope that you continue developing your data analysis skills.

References

Cameron, A. C., and P. K. Trivedi. *Regression Analysis of Count Data*. Econometric Society Monographs. Cambridge University Press, Cambridge, 1998.

de Jong, P., and G. Z. Heller. *Generalized Linear Models for Insurance Data*. International Series on Actuarial Science. Cambridge University Press, Cambridge, 2008.

Frees, E. W. *Regression Modeling with Actuarial and Financial Applications*. International Series on Actuarial Science. Cambridge University Press, Cambridge, 2010.

Frees, E. W., R. A. Derrig, and G. Meyers, editors. *Predictive Modeling Applications in Actuarial Science: Volume 1, Predictive Modeling Techniques*. International Series on Actuarial Science. Cambridge University Press, Cambridge, 2014.

Frees, E. W. (Jed), G. Meyers, and A. D. Cummings. Insurance ratemaking and a Gini index. *Journal of Risk and Insurance*, 81(2):335–366, 2014.

Gelman, A., and J. Hill. *Data Analysis Using Regression and Multilevel/ Hierarchical Models*. Analytical Methods for Social Research. Cambridge University Press, Cambridge, 2007.

Hardin, J., and J. Hilbe. *Generalized Linear Models and Extensions*. Stata Press, College Station, TX, 2001.

Khun, M., and K. Johnson. *Applied Predictive Modeling*. Springer, New York, 2013.

McCullagh, P., and J. A. Nelder. *Generalized Linear Models*. Chapman and Hall, London, 1998.

Steyerberg, E. W. *Clinical Prediction Models*. Statistics for Biology and Health. Springer, New York, 2009.

Werner, G., and C. Modlin. *Basic Ratemaking*. 4th ed. Casualty Acturial Society, Arlington, VA, 2010.

Zumel, N., and J. Mount. *Practical Data Science with R*. Manning, Shelter Island, NY, 2014.

2

Applying Generalized Linear Models to Insurance Data

Frequency/Severity versus Pure Premium Modeling

Dan Tevet

Chapter Preview. This chapter is a case study on modeling loss costs for motorcycle collision insurance. It covers two approaches to loss cost modeling: fitting separate models for claim frequency and claim severity and fitting one model for pure premium. Exploratory data analysis, construction of the models, and evaluation and comparisons of the results are all discussed.

2.1 Introduction

When modeling insurance claims data using generalized linear models (GLM), actuaries have two choices for the model form:

1. create two models – one for the frequency of claims and one for the average severity of claims;
2. create a single model for pure premium (i.e., average claim cost).

Actuaries have traditionally used the frequency/severity approach, but in recent years pure premium modeling has gained popularity. The main reason for this development is the growing acceptance and use of the Tweedie distribution.

In a typical insurance dataset, the value of pure premium is zero for the vast majority of records, since most policies incur no claims; but, where a claim does occur, pure premium tends to be large. Unfortunately, most "traditional" probability distributions – Gaussian, Poisson, gamma, lognormal, inverse Gaussian, and so on – cannot be used to describe pure premium data. Gaussian assumes that negative values are possible; the Poisson is generally too thin-tailed to adequately capture the skewed nature of insurance data; and the gamma, lognormal, and inverse Gaussian distributions do not allow for values of zero.

Fortunately, there is a distribution that does adequately describe pure premium for most insurance datasets – the Tweedie distribution. The Tweedie is essentially a compound Poisson-gamma process, whereby claims occur according to a Poisson distribution and claim severity, given that a claim occurs, follows a gamma distribution. This is very convenient since actuaries have traditionally modeled claim frequency with a Poisson distribution and claim severity with a gamma distribution.

In this chapter, we explore three procedures for modeling insurance data:

1. modeling frequency and severity separately;
2. modeling pure premium using the Tweedie distribution (without modeling dispersion; in practice, this is the most common implementation of pure premium modeling;
3. modeling pure premium using a "double GLM approach"; that is, modeling both the mean and dispersion of pure premium.

We compare the results of each approach and assess the approaches' advantages and disadvantages.

2.2 Comparing Model Forms

2.2.1 Modeling Claim Frequency

The term *frequency modeling* is vague, so it is important to clarify the exact model being discussed. In particular, there are three general forms for a frequency model:

1. Model the number of claims on each record as the target variable and offset for the exposure volume. With this specification, there is generally no GLM weight. The Poisson and the negative binomial are the most common choices for the distribution of claims.
2. Model claim frequency, calculated as claim count divided by exposures, as the target variable and weight each record by exposures. The Poisson distribution can be used to model claim frequency.
3. Model the probability of a claim using logistic regression.

It's interesting to note that, if the Poisson distribution is chosen, options 1 and 2 produce identical results.

In this case study, we construct three models for claim frequency:

1. model claim count using a Poisson distribution;
2. model claim count using a negative binomial distribution;
3. model the probability of a claim using logistic regression.

2.2.2 Modeling Claim Severity

Severity is defined as the dollars of loss per claim, conditional on one or more claims occurring. Thus, when modeling claim severity, only records for which there is a nonzero claim count are used. Since records with more claims are expected to have more stable experience, claim count is set as the GLM weight. For the distribution of severity, the most common choice is gamma, followed by inverse Gaussian.

The key difference between the gamma and inverse Gaussian distributions is in their implicit assumptions about volatility. The GLM variance function for a gamma distribution is $V(\mu) = \mu^2$, whereas for an inverse Gaussian distribution it is $V(\mu) = \mu^3$. So, as expected severity increases, an inverse Gaussian model assumes volatility increases at a faster rate than does a gamma distribution. For high-frequency, low-severity lines like private passenger automobile, the gamma distribution is generally the more appropriate choice, since claim costs can be expected to be relatively stable. Conversely, for low-frequency, high-severity lines like general liability, where a high degree of volatility in claim cost is the norm, an inverse Gaussian model may be more appropriate.

In this case study, we construct two models for claim severity:

1. model severity using a gamma distribution;
2. model severity using an inverse Gaussian distribution.

2.2.3 Modeling Pure Premium

As an alternative to building separate models for claim frequency and claim severity, one can directly model pure premium using the Tweedie distribution.

For pure premium modeling, there are two possible specifications:

1. Set pure premium, calculated as dollars of loss divided by exposures, as the target variable. With this option, exposures are generally used as the weight since records with a higher exposure volume are expected to have more stable experience.
2. Set dollars of loss as the target variable, offset for the exposure volume, and set $(\text{exposure})^{(p-1)}$ as the weight, where p is the Tweedie power parameter.

These are equivalent representations for estimating regression coefficients (see Appendix 2.A for proof).

The Tweedie distribution is a relatively new and very convenient distribution for modeling pure premium, but it does have one important limitation: buried in the Tweedie parameterization is the assumption of a positive correlation between claim frequencies and claim severity. That is, the Tweedie distribution, as commonly implemented in a GLM, implicitly assumes that each covariate impacts frequency and severity in the same direction.

Recall that the Tweedie is essentially a compound Poisson-gamma process, whereby claims occur according to a Poisson distribution and claim severity, given that a claim occurs, follows a gamma distribution. Smyth and Jørgensen (2002) use the following parameterization for the Tweedie distribution:

$$\mu = \lambda \cdot \alpha \cdot \theta, \quad p = \frac{\alpha + 2}{\alpha + 1}, \quad \varphi = \frac{\lambda^{1-p} \cdot (\alpha \cdot \theta)^{2-p}}{2 - p}$$

where λ is the mean of the underlying Poisson distribution, α is the shape parameter of the underlying gamma distribution, and θ is the scale parameter of the underlying gamma distribution.

The p parameter is constant across the dataset and is typically input by the modeler. Due to the constraint that $\alpha > 0$, $1 < p < 2$. In most applications of Tweedie GLMs, the dispersion parameter φ is assumed to be constant across the dataset.

Since p is assumed to be constant and $1 < p < 2$, the parameter φ has the following property:

$$\varphi \sim \frac{(\alpha \cdot \theta)^{2-p}}{\lambda^{p-1}}$$

In words, φ is proportional to the mean severity raised to some positive power divided by the mean frequency raised to some positive power. Therefore, if φ is constant across the dataset, then any factor which increases mean severity (and thus increases the numerator of the above equation) must also increase the mean frequency. Put simply, to preserve the constancy of φ, mean frequency and mean severity must move in the same direction.

Unfortunately, this assumption of positive correlation between frequency and severity is often unrealistic. For example, some classes of business (like chemical manufacturing plants) may have a low claim frequency but high severity once a claim occurs, while other classes may be high-frequency, low-severity.

However, the Tweedie distribution can still be used to model data for which frequency and severity move in opposite directions, as long as one models dispersion (φ) as well as the mean (μ). This procedure is commonly known as a "double generalized linear model" and is described in detail in Smyth and Jørgensen's 2002 paper. As explained, the assumption of positive correlation between frequency and severity stems from the assumption of a constant dispersion parameter across the dataset. However, if the dispersion (as well as the mean) is allowed to vary by record, then the constraint no longer applies.

The steps for running a Tweedie double GLM are as follows:

1. Fit a GLM for the mean. The target variable is (in our case) pure premium, the distribution is Tweedie, the weight is exposures divided by the dispersion parameter, and we initially set the dispersion parameter for all records to 1.

2. Based on the results in step 1, calculate the (weighted) deviance for each record in the dataset. The sum of these unit deviances equals the total deviance for the model run in step 1.
3. Fita GLM for dispersion. The target variable is the unit deviances (calculated in step 2), the distribution is gamma, and there is no weight. The predicted value from this step is now the new dispersion parameter for each record.
4. Refit the GLM for the mean as described in step 1, but this time we have a unique dispersion parameter for each record. The weight for this GLM is exposure divided by the dispersion parameter, as calculated in step 3.

2.2.4 Comparing the Frequency/Severity and Pure Premium Approaches

Both model forms have advantages and disadvantages of which the modeler should be aware.

The advantages of modeling frequency and severity separately include the following:

1. The modeler gains a greater intuition for how each variable impacts both frequency and severity. In this case study, which involves motorcycles collision coverage, one of the variables is the manufacturer suggested retail price (MSRP) of the bike. Obviously, as MSRP increases, so does severity. But what, if any, is the relationship between MSRP and claim frequency? That is, do more expensive bikes have more or fewer claims than less expensive ones? Intuitively there is no way to tell, and modeling pure premium will not provide an answer.
2. The Tweedie distribution is relatively new and is quite mathematically complex. The distributions commonly used to model frequency and severity though have been around for many years and are very well understood.
3. When modeling frequency and severity separately, one can include a different set of variables in each model, whereas pure premium modeling requires one set of common variables.
4. When modeling pure premium, if a double GLM approach is not used, then the modeler is implicitly assuming a positive correlation between frequency and severity.

The advantages of modeling pure premium include the following:

1. Only one model must be built, as opposed to two for frequency/severity, so there is time savings.
2. Since actuaries generally don't model an entire rating plan at once, it is common to off-set for variables not being modeled. For example, territorial base rate is often included as an offset in insurance models. Rates and rating factors are expressed in terms of pure premium though, and splitting variables like territorial base rate into separate frequency and severity components can be complicated and imprecise.

3. Pure premium models typically have fewer parameters than do models constructed for claim frequency and severity. This simplicity is helpful when conducting out-of-sample exercises, such as model validation.

2.3 The Dataset and Model Forms

The dataset that is used throughout this case study pertains to first-party coverage that insures against damage to a policyholder's motorcycle (aka motorcycles collision coverage). It is very important to note that, while this dataset is patterned on actual insurance data and thus is useful for pedagogic purposes, it does not comprise real data. Any results drawn from these data do not necessarily bear any resemblance to reality, so one should not act on any modeling results from these data or try to learn anything about the motorcycle insurance market from these data.

The dataset has five calendar/accident years of data (2008–2012) and contains the following fields:

- Bike Type: the type of motorcycle being insured; there are seven bike types, with cruisers being the base level
- Bike Age: the age of the motorcycle, which ranges from new to 12 years old
- Winter Temp: the average daily temperature during winter months for the location in which the motorcycle is insured
- MSRP: the manufacturer suggested retail price of the motorcycle
- Territory LC: the loss cost for the territory in which the motorcycle is insured
- Losses: incurred losses
- Claims: incurred claim count
- Bike Years: the exposure base for motorcycles

A few key summary statistics for this dataset:

Number of observations	1,000,000
Number of claims	31,047
Sum of earned exposures	500,249
Sum of loss dollars	$111,994,068
Average claim frequency	6.2%
Average claim severity	$3,607
Average pure premium	$224

Using this dataset, we will construct, evaluate, and compare the following models:

- Model F1: model claim count using a Poisson distribution
- Model F2: model claim count using a negative binomial distribution
- Model F3: model the probability of a claim using logistic regression
- Model S1: model severity using a gamma distribution

- Model S2: model severity using an inverse Gaussian distribution
- Model P1: model pure premium using a Tweedie distribution
- Model P2: model pure premium using a Tweedie distribution and a "double GLM" approach

All models will include bike type and bike age as discrete variables, and the log of winter temperature and the log of MSRP as continuous variables. Bike type is a categorical variable, whereas bike age is an ordinal variable since we expect a certain progression as a motorcycle ages. In all models, we will offset for the log of the territorial loss cost since we assume that the scope of this project does not include changing territorial loss costs. This is a common practice, as territorial loss costs are not usually determined via a GLM analysis but rather are calculated via techniques like spatial smoothing.

For all models, except for F3, we will use a GLM with a log-link (F3 uses a logit link, which is explained in Section 2.4.1.3). Thus, for the continuous covariates in the model, as well as for the offset terms, we use the natural log of the variable rather than the variable itself.

2.3.1 Splitting the Offset in Frequency/Severity Approach

As explained in Section 2.2.4, one drawback of modeling frequency and severity separately is that the modeler must split the offset term into a frequency component and a severity component. In this case, the challenge is to divide the territorial loss cost.

Ideally, such a split of territorial loss cost would be based on an analysis of the loss experience that went into the calculation of the loss costs. The relative effects of frequency and severity on the loss cost can vary by territory, so it would be desirable for such territorial differences to be reflected in the split. However, for simplicity, we consider an approach that uniformly allocates a portion of each loss costs to frequency and the remainder to severity.

As a first pass, let's run models F1 and S1, including the log of the territorial loss cost as a continuous variable in each model. Suppose that the coefficient for the log of territorial loss cost turns out to be 0.70 in the frequency model and 0.30 in the severity model. In that case, the task of dividing the territorial loss cost into frequency and severity components would be easy, since the coefficients sum to unity. We could simply offset for $0.70 \cdot$ (log of territorial loss cost) in model F1 and offset for $0.30 \cdot$ (log of territorial loss cost) in model S1.

Unfortunately, reality is not so simple. The coefficient in model F1 is 1.3989 and the coefficient in model S1 is 0.1431, which sum to 1.5420. We have a few options for splitting the territorial loss cost, but the main ones are as follows:

1. Proportionally assign the territorial loss cost to the frequency and severity models. The frequency portion is $1.3989/(1.3989 + 0.1431) = 0.907$, and the severity portion is $0.1431/(1.3989 + 0.1431) = 0.093$. So, the offset in F1 is $0.907 \cdot$ (log of territorial loss cost) and the offset in model S1 is $0.093 \cdot$ (log of territorial loss cost).
2. Since the territorial loss cost is a much more important driver of claim frequency than it is of claim severity (which we can see by looking at the magnitude of the coefficients, and can be further confirmed by looking at the confidence intervals), we can just offset for the log of the territorial loss cost in the frequency model and ignore it in the severity model.

For simplicity, we'll go with option 2, though in practice both options should be considered and tested.

2.3.2 Splitting the Dataset

To determine model performance, it is important to assess the models on holdout data. We could randomly split the dataset into training and test components (with training data used to build the model and test data used to determine model performance). Alternatively, we can split the dataset based on year. The latter approach allows for out-of-time validation, which is important because we want our model to be stable over short time periods. Therefore, we assign the last three years (2010, 2011, and 2012) to the training dataset and assign the first two years to holdout data. This roughly corresponds to a 70–30 split, with about 70% of exposures assigned to training data and 30% assigned to holdout data.

2.3.3 Interpreting Parameter Estimates

For GLMs with a log-link, the interpretation of parameter estimates is as follows. For discrete variables, a rating factor can be calculated for each level of the variable as $\exp(\beta)$, where β is the parameter estimate. These rating factors are relative to the base level, which by definition has a coefficient of 0 and thus has a rating factor of 1.

For continuous variables, we generally model the log of the variable rather than the variable itself. Then, the interpretation of the GLM coefficient is (target variable) $\propto$ (predictor variable)$^\beta$, where β is the GLM coefficient. So, if $\beta = 0.5$, then doubling the predictor variable causes the target variable to increase by $2^{0.50} - 1 = 41.4\%$, all else equal.

Note that this explanation only applies to GLMs with a log-link. For model F3, which has a logit link, the interpretation is different and is explained in Section 2.4.1.3.

2.3.4 Determining the Winning Model

Since we are comparing multiple models, we need some objective criterion for determining the superior model. For that, we will use the Gini index. Please see Appendix 2.B for more information on the Gini index.

2.4 Results

2.4.1 Frequency Models

2.4.1.1 Model F1

In Model F1, the target variable is claim count, the assumed distribution is Poisson, and the offset term is the log of the territorial loss cost plus the log of bike years.

The model output is shown in Figure 2.1.

MOTORCYCLE COLLISION SAMPLE DATASET
MODEL F1 RESULTS
FREQUENCY MODEL WITH POISSON DISTRIBUTION

Parameter	Level	Parameter Estimate	Standard Error	Wald Chi-Square	P Value
Intercept	–	−13.5074	0.2244	3,623.03	0.0000
Bike Type	Chopper	0.1732	0.1064	2.65	0.1037
Bike Type	Off-Road	−0.7714	0.0871	78.41	0.0000
Bike Type	Sport	1.0904	0.0203	2,881.79	0.0000
Bike Type	Sport-Touring	−0.0872	0.0621	1.97	0.1602
Bike Type	Standard	0.2570	0.0282	82.92	0.0000
Bike Type	Touring	0.0683	0.0218	9.83	0.0017
Bike Type	Cruiser (base)	0.0000	0.0000	–	–
Bike Age	2	−0.4294	0.0241	317.05	0.0000
Bike Age	3	−0.7984	0.0259	947.99	0.0000
Bike Age	4	−0.9507	0.0277	1,174.04	0.0000
Bike Age	5	−1.0968	0.0324	1,147.00	0.0000
Bike Age	6	−1.0961	0.0366	898.45	0.0000
Bike Age	7	−0.8076	0.0352	527.23	0.0000
Bike Age	8	−1.3377	0.0467	820.09	0.0000
Bike Age	9	−0.9132	0.0430	450.90	0.0000
Bike Age	10	−0.7522	0.0470	256.51	0.0000
Bike Age	11	−0.7188	0.0599	144.15	0.0000
Bike Age	12	−1.2259	0.0702	304.85	0.0000
Bike Age	1 (base)	0.0000	0.0000	–	–
Winter Temp	–	0.7640	0.0256	889.34	0.0000
MSRP	–	0.3225	0.0225	205.80	0.0000

Fig. 2.1. Motorcycle collision sample dataset: Model F1 results.

The Wald chi-squared statistic is calculated as the parameter estimate divided by the standard error, quantity squared. The larger the chi-squared static is, the more significant is the parameter. The Wald chi-squared statistic is so named because it can be compared to a chi-squared distribution with one degree of freedom. The *p*-value for each parameter estimate is then the probability of obtaining the observed Wald test statistic, or one of greater magnitude, by pure chance. Smaller *p*-values indicate greater parameter significance. To be clear though, for classification variables, this tests whether individual parameter estimates are significantly different from the base level for that variable, not whether the variable itself is significant. For example, in Model F1, the *p*-value for the chopper bike type is 0.1037. Since a popular cutoff for significance is a *p*-value of 0.05, we can conclude that the chopper bike type is not significantly different from the base level of cruisers. However, we would not conclude the bike type variable as a whole is insignificant, since sport bikes have a very high Wald chi-squared statistic.

The primary takeaways from the model output are as follows:

- The intercept is very small, but that can be ignored. Winter temperature, MSRP, and the territorial loss cost take on large values, so the intercept is merely compensating for that.
- Some bike types are significantly different from the base level, and others aren't. The sport bike type is very significant, though, and has a large parameter estimate, indicating the sport bikes are $\exp(1.0904) = 2.98$ times more likely to cause a claim than are cruisers (all else equal).
- All levels of bike age are very significant and indicate steep discounts. Note, though, that this is entirely a function of the chosen base level, which is new bikes. If we had set the base level to be bikes that are three years old, many of the levels would be insignificant.
- Winter temperature has a positive coefficient and is very significant. The coefficient of 0.7640 means that, as winter temperature doubles, the expected claim count increases by $2^{0.7640} - 1 \approx 70\%$.
- MSRP is significant and has a positive coefficient. This is an interesting result because it is unintuitive, and we would not have learned this information if we had only built a pure premium model.

2.4.1.2 Model F2

Model F2 is very similar to Model F1, but rather than using a Poisson distribution to model claim counts, a negative binomial distribution is used.

The parameter estimates for Model F2 are shown in Figure 2.2.

The conclusions of this model are generally the same as those for Model F1, so we won't elaborate on them.

2.4.1.3 Model F3

Model F3 is a logistic regression, in which we are modeling the probably of a record having one or more claims. There are only a handful of records with multiple claims, so for simplicity we can say that we're modeling the probably of a claim occurring.

The parameter estimates for Model F3 are shown in Figure 2.2.

Note that, because of the logit link function, the interpretation of the model output is very different from that of the models presented above. For Model F1, for example, we concluded that sport bikes are 2.98 times more likely to cause a claim than are cruisers (all else equal). For the logistic model, though, we cannot draw such conclusions. The closest we can come is to create certain scenarios. For example, say that bike age is 3, winter temperature is 40, the MSRP is 5,000, and the offset is 0.45. For a cruiser, the linear predictor is

$$-8.1326 + 0.0000 - 1.0895 + 1.0567 \cdot \log(40) + 0.4000 \cdot \log(5,000) = -1.9172$$

Thus, the probability of a claim is

$$0.45 \cdot \left[\frac{\exp(-1.9172)}{1 + \exp(-1.9172)} \right] = 58\%$$

For a sport bike with otherwise equivalent fields, the linear predictor is

$$-8.1326 + 1.8259 - 1.0895 + 1.0567 \cdot \log(40) + 0.4000 \cdot \log(5,000) = -0.0913$$

Thus, the probability of a claim is

$$0.45 \cdot \left[\frac{\exp(-0.0913)}{1 + \exp(-0.0913)} \right] = 215\%$$

So, in this case, the probability of having a claim with a sport bike is 3.7 times higher than the corresponding probability with a cruiser. However, if instead we have a new bike rather than a three-year-old one, the associated probabilities become 13.7% for cruisers and 32.9% for sport bikes, and the probability of having a claim is now 2.4 times higher for sport bikes than it is for cruisers.

2.4.1.4 Picking a Frequency Model

Figure 2.2 summarizes the parameter estimates for Models F1, F2, and F3.

We now have three models for claims frequency, and the question is, which model performs the best on the holdout data? To answer this, we will calculate Gini indexes for each model, with the x-axis being the cumulative percentage of bike years and the y-axis being the cumulative percentage of claims. For Models F1 and F2, the

MOTORCYCLE COLLISION SAMPLE DATASET
MODELS F1-F3 RESULTS

Parameter	Level	Model F1 Parameter Estimate		Model F2 Parameter Estimate		Model F3 Parameter Estimate	
Bike Type	Chopper	0.1732		0.1455		0.2580	
Bike Type	Off-Road	−0.7714	*	−0.7637	*	−0.8124	*
Bike Type	Sport	1.0904	*	1.1295	*	1.8259	*
Bike Type	Sport-Touring	−0.0872		−0.0425		0.0962	
Bike Type	Standard	0.2570	*	0.2588	*	0.3789	*
Bike Type	Touring	0.0683	*	0.0651	*	0.0802	*
Bike Type	Cruiser (base)	0.0000		0.0000		0.0000	
Bike Age	2	−0.4294	*	−0.4488	*	−0.7179	*
Bike Age	3	−0.7984	*	−0.7954	*	−1.0895	*
Bike Age	4	−0.9507	*	−0.9352	*	−1.2573	*
Bike Age	5	−1.0968	*	−1.0933	*	−1.4701	*
Bike Age	6	−1.0961	*	−1.0762	*	−1.4511	*
Bike Age	7	−0.8076	*	−0.8006	*	−1.1919	*
Bike Age	8	−1.3377	*	−1.3366	*	−1.7043	*
Bike Age	9	−0.9132	*	−0.9401	*	−1.3248	*
Bike Age	10	−0.7522	*	−0.7504	*	−1.1115	*
Bike Age	11	−0.7188	*	−0.7644	*	−1.1814	*
Bike Age	12	−1.2259	*	−1.2159	*	−1.6274	*
Bike Age	1 (base)	0.0000		0.0000		0.0000	
Winter Temp	−	0.7640	*	0.7944	*	1.0567	*
MSRP	−	0.3225	*	0.3145	*	0.4000	*

Fig. 2.2. Motorcycle collision sample dataset: Models F1–F3 results. The * denotes parameters with a p-value of less than 0.05.

sort order is the predicted claim count divided by bike years (we can call this predicted frequency). For F3, the sort order is the predicted probability of a claim divided by bike years (we can call this the predicted claim probability per unit of exposure).

The results are as follows:

Model	Gini Index
F1	35.02
F2	35.15
F3	34.68

Models F1 and F2 perform similarly (which is not surprising since they have similar parameter estimates), while the Gini index for Model F3 is slightly lower. Since Model F2 has the highest Gini index, we choose it as our model for claim frequency.

To determine how significant the differences are in these Gini indexes, the modeler can create bootstrapped confidence intervals. The involves creating several bootstrapped datasets (say, 20), determining the Gini index for each model on each dataset, and determining a standard error based on the standard deviationof these estimates.

2.4.2 Severity Models

2.4.2.1 Model S1

We now turn to the task of selecting a severity model. In Model S1, the target variable is claim severity (dollars of loss divided by claim count, conditional on there being one or more claims), the assumed distribution is gamma, and there is no offset term.

The model output is shown in Figure 2.3.

MOTORCYCLE COLLISION SAMPLE DATASET
MODEL S1 RESULTS
SEVERITY MODEL WITH GAMMA DISTRIBUTION

Parameter	Level	Parameter Estimate	Standard Error	Wald Chi-Square	P Value
Intercept	–	1.6318	0.1821	80.33	0.0000
Bike Type	Chopper	0.8227	0.0829	98.44	0.0000
Bike Type	Off-Road	−0.1906	0.0677	7.92	0.0049
Bike Type	Sport	0.0166	0.0161	1.07	0.3002
Bike Type	Sport-Touring	0.2029	0.0486	17.41	0.0000
Bike Type	Standard	0.1795	0.0221	66.04	0.0000
Bike Type	Touring	0.1163	0.0171	46.49	0.0000
Bike Type	Cruiser (base)	0.0000	0.0000	–	–
Bike Age	2	−0.0696	0.0188	13.65	0.0002
Bike Age	3	0.0438	0.0203	4.63	0.0314
Bike Age	4	0.0015	0.0220	0.00	0.9449
Bike Age	5	−0.0015	0.0253	0.00	0.9531
Bike Age	6	−0.0591	0.0288	4.21	0.0402
Bike Age	7	−0.0948	0.0276	11.77	0.0006
Bike Age	8	−0.1971	0.0365	29.15	0.0000
Bike Age	9	−0.1150	0.0336	11.74	0.0006
Bike Age	10	−0.1246	0.0368	11.46	0.0007
Bike Age	11	−0.1904	0.0471	16.37	0.0001
Bike Age	12	−0.2514	0.0549	20.95	0.0000
Bike Age	1 (base)	0.0000	0.0000	–	–
Winter Temp	–	−0.1060	0.0201	27.71	0.0000
MSRP	–	0.7313	0.0181	1,626.00	0.0000

Fig. 2.3. Motorcycle collision sample dataset: Model S1 results.

The primary takeaways from the model output are as follows:

- Many of the bike types that were significant in Model F1 are insignificant in this model, and vice versa. For example, choppers were insignificant in F1 but are significant (with a large surcharge) in S1, whereas sport bikes were very significant in F1 but insignificant in S1. So, for some bike types, losses are primarily frequency driven, while for others, losses are primarily a function of severity.
- Bike age is far less significant in this model than it was in the frequency models.
- The coefficient for winter temperature is negative. So, while warmer areas have a much higher frequency of claims than do colder areas, they have a slightly lower severity.
- The coefficient for MSRP is positive and is very significant, as expected.

2.4.2.2 Model S2

This model is very similar to S1, but rather than modeling severity using a gamma distribution, we do so with an inverse Gaussian distribution.

This model actually failed to converge. Intuitively, an inverse Gaussian distribution is probably not appropriate for this dataset. Whereas the gamma distribution assumes that variance is proportional to mean squared, the inverse Gaussian distribution assumes that variance is proportional to mean cubed. So, an inverse Gaussian is appropriate for highly volatile data (which, in the insurance context, is low-frequency, high-severity data). The motorcycles collision data would be more accurate described as high-frequency, low-severity though, so intuition would tell us that a gamma model would be more appropriate. Therefore, we discount this model and settle on S1 as our severity model.

2.4.3 Pure Premium Models

2.4.3.1 Model P1

For Model P1, the target variable is pure premium (dollars of loss divided by bike years), the assumed distribution is Tweedie, and the offset is the log of the territorial loss cost. Additionally, for a Tweedie distribution, we must select the Tweedie power parameter (p), which is a function of the coefficient of variation of the underlying severity distribution. We choose the value that minimizes the deviance of the model, which is $p = 1.45$.

The model output is shown in Figure 2.4.

The coefficients for Model P1 are generally similar to the sum of the coefficients for Models F1 and S1. For example, consider bike age 2. The sum of the coefficients for Models F1 and S1 are $-0.4294 - 0.0696 = -0.4991$, which is very close to the -0.4844 coefficient for Model P1. This isn't surprising, since combining a claim frequency and claim severity models should yield results that are similar

MOTORCYCLE COLLISION SAMPLE DATASET
MODEL P1 RESULTS
PURE PREMIUM MODEL WITH TWEEDIE DISTRIBUTION

Parameter	Level	Parameter Estimate	Standard Error	Wald Chi-Square	P Value
Intercept	–	−11.8335	0.3097	1,460.43	0.0000
Bike Type	Chopper	0.7852	0.1094	51.53	0.0000
Bike Type	Off-Road	−0.8695	0.0995	76.33	0.0000
Bike Type	Sport	1.0808	0.0311	1,210.64	0.0000
Bike Type	Sport-Touring	0.2108	0.0680	9.62	0.0019
Bike Type	Standard	0.4225	0.0373	128.37	0.0000
Bike Type	Touring	0.1780	0.0266	44.89	0.0000
Bike Type	Cruiser (base)	0.0000	0.0000	–	–
Bike Age	2	−0.4844	0.0364	176.84	0.0000
Bike Age	3	−0.7114	0.0365	380.86	0.0000
Bike Age	4	−0.8233	0.0375	480.93	0.0000
Bike Age	5	−1.0551	0.0418	635.81	0.0000
Bike Age	6	−1.0885	0.0461	557.40	0.0000
Bike Age	7	−0.8365	0.0465	323.54	0.0000
Bike Age	8	−1.4863	0.0555	717.14	0.0000
Bike Age	9	−1.0085	0.0547	340.02	0.0000
Bike Age	10	−0.8549	0.0611	195.68	0.0000
Bike Age	11	−0.8263	0.0777	113.00	0.0000
Bike Age	12	−1.2975	0.0848	234.33	0.0000
Bike Age	1 (base)	0.0000	0.0000	–	–
Winter Temp	–	0.6492	0.0321	410.03	0.0000
MSRP	–	1.0477	0.0311	1,137.88	0.0000

Fig. 2.4. Motorcycle collision sample dataset: Model P1 results.

to a model for pure premium, assuming that the same variables are used in all models.

2.4.3.2 Model P2

Model P2 is a Tweedie double GLM, the procedure for which is described in Section 2.2.3.

The model output is shown in Figure 2.5.

In some cases the parameter estimates produced by Models P1 and P2 are similar, and in other cases they are quite different (like for touring bikes).

2.4.3.3 Picking a Pure Premium Model

To calculate Gini indexes for a pure premium model, the *x*-axis is the cumulative percentage of bike years, the *y*-axis is the cumulative percentage of losses, and the sort order is the predicted pure premium.

MOTORCYCLE COLLISION SAMPLE DATASET
MODEL P2 RESULTS
DOUBLE GLM PURE PREMIUM MODEL

Parameter	Level	Parameter Estimate	Standard Error	Wald Chi-Square	P Value
Intercept	–	−13.1007	0.2999	1,907.88	0.0000
Bike Type	Chopper	0.6227	0.1573	15.67	0.0001
Bike Type	Off-Road	−0.9087	0.0738	151.52	0.0000
Bike Type	Sport	1.0524	0.0380	767.68	0.0000
Bike Type	Sport-Touring	0.2421	0.0782	9.57	0.0020
Bike Type	Standard	0.4395	0.0379	134.75	0.0000
Bike Type	Touring	0.1226	0.0305	16.15	0.0001
Bike Type	Cruiser (base)	0.0000	0.0000	–	–
Bike Age	2	−0.4670	0.0456	104.73	0.0000
Bike Age	3	−0.6809	0.0448	230.93	0.0000
Bike Age	4	−0.7891	0.0456	298.98	0.0000
Bike Age	5	−1.0177	0.0482	445.83	0.0000
Bike Age	6	−0.9809	0.0515	363.17	0.0000
Bike Age	7	−0.8734	0.0537	264.95	0.0000
Bike Age	8	−1.4492	0.0568	651.17	0.0000
Bike Age	9	−1.1035	0.0606	331.59	0.0000
Bike Age	10	−0.9096	0.0689	174.13	0.0000
Bike Age	11	−0.9608	0.0859	125.21	0.0000
Bike Age	12	−1.2918	0.0757	291.52	0.0000
Bike Age	1 (base)	0.0000	0.0000	–	–
Winter Temp	–	0.6170	0.0346	317.69	0.0000
MSRP	–	1.1934	0.0299	1,593.42	0.0000

Fig. 2.5. Motorcycle collision sample dataset: Model P2 results.

The results are as follows:

Model	Gini Index
P1	40.68
P2	40.33

So, the single GLM slightly outperforms the double GLM.

2.4.4 Comparison of Performance: Frequency/Severity versus Pure Premium

The final question we must answer is, which modeling approach performs better on this dataset – modeling frequency and severity separately or building one model for pure premium?

To determine this, we'll combine Models F2 and S1 and call that the frequency/ severity answer, and we'll compare the Gini index of that combination to the Gini index for P1.

To combine F2 and S1, we will simply add the parameter estimates for the two models. For example, for the chopper bike type, the frequency/severity answer is $0.1455 + 0.8227 = 0.9682$. Thus, the frequency/severity rating factor for choppers is $\exp(0.9682) = 2.63$. By contrast, the rating factor for choppers indicated by Model P1 is $\exp(0.7852) = 2.19$.

The Gini index for the frequency/severity approach (combining Models F2 and S1) is 40.63. And, as shown earlier, the Gini index for Model P2 is 40.68. So, P2 wins, but by a razor-thin margin. Realistically, we can call this one a tie.

Appendix 2.A Proof of Equivalence between Pure Premium Model Forms

As stated in Section 2.2.3, there is an exact equivalence between the following two model specifications:

1. Target variable = pure premium, calculated as dollars of loss divided by exposures.
   Weight = exposures.
   Distribution = Tweedie.
2. Target variable = dollars of loss.
   Weight = (exposure)$^{(p-1)}$.
   Offset for exposure volume.
   Distribution = Tweedie.

Here is the proof of that equivalence. Klinker (2011) defines the normal equation for a GLM as

$$0 = \sum_j w_j \cdot \frac{(y_j - \mu_j)}{V(\mu_j) \cdot g'(\mu_j)}$$

where

- w_j is the weight for record j;
- y_j is the actual value of the target variable for record j;
- μ_j is the fitted value of the target variable for record j;
- $V(\mu)$ is the GLM variance function;
- $g'(\mu)$ is the derivative of the link function.

The normal equation holds for every level of each variable and for the entire dataset.
   Recall that the variance function for the Tweedie distribution is

$$V(\mu) = \mu^p.$$

For a log-link,

$$g(\mu) = \ln(\mu)$$

and thus

$$g'(\mu) = 1/\mu.$$

Therefore, for a GLM with a Tweedie distribution and a log-link,

$$V(\mu) \cdot g'(\mu) = \mu^{(p-1)}.$$

In comparing the GLM normal equations for the two model specifications described above, we use the following notation:

- L_j = actual dollars of loss on record j;
- $\acute{L}_j$ = fitted value for dollars of loss on record j;
- E_j = exposures on record j;

Case 1: Model pure premium with exposures as weight
Using the notation for the GLM normal equation above:

- $w_j = E_j$;
- $y_j = L_j/E_j$;
- $\mu_j = \acute{L}_j/E_j$;
- $V(\mu) \cdot g'(\mu) = (\acute{L}_j/E_j)^{(p-1)}$.

Thus, the normal equation is:

$$\sum_j w_j \cdot \frac{(y_j - \mu_j)}{V(\mu_j) \cdot g'(\mu_j)} = \sum_j E_j \cdot \frac{(L_j/E_j - \acute{L}_j/E_j)}{(\acute{L}_j/E_j)^{(p-1)}}$$

$$= \sum_j (L_j - \acute{L}_j) \cdot [\acute{L}_j/\acute{L}_j/E_j]^{(1-p)}.$$

Case 2: Model dollars of loss with exposures$^{(p-1)}$ as weight
Using the notation for the GLM normal equation above:

- $w_j = E_j^{(p-1)}$;
- $y_j = L_j$;
- $\mu_j = \acute{L}_j$;
- $V(\mu) \cdot g'(\mu) = \acute{L}_j^{(p-1)}$.

Thus, the normal equation is:

$$\sum_j w_j \cdot \frac{(y_j - \mu_j)}{V(\mu_j) \cdot g'(\mu_j)} = \sum_j E_j^{(p-1)} \cdot \frac{(L_j - \acute{L}_j)}{\acute{L}_j^{(p-1)}}$$

$$= \sum_j (L_j - \acute{L}_j)[\acute{L}_j/\acute{L}_j/E_j]^{(1-p)}.$$

Conclusion

Since both model forms produce the same normal equations, they must produce identical output.

Appendix 2.B The Gini Index

Since we are comparing multiple models, we need some objective criterion for determining the superior model. For that, we will use the Gini index.

The Gini index, named for statistician and sociologist Corrado Gini, is commonly used in economics to quantify national income inequality. Figure 2.B.1 is a Gini index plot for the United States.

The national income inequality Gini index is calculated as follows:

1. Sort the population based on earnings, from those with the lowest earnings to those with the highest earnings. (If one wishes to measure wealth inequality rather than income inequality, the sorting is based on wealth.)
2. The x-axis is the cumulative percentage of earners.
3. The y-axis is the cumulative percentage of earnings.

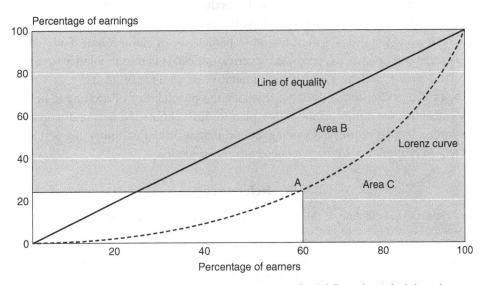

Fig. 2.B.1. Gini index for the United States. *Source:* Social Security Administration.

The locus of points created by plotting the cumulative percentage of earnings against the cumulative percentage of earners is called the Lorenz curve. The 45-degree line is called the line of equality, so named because if everyone earned the same exact income, the Lorenz curve would be that line. As an illustration, if there are 100 people in such a society, then each person represents 1% of the population and would earn 1% of the income, resulting in a perfectly diagonal Lorenz curve. Everyone doesn't earn the same income though, so the Lorenz curve is bow-shaped. As the chart above shows, the poorest 60% of earners earn roughly 20% of the total income. The Gini index is calculated as twice the area between the Lorenz curve and the line of equality.

The Gini index can also be used to measure the lift of an insurance rating plan by quantifying its ability to segment the population into the best and worst risks. The Gini index for an insurance rating plan model is calculated as follows:

1. Sort the dataset based on the loss cost predicted by the model. The records at the top of the dataset are then the risks which the model believes are best, and the records at the bottom of the dataset are the risks which the model believes are worst.
2. On the *x*-axis, plot the cumulative percentage of exposures.
3. On the *y*-axis, plot the cumulative percentage of losses.

The locus of points is the Lorenz curve, and the Gini index is twice the area between the Lorenz curve and the line of equality.

If a model produced the Gini index plot above, then it would have identified 60% of exposures which contribute only 20% of the total losses.

The steps above describe using the Gini index to assess a model (or models) that calculate expected pure premium, but the Gini index can also be used to measure the performance of a frequency or a severity model. In the case of a frequency model, the sort order is the predicted frequency, the *x*-axis is the cumulative percentage of exposures, and the *y*-axis is the cumulative percentage of claim counts. For a severity model, the sort order is the predicted severity, the *x*-axis is the cumulative percentage of claim counts, and the *y*-axis is the cumulative percentage of losses.

Note that a Gini index does not quantify the profitability of a rating plan, but it does quantify the ability of the rating plan to differentiate the best and worst risks. Assuming that an insurer has pricing and/or underwriting flexibility, this will lead to increased profitability through reduced adverse selection.

References

Anderson, D., S. Feldblum, C. Modlin, D. Schirmacher, E. Schirmacher, and N. Thandi. A practitioner's guide to generalized linear models. *Casualty Actuarial Society Discussion Paper Program*, 2004.

de Jong, P., and G. Heller. *Generalized Linear Models for Insurance Data*. International Series on Actuarial Science. Cambridge University Press, Cambridge, 2008.

Klinker, F. GLM invariants. *Casualty Actuarial Society E-Forum*, Summer 2011.

McCullagh, P., and J. A. Nelder. *Generalized Linear Models*. 2nd ed. Chapman and Hall/CRC, Boca Raton, 1989.

Smyth, G., and B. Jørgensen. Fitting Tweedie's compound Poisson model to insurance claims data: Dispersion modeling. *Astin Bulletin*, 32(1): 143–157, 2002.

Yan, J., J. Guszcza, M. Flynn, and C.-S. P. Wu. Applications of the offset in property-casualty predictive modeling. *Casualty Actuarial Society E-Forum*, Winter 2009.

3

Generalized Linear Models as Predictive Claim Models

Greg Taylor and James Sullivan

3.1 Review of Loss Reserving

3.1.1 Background

A typical property and casualty (P&C) insurance will indemnify the insured against events that occur within a defined period. From an accounting viewpoint, a liability accrues to the insurer at the date of occurrence of an indemnified event. From that date the insurer's accounts are therefore required to recognize the quantum of this liability to the extent that it has not been settled.

However, there will be an inevitable delay between the occurrence of the event and notification of an associated claim to the insurer, and a further delay between notification and settlement of the claim. These delays can be considerable. For example, in casualty classes of business, such as auto bodily injury liability, a typical average period from claim occurrence to settlement might be 3 or 4 years, with some claims remaining unsettled for 10 to 20 years.

During the period between occurrence and notification, even the existence of the claim will be unknown to the insurer. Between notification and settlement its existence will be known but its ultimate quantum unknown since it may depend on the outcome of negotiation between insurer and insured, or on an adversarial legal process. The insurer is obliged to make accounting provision for the claim despite these shortfalls in knowledge.

The balance sheet item recognizing the insurer's liability is called the *loss reserve*, and the determination of this reserve as *loss reserving*. The reserve will certainly include the liability for the cost of the claims themselves but, depending on the accounting regime, may also include allowance for other associated costs such as loss adjustment expenses.

For long tail lines of insurance, the loss reserve may amount to several times annual premium income, and therefore may amount to a large multiple of typical annual profit. As a result, a modest proportionate error in the loss reserve can impinge heavily on annual profit, and so accuracy of the reserve is a matter of considerable importance.

The estimation of loss reserves in practice relies on a wide variety of models and methodologies. It is not feasible to review them all here. For that, refer to Taylor (2000) and Wüthrich and Merz (2008). Suffice to say that, of all models in use, the so-called *chain ladder* is the most commonly encountered. Accordingly, much of Chapter 18 of Volume I (this will be referred to as [I:18], and subsequent references to Volume I similarly) was concerned with this model, with later sections of the chapter examining variations of it and some further models.

The chain ladder model was formulated in [I:18.2.2], naturally involving specific assumptions about the behaviour of the observed claims data. These assumptions are restrictive, proving not to be representative for many datasets, and with some datasets breaching all assumptions. Accurate representation of these datasets requires different model formulation, and this is the reason for the introduction of the modeling in [I:18].

But, in any event, it is suggested that, even if a dataset appears to conform with chain ladder assumptions, the additional modeling in [I:18] is worthwhile and should be carried out. It provides a full stochastic framework within which to test those assumptions rigorously, and respond to any detected failures. It also provides a statistical framework designed to simplify decision making, and these features outweigh the ease and familiarity of the chain ladder.

The present chapter is concerned with a dataset that is in fact far from conformity with the chain ladder assumptions. Its modeling requires a great deal more structure than provided by the chain ladder, so that informed decision-making will be achieved only by means of statistical methods. The chapter is concerned with the physical circumstances accounting for the breach of chain ladder assumptions, the recognition of these circumstances in the model formulation, and the representation of the resulting model in the form of a generalized linear model (GLM).

3.1.2 Data and Notation

The conventional representation of claims experience as a *claims triangle* was described in [I:18.1.2]. In that case the available data were represented by a triangular array of observations y_{ij}, denoted $\mathcal{D}_K = \{y_{ij}: 1 \le i \le K, 1 \le j \le K - i + 1\}$ where i, j denote *accident period* and *development period* respectively (actually that discussion used k in place of i, but i will be more convenient here). These concepts were described in [I:18.1.2], except that only *accident year* and *development year* were considered there. The present chapter will often refer to periods more general than a year and so the more general terminology is preferred. The choice of time unit is essentially irrelevant to the logic of model formulation.

The precise nature of the observations is left unspecified at this stage. Indeed, their nature will vary from point to point through the development of this chapter.

In the present case, modeling will often revert to the use of claims triangles. However, it is to be emphasized that the actual dataset is a unit record claim file, that is, a file containing one record per claim, that record including various details of the claim concerned. The dataset will be addressed in detail in Sections 3.2 and 3.6.1. Thus all claim triangles are extracts from the dataset.

The following additional definitions were also given in [I:18.1.2]:

$$\mathcal{D}_K^c = \{y_{ij} : 2 \le i \le K, K - i + 1 < j \le K\}$$
$$\mathcal{D}_K^+ = \mathcal{D}_K \cup \mathcal{D}_K^c$$

where $\mathcal{D}_K$ denotes observations (the past), $\mathcal{D}_K^c$ observations yet to occur in the same accident periods as included in $\mathcal{D}_K$ (the future), and $\mathcal{D}_K^+$ the totality of observations on these accident years when they have finally occurred.

3.1.3 Modeling and Forecasting

As explained in [I:18.1.3], a loss reserve requires a forecast of future claim payments. In the case where the dataset $\mathcal{D}_K$ consists of claim payments, the requirement is the forecast of $\mathcal{D}_K^c$ on the basis of observations $\mathcal{D}_K$. A model of the $y_{ij} \in \mathcal{D}_K$ is formulated, with y_{ij} dependent on i, j and possibly other quantities. This model is then calibrated against $\mathcal{D}_K$, and the calibrated model used to forecast the $y_{ij} \in \mathcal{D}_K^c$.

Emphasis was placed on the chain ladder model in [I:18]. It is therefore convenient to restate that model here. The model has two distinct forms, generally known as the *Mack* and *cross-classified* forms. The latter is better adapted to conversion to GLM, and the following description of the *overdispersed Poisson* (ODP) version of it is reproduced from [I:18.2.2].

ODP cross-classified model

(ODPCC1)   The random variables $y_{ij} \in \mathcal{D}_K^+$ are stochastically independent.
(ODPCC2)   For each $i, j = 1, 2, \ldots, K$,
        (a) $y_{ij} \sim ODP(\alpha_i \gamma_j, \varphi)$ for some parameters $\alpha_i, \gamma_j, \varphi > 0$;
        (b) $\sum_{j=1}^{K} \gamma_j = 1$.

GLM representations of claims models were discussed in [I:18.3]. The components required generally for the specifications of such models, defined in [I:5], are set out in

Table 3.1. *GLM Representation of Claims Models*

General	Specific to ODP Cross-Classified Model
	GLM Component
Response variate	y_{ij}
Covariates (categorical)	Accident years i, development years j
Link function	Log
Error structure	ODP
Weights	None
Offset	None
Linear response	$\ln \alpha_i + \ln \gamma_j$

Table 3.1, as are their specific definitions for the ODP cross-classified model (reproduced from [I:Table 18.1]).

3.2 Additional Notation

For the purpose of this chapter, let the following notation be adopted:

i = accident quarter, $i = 1, 2, 3, \ldots, 82$, and $1 = $ Sep-94, $2 = $ Dec-94...., $82 = $ Dec-14;

j = development quarter, $j = 0, 1, 2, \ldots, 81$;

k = calendar quarter of finalization, $k = 1, 2, 3, \ldots, 82$, and $1 = $ Sep-94, $2 = $ Dec-94...., $82 = $ Dec-14;

s = injury severity, a ranking based on the bodily injury of the claimant;

$Y^s_{i[r]}$ = aggregate claim payment of the rth individual claim from accident quarter i with injury severity s, with r ordering claims by say date of occurrence;

Y^s_{ij} = average size of claims from accident quarter i with injury severity s, and finalized in development quarter j;

N^s_i = estimated number of claims incurred in accident quarter i with injury severity s;

G^s_{ij} = cumulative number of claims finalized to development quarter j for accident quarter i and injury severity s;

The term (i, j, s) cell will be used to refer to those claims of injury severity s with accident quarter i and finalized in development quarter j.

It is assumed that the date at which the dataset is available, being the end of calendar quarter $k = k_0$, will be referred to as the valuation date. The objective of the modeling is to estimate the ultimate claim cost of each accident quarter, on the basis of the information up to the valuation date.

A number of the quantities just defined are dollar amounts, and therefore subject to inflation over time. Their analysis will be facilitated if they are adjusted to a constant dollar base on the basis of some reasonable assumed inflation index.

The numerical example dealt with in Section 3.6 involves auto liability claims. As these claims are made within a common law environment, seeking restitution of personal income and other amenities, a reasonable normative inflation index is an index of average wages. One is free, of course, to make alternative choices, but this one has been assumed for the purpose of the present chapter.

All quantities defined in dollar amounts in this chapter will to taken to have been so adjusted to dollar amounts of the valuation date. All amounts appearing in tables and charts have been adjusted, and all defined quantities, such as immediately above, are also adjusted to these dollar values without explicit statement on each occasion.

3.3 GLM Background

3.3.1 Statistical Framework

Consider observations that take the form

$$y_{ij} \sim Dist(\theta_{ij}, \phi_{ij}) \tag{3.1}$$

for some distribution denoted *Dist* and *location and dispersion parameters* θ_{ij}, ϕ_{ij} respectively.

Now suppose further that the cell means may be expressed in the form

$$\mu_{ij} = E[y_{ij}] = g^{-1}(\eta_{ij}) \tag{3.2}$$

for some one-one and twice differentiable function g, with

$$\eta_{ij} = \sum_{h=1}^{H} \beta_h X_{h:ij} \tag{3.3}$$

and where $X_1, \ldots, X_H$ are explanatory variables, with $X_{h:ij}$ denoting the value of X_h taken in the (i, j) cell, and the β_h are fixed but unknown constants.

A GLM is a model in which observations satisfy (3.1) and (3.2) and *Dist* is drawn from the so-called *exponential dispersion family* (EDF) (Nelder and Wedderburn, 1972). The EDF is an extensive family, including many commonly used distributions (normal, gamma, Poisson, inverse Gaussian, compound Poisson-gamma), and so modeling of a claims triangle by means of a GLM provides a wide choice of distributions for the representation of the observations. See McCullagh and Nelder (1989) for an extensive treatment of GLMs.

A GLM provides a framework in which one can obtain a formal estimate of claim behaviour for each (i, j, s) cell, with due account taken of the distribution of the content of that cell. The chain ladder, on the contrary, or indeed any other conventional actuarial method consisting of row and column manipulations, is unable to estimate cell-specific effects other than those specified within those models' limited and often unrealistic, assumptions.

In GLM terminology, g is called the *link function*, and η_{ij} the *linear predictor* (associated with observation y_{ij}).

Calibration of the model involves estimation of the unknown quantities β_h, with estimates denoted $\hat{\beta}_h$ say. This yields estimates of the linear predictor, and the cell mean, as follows:

$$\hat{\eta}_{ij} = \sum_{h=1}^{H} \hat{\beta}_h X_{h:ij} \tag{3.4}$$

$$\hat{\mu}_{ij} = g^{-1}(\hat{\eta}_{ij}) \tag{3.5}$$

and the $\hat{\mu}_{kj}$ are referred to as *fitted values*.

Later development of this chapter will require the concept of a *residual* associated with observation y_{ij}. The simplest form of residual, the *Pearson residual*, is defined as

$$R_{ij}^P = (y_{ij} - \hat{\mu}_{ij})/\sigma_{ij} \tag{3.6}$$

Although simple, this form of residual is of limited use when observations are markedly non-normally distributed. For non-normal data, *deviance residuals* are usually more useful since they have been shown to be normally distributed with error of order $m^{-1/2}$, where m is a certain index derived from the specific member of the EDF under consideration (Pierce and Schafer, 1986).

The *standardized deviance residual* associated with observation y_{ij} is defined as

$$R_{ij}^D = sgn(y_{ij} - \hat{\mu}_{ij})(d_{ij}/\hat{\phi})^{1/2} \tag{3.7}$$

in the case $\phi_{ij} = \phi$, with $\hat{\phi}$ an estimate of ϕ, and

$$d_{ij} = 2[\ln \pi(y_{ij}; y_{ij}, \phi = 1) - \ln \pi(y_{ij}; \hat{\theta}_{ij}, \phi = 1)] \tag{3.8}$$

with $\pi(y_{ij}; \theta_{ij}, \phi_{ij})$ denoting the GLM likelihood of observation y_{ij} in the presence of parameters θ_{ij}, ϕ_{ij} (see (3.7)), and $\hat{\theta}_{ij}$ the GLM estimate of θ_{ij}. The first of the two members in the square bracket is the likelihood associated with the observation y_{ij} in the case of the so-called *saturated model*, which fits every observation with its own value.

3.3.2 Calibration

In the fitting of a model to a dataset one is assisted by a set of *diagnostics*. In general terms, a diagnostic is a statistic that in some sense compares the fitted values with their counterpart observations, that is, compares the $\hat{\mu}_{ij}$ with the y_{ij}.

Such comparisons are facilitated by the availability of the stochastic properties, particularly the dispersion, of the $\hat{\mu}_{ij}$. These enable an assessment of the statistical significance of the differences from the y_{ij}. Since the stochastic properties of a GLM (or any other stochastic model) are specified, the properties of all derivative quantities, including diagnostics, may be deduced. This contrasts with the fitting of nonstochastic models, which tends to be ad hoc.

As will be seen in the example of Section 3.6, a GLM of claims data may involve many explanatory variables, combined in a complex matter. This form of model will usually need to be identified by degrees, with the gradual introduction of individual explanatory variables, or small collections of them, into the model.

Thus, the fitting procedure is iterative, according to the following steps:

1. Examine diagnostics of the current form of model (initially, this might be some primitive form, such as chain ladder);
2. Where the diagnostics indicate a possible failure in the fit of the current model to the data, hypothesize additional explanatory variables that might be expected to correct or mitigate this failure;
3. Refit the model with these additional terms incorporated;
4. Repeat steps 1–3 until satisfied that all model failures have been eliminated or sufficiently mitigated.

The clear formulation of the GLM's linear predictor and the transparency added by its linear form facilitate this process.

3.4 Advantages of GLMs

Conventional actuarial analysis of claims triangles tends to consist of averaging over (possibly partial) rows and columns, the formation of ratios between rows and columns, and various other row-and-column manoeuvres. The averaging period is usually judgmental, requiring an assumption of similarity of claims behavior across averaging period.

Furthermore, missing cells in a triangle may upset this averaging calculation. At the very least, the form of calculation will probably require revision. A GLM, alternatively, enables estimation of the statistically preferred averaging period and accommodates missing cells without any revision.

Row-and-column averaging is often readily adapted to the estimation of trends in two dimensions, e.g. row and column trends within the cross-classified chain ladder model, and column and diagonal trends within the separation method (Taylor, 1977). However, estimation of trends in three dimensions is cumbersome. For an illustration, see Taylor (2000, Section 4.3.5). Again, GLMs provide simple facilities for the exploration and estimation of multiple trends within the data.

There are a number of other areas, of a more technical statistical nature, in which GLMs provide far greater model generality and flexibility of model calibration than can be achieved by conventional actuarial means. These are discussed in the remainder of the present subsection.

3.4.1 Prediction Error

Section 3.1.3 notes that loss reserving consists of the derivation of forecasts from a model. The forecasts are derived from observations that are random variables, by means of a model whose true form is unknown and is therefore merely approximated. Hence the forecasts are themselves random variables of unknown accuracy. In short, they are accompanied by *forecast error*, or *prediction error*.

The forecasts themselves are not especially informative unless accompanied by some indication of the magnitude of prediction error. This requires formal recognition of the stochastic nature of the dataset; that is it requires the claims model to be formulated as a *stochastic model*. The properties of the stochastic model may then be used to produce an estimate of prediction error. These matters are discussed in [I:18.3.7,I:18.3.8].

The conventional actuarial approach to claims modeling does not lend itself easily to stochastic formulation. A GLM, conversely, is by its nature a stochastic model. It provides a ready-made framework within which to estimate prediction error. Some theoretical basics of this are set out in [I:18.3.8].

3.4.2 Nonlinearity

The link function of a GLM is introduced in [I:5.3] and again in Section 3.3.1 here. The link function may be linear or nonlinear, and hence the relation between the cell means μ_{ij} and the explanatory variables may be *linear or nonlinear*. In principle, the link function might be any one-one and twice differentiable function with range equal to the real line, though in practice, it is usually limited to specific functional forms incorporated in GLM software.

3.4.3 Nonnormality

Conventional row and column manipulations are typically not based on any assumptions about the distribution of observations. Typically, they do not even rest on any assumptions about the dispersion of observations. In particular, the response of the chain ladder to the frequency and magnitude of large losses will be unknown.

A stochastic model, conversely, will include such distributional assumptions. A stochastic model of the observations y_{ij} of the form (3.1), as in a GLM, can specify either *normal or nonnormal* observations.

3.4.4 Emerging Claims Experience

Prior sections have been concerned with the fitting of a model to the data available at the time of fitting. However, as further data accumulate subsequently, one will be concerned with the ongoing quality of fit.

This can be achieved by means of post hoc diagnostics. The subject of diagnostics generally is discussed in Section 3.5. As will be seen there, these compare the difference between the $\hat{\mu}_{ij}$ and the y_{ij}, in terms of statistical significance, but this time the observations y_{ij} are subsequent to those included in the dataset underpinning the model. They are said to be *out-of-sample* with respect to the model.

The GLM provides a stochastic framework for the construction of relevant diagnostics, just as in Section 3.5. The construction of diagnostics is discussed in some detail in Taylor (2011). The diagnostics there, and in general, concentrate heavily on *actual versus forecast* (AvF) comparisons, using either the arithmetic difference or the ratio between actual (out-of-sample observation) and forecast (the forecast of that observation by the model under test).

3.5 Diagnostics

The process of fitting a GLM is discussed in Section 3.3. This process involves examining diagnostics in order to test the validity of the assumptions underlying the model. Diagnostics visually illustrate any deficiencies of the model, both distributional assumptions and goodness-of-fit, that is, in general terms, closeness of the model's fitted values to the corresponding observations.

3.5.1 Distributional Assumptions

The first step in fitting a GLM is the choice of error distribution and link function. The link function is usually determined by the model structure as being that transformation of a cell mean that produces a linear predictor. Commonly, a multiplicative model implies a log-link, while an additive model uses an identity link. The selection of an error distribution, however, is based on an iterative process that examines error distribution and goodness-of-fit alternately.

The choice of error distribution is guided by examining the observed residuals, which depend on the fitted model. Therefore, model calibration proceeds by iteration between fitting of model covariates and choice of error distribution, as follows:

1. Select the appropriate link function;
2. Select a reasonable error distribution, based on common sense arguments;
3. Fit a simple model, comprising main effects and any obvious interactions (these terms will be defined in Section 3.6.6.1);
4. Examine the residual diagnostics to identify any deficiencies in the distributional assumption, and make changes if necessary;
5. Continue modification of covariates to improve the model fit, while re-examining the goodness-of-fit diagnostics tests. Accept the choice of error distribution when a model is obtained which displays satisfactory residual diagnostics. Otherwise repeat Steps 4 and 5.

3.5.2 Residual Diagnostics

Residual diagnostics can come in many forms, but the simplest is a scatterplot. A scatterplot displays the residuals of the model (as defined in Section 3.3) against some particular variable. Most often in the current loss reserving environment, this variable will be fitted value or linear predictor from the model, or else accident, development or calendar period. Figure 3.1 provides an example of a scatterplot where the standardized deviance residuals are plotted against the linear predictor.

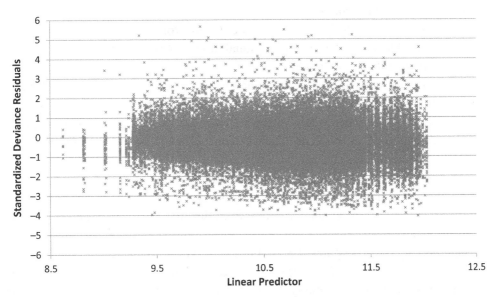

Fig. 3.1. Scatterplot of standardized deviance residuals versus the linear predictor.

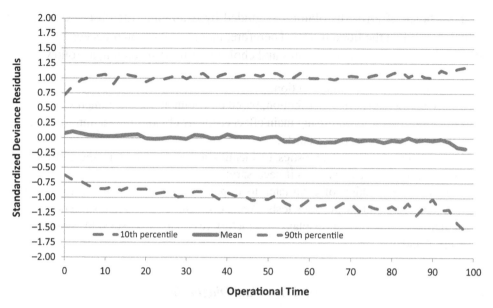

Fig. 3.2. Spread plot of standardized deviance residuals versus operational time.

A satisfactory model will show random, homoscedastic deviance residuals, that is, exhibiting no marked variation in vertical dispersion as one moves across the plot from left to right. A trend in the residuals potentially indicates goodness-of-fit issues, while heteroscedasticity (the absence of homoscedasticity) indicates that dispersion assumptions are inappropriate.

The following residual diagnostics are taken from the model presented in Section 3.6.7. As shown, the deviance residuals appear to be random and homoscedastic, indicating a satisfactory model.

Alternatively, residuals can be examined using a spread plot. A spread plot displays the mean and a pair of percentiles (commonly the 10th and 90th of the residuals for each value of the independent variable. Figure 3.2 shows an example of a spread plot, whereby the standardized deviance residuals are plotted against operational time (defined in Section 3.6.5).

As shown, the range between the 10th and 90th percentiles is reasonably constant, while the mean fluctuates around zero, suggesting homoscedasticity and reasonable goodness-of-fit. Any systematic departure from this may indicate a problem with the model assumptions.

Another diagnostic that may be used to check the distributional assumptions is a histogram of standardized deviance residuals. If the model is appropriate, the residuals should be approximately normally distributed, as shown in Figure 3.3. The solid line is a normal distribution, fitted using the method of moments.

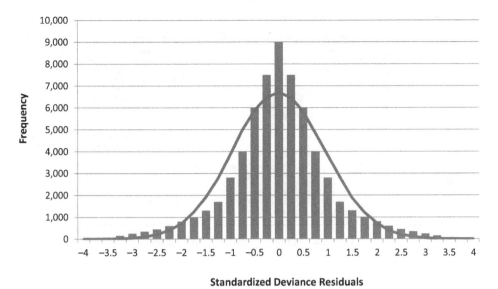

Fig. 3.3. Histogram of standardized deviance residuals.

3.5.3 Goodness-Of-Fit

Goodness-of-fit, as defined earlier, is achieved by satisfactory identification of the drivers of the fitted value. In claims reserving, this amounts largely to reviewing diagnostics in which accident, development and calendar periods serve as the independent variables. In simple terms, each cell can be examined in comparison with its fitted value from the model.

A heat map is an ideal way to illustrate goodness-of-fit. The map shows, by accident and development period, the AvF ratio defined in Section 3.4.4. A typical heat map is color coded with, for example, red indicating a ratio greater than 100%, and blue less than 100%, with gradations of color to indicate the degree by which the ratio exceeds or falls short of 100%.

Owing to the limitations of black-and-white publishing, it has been necessary to represent the example heat map in Figure 3.4 in less graphic style, using shades of gray, dark gray indicating a ratio greater than 100%, and lighter gray or white indicating a ratio less than 100%.

The following goodness-of-fit diagnostics are taken from the model presented in Section 3.6.6.

A satisfactory model will generate a heat map in which cell colorings are randomly scattered. Any systematic coloring of the grid will indicate regions in which the model consistently over- or underpredicts.

In Figure 3.4 the distribution of AvF is nonrandom, with clusters of ratios greater and less than 100%. Since the clusters appear to be located within specific areas (i.e.,

Accident Year / Development Quarter	1	2	3	4	5	6	7	8	9	10	11	12	13	14	15	16
							Actual versus Forecast									
1994/1995		132%	129%	121%	120%	89%	81%	78%	73%	93%	94%	83%	86%	80%	109%	100%
1995/1996	326%	146%	141%	116%	100%	78%	77%	81%	90%	89%	100%	99%	122%	101%	89%	115%
1996/1997	98%	133%	121%	105%	97%	83%	90%	91%	89%	96%	91%	109%	107%	112%	112%	105%
1997/1998	80%	103%	103%	97%	94%	88%	89%	103%	107%	106%	96%	119%	96%	107%	89%	99%
1998/1999		120%	106%	106%	104%	102%	99%	99%	104%	98%	103%	107%	96%	92%	93%	109%
1999/2000		99%	108%	107%	100%	101%	102%	96%	99%	102%	98%	90%	109%	102%	107%	98%
2000/2001	104%	98%	91%	110%	91%	102%	94%	104%	105%	106%	107%	111%	100%	107%	92%	92%
2001/2002		83%	71%	100%	115%	106%	119%	112%	111%	94%	88%	90%	86%	90%	84%	87%
2002/2003	107%	72%	108%	133%	122%	120%	99%	99%	88%	95%	87%	85%	90%	89%	89%	104%
2003/2004		77%	93%	55%	65%	58%	65%	70%	83%	87%	105%	105%	100%	112%	134%	121%
2004/2005	26%	45%	49%	35%	35%	54%	65%	84%	87%	114%	105%	128%	128%	112%	132%	124%
2005/2006		32%	40%	37%	51%	73%	95%	98%	106%	117%	134%	108%	107%	110%	111%	91%
2006/2007		31%	43%	45%	85%	108%	104%	113%	111%	116%	105%	109%	102%	104%	103%	72%
2007/2008	1%	67%	63%	54%	88%	130%	122%	123%	112%	101%	96%	89%	84%	90%	78%	105%
2008/2009		58%	78%	72%	104%	121%	113%	106%	107%	110%	96%	97%	102%	89%	83%	82%
2009/2010		85%	61%	69%	99%	107%	115%	111%	106%	98%	103%	93%	103%	93%	80%	63%
2010/2011		95%	82%	76%	100%	123%	114%	107%	111%	98%	96%	84%	83%	93%	69%	75%
2011/2012		42%	42%	86%	112%	116%	107%	100%	98%	92%	99%	81%				
2012/2013	44%	66%	62%	87%	106%	104%	114%	96%								
2013/2014		61%	67%	79%												

Fig. 3.4. Actual versus forecast heat map.

specific combinations of accident and development periods), an interaction between accident and development period or calendar period may improve the goodness-of-fit.

To illustrate this further, Figure 3.5 collapses Figure 3.4 onto diagonals to show the AvF for calendar period only, for accident periods both pre-2002/2003 and post-2003/2004. There are clear trends in calendar period for these two distinct sets of accident periods, indicating that different forms of model are required for those two sets.

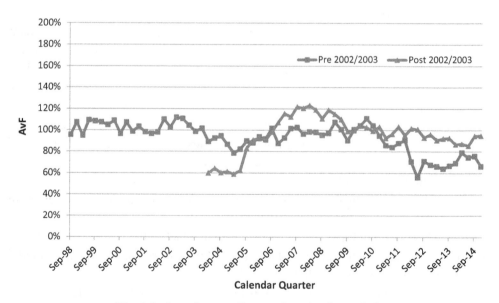

Fig. 3.5. Actual versus forecast by calendar period.

3.6 Example

The use of generalized linear models (GLMs) to model automobile bodily injury insurance data was discussed in Taylor and McGuire (2004) and McGuire (2007). Both found that the use of individual claim data to model finalized claim size using a GLM had advantages over a chain ladder model, leading to a more parsimonious, interpretable model.

Taylor and McGuire (2004) summarized the disadvantages of the use of a chain ladder for this dataset specifically,

- there are no criteria to assist in deciding whether a chain ladder is appropriate for loss reserving; and
- the chain ladder's treatment of time trends is unsatisfying.

Taylor and McGuire (2004) also concluded that

- the conventional application of the chain ladder to the data is dubious;
- the analysis of average claim sizes of individual finalized claims may be preferable to analysis of total claim payments aggregated over cells of a conventional claim triangle;
- it is desirable that model claim size is a function of operational time (defined in Section 3.6.5); and
- the use of regression can simultaneously identify time trends and loss development.

McGuire (2007) extended the observations concluded by Taylor and McGuire (2004). In particular,

- owing to decreases in claim frequency and a resultant change in mix of claims, simple extrapolation of time trends is unlikely to give the correct result; and
- the impact of legislative change on finalized claim size is different for different types of injury; hence, a need for more granularity within the model.

All of the observations made by Taylor and McGuire (2004) and McGuire (2007) are confirmed within the example discussed in the present chapter. However, this example focuses on the identification, modeling and forecasting benefits of

1. differentiation of finalized claim size by severity;
2. variation of claims inflation for different operational times; and
3. recognition of certain aspects of changing claim frequency by the warping of operational times (see Section 3.6.5).

3.6.1 Data

The dataset relating to this example is sourced from a statewide auto bodily injury insurance scheme in Australia. The insurance is compulsory and excludes any property coverage. The scheme is legislated but is underwritten by private insurers subject to regulation.

Insurers participating in the underwriting of the scheme are required to submit their claims data to a centralized data base. The dataset used in this example is an extract of this centralized data base. The dataset comprises a unit record claim file, containing

- date of injury;
- date of notification;
- histories, including dates, of
    o claim status (unfinalized, finalized, or reopened);
    o paid losses;
    o case estimates (sometimes known as physical estimates, or manual estimates);
    o legal representation flag (whether or not the claimant is legally represented); and
    o injury codes and severity (as defined below).
- operational time (as defined in Section 3.6.5); and
- various other claim characteristics not used in this example.

3.6.2 Claim Frequency and Severity

Many actuarial approaches to the forecast of insurance claim costs work with *aggregate* costs, that is, the total cost of claims in each future period. The present chapter is concerned with an example in which these costs are disaggregated in two ways:

1. *claim frequency* and *average claim size* of each accident period are estimated separately; and
2. expected claim size is estimated separately *for each claim* of each accident period, consistently with the form of data on individual claims described in Section 3.6.1.

Space restrictions of the chapter require that estimation of claim frequency be considered out-of-scope. It will be assumed that the number of claims incurred in each accident period and their distribution over notification periods, have already been estimated and that these results are available.

Attention will be concentrated on estimation of individual claim sizes. At the point of evaluation, some claims of each accident period will already have been finalized, and their claim sizes fixed. Consideration will therefore be reserved for claims that are unfinalized at the point of evaluation.

In practice, finalized claims are occasionally re-opened. As a result, the sizes of some finalized claims may not be fixed, in fact, as assumed in the preceding paragraph. This creates an additional level of complexity in the practical application of the model described in this chapter. However, it is regarded as out-of-scope for current purposes.

3.6.3 Modeling According to Injury Severity

Within the dataset that serves as the basis of this example, each injury is coded with an *injury severity*. The briefest investigation of the data indicates that, on average, claim sizes increase strongly with injury severity. Injury severity thus becomes a valuable predictor in any model of the ultimate sizes of claims that are currently open.

Injuries are recorded using a coding system for nature of injury. This coding system is called the *Abbreviated Injury Scale* (AIS) and defines approximately 70,000 injuries. Each claim can be assigned up to thirty injury codes. AIS codes consist of seven digits: the first six digits detail the injury type, while the seventh digit refers to the severity of the injury, ranging from 1 (least severe) to 5 (catastrophically injured) and 6 (death). The measure of severity recorded against a claim is defined as follows:

- the maximum injury severity of all injury codes, ranging between 1 and 6;
- when the maximum injury severity is 1,
  - o no legal representation, denoted as severity 0; and
  - o legal representation, denoted as severity 1 (it is rare that a claimant with severity greater than 1 is unrepresented);
- from time to time, severity 9 that indicates insufficient medical advice to define a severity.

To provide a numerical perspective, Table 3.2 displays the proportions of claims, by number, according to injury severity. These proportions vary from time to time, of course, but those appearing in the table are representative of an accident period toward the end of the dataset.

A claim may undergo many reassessments over its lifetime, and its assessed injury severity may change. A forecast of a claim's ultimate claim size will require an estimate of the distribution of its injury severity at the time of finalization. This was

Table 3.2. *Proportions of Claims (by Number) According to Injury Severity*

Injury Severity	Proportion of Claims by Number (%)
0	17.3
1	50.6
2	15.4
3	6.8
4	1.0
5	0.4
6	1.8
9	6.7

obtained by the means of a (nonhomogeneous) Markov chain of transitions between severities, applied to the injury severity at the valuation date.

Once again, this submodel of the entire claim size model is beyond the scope of this chapter. The forecasting task will be assumed limited to the estimation of the expected size of a claim from accident quarter i, finalized in development quarter j with injury severity s, that is, estimation of $E[Y_{ij}^s]$. For brevity, the remainder of this chapter deals with severity 1 only.

3.6.4 Conventional Triangular Modeling of Claim Severity

The simplest approach to the situation described in the preceding subsection would consist of the application of a separate chain ladder to the claims experience of each injury severity. Each chain ladder could be implemented by a GLM of a form similar to that described by (ODPCC1-2) in Section 3.1.3, but with these conditions replaced by the following, where y_{ij}^s denotes a realization of the variable Y_{ij}^s:

(ODPCCs1) The random variables y_{ij}^s are stochastically independent.
(ODPCCs2) For each $i, j = 1, 2, \ldots, K$ and each s,

$$\text{(a) } y_{ij}^s \sim ODP(\alpha_i^s, \gamma_j^s, \varphi^s) \text{ for some parameters } \alpha_i^s, \gamma_j^s, \varphi^s > 0;$$

$$\text{(b) } \sum_{j=1}^{K} , \gamma_j^s = 1.$$

Figure 3.6 displays heat maps, as defined in Section 3.5, arising from a chain ladder model fitted to data for injury severity 1. Accident quarters have been collapsed to accident years here to contain the size of the figures. These are Australian financial years with year-end June 30. Thus, for example, "1994/95" denotes the year ended June 30, 1995.

Development Quarter	1	2	3	4	5	6	7	8	9	10	11	12	13	14	15	16
1994/1995	466668%	78%	84%	72%	68%	81%	91%	99%	104%	100%	104%	104%	102%	104%	105%	105%
1995/1996	51%	81%	77%	89%	79%	81%	95%	101%	100%	101%	103%	103%	102%	100%	102%	103%
1996/1997	107%	130%	93%	84%	79%	89%	95%	96%	100%	99%	101%	99%	100%	100%	100%	98%
1997/1998	85%	126%	85%	84%	81%	87%	93%	100%	96%	97%	100%	95%	97%	99%	100%	101%
1998/1999	365311%	135%	103%	90%	83%	82%	89%	90%	92%	98%	98%	100%	99%	100%	101%	100%
1999/2000	89%	97%	92%	76%	79%	91%	94%	104%	104%	99%	99%	98%	99%	100%	100%	99%
2000/2001	242866%	70%	107%	105%	107%	99%	106%	98%	98%	98%	100%	100%	101%	98%	98%	100%
2001/2002	208902%	122%	129%	108%	91%	93%	94%	94%	96%	97%	98%	101%	99%	100%	102%	100%
2002/2003	8%	89%	140%	96%	96%	97%	97%	100%	103%	106%	108%	108%	109%	108%	106%	102%
2003/2004	51%	80%	88%	100%	115%	131%	132%	130%	124%	121%	113%	112%	110%	110%	107%	105%
2004/2005	127097%	239%	79%	99%	160%	164%	125%	123%	118%	118%	113%	109%	105%	105%	102%	101%
2005/2006	288015%	85%	85%	178%	155%	149%	130%	116%	112%	105%	102%	105%	102%	101%	99%	99%
2006/2007	946%	62%	112%	145%	215%	144%	116%	105%	106%	101%	99%	99%	103%	102%	101%	100%
2007/2008	81400%	65%	104%	142%	186%	124%	113%	103%	102%	101%	103%	100%	100%	100%	102%	103%
2008/2009	66415%	84%	80%	173%	151%	122%	120%	106%	104%	104%	100%	102%	100%	100%	98%	101%
2009/2010	63931%	76%	104%	164%	165%	136%	107%	103%	102%	101%	99%	100%	100%	99%	98%	99%
2010/2011	135479%	194%	160%	201%	167%	121%	103%	104%	99%	98%	98%	96%	97%	99%	97%	97%
2011/2012	401899%	79%	264%	150%	133%	112%	99%	98%	99%	99%	96%	93%				
2012/2013	26%	122%	152%	188%	130%	106%	91%	89%								
2013/2014	77090%	96%	140%	110%												

Fig. 3.6. AvF of the GLM chain ladder model for injury severity 1.

3.6.5 Operational Time

The heat maps in Figure 3.6 exhibit distinctly nonrandom features. The patches of dark gray and white in the first column can probably be disregarded, as the long-tail nature of this experience results in light (and therefore unstable) paid loss experience in the first development year.

However, the tendency for the coloring of the maps to trend from light to dark gray down columns is more disturbing. This indicates that the chain ladder tends to overestimate paid losses in the earlier years and underestimate more recently.

A suspicion of a rate of claim settlement that varies with accident period might cause one to examine the development of each accident period in terms of the cumulative amounts of paid losses (in respect of only finalized claims) per claim incurred by development period. The so-called cumulative payments per claim incurred (PPCI) in the (i, j, s) cell, that is, cumulative to the end of development quarter j of accident quarter i, is defined as

$$PPCI\,(i, j, s) = \sum_{h=1}^{j} Y_{ih}^s \big/ N_i^s \tag{3.9}$$

This form of claims development is discussed by Taylor (2000, Section 4.2). Figure 3.7 displays the development of PPCI for a sample of accident years.

The figure shows quite clearly the varying rate of claim settlement. The average amounts paid per claim in the earlier development quarters are seen to be dramatically

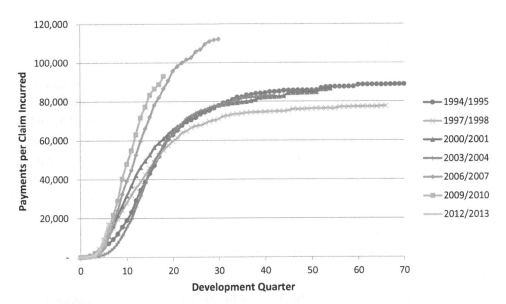

Fig. 3.7. Payments per claim incurred for sample accident quarters.

higher for more recent accident years than for earlier ones. Either the rate at which claims are settled has increased over time, or the cost of claims has increased, or both.

A possible explanation of the changing rate of settlement of claims in dollars is a changing rate of settlement in claim numbers, and this source of variation would typically be checked in practice. The checking involves an investigation of operational time (OT), which was introduced in [I:18.3.4].

The concept of OT is to be contrasted with that of (real) development time, which commences at time zero at the commencement of an accident period and proceeds linearly and continuously, attaining development time j at the end development period j. Thus, for example, development time $j + \frac{1}{2}$ corresponds to the mid-point of development period $j + 1$.

Henceforth, the quantity G_{ij}^s, defined in Section 3.2 in terms of development period j, will be interpreted as defined for development time j; that is, for nonintegral j, G_{ij}^s will denote the cumulative number of claims finalized up to development time j.

In the notation of the present chapter the OT associated with development time j of accident period i for claims of severity s is defined as follows:

$$t_i^s(j) = G_{ij}^s / N_i^s \qquad (3.10)$$

When OT is introduced into a model, it is typical to regard expected claim size as a function of OT (and possibly other covariates) instead of development time as in more conventional models. This is the case in, for example, Reid (1978), Taylor and McGuire (2004), and others and is discussed briefly in [I:18.3.4].

Consider a specific severity s. Since the dataset described in Section 3.6.1 consists of unit record claim data, a GLM of individual claim sizes for this severity can be constructed, as follows:

(ICGLM1)   The random variables $Y_{i[r]}^s$ are stochastically independent.

(ICGLM2) $Y_{i[r]}^s \sim gamma(\theta_{i[r]}^s, \phi_{i[r]}^s)$ where $\theta_{i[r]}^s, \phi_{i[r]}^s$ are location and scale parameters, as in (3.1), but specific to the individual claim.

(ICGLM3) $\mu_{i[r]}^s = E[Y_{i[r]}^s] = \exp(\sum_{h=1}^{H} \beta_h^s X_{h:i[r]}^s)$ as in (3.2) and (3.3), where $X_1^s, \ldots, X_H^s$ are explanatory variables, with $X_{h:i[r]}^s$ denoting the value of X_h^s taken by the individual claim under discussion, and the β_h^s are fixed but unknown constants.

(ICGLM4)   The leading terms of the linear predictor in (ICGLM3) are $\sum_{h=1}^{v} \beta_h^s X_{h:i[r]}^s = \sum_{h=1}^{v} \beta_h^s f_h^s(t_i^s(j_{i[r]}^s))$ for functions f_h^s yet to be defined, and $j_{i[r]}^s$ is the (real) development time at which the rth claim from accident period i with severity s is finalized.

The part of the linear predictor displayed in (ICGLM4) is indeed a function of OT, as promised in the preamble to the statement of the model. It is, in fact, a special form of function that consists of a linear combination of simpler functions called basis functions to conform with the definition of GLM in Section 3.3.1. A GLM that incorporates a set of basis function within its linear predictor is called a generalized additive model (GAM) (Hastie and Tibshirani, 1990).

The selection of the gamma assumption in (ICGLM2) is not automatic but has been separately justified for the dataset under consideration here in work that is not included in this chapter. A log-link is assumed in (ICGLM3). This is justified empirically, but it is also a matter of great convenience because it causes risk factors to contribute multiplicatively to the mean values of observations, thus

$$\mu^s_{i[r]} = \prod_{h=1}^{H} \exp\left(\beta^s_h X^s_{h:i[r]}\right)$$

Consider now the leading terms of the linear predictor mentioned in (ICGLM4). These described the functional dependence of mean individual claim size on OT. The simplest conceivable case would be that in which $v = 1$ and the single basis function f^s_1 were linear. In this case, (ICGLM3) reduces to the following:

$$\mu^s_{i[r]} = \exp\left(\beta^s_1 t^s_i\left(j^s_{i[r]}\right) + \sum_{h=2}^{H} \beta^s_h X^s_{h:i[r]}\right) \tag{3.11}$$

where all functional dependence on OT is confined to the first summand.

In fact, the situation is not quite as simple as this, but also not too much more complicated. Figure 3.8 plots the linear predictor for injury severity 1 when OT is included as a categorical variate over 2% intervals, that is, 0%–2%, 2%–4%, and so on. The model here is restricted to the early accident quarters Sept-94 to Dec-02, over which the OT effect is relatively consistent. The linear predictor at this stage includes no effects other than OT.

The figure suggests that the OT effect might be approximated reasonably well by a linear spline with knots at OT values 10% and 80%. This spline may be constructed from the basis functions

$$f^s_1(t) = \min(0.1, t)$$

$$f^s_2(t) = \max[0.7, \min(0, t - 0.1)]$$

$$f^s_3(t) = \min(0, t - 0.8)$$

with the entire spline represented by $\sum_{h=1}^{3} \beta^s_h f^s_h(t)$ and the model (3.11) now taking the form

$$\mu^s_{i[r]} = \exp\left(\sum_{h=1}^{3} \beta^s_h f^s_h(t_{i[r]})\right) \tag{3.12}$$

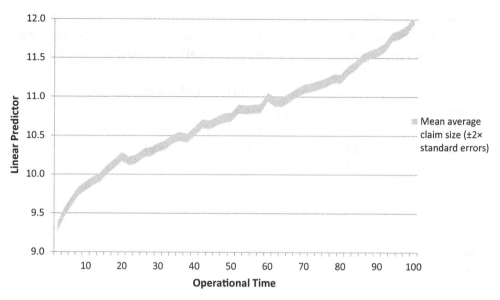

Fig. 3.8. Empirical relation between mean individual claim size and operational time (injury severity 1).

where $t_{i[r]}$ has been written as an abbreviation for the term $t_i^s(j_{i[r]}^{is})$ that appears in (3.11).

Figure 3.9 displays the spline of this form fitted to the data of accident quarters Sept-94 to Dec-2, with empirical plot of Figure 3.8 overlaid for comparison.

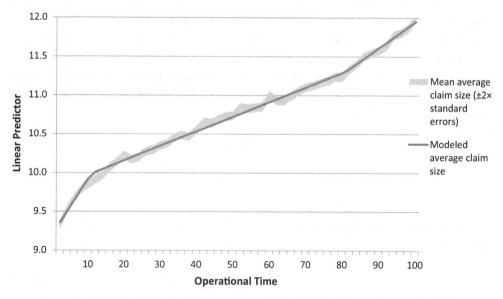

Fig. 3.9. Modeled relation between mean individual claim size and operational time (injury severity 1).

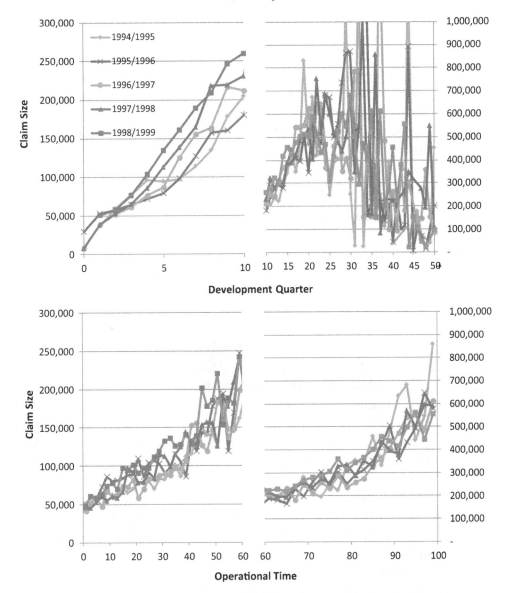

Fig. 3.10. Average claim size by development time and OT (injury severity 1).

These results are interesting because they show that the entire claims development over time can be represented very economically by just three parameters β_h^s, $h = 1, 2, 3$. By comparison, the chain ladder would require 81 age-to-age factors.

Moreover, modeling in terms of OT fulfils its purpose. Figure 3.10 plots, for a sample of accident quarters Sep-94 to Dec-02 (represented by the different trajectories plotted), the average claim size of finalizations occurring in each development quarter, together with the fitted values according to model illustrated in Figure 3.9. These fitted values have been calculated at the average OT for the development quarter, that is, the average of OT at the start and end of that quarter.

It can be seen in Figure 3.10 that the relation between development time and average claim size varies over accident quarters. Development quarters 0 to 10 are characterized by a systematic shift upward in claim sizes as accident year advances (see also Figure 3.7), which is partially corrected by the use of an OT time scale. Claim sizes display erratic behavior over development quarters higher than 10, but quite a clear trend when related to OTs.

3.6.6 Row and Diagonal Effects

Some datasets contain features whereby the experience of particular accident periods (rows), or groups of accident periods, differs fundamentally from that of other accident periods. A similar phenomenon may affect calendar periods (diagonals). The dataset described in Section 3.6.1 exhibits both features. The row effects arise from legislative change; the diagonal effects from superimposed inflation (SI). These two subjects are treated in the following two sub-sections.

3.6.6.1 Superimposed Inflation

As noted in Section 3.2, claim costs are adjusted to constant dollar values, taking into account "normal" inflation. SI refers to any difference between the "normal" rate and the rate of inflation actually experienced.

Suppose that experience has been modeled according to (ICGLM3), but with none of the covariates $X^s_{h:i[r]}$ defined in terms of calendar period k. An example is provide by the model underlying Figure 3.9. Figure 3.11 tests whether the omission of calendar period terms is valid.

Figure 3.11 plots the average standardized deviance residuals (see Section 3.3.1) against calendar quarter, for an (ICGLM3) form of model, calibrated against data from accident quarters 2002Q4 and earlier, that is, those accident quarters unaffected by the legislative change that occurred toward the end of 2002Q4. The figure displays the calendar quarter experience of these claims up to and including 2007Q2. Beyond that, claims remaining unfinalized become relatively sparse, and the residuals erratic.

The figure identifies a model failure in that residuals shift from systematically negative in the marked early periods to systematically positive in the later periods. There is also a downward trend in the very earliest quarters which might or might not be significant, as these quarters correspond to the commencement of the scheme of insurance, and contain relatively few claim finalizations. Since the model assumes no trend across calendar quarters, the residual plot indicates

- an upward movement in inflation-adjusted claim sizes from late 1997 to the end of 2002; followed by
- a downward movement from 2003 to early 2005.

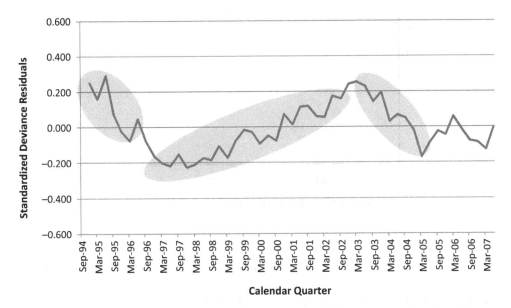

Fig. 3.11. Average claim size by development time and OT (injury severity 1): residual plot against calendar quarter.

The significance or otherwise of the residual pattern in the earliest periods requires investigation.

One might reasonably guess that modeling of these changes requires the inclusion in (3.12) of additional basis functions, as follows:

$$\mu_{i[r]}^s = \exp\left(\sum_{h=1}^{3} \beta_h^s f_h^s(t_{i[r]}) + \beta_4^s[1 - H_{11}(k_{i[r]})] + \beta_5^s L_{1:25}(k_{i[r]}) + \beta_6^s L_{25:34}(k_{i[r]})\right)$$

(3.13)

where $k_{i[r]}$ is the quarter of finalization of the rth claim in accident quarter i and $H_{k^*}(k)L_{mM}(k)$ are the Heaviside and ramp functions

$$H_{k^*}(k) = 1 \quad \text{if } k \geq k^*$$

$$= 0 \quad \text{otherwise}$$

(3.14)

$$L_{mM}(k) = \min[M - m, \max(0, k - m)] \quad \text{with } m < M$$

(3.15)

Note that $L_{mM}(k)$ is linear with unit gradient between m and M, and constant outside this range, as illustrated in Figure 3.12.

In fact, experimentation reveals one or two other subtleties in the modeling, concerning the period 1997Q1 to 2002Q4. Although Figure 3.11 suggests a more or less linear increase in claim sizes over this period, investigation reveals that the linear increase occurred at different rates for claims finalized at different OTs. To be specific, the rate of increase was estimated

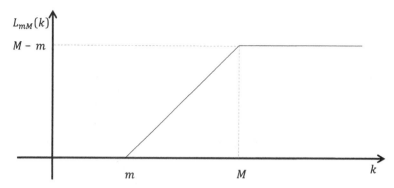

Fig. 3.12. Illustration of the function $L_{mM}(k)$.

(a) to be low for the very earliest finalizations, that is, OT $\cong 0$;
(b) to increase (i.e., increase in the rate of increase) linearly as OT increases from 0 to 0.1;
(c) to decrease linearly as OT increases from 0.1 to 1.

Moreover, within this framework, the rates of increase underwent some change at calendar quarter 2000Q4.

The anecdotal evidence suggested the following explanation for these trends. Claims in category (a) are very small in size, possibly nothing more than the cost of a police report. Their cost is subject to relatively little change in real terms. Claims at the high end of category (c) are of a catastrophic nature. The extent of injury is objectively evident, and their costs tend to move more or less in line with normal inflation.

However, claims intermediate between these two extremes include the important category of soft tissue injury, where the assessment of the extent of injury is much more subjective. The efforts of the claimants themselves, and their legal representatives, can cause the cost of these claims to escalate at a greater rate than normal inflation.

If the model is to make allowance for these additional features, then a fundamental revision of (3.13) is required, as follows, where the newly introduced terms appear in bold:

$$\mu_{i[r]}^s = \exp\left(\sum_{h=1}^{3} \beta_h^s f_h^s(t_{i[r]}) + \beta_4^s[1 - H_{11}(k_{i[r]})] + L_{1:25}(k_{i[r]})[\beta_5^s + \beta_6^s \lambda(t_{i[r]})] \right.$$

$$\left. + L_{25:34}(k_{i[r]})[\beta_7^s + \beta_8^s \lambda(t_{i[r]})] + \beta_9^s I(39 \leq k_{i[r]} \leq 44) + \beta_{10}^s \lambda(t_{i[r]}) \right)$$

(3.16)

Table 3.3. *Estimated Superimposed Inflation Parameters*

h	β_h^s
4	0.0608
5	0.0629
6	0.434
7	0.0667
8	0.0221
9	−0.1097
10	0.0441

where

$$\lambda(t) = \frac{\min(0.1, t)}{0.1} - \frac{\max(0, t - 0.1)}{0.9} \tag{3.17}$$

whose graph describes a triangle with [0, 1] on the *x*-axis as base, and apex of unit height at $t = 0.1$. This allows for the rate of SI to increase as OT increases from 0 to 0.1, and then decrease as OT increases from 0.1 to 1, as required earlier.

The terms associated with the coefficients β_6^s and β_8^s can be recognized as interaction terms, since each involves the joint effect of two covariates, calendar period k_i and OT t_i. Terms involving a single covariate are called main effects.

When model (3.16) is fitted to the data, the estimates of the newly added parameters are as set out in Table 3.3.

This shows, for example, that, in the years up to and including 1996, claim sizes were higher then immediately subsequently by a factor of exp(0.0608), that is, higher by 63%. Similarly, relative to the situation at the end of 2002, claim sizes were 10.6% lower in the six quarters after that.

The parameters β_5^s, β_6^s describe SI over the period up to the end of 1996. The *quarterly* rate of SI over this period is estimated as exp[0.0629 + 0.0434$\lambda(t)$] − 1 for OT t, that is, 6.5% for $t = 0$, increasing to 11.2% at $t = 0.1$, and then returning to 6.5% for $t = 1$.

These are, of course, very high rates of SI (note even higher over the period 2001 and 2002), and drove the Scheme to crisis. The legislative change was a response to this. Although, according to strict legal interpretation, it was not to affect claims that occurred before it became effective, it appears that it did affect the costs of those claims by some mechanism.

Residual plot Figure 3.11, after adjustment of the model to incorporate SI, changes to that appearing in Figure 3.13.

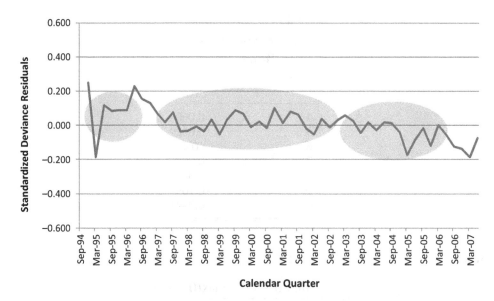

Fig. 3.13. Average claim size by development time and OT (injury severity 1): residual plot against calendar quarter (after allowance for superimposed inflation).

It is seen that the insertion in the model of the additional covariates appearing in (3.16) has had the desired effect of largely flattening the peaks and troughs that appeared in residual plot Figure 3.11. Some further analysis might be required in respect of calendar years 2005 and later.

3.6.6.2 *Legislative Change*

The legislation governing the scheme of auto bodily injury insurance underwent fundamental change, effective early December 2002, that is, toward the end of accident quarter 34. The change affected only claims with accident dates later than the effective date. Hence, any changes in claims experience induced by the legislative change affect all accident quarters 34 and later.

The 2002 legislation included a number of provisions with the potential to affect claims experience. Major among these were provisions aimed at controlling costs awarded to claimants under the common law head of damage. This required that a court assign a semiobjective rating to a claim's AIS codes and that this be mapped by formula (more or less) to an amount of common law award.

Section 3.6.6.1 examined the modeling of claims that occurred before the legislative change. It is necessary, of course, to model the later claims in addition. Although the respective experiences of claims occurring pre- and postchange are expected to exhibit distinct differences, there are also expected to be similarities. For example, it was anticipated that the change would not affect the smaller claims, which receive little or no common law payment, nor the largest claims, whose assessment had always been relatively objective.

It would be undesirable, therefore, to create separate models for claims experience pre- and postchange. In the early periods following the legislative change there would be little postchange experience. A preferable course would consist of the creation of a single model for all claims, but with appropriate differentiation between pre- and postchange accident periods.

Consider how this might be done in real time. At the end of 2002, one would have a model calibrated against data (almost) entirely pre-change. During 2003 and subsequent years, postchange data would accumulate and, to the extent that they differed from prechange, would display a drift away from the predictions of the prechange model.

To illustrate this on the basis of a meaningful quantity of post-change data, the point of observation of the claims experience is shifted forward to December 31, 2008. At this point, there is six years' experience of the postchange claims, those from accident years 2002 to 2008.

Figure 3.14 consists of two AvF plots where the forecast component is based on the prechange model (3.16) in both cases. In the second of the plots, the Actual component represents the experience of post-change claim occurrences, and the AvF is plotted against *accident quarter*, since the change directly influences claims of accident quarters 2003Q1 and later. The plot also includes the experience of pre-change claim occurrences (accident years up to and including 2002) for comparison.

It is possible (and indeed will be seen to be the case) that the postchange experience includes effects other than those directly related to the legislation affecting accident periods, and that these other effects confound the accident period effects. These are best inferred from the experience of prechange claims, which are at most only indirectly affected by the legislation. Therefore, Figure 3.14 also includes, as the first plot, the AvF, where the actual relates to prechange claims and the AvF is plotted against calendar quarter.

The second plot in Figure 3.14 illustrates how the change in legislation produced the desired effect, at least temporarily, with a reduction of about 20%–30% in average claim size in the accident quarters immediately following the change. However, this reduction is seen to be rapidly eroded in subsequent accident quarters and has diminished to virtually nil by 2004Q2, only 18 months after the change.

The erosion of the legislative benefit raises a question as to its source: whether it is specific to the postchange accident periods, or a more general phenomenon, affecting all claims. It was seen in model (3.16) and its associated discussion that high rates of SI had occurred in some early years of the Scheme, and this naturally raises a question as to whether a recurrence of it occurred in the years subsequent to 2003.

Prechange claim occurrences

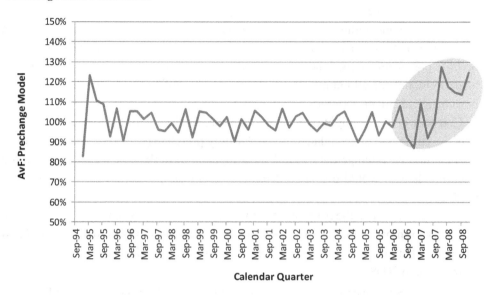

Postchange claim occurrences

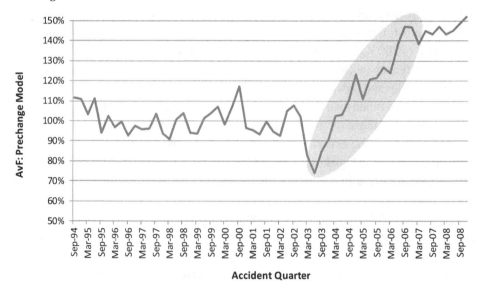

Fig. 3.14. AvF plot of pre- and postchange claims experiences against prechange model.

The purpose of the first plot in Figure 3.14 is to assist in resolving this question. Recall the plot that displays the experience of prechange claims occurrences only. It indicates quite clearly that these have been affected by large-scale SI over the period from about 2006Q3.

While the legislative change was expected to cause a step down in claim sizes (and did), its provisions were not such as to confer immunity against subsequent upward creep. It is therefore necessary that further modeling recognize simultaneous accident quarter and calendar quarter effects in the claims experience of calendar years 2003 and later; and with the calendar quarter effects possibly differentiated between pre- and postchange claim occurrences.

In accordance with the preceding discussion, the model (3.16) was first adjusted further to incorporate SI up to the end of 2008. The adjusted model took the form

$$\mu_{i[r]}^s = \exp \left(\sum_{h=1}^{3} \beta_h^s f_h^s(t_{i[r]}) + \beta_4^s[1 - H_{11}(k_{i[r]})] + L_{1:25}(k_{i[r]})[\beta_5^s + \beta_6^s \lambda(t_{i[r]})] \right.$$

$$+ L_{25:34}(k_{i[r]})[\beta_7^s + \beta_8^s \lambda(t_{i[r]})] + \beta_9^s I(pre) I(39 \le k_{i[r]} \le 44) + \beta_{10}^s \lambda(t_{i[r]})$$

$$\left. + \beta_{11}^s I(post) I(41 \le k_{i[r]} \le 45) + \beta_{12}^s[1 - t_{i[r]}] L_{48:55}(k_{i[r]}) \right) \qquad (3.18)$$

where $I(pre) = 1$ if and only if accident quarter i belongs to the prechange period of the scheme, and $I(post)$ is similarly defined.

The additional terms comprise

- a temporary downward shift of 21.8% in the size of all postchange claims over finalization quarters 41 to 45 (2004Q3 to 2005Q3), a slightly different period from that of the corresponding shift for pre-change claims;
- an exponential increase in claim sizes (linear in the linear predictor) from finalization quarter 48 to 55 (2006Q2 to 2008Q1), with rates of increase that depend on OT, specifically, a rate of 1.8% per quarter at OT = 0, reducing to 0% at OT = 1.

These changes are also accompanied by some changes to the OT main effect terms, not displayed here for the sake of brevity.

When the forecast components of the two AvF plots that appear in Figure 3.14 are adjusted in accordance with this model revision, those plots appear as in Figure 3.15.

The first plot in Figure 3.15 demonstrates that the additional terms included in (3.18) have largely accounted for SI over the postchange period in relation to prechange claim occurrences. There remains, however, a hint of some further SI, not accounted for, during 2008. This matter will be investigated further in Section 3.6.7.

The second plot in Figure 3.15, alternatively, presents a very different picture. In this case, the model of claim size of prechange occurrences, adjusted for SI as in (3.18), fail spectacularly to match the experience of postchange occurrences. There is a rapid increase in the sizes of postchange claim occurrences not accounted for by the model.

Prechange claim occurrences

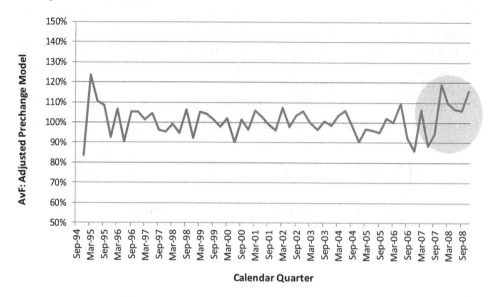

Postchange claim occurrences

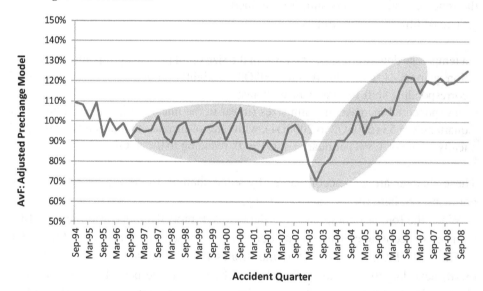

Fig. 3.15. AvF plot of pre- and postchange claims experiences against prechange model, adjusted for superimposed inflation.

This rapid increase appeared in Figure 3.14, and it has been materially attenuated in Figure 3.15, reflecting the adjustment of the model from (3.16) to (3.18). However, the attenuation is not nearly enough. With calendar period effects accounted for, the reasoning given in the text relating to Figure 3.14 suggests that these may be accident period effects. This is supported by the second plot in Figure 3.15, in which accident year 2003 exhibits claims sizes dramatically lower than model forecasts.

Model (3.18) has therefore been further adjusted to the following:

$$\mu_{i[r]}^s = \exp\left(\sum_{h=1}^{3} \beta_h^s f_h^s(t_{i[r]}) + \beta_4^s[1 - H_{11}(k_{i[r]})] + L_{1:25}(k_{i[r]})[\beta_5^s + \beta_6^s\lambda(t_{i[r]})]\right.$$

$$+ L_{25:34}(k_{i[r]})[\beta_7^s + \beta_8^s\lambda(t_{i[r]})] + \beta_9^s I(pre)I(39 \leq k_{i[r]} \leq 44) + \beta_{10}^s\lambda(t_{i[r]})$$

$$+ \beta_{11}^s I(post) I(41 \leq k_{i[r]} \leq 45) + \beta_{12}^s[1 - t_{i[r]}]L_{48:55}(k_{i[r]})$$

$$\left. + \beta_{13}^s I(35 \leq i \leq 38)\right) \tag{3.19}$$

Calibration of this model estimates a temporary downward shift of 107% in the size of all claims occurring in the immediate post-change quarters 35 to 38 (accident year 2003). This largely substitutes for the previously estimated 21.8% temporary downward shift over finalization quarters 41 to 45, and the estimated size of this shift is now reduced to only 25%.

With the replacement of model (3.18) by (3.19), the second plot in Figure 3.15 is adjusted to that in Figure 3.16. Limited improvement can be seen in that the AvF ratio

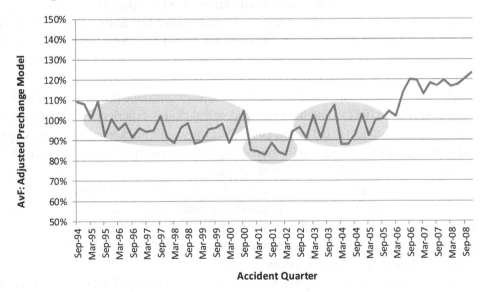

Fig. 3.16. AvF plot of postchange claims experience against prechange model, adjusted for superimposed inflation and accident quarter effects.

now varies from about 83% to 123% over the period 2001 to 2008, compared with variation from about 70% to 123% in Figure 3.15.

However, this remains far from acceptable. Furthermore, Figure 3.16 exhibits a rather unsatisfactory slow downward trend over the period 1995 to 2000. These features will be subjected to further analysis in Section 3.6.7.

3.6.7 Warped Operational Time

The introduction of the legislation discussed in Section 3.6.6.2 had the effect of reducing the common law award to nil for some claims. As a result, it became uneconomic for some claimants to lodge claims that would have been lodged under previous legislation, and the effect of this was to distort the OT scale. The situation can be visualized as follows.

Imagine all the claims of an accident period assembled in an ascending order of time of finalization, that is, at equally spaced points along the OT interval [0,1]. The sizes of these claims will exhibit the relation between OT and average claim size.

Now suppose that a substantial body of the smaller claims are deleted from the sequence. These claims will lie predominantly at the lower values of OT. The remaining claims will be finalized at equally spaced points on a newly defined OT interval [0,1]. In general terms, the OT of a specific claim before the deletion will be mapped to a lower OT after it. In this sense, the OT scale has been warped, and the new scale will be referred to as *warped operational time*.

The situation may be represented diagrammatically as in Figure 3.17. The upper half of the diagram illustrates individual claims of an accident period in the original regime, with their sizes at settlement plotted against OT. Some of the claims are marked with heavy lines. These are the ones that would have been eliminated had the new regime (after the legislative change) been in operation. It may be noted that they are concentrated among the smaller claims settled at the lower OTs.

The lower half of the diagram illustrates a later accident period, with identical injury experience (i.e., would have led to identical claims experience under the original regime), but subject to the new regime. Here the claims marked in bold in the upper half have been deleted, causing the remaining claims to shift to lower OTs. This shift is marked by broken arrows in a couple of cases.

Accounting for this change requires reasoning of the following sort. Suppose that the last accident quarter prior to the legislative change is $i = i_0$, and consider a later accident quarter $i > i_0$. According to the preceding explanation, there will exist a mapping $\tau_i(t)$ from OT t in accident quarter i_0 to the "equivalent" OT in accident quarter i, that is, subject to the same expected claim size.

The function τ_i is the *warping function*, and the subscript i allows for different warping in different accident quarters, since some time may be required for the effect of the change in legislation to become fully manifest. It is assumed that the warping function satisfies the following requirements:

Original regime (prior to legislation)

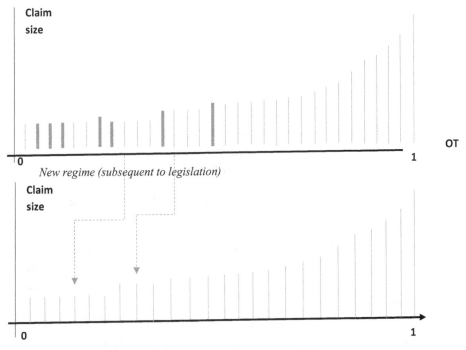

Fig. 3.17. Diagrammatic illustration of OT warping.

- it is one-one (therefore invertible) and smooth (continuously differentiable);
- $\tau_i(t) = t$ for $i = i_0$;
- $\tau_i(t) \leq t$ for $i > i_0$.

For purposes of the analysis of claim sizes, it is helpful to adopt the relation between OT and claim size in accident quarter i_0 as the standard and standardize all subsequent accident quarters on an *"as if* accident quarter i_0" basis, that is, replace their OTs by those that would have arisen prior to the legislation. Thus a claim finalized at OT t in accident quarter i is assigned the *warped OT* $\tau_i^{-1}(t) \geq t$. With all accident quarters standardized in this way, analysis of claim sizes then proceeds as previously.

In the selection of suitable warping functions, it is assumed that there exists an operational time threshold (denote it t^*) above which claim sizes are sufficiently large that the legislation does not eliminate any. Nonetheless, the OTs of these claims will be warped as a result of elimination of claims at lesser OTs.

In fact, these claims, which account for the last $1 - t^*$ of OT in the new regime, would have accounted for the last $(1 - t^*)f_{i_0}/f_i$, where f_i denotes the claim frequency experienced in accident quarter i, and it is assumes for the sake of this example that the change in claim frequency over accident quarters is due solely to the elimination of the claims under discussion here (the actual case study also exhibited longer term trends, which added considerably to the complexity of the analysis).

According to the preceding reasoning,

$$\tau_i^{-1}(t) = 1 - \rho_i(1 - t) \quad \text{for } t \geq t^* \tag{3.20}$$

where

$$\rho_i = f_{i_0}/f_i \tag{3.21}$$

It also follows from the preceding reasoning that the shift in operational time must be greater than in (3.20) for $t \leq t^*$. The shape of the warping function will need to found empirically. In the present case study, the following form was found suitable:

$$\tau_i^{-1}(t) = [1 - \rho_i(1 - t^*)]t/t^* + a\rho_i[1 + \sin 2\pi(t/t^* - 1/4)]^{1/2} \quad \text{for } t \leq t^* \tag{3.22}$$

where $a > 0$ is a constant to be estimated from the data.

Note that, as t varies from 0 to t^*, the first member on the right varies linearly from 0 to $[1 - \rho_i(1 - t^*)]$. The final square bracket starts at 0, increases to a maximum of 2 at $t = 1/2t^*$ and then decreases to 0 at $t = t^*$, so that (3.22) reduces to (3.20) at the two end points $t = 0, t^*$.

Calibration of this model requires estimation of its two parameters t^* and a. This cannot be achieved within the GLM itself, as it amounts to an adjustment of the OT covariate in that model. In the event, the two parameters concerned were selected after an extensive iterative process. A plot of average claim size against warped OT, with t^* and a fixed, was examined for a variety of accident quarters. The values of t^* and

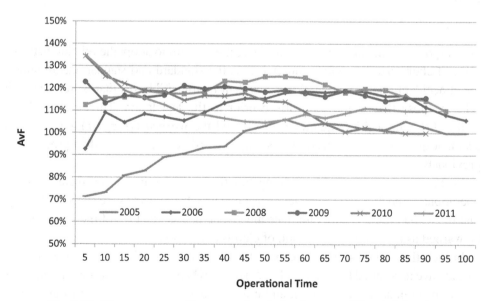

Fig. 3.18. Change over accident years in relation between OT and claim size.

Table 3.4. *Estimated Warping*
Function Parameters

Parameter	Value
t^*	0.700
a	0.116

a were varied until the plots for all the accident quarters assumed approximately the same *shape*, possibly shifted by accident period effects. A more methodical approach may well exist.

Care is required in the selection of parameter values. It is inherent in the description of OT in Section 3.6.5 that the function τ_i, and hence τ_i^{-1}, should be strictly one-one. Since the two components of (3.22) can take opposite gradients, τ_i^{-1} will have the one-one property only for suitable combinations of the parameters ρ_i, t^*, a.

Figure 3.18 plots a lightly smoothed version of the AvF against OT for a sequence of accident years, where the forecast is based on model (3.19). The progressive change in shape with advancing accident year is evident. In the earliest accident years, the model overestimates claim sizes at the low OTs, whereas it underestimates them in the latest accident years.

This is consistent with the phenomenon of OT warping described earlier in this subsection. The elimination of smaller low-OT claims from the experience causes larger, higher-OT claims to appear at lower OTs. As the degree of elimination steadily increases with accident year, claims finalized at the low OTs steadily increase in size, as in Figure 3.18.

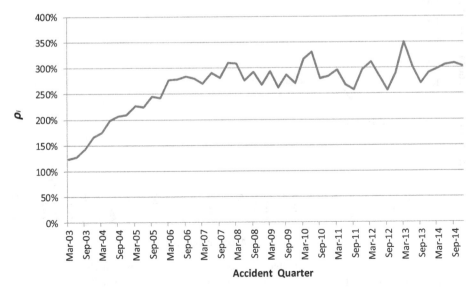

Fig. 3.19. Estimate of ρ_i *for accident quarters post legislation change.*

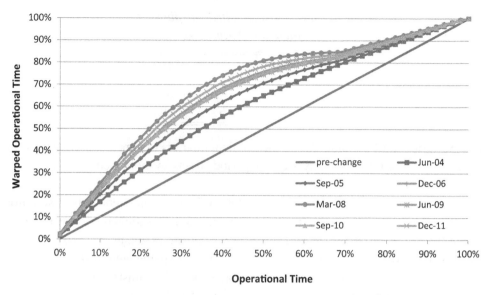

Fig. 3.20. Diagrammatic illustration of OT warping.

For the warping function (3.22), the selected parameter values were as set out in Table 3.4 and Figure 3.19, and the functions τ_i^{-1} in Figure 3.20.

Figure 3.21 adjusts Figure 3.16 by substituting warped OT $\tau_i^{-1}(t)$ in place of OT t in model (3.19). It is seen that the OT warping eliminates the upward trend on

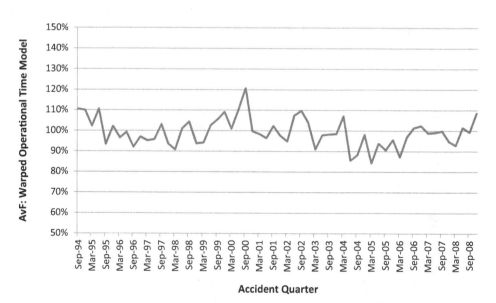

Fig. 3.21. AvF plot of postchange claims experience against prechange model, adjusted for superimposed inflation, accident quarter effects, and OT warping.

the right of the earlier figure, as well as the slight downward trend on the left. One or two minor spikes remain that might warrant further investigation, but the AvF profile in Figure 3.21 now appears acceptably flat for the purposes of the current chapter.

3.7 Conclusion

The purpose of the present chapter has been to illustrate the use of GLMs in the modeling of an insurance claims experience with a view to loss reserving for the portfolio concerned.

It is mentioned in [I:18] that the chain ladder is ubiquitous in loss reserving. As remarked in the same source [I:18.2.2], the chain ladder may be concisely described as a multiplicative model with row and column effects, e.g. $E[Y_{kj}] = \alpha_k \beta_j$.

An application of the chain ladder therefore lacks validity in the event of any inconsistency between the claim data and this algebraic structure. Too often in practice, no check for consistency (or at least the absence of inconsistency) is applied. Or else, inconsistency is detected but disregarded, or addressed in some unsatisfying ad hoc manner. In the present case, Figure 3.6 amply demonstrates the failings of the assumed multiplicative structure.

For the more general case, Section 3.5 provides an array of diagnostics that could have been used to submit the dataset to test. In fact, this formality has not been carried out because of Figure 3.6, and because the data contain a variety of unusual effects and are known to be highly inconsistent with the stated multiplicative model.

First, it is known that claim sizes are highly differentiated by injury severity (Section 3.6.2), and so injury severity is a covariate in the model. The example in Section 3.6 presents only the segment of the model that addresses injury severity 1. However, it is to be emphasized that the total model is a single algebraic structure that includes all injury severities.

This enables the inclusion of features that are common to a number of injury severities to be reflected and modeled on the basis of data from all of those injury severities. Differentiation between the effects of different injury severities is included in the model by means of interactions. For example, when the graph of average claim size against OT varies by injury severity, the model must include an interaction between OT and injury severity.

This sort of approach will usually be preferable to the creation of a multiplicity of models, one for each injury severity. In the latter case, each model would need to be estimated on the basis of data in respect of just its own severity, and these data may be sparse in some cases, generating unnecessarily large prediction errors.

There are two data features that, perhaps more frequently than any others that distort paid loss triangles away from the multiplicative form that is required by the chain ladder:

- changes over time in the rate of finalization of claims; and
- superimposed inflation.

Both are found to be present in the example dataset. The response to the first is to model claim sizes in terms of OT rather than real development time (Section 3.6.5). The response to the second is the study and identification of "diagonal effects" (Section 3.6.6.1). It is well known that the chain ladder is particularly ill adapted to these diagonal trends.

As it happens, the data also include row effects, resulting from legislation that affected only accident periods beyond the effective date of the legislation. These are investigated in Section 3.6.6.2. The same legislative change indirectly resulted in the reduction of claim frequency by the selective elimination of certain types of claims. This, in turn, caused a shift over accident periods (rows) in the relation between OT and claim size. The model required extension to account for this further effect, an extension that was incorporated by means of the device of warping OT (Section 3.6.7).

The dataset is thus seen to be far from the multiplicative structure assumed by the chain ladder, but rather a rich tapestry of row, quasi-column (OT), diagonal and other main effects, together with interactions between them. A model that addresses all of these features adequately and effectively within a unified stochastic structure will necessarily be a GLM or some close relative. Section 3.6 illustrates a number of aspects of the application of a GLM to the modeling.

References

Hastie, T. J., and R. J. Tibshirani. *Generalized Additive Models.* Chapman and Hall, New York, 1990.

McCullagh, P., and J. A. Nelder. *Generalized Linear Models.* 2nd ed. Chapman and Hall, Boca Raton, 1989.

McGuire, G. Individual claim modelling of CTP data. Insititute of Actuaries of Australian XIth Accident Compensation Seminar, Melbourne, Australia. http://actuaries.asn.au/Library/6.a_ACS07_paper_McGuire_Individual%20claim%20 modelling%20of%20CTP%20data.pdf, 2007.

Nelder, J. A., and R. W. M. Wedderburn. Generalized linear models. *Journal of the Royal Statistical Society, Series A,* 135: 370–384, 1972.

Pierce, D. A., and D. W. Shafer. Residuals in generalised linear models. *Journal of the American Statistical Association,* 81: 977–986, 1986.

Reid, D. H. Claim reserves in general insurance. *Journal of the Institute of Actuaries,* 105: 211–296, 1978.

Taylor, G. C. Separation of inflation and other effects from the distribution of non-life insurance claim delays. *Astin Bulletin,* 9: 217–230, 1977.

Taylor, G. *Loss Reserving: An Actuarial Perspective*. Kluwer Academic, Boston, 2000.

Taylor, G. Maximum likelihood and estimation efficiency of the chain ladder. *Astin Bulletin*, 41(1): 131–155, 2011.

Taylor, G., and G. McGuire. Loss reserving with GLMs: A case study. Casualty Actuarial Society 2004 Discussion Paper Program, 327–392, 2004.

Wüthrich, M. V., and M. Merz. *Stochastic Claims Reserving Methods in Insurance*. John Wiley, Chichester, UK, 2008.

4

Frameworks for General Insurance Ratemaking

Beyond the Generalized Linear Model

Peng Shi and James Guszcza

Chapter Preview. This chapter illustrates the applications of various predictive modeling strategies for determining pure premiums in property-casualty insurance. Consistent with standard predictive modeling practice, we focus on methodologies capable of harnessing risk-level information in the ratemaking process. The use of such micro-level data yields statistical models capable of making finer-grained distinctions between risks, thereby enabling more accurate predictions. This chapter will compare multiple analytical approaches for determining risk-level pure premium. A database of personal automobile risks will be used to illustrate the various approaches. A distinctive feature of our approach is the comparison of two broad classes of modeling frameworks: univariate and multivariate. The univariate approach, most commonly used in industry, specifies a separate model for each outcome variable. The multivariate approach specifies a single model for a vector of outcome variables. Comparing the performance of different models reveals that there is no unique solution, and each approach has its own strengths and weaknesses.

4.1 Introduction

Ratemaking, the estimation of policy- or risk-level pure premium for the purpose of pricing insurance contracts, is one of the classical problems of general insurance (aka "nonlife," aka "property-casualty") actuarial science. For most of the 20th century, ratemaking practice was largely restricted to the one-way analyses of various rating dimensions (such as risk class, prior claims, geographical territory, and so on) with pure premium. Insurers would occasionally employ Bailey-Simon minimum bias methods to account for dependencies amongst rating dimensions. However, the multivariate approach to ratemaking was typically more honored in the breach than the observance due to the information technology limitations of the time and the difficulty of running the iterative Bailey-Simon computational routines. Neither the one-way nor the Bailey-Simon approach was founded in mainstream statistical modeling concepts.

This state of affairs began to change rapidly starting in the mid-1990s thanks partly to increasing availability of computing technology, and partly to the recognition that generalized linear models (GLM) offers practitioners a rigorous, mainstream statistical framework within which Bailey-Simon type calculations, and much else, can be performed (see, e.g., Mildenhall, 1999). GLM methodology offers the ability to move beyond fairly rudimentary analyses of low-dimensional aggregated data to the creation of sophisticated statistical models, containing numerous predictive variables, that estimate expected pure premium at the risk rather than class level. From a methodological point of view, the adoption of GLM has brought into the ratemaking fold such mainstream methodologies such as graphical exploratory data analysis (EDA), formal variable significance testing, graphical residual analysis and model criticism, and the use of cross-validation to evaluate model accuracy. From a business strategy point of view, the use of rigorous, granular models for pricing and underwriting enables analytically sophisticated insurers to grow profitably and avoid adverse selection.

From a purely technical point of view, it is common to identify pure premium ratemaking with the use of Poisson and gamma regression to model claim frequency and severity, respectively. For example, Werner and Guven (2007) state, "It is widely accepted that there are standard distributions for frequency and severity. Generally speaking, a Poisson error structure is appropriate for frequency modeling and a gamma error structure is appropriate for severity modeling." They go on to consider the use of Tweedie (compound Poisson-gamma) regression to model pure premium directly, but advise against doing so without simultaneously modeling the Tweedie dispersion parameter.

The goal of this chapter is to advance the conversation by placing pure premium ratemaking within a broader statistical modeling framework than typically found in the literature. While the GLM framework is a major advance over prestatistical ratemaking practice, there is in principle no reason why actuaries should restrict themselves to distributions that happen to belong to the exponential family central to GLM theory. Furthermore, the decision of whether to model pure premium directly or in stages through separate frequency and severity models should be viewed as an empirically informed one rather than a decision determined by tradition and/or a priori assumptions about the (in)adequacy of certain model forms.

Beyond their mixed discrete/continuous character, risk- or policy-level general insurance losses are also distinctive in that they can be viewed as the sum of losses from multiple hazard or coverage types. For example, standard comprehensive automobile insurance policies cover both third party bodily injury and property damage as well as the damage to the policyholder's own vehicle; multiperil homeowner insurance policies cover property damage caused by different hazards; medical insurance policies often compensate care costs associated with office-based visits, hospital stays, or emergency room visits. Insurers must typically analyze payments separately by coverage type both because of differing contract features specific to coverage types (such as limits and deductibles) and because predictive dimensions generally relate differently to the various coverage types. The default option is a *univariate* modeling approach: one builds a separate model for each coverage type. In contrast, a *multivariate* approach, two of examples of which will be explored in what follows, builds a single model of a vector of outcome variables.[1]

This chapter will illustrate a variety of approaches to pure premium ratemaking using a sample of policy-level personal automobile data from the state of Massachusetts. Details of this data are provided in Section 4.2. Sections 4.3 and 4.4 discuss various univariate and multivariate approaches, respectively. In Section 4.3, we consider two standard methods that are widely used in the actuarial practice: the two-part frequency/severity model and the Tweedie generalized linear model. In contrast with much of the literature, not all of the frequency and severity model forms discussed fall within the GLM framework. To jointly model claims of multiple types, we extend the standard frequency-severity model in two ways in Section 4.4. One approach is to employ multivariate copula regression; the other is a "hierarchical" approach in which model claim type is also modeled, with the resulting model being combined with claim frequency and severity models. Section 4.5 compares several of the alternative models using out-of-sample validation data. Concluding remarks are provided in Section 4.6.

4.2 Data

In the case study, we consider a portfolio of automobile policyholders obtained from the Commonwealth Automobile Reinsurers (CAR) in the state of Massachusetts in the United States. As a statistical agent for motor vehicle insurance in the Commonwealth of Massachusetts, the CAR collects insurance claim data for private passengers and commercial automobiles in Massachusetts and takes steps to ensure the highest standard of data quality.

We take a random sample of 150,000 policyholders with compulsory coverage in the 2006 policy year. We use a random sample of one hundred thousand policyholders to develop models, and set aside the other 50,000 policyholders for out-of-sample analysis. For each individual driver, the dataset contains the information on the number of claims made over the year. When claims are present, we also have access to the amount of payments for two types of coverage: third party liability (property damage and bodily injury) and personal injury protection (PIP). Table 4.1 displays the claim frequency for the portfolio of policyholders. As anticipated, we observe that only a

---

[1] This chapter uses the terms *univariate* and *multivariate* to denote models of a single outcome variable and a vector of outcome variables, respectively. This is consistent with mainstream statistical usage of these terms, and in contrast with the common use of the terms to denote analyses that employ one or multiple explanatory variables, respectively.

Table 4.1. *Claim Frequency of the Insurance Portfolio*

Count	0	1	2	3	4
Frequency	95,443	4,324	219	12	2
Percentage	95.44	4.32	0.22	0.01	0.00

Table 4.2. *Claim Frequency of the Insurance Portfolio*

		PIP				
		0	1	Total	χ^2-statistic	881.32
	0	95,443	453	95,896	p-value	<0.001
Liability	1	3,821	283	4,104	ϕ-coefficient	0.1491
	Total	99,264	736	100,000		

Table 4.3. *Percentiles of Claim Size by Type*

	5%	10%	25%	50%	75%	90%	95%
Third party liability	237	350	676	1,464	3,465	10,597	19,959
PIP	2	5	84	1,372	3,300	7,549	8,232

Table 4.4. *Description and Summary Statistics of Explanatory Variables*

			Mean	
Variable	Description	Overall	No Accident	With Accident
Rating group	1. if adults	0.747	0.749	0.703
	2. if business	0.014	0.014	0.014
	3. if <3 years experience	0.043	0.042	0.078
	4. if 3–6 years experience	0.044	0.043	0.067
	5. if senior citizens	0.152	0.153	0.138
Territory group	1. if the least risky territory	0.185	0.189	0.132
	2. if the second to least risky territory	0.193	0.194	0.168
	3. if the fourth risky territory	0.113	0.114	0.091
	4. if the third risky territory	0.201	0.201	0.194
	5. if the second risky territory	0.189	0.187	0.227
	6. if the most risky territory	0.120	0.117	0.189

small portion (less than 5%) of policyholders incurred accident(s) during the year. This explains the semicontinuous nature of the claims data, in which a significant fraction of zeros corresponds to no claims and a small percentage of positive values corresponds to the aggregate claim amount in the event of one or more claims.

Table 4.2 further shows the two-way frequency table indicating the occurrence of either type of claims. The result suggests some positive relationships between the the two types of occurrence, which is supported by the χ^2 statistic and ϕ coefficient. For instance, among policyholders with liability claim, the chance of filing a PIP claim is 6.9%, compared with 0.47% for policyholders without liability claim. This result motivates the multivariate modeling approaches discussed in Section 4.4. Note that this analysis does not account for the correlation introduced by the covariates. Section 4.4 will address this issue in a regression setup and introduce different methods to capture the positive relationship.

Another characteristic feature of insurance data is the long tail of the claim size distribution. To illustrate, Table 4.3 displays the percentiles of the total claim amount per policy year of third party liability and PIP coverage conditional on the occurrence of a claim. In addition to the skewness and heavy tails, one also observes that claims of liability coverage are generally greater than those of PIP coverage. This is not surprising because liability coverage usually has a higher policy limit than the PIP coverage.

In addition to claim information, the dataset also contains standard rating factors to be considered for inclusion as explanatory variables in the regression analysis. The description of these variables and their sample means are displayed in Table 4.4. We have five rating groups of drivers differed by age, driving experience, or usage of the vehicle. For example, the majority (about 75%) of policyholders are adult drivers with more than six years of driving experience. Policyholders are also categorized into six groups according to the riskiness of the driving territory. It appears that the policyholders are fairly evenly sampled from the various territories. Table 4.4 also displays the sample means of rating factors for policyholders with and without accidents, respectively. The sample means for claim-free policyholders are close to the overall mean because only a small percent of drivers have one or more claims over the year. However, the heterogeneity introduced by these observables are apparent. For example, when compared with policyholders without accidents, a higher (lower) percentage of policyholders with accidents are from more (less) risky driving territories.

4.3 Univariate Ratemaking Framework

This section illustrates ratemaking using a univariate modeling framework. Here we analyze aggregate claims per year at policy level, not broken down by coverage type. Here "univariate" refers to the class of methods that models a single outcome variable.

In particular, we discuss two ratemaking approaches that are widely used in current practice, the Tweedie compound Poisson-gamma model and the frequency-severity model.

4.3.1 Tweedie Model

For short-term products such as automobile insurance, an initial estimate of the annual premium for a given policy should be the expected amount of total claims per policy term. A straightforward approach is to directly model the aggregate claims. As noted earlier, the distribution of this quantity is characterized by a probability mass at zero. The Tweedie generalized linear model is a commonly used model of an otherwise continuous variable with a point mass at zero.

The Tweedie distribution is defined as a Poisson sum of gamma-distributed random variables (see Tweedie, 1984). Specifically, let Y_i denote the total claims observed for individual i per unit of exposure. Then Y_i could be expressed in terms of an aggregate loss model as $Y_i = (Z_{i1} + \cdots + Z_{iN_i})/\omega_i$, where N_i represents the number of claims; Z_{ij} $(j = 1, \cdots, N_i)$, independent of N_i, is an i.i.d. sequence indicating the corresponding claim amounts; and ω_i denotes the exposure. The Tweedie compound Poisson model is derived by assuming that N_i is Poisson distributed with mean $\omega_i \lambda_i$ and Z_{ij} are i.i.d. gamma distributed with shape parameter α and scale parameter γ_i. It is straightforward to see that Y_i has a positive probability at zero when $N_i = 0$ (zero claim) and follows a gamma distribution when $N_i = n > 0$ (one or more claims).

The Tweedie GLM is derived under the following reparameterizations:

$$\lambda_i = \frac{\mu_i^{2-p}}{\phi(2-p)}, \quad \alpha = \frac{2-p}{p-1}, \quad \gamma_i = \phi(p-1)\mu_i^{p-1} \quad (4.1)$$

Note that here the dispersion parameter ϕ is assumed to be constant and this assumption could be relaxed as discussed in the following analysis. With the preceding relationships, we consider two cases. First, the total cost of claims as well as the number of claims are observed for each individual, i.e. both Y_i and N_i are recorded. As shown by Jørgensen and de Souza (1994), the joint density function of Y_i and N_i could be expressed as

$$f_i(n, y) = a(n, y; \phi/\omega_i, p) \exp\left\{\frac{\omega_i}{\phi} b(y; \mu_i, p)\right\} \quad (4.2)$$

with

$$a(n, y; \phi/\omega_i, p) = \left\{\frac{(\omega_i/\phi)^{1/(p-1)} y^{(2-p)/(p-1)}}{(2-p)(p-1)^{(2-p)/(p-1)}}\right\}^n \frac{1}{n!\Gamma(n(2-p)/(p-1))y}$$

and

$$b(y; \mu_i, p) = \frac{-y}{(p-1)\mu_i^{p-1}} - \frac{\mu_i^{2-p}}{2-p}$$

in the second case, only the total cost of claims Y_i but not the number of claims N_i has been recorded. In this case, the quantity being modeled is the marginal distribution of Y_i. From (4.2) one can show

$$f_i(y) = \exp\left[\frac{\omega_i}{\phi_i} b(y; \mu_i, p) + S(y; \phi/\omega_i)\right] \tag{4.3}$$

where

$$S(y; \phi/\omega_i) = \begin{cases} 0 & \text{if } y = 0 \\ \ln\left\{\sum_{n\geq 1} a(n, y; \phi/\omega_i, p)\right\} & \text{if } y > 0 \end{cases}$$

Hence, the distribution of Y_i belongs to the exponential family with parameters μ_i, ϕ, and $p \in (1, 2)$, and we have

$$E(Y_i) = \mu_i \quad \text{and} \quad \text{Var}(Y_i) = \frac{\phi}{\omega_i}\mu_i^p$$

The general theoretical foundations of GLM (see, e.g., Dean, 2014) is therefore applicable to the Tweedie model. It is also worth mentioning the two limiting cases of the Tweedie model: $p \to 1$ results in the overdispersed Poisson model and $p \to 2$ results in the gamma GLM. The Tweedie compound Poisson model accommodates the situations in between.

A regression model is achieved by relating the expected value of the outcome variable with covariates through a link function:

$$g_\mu(\mu_i) = \mathbf{x}_i'\boldsymbol{\beta}$$

where $\mathbf{x}_i$ is the vector of covariates and $\boldsymbol{\beta}$ is the vector of corresponding regression coefficients. In the preceding formulation, one focuses on the expected cost of claims per unit at risk μ_i and assumes a constant dispersion ϕ. As pointed out in Smyth and Jørgensen (2002), when modeling the cost of claims, it is useful to model the dispersion as well as the mean. This could be implemented in a double generalized linear model framework, where one allows both mean μ_i and dispersion ϕ_i to vary across individuals. That is, in addition to the mean model, one uses another link function for the dispersion

$$g_\phi(\phi_i) = \mathbf{z}_i'\boldsymbol{\eta}$$

where $\mathbf{z}_i$ and $\boldsymbol{\eta}$ are the vector of covariates and regression parameters in the dispersion model respectively. The particular parametrization (4.1) of the Tweedie distribution guarantees that μ_i and ϕ_i, and thus $\boldsymbol{\beta}$ and $\boldsymbol{\eta}$ are orthogonal.

Estimation results of the various Tweedie models are summarized in Table 4.5. Again, the variable of interest is the total liability and PIP claim cost. "Cost and Claim Counts" model refers to the case that totoal number of claims in each policy year is available in addition to the claim cost. The model corresponds to the Tweedie density defined by equation (4.2). "Cost Only" model refers to the case that totoal number of claims in each policy year is not available in the database. The model corresponds to the Tweedie density defined by equation (4.3). The effects of rating factors are as expected. For example, policyholders with less driving experience and policyholders from riskier territories are more likely to incur higher claims cost. We fit models corresponding to the cases in which claim counts are and are not available. The additional information contained in claim counts does not substantially affect the estimation of regression coefficients. In the double generalized linear modeling framework, we observe the significant effects of explanatory variables on the dispersion. However, this does not substantially influence the mean regression because the regressions for the mean and the dispersion are parameterized orthogonally. Finally, it is worth pointing out that AIC/BIC statistics suggest using the more complex generalized gamma regression model.

4.3.2 Frequency-Severity Model

The alternative approach to modeling the semicontinuous claim costs is through a two-step analysis. First one models the frequency of claims per exposure, in the second step, one models the claim amount given the the occurrence of one or more claims. This is known as frequency-severity or two-part model in the literature. See Frees (2014) for details.

The two-part model can take different forms depending on the specifics of the available data. Consider the insurance claims data. If the total claim cost is the only observed information for each policyholder, the two-part framework consists of a frequency model that estimates the probability of one or more claims and the severity model of the size of total claims conditioning on this occurrence. Or in another scenario we might have more information than total claim costs. For example, an insurer might also record the number of claims of each policyholder and the associated cost of each claim. In this case, the more appropriate two-part framework could be modeling the number rather than the probability of claims in the first part, and then the cost per claim rather than an aggregated cost in the second part. We focus on the second option in this application since all relevant information are available. We will revisit the first option in the multivariate modeling section.

Table 4.5. *Estimation of the Tweedie Models*

| | Cost and Claim Counts | | | | Cost Only | | | |
| | Mean Model | | Dispersion Model | | Mean Model | | Dispersion Model | |
Parameter	Estimate	StdErr	Estimate	StdErr	Estimate	StdErr	Estimate	StdErr
intercept	5.634	0.087	5.647	0.083	5.634	0.088	5.646	0.084
rating group = 1	0.267	0.070	0.263	0.071	0.267	0.071	0.263	0.072
rating group = 2	0.499	0.206	0.504	0.211	0.500	0.209	0.506	0.213
rating group = 3	1.040	0.120	1.054	0.106	1.040	0.121	1.054	0.108
rating group = 4	0.811	0.122	0.835	0.113	0.811	0.123	0.834	0.114
territory group = 1	−1.209	0.086	−1.226	0.086	−1.210	0.087	−1.226	0.087
territory group = 2	−0.830	0.083	−0.850	0.080	−0.831	0.084	−0.850	0.081
territory group = 3	−0.845	0.095	−0.863	0.097	−0.845	0.097	−0.862	0.098
territory group = 4	−0.641	0.081	−0.652	0.077	−0.641	0.082	−0.652	0.078
territory group = 5	−0.359	0.080	−0.368	0.074	−0.360	0.081	−0.368	0.075
p	1.631	0.004	1.637	0.004	1.629	0.004	1.634	0.004
dispersion								
intercept	5.932	0.015	5.670	0.041	5.968	0.016	5.721	0.043
rating group = 1			0.072	0.034			0.064	0.035
rating group = 2			0.006	0.101			0.010	0.105
rating group = 3			−0.365	0.051			−0.356	0.054
rating group = 4			−0.206	0.054			−0.209	0.056
territory group = 1			0.401	0.042			0.374	0.043
territory group = 2			0.323	0.039			0.301	0.040
territory group = 3			0.377	0.047			0.365	0.048
territory group = 4			0.266	0.037			0.260	0.039
territory group = 5			0.141	0.036			0.132	0.037
loglik	−61,121		−60,988		−60,142		−60,030	
AIC	122,266		122,018		120,308		120,036	
BIC	122,380		122,218		120,422		119,922	

Let N denote the number of claims per year and Y denote the severity of each claim. The frequency-severity model could be formulated as

$$f(N, Y) = f(N) \times f(Y|N)$$

Here all the information contained in the observed data are captured by the joint distribution $f(N, Y)$ which can further be decomposed into two components. The first one $f(N)$ models the distribution of the number of claims, and the second one $f(Y|N)$ models the amount of each claim given occurrence. Note that the preceding decomposition is based on conditional probability and does not require an assumption about the independence of the two components. The decoupling result implies that we may build and estimate the two components separately in two independent steps. We discuss this two-part model as a univariate modeling framework because, despite the presence of two components, each of them involves only a single outcome.

Unlike the Tweedie GLM, the two-part model allows for the inclusion of different sets of explanatory variables in the frequency and the severity models. This could be useful if, for instance, the factors affecting the probability of accidents differ from those determining the severity of accidents. In fact, the two-part formulation was originally motivated by the two-step decision in the determination of health care demand. In this context, the individual decides to seek treatment, whereas the physician makes decisions determining the amount of expenditures. In contrast, the Tweedie model uses a single set of covariates to explain the total cost of claims and thus does not differentiate between the two components. However, it is a more parsimonious formulation which simplifies the process of variable selection.

4.3.2.1 Frequency

Applying the two-part model requires that we consider various techniques for modeling the frequency and severity components. The frequency part uses regression models for count data. The count regression models are discussed in Boucher (2014). The simplest form of count regression assumes that the number of claims follow a Poisson distribution, that is,

$$\Pr(N_i = n_i) = \frac{\lambda_i^{n_i} e^{-\lambda_i}}{n_i!}, \quad \text{for } n_i = 0, 1, 2, \ldots \tag{4.4}$$

with $\lambda_i = \omega_i \exp(\mathbf{x}_i' \boldsymbol{\beta})$. Here, ω_i represents exposure, such as the length of time the policy is in force. Vector $\mathbf{x}_i$ is the vector of covariates for policyholder i, and $\boldsymbol{\beta}$ represents the vector of corresponding regression coefficients. It is well known that the Poisson distribution implies equi-dispersion, that is, $E[N_i] = \text{Var}[N_i] = \lambda_i$. The Poisson regression model can be viewed as a generalized linear model. It is straightforward to show that the Poisson distribution belongs to the exponential family and that the preceding model employs the canonical log-link function for the mean.

The phenomenon of overdispersion (variance of claim count being greater than the expected value) is often associated with insurance claims count, which makes the Poisson model unsuitable in a cross-sectional context. Negative binomial regression is another popular choice for modeling count data and offers the advantage of capturing overdispersion, compared with the Poisson model. Different formulations of the negative binomial distribution are available for modeling count data. We consider the following formulation that is of particular interest in the present context:

$$\Pr(N_i = n_i) = \frac{\Gamma(\eta + n_i)}{\Gamma(\eta)\Gamma(n_i + 1)} \left(\frac{1}{1 + \psi_i}\right)^{\eta} \left(\frac{\psi_i}{1 + \psi_i}\right)^{n_i}, \quad \text{for } n_i = 0, 1, 2, \ldots$$

$$(4.5)$$

and $\eta > 0$. The mean and variance of N_i are $\mathrm{E}(N_i) = \eta \psi_i$ and $\mathrm{Var}(N_i) = \eta \psi_i(1 + \psi_i)$, respectively. To incorporate explanatory variables, it is conventional to employ a log-link function to form a mean regression that could be specified in terms of covariates $\eta \psi_i = \exp(\mathbf{x}_i'\boldsymbol{\beta})$. Compared with the Poisson distribution, the negative binomial accommodates overdispersion via the parameter ψ. As $\psi \to 0$, overdispersion vanishes, and the negative binomial converges to the Poisson distribution. In the preceding formulation, not only is overdispersion allowed for but also the subject heterogeneity in the dispersion.

Another phenomenon occasionally encountered in claim count data is the excess of zeros. For example, this could result from the underreporting of claims that would result in compensation less than subsequent premium increase. This feature of the data is not readily captured by either the Poisson or negative binomial distributions. One solution is to use the zero-inflated count regressions. Zero-inflated models can be viewed as a mixture of two stochastic processes, one only generating zeros and the other generating nonnegative counts according to a standard count distribution. The probability that an individual count outcome is from the zero-generating process is usually modeled by a binary regression model, for example, a logit model with a binomial distribution assumption. In this application, we consider the following formulation:

$$\Pr(N_i = n_i) = \begin{cases} \pi_i + (1 - \pi_i)f(n_{it}) & \text{if } n_i = 0 \\ (1 - \pi_i)f(n_i) & \text{if } n_i > 0 \end{cases} \qquad (4.6)$$

In this model, π_i represents the probability that the observation n_i is from the zero-only process, and $f(n_i)$ represents a standard count regression. In particular, we consider a zero-inflated Poisson model (ZIP) with $f(n_i)$, following (4.4), and a zero-inflated negative binomial model (ZINB) with $f(n_i)$, following (4.5). The probability π_i is determined by a logistic regression of the form

$$\log\left(\frac{\pi_i}{1 - \pi_i}\right) = \mathbf{z}_i'\boldsymbol{\gamma}$$

where $\mathbf{z}_i$ is a set of covariates that could be different from the standard count data model and $\boldsymbol{\gamma}$ is the corresponding vector of regression coefficients.

In the data analysis, we study the total number of claims per policy year for the policyholder. Table 4.6 displays the estimates of alternative count regression models. Both rating group and territory group are important predictors of claim count. A comparison of the Poisson and negative binomial models provides evidence of overdispersion associated with the claim counts. In the zero-inflated models, the rating factors have little statistical significance in the zero model. Not surprisingly, the AIC and BIC statistics, penalizing the complexity of the model, support the more parsimonious negative binomial regression.

4.3.2.2 Severity

The severity part concerns the modeling of the size of each claim, conditioned on the occurrence of at least one claim. In this section of univariate analysis, our variable of interest is the sum of liability and PIP claim cost. It is well known that claim size distributions often exhibit skewness and long tails, indicating that large claims are more likely to occur than implied by the normal distribution. To accommodate long tails, we employ three heavy-tailed regression techniques discussed in Shi (2014). The first is the lognormal model. One can view lognormal regression as a transformation method, in which one employs the logarithm of claim amount as the outcome variable of a standard ordinary least squares (OLS) linear model (see Rosenberg and Guszcza, 2014). The second is a GLM. Recall that in the exponential family, the gamma distribution and inverse Gaussian distribution have the potential to capture moderate and heavy tails, respectively. We demonstrate this with a gamma regression model. The log-link function instead of the canonical inverse link function is used so that the regression coefficients are interpretable and comparable to those of other models. The third is a parametric regression based on distributions that do not happen to fall within the exponential family. Refer to Klugman et al. (2012) for heavy-tailed distributions commonly used in actuarial science. As a demonstration, we consider the generalized gamma distribution, whose density is given by

$$f(y_i) = \frac{\lambda^\lambda}{y\Gamma(\lambda)\sigma} \exp\left(\text{sign}(\kappa)u_i\sqrt{\lambda} - \lambda\exp(\kappa u_i)\right) \qquad (4.7)$$

with $\lambda = |\kappa|^{-2}$, $\sigma = \omega\sqrt{(\lambda)}$, and $u_i = (\ln y - \eta_i)/\omega$. Furthermore, the explanatory variables are included through $\eta_i = \mathbf{x}_i'\boldsymbol{\beta}$.

Results of the three long-tail regression models are exhibited in Table 4.7. We observe that the explanatory variables significantly determine not only the frequency but also the severity. Although the two-part framework has the flexibility of allowing for different sets of covariates for the two modeling components, variable selection is out of the scope of this study due to the small number of predictors available. Both

Table 4.6. *Estimation of Univariate Frequency Models*

Parameter	Poisson Estimate	Poisson StdErr	NegBin Estimate	NegBin StdErr	ZIP Estimate	ZIP StdErr	ZINB Estimate	ZINB StdErr
intercept	−2.561	0.050	−2.559	0.051	−1.501	0.192	−2.185	0.865
rating group = 1	0.039	0.043	0.039	0.044	−0.303	0.155	−0.133	0.678
rating group = 2	0.189	0.127	0.186	0.130	−0.389	0.434	−0.025	0.835
rating group = 3	0.794	0.064	0.793	0.067	0.274	0.226	0.551	0.873
rating group = 4	0.551	0.068	0.550	0.070	0.026	0.224	0.398	0.683
territory group = 1	−0.865	0.052	−0.866	0.053	−1.225	0.195	−1.068	0.121
territory group = 2	−0.646	0.048	−0.647	0.050	−0.995	0.177	−0.867	0.128
territory group = 3	−0.702	0.058	−0.703	0.060	−0.599	0.249	−0.777	0.111
territory group = 4	−0.516	0.046	−0.517	0.048	−0.487	0.182	−0.655	0.091
territory group = 5	−0.283	0.045	−0.283	0.046	−0.409	0.200	−0.451	0.112
ln η			−0.032	0.131			−0.248	0.628
zero model								
intercept					0.706	0.337	−0.104	1.709
rating group = 1					−0.661	0.272	−1.507	0.818
rating group = 2					−1.314	1.383	−2.916	3.411
rating group = 3					−1.118	0.539	−5.079	5.649
rating group = 4					−1.121	0.539	−1.260	1.388
territory group = 1					−0.874	0.542	−2.577	11.455
territory group = 2					−0.836	0.476	−3.894	52.505
territory group = 3					0.193	0.443	−0.509	0.965
territory group = 4					0.056	0.340	−1.145	2.264
territory group = 5					−0.264	0.411	−1.583	4.123
loglik	−19,195		−19,148		−19,145		−19,139	
AIC	38,410		38,317		38,329		38,320	
BIC	38,505		38,422		38,519		38,520	

Table 4.7. *Estimation of Univariate Severity Models*

Parameter	LN		Gamma		GG	
	Estimate	StdErr	Estimate	StdErr	Estimate	StdErr
intercept	7.045	0.087	8.179	0.066	7.601	0.079
rating group = 1	0.104	0.073	0.235	0.056	0.207	0.064
rating group = 2	0.242	0.218	0.382	0.167	0.306	0.190
rating group = 3	0.198	0.110	0.257	0.084	0.259	0.096
rating group = 4	0.009	0.117	0.284	0.089	0.208	0.102
territory group = 1	−0.060	0.090	−0.376	0.068	−0.245	0.079
territory group = 2	−0.017	0.084	−0.223	0.064	−0.166	0.073
territory group = 3	0.074	0.100	−0.168	0.077	−0.115	0.088
territory group = 4	0.015	0.080	−0.175	0.061	−0.119	0.070
territory group = 5	0.079	0.077	−0.117	0.059	−0.053	0.067
scale	0.543	0.010			1.504	0.017
shape			0.579	0.010	0.653	0.028
loglik	−43,815		−43,749		−43,505	
AIC	87,651		87,519		87,033	
BIC	87,722		87,590		87,111	

the gamma and generalized gamma regressions use the log-link function for the mean. Thus the regression coefficients of the two models are comparable and consistent. In contrast, the lognormal regression model involves transforming the observed outcome variable rather than employing a link function. Nevertheless, the regression parameter estimates can be interpreted as proportional changes to the outcome variable resulting from unit change to the various explanatory variables.

4.4 Multivariate Ratemaking Frameworks

This section illustrates ratemaking using a multivariate modeling framework. Motivated by the observation that insurance policies often provide multiple types of coverage with different features, we separate insurance claims by type rather than aggregating them at the policy level. Thus the outcome of interest is not a single variable but rather a vector of variables, each associated with one type of coverage. We use "multivariate" to refer to the class of models that treat a vector of outcome variables simultaneously. Here we discuss two advanced statistical modeling frameworks: first, a multivariate version of the frequency-severity model; and second, a multilevel insurance claims models.[2]

---

[2] We note that the Tweedie model can be extended to a multivariate context; see, for example, Shi (2016) for a recent development in the literature.

4.4.1 Multivariate Two-Part Model

In a multivariate two-part model, the outcomes of interest are vectors of both frequency and severity variables. In the present example, the auto insurance policy provides two types of coverage, third party liability and PIP. To formulate the multivariate model, we use $\mathbf{Y_i} = (Y_{i1}, Y_{i2})'$ to denote the vector of total cost of claims by type for the ith policyholder. Note that both elements Y_{i1} and Y_{i2} are semicontinuous. We jointly model Y_{i1} and Y_{i2}, and we show that under certain assumptions, a similar decoupling result as with the univariate two-part model can be derived in the multivariate context as well. That is, the model could be decomposed into a frequency component and a severity component.

Specifically, consider four scenarios, (1) $\{Y_{i1} = 0, Y_{i2} = 0\}$, (2) $\{Y_{i1} > 0, Y_{i2} = 0\}$, (3) $\{Y_{i1} = 0, Y_{i2} > 0\}$, (4) $\{Y_{i1} > 0, Y_{i2} > 0\}$, for the joint distribution. We have

$$
g(y_{i1}, y_{i2}) = \begin{cases} \Pr(Y_{i1} = 0, Y_{i2} = 0) & \text{if } y_{i1} = 0, y_{i2} = 0 \\ \Pr(Y_{i1} > 0, Y_{i2} = 0) \times f_1(y_{i1}|y_{i1} > 0, y_{i2} = 0) & \text{if } y_{i1} > 0, y_{i2} = 0 \\ \Pr(Y_{i1} = 0, Y_{i2} > 0) \times f_2(y_{i2}|y_{i1} = 0, y_{i2} > 0) & \text{if } y_{i1} = 0, y_{i2} > 0 \\ \Pr(Y_{i1} > 0, Y_{i2} > 0) \times f(y_{i1}, y_{i2}|y_{i1} > 0, y_{i2} > 0) & \text{if } y_{i1} > 0, y_{i2} > 0 \end{cases}
$$

It is straightforward to show that the total log-likelihood function has the following decomposition:

$$
ll = ll_{frequency} + ll_{severity}
$$

where

$$
ll_{frequency} = \sum_{\{i:y_{i1}=0,y_{i2}=0\}} \ln \Pr(Y_{i1} = 0, Y_{i2} = 0) + \sum_{\{i:y_{i1}>0,y_{i2}=0\}} \ln \Pr(Y_{i1} > 0, Y_{i2} = 0)
$$

$$
+ \sum_{\{i:y_{i1}=0,y_{i2}>0\}} \ln \Pr(Y_{i1} = 0, Y_{i2} > 0) + \sum_{\{i:y_{i1}>0,y_{i2}>0\}} \ln \Pr(Y_{i1} > 0, Y_{i2} > 0)
$$

and

$$
ll_{severity} = \sum_{\{i:y_{i1}>0,y_{i2}=0\}} \ln f_1(y_{i1}|y_{i1} > 0, y_{i2} = 0) + \sum_{\{i:y_{i1}=0,y_{i2}>0\}} \ln f_2(y_{i2}|y_{i1} = 0, y_{i2} > 0)
$$

$$
+ \sum_{\{i:y_{i1}>0,y_{i2}>0\}} \ln f(y_{i1}, y_{i2}|y_{i1} > 0, y_{i2} > 0)
$$

Here, f_1 and f_2 denote the conditional density for the claim size of the two types, and f denotes their joint (conditional) density. To simplify the model, we further assume that $f_1(y_{i1}|y_{i1} > 0, y_{i2} = 0) = f_1(y_{i1}|y_{i1} > 0)$ and $f_2(y_{i2}|y_{i1} = 0, y_{i2} > 0) = f_2(y_{i2}|y_{i2} > 0)$; that is, given occurrence of a certain type of claim, the size of the claim does not rely on the occurrence of other types of claims. Under this assumption, the likelihood of the severity component reduces to

$$ll_{severity} = \sum_{\{i:y_{i1}>0,y_{i2}=0\}} \ln f_1(y_{i1}|y_{i1} > 0) + \sum_{\{i:y_{i1}=0,y_{i2}>0\}} \ln f_2(y_{i2}|y_{i2} > 0)$$

$$+ \sum_{\{i:y_{i1}>0,y_{i2}>0\}} \ln f(y_{i1}, y_{i2}|y_{i1} > 0, y_{i2} > 0)$$

The preceding formulation shows that the maximization of the joint likelihood is equivalent to maximizing the two components of the log-likelihood function separately. Next, we discuss various approaches to constructing the multivariate frequency and severity models. The formulation of the severity model will assume the simplified version in the following discussion.

4.4.1.1 Multivariate Frequency

In the frequency part, we must model whether the policyholder has a certain type of claim. To simplify the presentation, we define $\mathbf{R} = (R_1, R_2)'$ with $R_{ij} = I(Y_{ij} > 0)$ for $j = 1, 2$. Thus each component of outcome $\mathbf{R}$ is a binary variable with 1 indicating the presence of the corresponding type and 0 otherwise. We discuss three techniques for the joint modeling of R_{i1} and R_{i2} that are built on the marginal regression models. The first is to use the *dependence ratio*, defined as

$$\theta_{12} = \frac{\Pr(R_{i1} = 1, R_{i2} = 1)}{\Pr(R_{i1} = 1)\Pr(R_{i2} = 1)}$$

The joint distribution can then be derived in terms of the marginals and the parameter θ_{12}:

$$\begin{cases} \Pr(R_{i1} = 1, R_{i2} = 1) = \theta_{12}\Pr(R_{i1} = 1)\Pr(R_{i2} = 1) \\ \Pr(R_{i1} = 1, R_{i2} = 0) = \Pr(R_{i1} = 1) - \Pr(R_{i1} = 1, R_{i2} = 1) \\ \Pr(R_{i1} = 0, R_{i2} = 1) = \Pr(R_{i1} = 1) - \Pr(R_{i1} = 1, R_{i2} = 1) \\ \Pr(R_{i1} = 0, R_{i2} = 0) = 1 - \Pr(R_{i1} = 1) - \Pr(R_{i1} = 1) + \Pr(R_{i1} = 1, R_{i2} = 1) \end{cases}$$

The parameter θ_{12} captures the relationship between the two outcomes; $\theta_{12} > 1 \, (< 1)$ indicates a positive (negative) relationship, and $\theta_{12} = 1$ indicates independence.

The second strategy is to construct the joint distribution using the *odds ratio* between R_{i1} and R_{i2}. This is defined as

$$\theta_{12} = \frac{odds(R_{i2}|R_{i1} = 1)}{odds(R_{i2}|R_{i1} = 0)} = \frac{\Pr(R_{i1} = 1, R_{i2} = 1)\Pr(R_{i1} = 0, R_{i2} = 0)}{\Pr(R_{i1} = 1, R_{i2} = 0)\Pr(R_{i1} = 0, R_{i2} = 1)}$$

From the preceding quadratic relationship, one can also solve $\Pr(R_{i1} = 1, R_{i2} = 1)$ as a function of the marginal distributions and parameter θ_{12}. As with the dependence ratio, the independence case corresponds to an odds ratio of one. A ratio greater and less than one indicates positive and negative relationship, respectively. We refer to Frees et al. (2013) and the literature therein for the details on dependence ratio and odds ratio.

The third approach is to join marginal models through parametric copulas. Using a copula $H(; \theta_{12})$ with association parameter θ_{12}, the joint distribution of R_{i1} and R_{i2} can be represented as follows (see, e.g., Shi and Zhang, 2013):

$$\begin{cases} \Pr(R_{i1} = 1, R_{i2} = 1) = 1 - F_1(0) - F_2(0) - H(F_1(0), F_2(0); \theta_{12}) \\ \Pr(R_{i1} = 1, R_{i2} = 0) = F_2(0) - H(F_1(0), F_2(0); \theta_{12}) \\ \Pr(R_{i1} = 0, R_{i2} = 1) = F_1(0) - H(F_1(0), F_2(0); \theta_{12}) \\ \Pr(R_{i1} = 0, R_{i2} = 0) = H(F_1(0), F_2(0); \theta_{12}) \end{cases}$$

where F_1 and F_2 are the cumulative distribution functions of R_1 and R_2, respectively. It is important to stress the identifiability issue with copulas on discrete data. Sklar's theorem guarantees that there exists a copula for **R**. However, the copula is unique only on the set $Range(F_1) \times Range(F_2)$. This unidentifiability issue does not invalidate construction of discrete distributions using copulas. Conversely, one wants to be cautious that some properties of copula models do not carry over from continuous to discrete case (see Genest and Nešlehová, 2007, for detailed discussion).

In each of the preceding three models, the marginal of R_{ij} could be modeled with usual binary regression models, be they logit or probit. Here we consider the logit formulation $\text{logit}(\pi_{ij}) = \mathbf{x}'_{ij}\boldsymbol{\beta}_j$ for $j = 1, 2$, where $\pi_{ij} = \Pr(R_{ij} = 1)$. Note that different sets of covariates and corresponding regression coefficients are permitted in the marginal models for the two types of claims.

Table 4.8 summarizes the model fit for the bivariate binary regressions using the dependence ratio, the odds ratio, as well as the Frank copula. It is not surprising to see the similarity among the estimates for the marginal models because all three approaches separate the marginal and joint distributions. The dependence ratio and odds ratio are greater than 1, and the association parameter in the Frank copula is greater than zero, indicating that the occurrence of the two types of claims are positively related. As a robustness check, we also perform a likelihood ratio test between each of the three models and the independence case. The large χ^2 statistics reported at the bottom of the table confirm the statistical significance of the positive association.

All three methods discussed previously aimed to construct the joint distribution of binary variables R_1 and R_2. It is worth mentioning that an alternative is to use multinomial regression to examine the possible combinations of the two outcomes. Specifically, there are four possibilities in our data, (0,0), (1,0), (0,1), and (1,1). The dependent variable in the multinomial regression model will be a categorical variable with these four levels. Though not explored here, the same idea is applied to the

Table 4.8. *Estimation of Multivariate Frequency Models*

Parameter	Dependence Ratio		Odds Ratio		Frank Copula	
	Estimate	StdErr	Estimate	StdErr	Estimate	StdErr
Third party liability						
intercept	−2.723	0.055	−2.684	0.055	−2.688	0.025
rating group = 1	−0.008	0.046	−0.003	0.046	−0.006	0.095
rating group = 2	0.210	0.137	0.202	0.137	0.206	0.094
rating group = 3	0.680	0.068	0.795	0.072	0.781	0.022
rating group = 4	0.415	0.075	0.471	0.077	0.455	0.019
territory group = 1	−0.739	0.057	−0.795	0.058	−0.788	0.023
territory group = 2	−0.502	0.054	−0.565	0.054	−0.555	0.043
territory group = 3	−0.585	0.064	−0.643	0.065	−0.635	0.054
territory group = 4	−0.397	0.052	−0.458	0.053	−0.448	0.037
territory group = 5	−0.184	0.050	−0.231	0.051	−0.226	0.038
PIP						
intercept	−4.354	0.133	−4.334	0.133	−4.336	0.026
rating group = 1	0.356	0.124	0.363	0.124	0.362	0.099
rating group = 2	0.223	0.373	0.217	0.372	0.224	0.598
rating group = 3	0.872	0.179	0.968	0.180	0.961	0.137
rating group = 4	1.039	0.170	1.094	0.170	1.083	0.130
territory group = 1	−1.466	0.137	−1.502	0.137	−1.498	0.124
territory group = 2	−1.182	0.123	−1.224	0.123	−1.218	0.118
territory group = 3	−1.298	0.156	−1.336	0.156	−1.331	0.144
territory group = 4	−0.874	0.110	−0.915	0.110	−0.909	0.110
territory group = 5	−0.650	0.105	−0.679	0.105	−0.677	0.080
dependence	6.893	0.309	13.847	1.094	10.182	1.084
loglik	−20,699		−20,669		−20,677	
Chi-square	799		859		843	
AIC	41,440		41,380		41,396	
BIC	41,639		41,580		41,596	

claim type component in the hierarchical model of Section 4.4.2. The model can be estimated using standard packages and results are readily interpretable.

4.4.1.2 Multivariate Severity

In the multivariate severity part, we jointly model the amount of different types of claims using copula regression models. Specifically, the (conditional) joint distribution $f(y_{i1}, y_{i2}|y_{i1} > 0, y_{i2} > 0)$ can be represented via the density function $h(.; \theta_{12})$ of a parametric copula:

$$f(y_{i1}, y_{i2}|y_{i1} > 0, y_{i2} > 0) = h(F_1(y_{i1}|y_{i1} > 0), F_2(y_{i2}|y_{i2} > 0); \theta_{12}) \prod_{j=1}^{2} f_j(y_{ij}|y_{ij} > 0)$$

Using preceding relation, the likelihood function of the severity part becomes

$$ll_{severity} = \sum_{\{i:y_{i1}>0\}} \ln f_1(y_{i1}|y_{i1} > 0) + \sum_{\{i:y_{i2}>0\}} \ln f_2(y_{i2}|y_{i2} > 0)$$

$$+ \sum_{\{i:y_{i1}>0, y_{i2}>0\}} \ln h(F_1(y_{i1}|y_{i1} > 0), F_2(y_{i2}|y_{i2} > 0); \theta_{12})$$

In the preceding copula model, both conditional marginals are specified using the generalized gamma regression given by equation (4.7). Note that in the multivariate two-part model, the frequency part models the probability of at least one claim. Thus the severity part models the aggregate cost of all claims of a given type over the exposure period.

We fit the multivariate severity model with various forms of copulas. Specifically, we consider the Gaussian and t copulas from the elliptical family and the Gumbel, Clayton, and Frank copulas from the Archimedean family. Because the copula preserves the marginals, the difference among estimates for the marginal models are insubstantial. As expected, one observes the different effects of covariates on the two types of claims. The association parameters in all five copulas indicate positive relationships among the claim amounts of two types, with statistical significance supported by both t and χ^2 statistics. The poor goodness-of-fit of the Clayton copula (the relative low likelihood) could be explained by its focus on the dependency in lower tails.

4.4.2 Hierarchical Insurance Claims Model

As an alternative multivariate modeling framework, this section specifies a hierarchical insurance claims model with three components.[3] The statistical model and data analysis are based on Frees and Valdez (2008) and Frees et al. (2009). To make the presentation self-contained, we briefly describe the idea of this multilevel model. The entire claim process is decomposed into three parts. The first part concerns the frequency of accidents. Conditional on an occurrence, the second part models the type of the claim. For a given claim type, the third part models the multivariate claim amount. Let N denote the number of claims, T denote the type given occurrence, and Y denote the claim amount given occurrence and type. The three-part model can be expressed as

$$f(N, T, Y) = f(N) \times f(T|N) \times f(Y|N, T)$$

---

[3] We use the word *hierarchical* in the sense of decomposing a process into parts, not in the sense of mixed effects models. See, for example, Gelman and Hill (2006).

Table 4.9. *Estimation of Multivariate Severity Models*

Parameter	Gaussian Copula Estimate	StdErr	t copula Estimate	StdErr	Gumbel Copula Estimate	StdErr	Clayton Copula Estimate	StdErr	Frank Copula Estimate	StdErr
Third party liability										
intercept	7.439	0.081	7.437	0.081	7.438	0.082	7.444	0.081	7.435	0.082
rating group = 1	0.268	0.065	0.269	0.065	0.269	0.065	0.267	0.065	0.261	0.065
rating group = 2	0.280	0.190	0.272	0.190	0.254	0.190	0.290	0.190	0.282	0.189
rating group = 3	0.420	0.098	0.417	0.098	0.416	0.098	0.418	0.099	0.410	0.098
rating group = 4	0.434	0.106	0.428	0.106	0.425	0.106	0.437	0.107	0.423	0.106
territory group = 1	−0.236	0.081	−0.233	0.081	−0.235	0.081	−0.243	0.081	−0.232	0.081
territory group = 2	−0.196	0.075	−0.196	0.075	−0.197	0.075	−0.202	0.075	−0.192	0.076
territory group = 3	−0.087	0.090	−0.090	0.090	−0.095	0.090	−0.093	0.090	−0.082	0.091
territory group = 4	−0.106	0.073	−0.105	0.073	−0.105	0.073	−0.110	0.073	−0.103	0.073
territory group = 5	−0.073	0.070	−0.073	0.070	−0.075	0.070	−0.074	0.070	−0.067	0.071
σ	1.426	0.016	1.428	0.016	1.429	0.016	1.428	0.016	1.427	0.016
κ	0.214	0.029	0.210	0.029	0.202	0.029	0.210	0.030	0.202	0.029
PIP										
intercept	8.111	0.226	7.955	0.220	7.921	0.216	8.270	0.237	8.079	0.225
rating group = 1	0.007	0.196	0.121	0.185	0.138	0.166	−0.054	0.207	−0.024	0.193
rating group = 2	−0.205	0.565	−0.156	0.523	−0.255	0.422	−0.061	0.604	−0.146	0.528
rating group = 3	−0.133	0.286	−0.033	0.275	−0.054	0.259	−0.123	0.304	−0.130	0.279
rating group = 4	−0.596	0.273	−0.448	0.263	−0.447	0.248	−0.675	0.283	−0.601	0.271
territory group = 1	−0.068	0.227	−0.049	0.226	−0.053	0.225	−0.132	0.233	−0.081	0.231
territory group = 2	−0.497	0.194	−0.519	0.190	−0.524	0.185	−0.475	0.203	−0.484	0.194
territory group = 3	−0.448	0.256	−0.427	0.249	−0.434	0.234	−0.521	0.261	−0.428	0.255
territory group = 4	−0.167	0.174	−0.178	0.171	−0.167	0.173	−0.143	0.182	−0.139	0.174
territory group = 5	−0.048	0.169	−0.100	0.164	−0.094	0.160	−0.081	0.176	−0.029	0.170
σ	1.670	0.064	1.673	0.062	1.673	0.060	1.655	0.067	1.711	0.067
κ	1.661	0.108	1.655	0.105	1.633	0.100	1.648	0.109	1.622	0.109
dependence	0.287	0.041	0.326	0.047	1.204	0.041	0.135	0.072	2.346	0.343
df			11.258	4.633						
loglik	−44,046		−44,042		−44,039		−44,064		−44,042	
Chi-square	41		48		54		4		48	
AIC	88,141		88,134		88,128		88,178		88,134	
BIC	88,302		88,295		88,289		88,338		88,295	

The conditional probability relationship implies that the joint distribution of three components can be decomposed into three independent segments. The first, $f(N)$, models the probability of having N claims. One could employ the count regression models discussion from the univariate modeling framework, such as Poisson or negative binomial models. The second, $f(T|N)$, denotes the probability of claim type T for a given accident. Because an insurance policy has two types of coverage, there are three possible claim types for a given claim. They are third party liability only, PIP only, and both liability and PIP together. These are denoted by $T = (Y_1), (Y_2), (Y_1, Y_2)$, respectively. A multinomial logit model is used to incorporate covaraites in the regression analysis. Specifically, the conditional distribution of T is

$$\Pr(T = (Y_1)) = \frac{\exp(\mathbf{x}'_{i1}\boldsymbol{\beta}_1)}{1 + \exp(\mathbf{x}'_{i1}\boldsymbol{\beta}_1) + \exp(\mathbf{x}'_{i2}\boldsymbol{\beta}_2)}$$

$$\Pr(T = (Y_2)) = \frac{\exp(\mathbf{x}'_{i2}\boldsymbol{\beta}_2)}{1 + \exp(\mathbf{x}'_{i1}\boldsymbol{\beta}_1) + \exp(\mathbf{x}'_{i2}\boldsymbol{\beta}_2)}$$

Here $\mathbf{x}_{ij}$ denotes the set of covariates for the jth ($j = 1, 2$) claim type and $\boldsymbol{\beta}_j$ denotes the corresponding regression coefficients. The final segment $f(Y|N, T)$ denotes the conditional density of the claim vector given the type. Here we assume that both Y_1 and Y_2 follow the generalized gamma distribution and their joint density is constructed using a parametric copula. It is worth mentioning the subtle difference between this step and the multivariate severity model in the two-part model, though they appear similar. The former models the amount of a single claim while the latter models the total cost of claims by coverage type per exposure period.

The estimation of the first component is the same as the univariate frequency model reported in Table 4.6. Recall that the negative binomial regression provides the most favorable results for this data. The multinomial logit model for the second component is reported in Table 4.10. The upper panel shows the estimates of regression coefficients and the lower panel shows variance analysis for the two rating factors. Overall both factors are significant determinants for the claim type. For the severity components, we use the Gumbel copula with generalized gamma marginals and we present the estimation result in Table 4.11. Comparing these with the Gumbel copula model results in Table 4.9, we find that the estimates of the two models are quite close. Recall that the difference between the two models is that the multivariate severity model looks into total cost of claims per exposure period and the hierarchical severity model examines the cost per claim. The consistent estimates is explained by the fact that only a small percentage of policyholders have multiple claims per year.

Table 4.10. *Estimation of the Multinomial Logit Model*

Parameter Estimates

Parameter	Third Party Liability		PIP	
	Estimate	StdErr	Estimate	StdErr
intercept	2.799	0.126	0.390	0.178
rating group = 1	0.091	0.135	0.403	0.188
rating group = 2	−0.225	0.381	−0.851	0.592
rating group = 3	−0.021	0.204	−0.170	0.276
rating group = 4	0.027	0.229	0.731	0.278
territory group = 1	0.429	0.200	0.287	0.232
territory group = 2	0.028	0.155	−0.210	0.191
territory group = 3	0.299	0.221	0.088	0.261
territory group = 4	−0.226	0.135	−0.254	0.166
territory group = 5	0.003	0.138	0.070	0.163

Maximum Likelihood Analysis of Variance

Source	DF	Chi-Square	p-Value
Intercept	2	766	<0.001
Rating group	8	26	0.001
Territory group	10	55	<0.001
Likelihood ratio	40	56	0.049

Table 4.11. *Estimation of Gumbel Copula*

Parameter	Liability		PIP	
	Estimate	StdErr	Estimate	StdErr
intercept	7.347	0.077	8.131	0.178
rating group = 1	0.226	0.061	0.102	0.132
rating group = 2	0.233	0.179	−0.036	0.315
rating group = 3	0.255	0.092	−0.245	0.202
rating group = 4	0.326	0.100	−0.507	0.191
territory group = 1	−0.152	0.077	0.028	0.178
territory group = 2	−0.132	0.071	−0.457	0.145
territory group = 3	−0.056	0.085	−0.368	0.189
territory group = 4	−0.088	0.068	−0.246	0.126
territory group = 5	−0.048	0.066	−0.013	0.128
σ	1.384	0.015	1.325	0.060
κ	0.242	0.029	2.198	0.141
dependence	1.207	0.042		
loglik	−45,209			

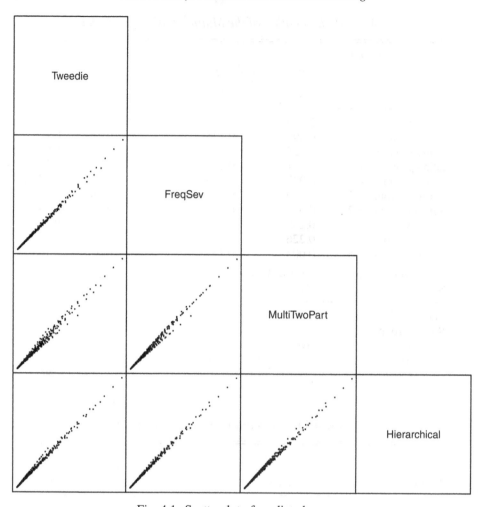

Fig. 4.1. Scatterplot of predicted scores.

4.5 Model Comparisons

This section analyzes the predictions of various models for the 50,000 policyholders in the hold-out sample. For brevity of exposition, we analyze the predictions of only four models, one from each of the four modeling frameworks. Specifically, they are the Tweedie GLM, the univariate two-part model with negative binomial frequency and generalized gamma severity, the multivariate two-part model with odds ratio frequency and the Gumbel copula severity, and the hierarchical insurance claims model.

The pairwise scatterplot of predicted scores from the four models is displayed in Figure 4.1. It appears that the predictions, at least for the expected cost of claims, are quite in line with each other, though divergence between multivariate two-part model and others are slightly higher. We also calculate the correlations among the predicted

Table 4.12. *Correlations of Predicted Scores*

		Spearman			
		Tweedie	FreqSev	MultiTwoPart	Hierarchical
	Tweedie	–	0.9970	0.9789	0.9814
Pearson	FreqSev	0.9984	–	0.9802	0.9837
	MultiTwoPart	0.9945	0.9969	–	0.9953
	Hierarchical	0.9967	0.9987	0.9981	–

scores, displayed in Table 4.12. The lower triangle reports Pearson correlation and the upper triangle reports Spearman correlation. As anticipated, both correlation measures indicate highly correlated predictions.

This analysis shows that the various modeling approaches yield highly consistent indications for pure premium determination. For model selection purposes, one could further calculate various measures of model segmentation power, such as gain charts or lift curves. However, the preceding correlation analysis implies that we would not expect material differences in model segmentation power. We should emphasize that the purpose of this modeling exercise has not been to identify the "best" model of this particular data in terms of goodness-of-fit and predictive performance. Rather, the goal has been to introduce practicing actuaries to various statistical modeling techniques that could be useful in pure premium determination.

4.6 Conclusion

This chapter has focused on the statistical problem of pure premium ratemaking. While pure premium is an important input into a process of pricing insurance contracts, it is not the sole input. Such market-based pricing considerations as competitor rates, consumer behavior, price elasticity, and customer lifetime value (CLV) are also important to insurance pricing but fall beyond the scope of this chapter.

Our discussion has been limited to the statistical realm, with the goal of providing the practitioner a broader framework for constructing pure premium models than is often discussed in the GLM-based ratemaking literature. While the GLM approach has been a significant improvement over pretheoretical ratemaking approaches, there is in principal no reason to restrict one's modeling activities to the GLM framework. The use of nonexponential family distributional forms and copula regression, illustrated here, exemplifies the possibilities.

A practical consideration is that certain probability functional forms are easier to work with than others. For example, when confronted with a large dataset containing many candidate predictive variables, a practitioner might well wish to start with gamma regression (which is supported by convenient statistical packages) rather than generalized gamma regression (which requires likelihood functions to be coded and maximized). Similarly, a practitioner might judge that the limited time available for model building is better spent identifying the appropriate predictive variables, interactions, and variable transformations than considering alternate distributional forms for the dependent variable.

We are sympathetic with such judgments, and the purpose of this chapter is not to argue against them. A useful bit of methodological advice is to start with simple, familiar models and gradually add complexity as the situation demands. The econometrician Arnold Zellner called this methodological precept "sophisticated simplicity" and recommended that "an initial, sophisticatedly simple model be formulated and tested in terms of explaining past data and in forecasting or predicting new data. If the model is successful in meeting these tests, it can be put into use. If not, usually the initial model can be modified or elaborated to improve performance" (see Zellner, 2002). The various modeling options illustrated in this chapter, it is hoped, will enhance the practitioner's ability to approach the ratemaking problem from the perspective of sophisticated simplicity.

Finally, we note that the alternatives discussed here by no means exhaust the methods available to augment the standard GLM-based ratemaking approach. Tree-structured statistical learning methods, "regularized" regression methods such as ridge and lasso, generalized additive models, multilevel/hierarchical modeling, and Bayesian data analysis can also be explored to improve various aspects of ratemaking.

References

Boucher, J.-P. Regression with count-dependent variables. In E. W. Frees, G. Meyers, and R. A. Derrig (eds.), *Predictive Modeling Applications in Actuarial Science: Volume 1, Predictive Modeling Techniques*, pp. 87–106. Cambridge University Press, Cambridge, 2014.

Dean, C. G. Generalized linear models. In E. W. Frees, G. Meyers, and R. A. Derrig (eds.), *Predictive Modeling Applications in Actuarial Science: Volume 1, Predictive Modeling Techniques*, pp. 107–137. Cambridge University Press, Cambridge, 2014.

Frees, E. W. Frequency and severity models. In E. W. Frees, G. Meyers, and R. A. Derrig (eds.), *Predictive Modeling Applications in Actuarial Science: Volume 1, Predictive Modeling Techniques*, pp. 138–164. Cambridge University Press, Cambridge, 2014.

Frees, E., X. Jin, and X. Lin. Actuarial applications of multivariate two-part regression models. *Annals of Actuarial Science*, 7(2): 71–30, 2013.

Frees, E., P. Shi, and E. Valdez. Actuarial applications of a hierarchical claims model. *ASTIN Bulletin*, 39(1): 165–197, 2009.

Frees, E., and E. Valdez. Hierarchical insurance claims modeling. *Journal of the American Statistical Association*, 103(484): 1457–1469, 2008.

Gelman, A., and J. Hill. *Data Analysis Using Regression and Multilevel/Hierarchical Models*. Cambridge University Press, Cambridge, 2006.

Genest, C., and J. Nešlehová. A primer on copulas for count data. *Astin Bulletin*, *37*(2): 475, 2007.

Jørgensen, B., and M. de Souza. Fitting Tweedies compound Poisson model to insurance claims data. *Scandinavian Actuarial Journal*, *1*(1): 69–93, 1994.

Klugman, S. A., H. H. Panjer, and G. E. Willmot. Loss models: From data to decisions, 2012.

Mildenhall, S. J. A systematic relationship between minimum bias and generalized linear models. *Proceedings of the Casualty Actuarial Society*, *LXXXVI*(164): 393–487, 1999.

Rosenberg, M., and J. Guszcza. Overview of linear models. In E. W. Frees, G. Meyers, and R. A. Derrig (eds.), *Predictive Modeling Applications in Actuarial Science: Volume 1, Predictive Modeling Techniques*, pp. 13–64. Cambridge University Press, Cambridge, 2014.

Shi, P. Fat-tailed regression models. In E. W. Frees, G. Meyers, and R. A. Derrig (eds.), *Predictive Modeling Applications in Actuarial Science: Volume 1, Predictive Modeling Techniques*, pp. 236–259. Cambridge University Press, Cambridge, 2014.

Shi, P. Insurance ratemaking using a copula-based multivariate Tweedie model. *Scandinavian Actuarial Journal*, *2016*(3): 198–215, 2016.

Shi, P., and W. Zhang. Managed care and health care utilization: Specification of bivariate models using copulas. *North American Actuarial Journal*, *17*(4): 306–324, 2013.

Smyth, G., and B. Jørgensen. Fitting Tweedie's compound Poisson model to insurance claims data: dispersion modelling. *ASTIN Bulletin*, *32*(1): 143–157, 2002.

Tweedie, M. An index which distinguishes between some important exponential families. In J. Ghosh and J. Roy (eds.), *Statistics: Applications and New Directions. Proceedings of the Indian Statistical Institute Golden Jubilee International Conference*, pp. 579–604. Indian Statistical Institute, Calcutta, 1984.

Werner, G., and S. Guven. GLM basic modeling: Avoiding common pitfalls. *CAS Forum*, Winter 2007.

Zellner, A. My experiences with nonlinear dynamic models in economics. *Studies in Nonlinear Dynamics and Econometrics*, *6*(2): 1–18, 2002.

5

Using Multilevel Modeling for Group Health Insurance Ratemaking

A Case Study from the Egyptian Market

Mona S. A. Hammad and Galal A. H. Harby

Chapter Preview. As explained in more detail in Volume I of this book, multi-level modeling represents a powerful tool that recently gained popularity in actuarial research. It builds on recent findings linking credibility theory in actuarial science to the linear mixed model in statistics. In this chapter, we present a practical application of multilevel modeling in dealing with the complex nature of group health insurance policies within a ratemaking context. In particular, using a real dataset from one of the major insurance companies in Egypt, we illustrate how the pure premiums for these policies can be estimated using both these advanced models and traditional (single-level) general linear models. The results are compared using both in-sample goodness of fit tests and out-of-sample validation.

The overall aim is to illustrate the additional advantages gained by using these advanced types of models, more specifically, its ability to allow for the complex data structures underlying group health insurance policies. These include, for example, multidimensional benefit packages and panel/longitudinal aspects, which are often necessary for experience rating purposes.

Interested readers may refer to Chapters 2, 7, 8, and 9 in Volume I of this book for more detail regarding the models used in this chapter.

5.1 Motivation and Background

Motivation behind this research can be attributed to four main factors: (1) the difficulties associated with insurance ratemaking in general; (2) the complex nature of group health insurance policies in particular; (3) the high potential for multilevel modeling to handle this complexity; and (4) the importance of this application for the Egyptian market context. Each of these factors is considered in more detail in the following subsections.

5.1.1 Insurance Ratemaking

Adequate ratemaking represents a continuous concern for most actuaries worldwide. This is due to its significant impact on the profitability and sustainability of insurance business. It also reflects the distinctive nature of this business as opposed to other types of business. For example, in general the true cost of issuing a particular insurance policy is usually not known with certainty at time of sale, as it depends on future uncertain claims. This is different from most other types of products, where all production costs are usually known prior to sale (Werner and Modlin, 2010). Accordingly, calculating suitable rates for insurance products is usually not an easy process. In fact, it is often described as combining art with science (see, e.g., McClenahan, 2001).

5.1.2 Group Health Insurance Policies

In this chapter, we address ratemaking for one of the most complex yet very important insurance products. That is group health insurance policies. We use this term to refer to indemnity-type group health insurance policies sold by insurance companies, which aim to reimburse health care costs. This product is known in different markets (and accordingly literature) by different alternative names. For instance, in the United Kingdom this is usually known as *private medical insurance* or more simply *PMI* (see, e.g., Alexander et al., 2001; Foubister et al., 2006). In North America, the term *medical expense insurance* is more often used (see, e.g., O'Grady, 1988; Orros and Webber, 1988). The simpler term *group health insurance* is also frequently used to refer to these types of policies, especially when there is no risk of confusion with another product type (see, e.g., Beam, 1997). This will be the term used here.

Due to the indemnity nature of this product, it is usually classified as a non-life insurance product (see, e.g., Foubister et al., 2006; Orros and Webber, 1988; Skipper, 2001).[1] It is also worth noting that in general this product can be also offered on an individual basis. However, the group version tends to be more common. Therefore, it is the focus of this research.

Group health insurance policies are usually characterized by certain special features that further complicate the ratemaking modeling process. These include the following.

5.1.2.1 Multilevel Data

Datasets for group health insurance policies are usually multilevel in nature. In other words, the variables contained in these datasets are usually defined at different levels. For example, as shown later, some of the variables may be defined at the policy level

---

[1] This is also consistent with insurance regulations in Egypt for short-term policies (less than one year). However, some authors also consider health insurance as a separate category of its own that is, neither life insurance nor non-life insurance (see, e.g., Taylor, 2004).

such as the industrial classification of the policyholder and the total number of insureds under the policy; while others can be defined at the coverage level (e.g., cost-sharing details), or even the insured level (e.g., gender and age[2]).

5.1.2.2 *Multidimensional Nonstandardized Benefit Packages*

A typical coverage under this product usually includes multiple categories of health care services depending on the requirements of the policyholder (often an employer). Therefore, these policies are characterized by nonstandardized benefit packages that tend to be tailored to meet policyholders' needs. In fact, even within the same policy, benefits can differ between classes of insureds (often employees working for this employer).

These differences are also usually multidimensional in nature. For example, as explained in more detail later (Section 5.2.3.1), the dataset used in this research contained in total five dimensions to define the benefit package. These related to type and quality of health service covered, in addition to cost-sharing arrangements.

5.1.2.3 *Panel/Longitudinal Aspects and Experience Rating*

As we are dealing with group policies, experience rating is often important both from a technical and marketing perspectives. Therefore, it is usually useful to build the models to benefit from the information contained in the correlations among related observations. In particular, records related to the same subject (e.g., policyholder, or even insured) over the years of available data. This is referred to as panel or longitudinal aspects of the dataset, which were considered in more detail in Chapter 7 of Volume I.

5.1.2.4 *Large Volume of Unbalanced Records*

Datasets for group health insurance policies are typically very large, especially if records are considered at the insured level. They are also usually *unbalanced*. In other words, the number of observations differs from one policy to another, as not all policies will be in force for the full observation period. Therefore, the selected modeling approach should allow for this aspect.

5.1.3 *Multilevel Modeling*

To address the special nature of group insurance policies, as described before, we focus in this research on multilevel modeling. This is a powerful statistical

---

[2] Unfortunately, no information related to age was supplied by the insurance company for this research. However, this is an important rating factor that should be considered in future similar research.

modeling approach, which recently found its way to actuarial literature. As explained in more details in Chapters 8 and 9 in Volume I, it builds on the linear mixed model theory. Recent researches showed links between this advanced theory in statistics and credibility theory in actuarial science. In fact, as illustrated by such research, most credibility models can be considered a special case of these more general models. Therefore, it is often more beneficial to use these models.

In particular, as argued by Frees et al. (1999) and Frees (2004a, 2010), this helps to overcome some of the common challenges associated with the selection of credibility models by providing a more general and flexible statistical modeling framework. It also provides some additional advantages such as (1) offering a much wider range of models to choose from; (2) the possibility of using standard software for statistical modeling to analyze data; (3) the possibility of using of standard diagnostic & graphical tools for statistical modeling to assess the results; and (4) offering actuaries a new way to explain the ratemaking process. Multilevel modeling is also better equipped to handle complex data structures as opposed to single-level models, as illustrated in the empirical work in this research.

5.1.4 The Egyptian Market Context

Group health insurance policies (and private health insurance in general) represent an important line of business for the Egyptian insurance market, which has not reached its full potential yet. In particular, the Egyptian population suffers from a high percentage of out-of-pocket spending on health. Based on most recent available statistics from World Health Organization (WHO) website, out-of-pocket expenditure on health as a percentage of total expenditure on health is estimated to be about 60% on 2012. This can be attributed to the inability of the social health scheme to date to adequately meet the needs of its clients. Based on most recent official statistics available on the Health Insurance Organization (HIO) website,[3] the scheme currently covers about 58% of the population. It owns its own hospital and clinics. Therefore, it is responsible not only for the finances, but also the provision of most health care services. Many studies and surveys show that most Egyptians perceive these services to be of poor quality and prefer to seek treatment from private health care providers, whenever they can afford it. This is particularly true for outpatient services.

There have been continuous plans to expand the coverage of the social health insurance scheme to cover 100% of the population and to improve the quality of its services

---

[3] HIO is the organization responsible for the social health insurance scheme in Egypt. Its website is http://www.hio.gov.eg.

by separating financing from service provision and contracting with private health care providers. However, these plans failed to date due to various reasons including: (1) frequent changes in government (especially over the last few years), which interrupts ongoing efforts; (2) lack of sufficient financial resources and the political sensitivity of attempting to raise more contributions, as it will be perceived by an average citizen as additional taxes; and (3) the difficulty of targeting the remaining members of population, as they fall mainly in the informal sector.

All these issues increase the potential for private health insurance, especially with the increasing number of private and multinational employers who seek good coverage for their employees. However, one of the key factors that has been hindering the adequate growth of this market is difficulty of pricing these policies, especially in light of lack of specialized local health actuaries. The deficiency of current regulations also encouraged some noninsurance firms to enter into this market without having to comply with the legal requirements for insurance companies. This in turn led to unhealthy competitions on prices. However, there are currently important efforts within the Egyptian Financial Supervisory Authority (EFSA) to amend current laws to solve this problem. Thus, the market is expected to prosper more over the coming years. Accordingly, this research can be of useful practical application to insurers operating (or planning to operate) in this field.

The remainder of this chapter is organized as follows: Section 5.2 describes the nature of the real dataset used in this research and key variables. Section 5.3 summarizes the model development process, including the model building strategy used. This is then followed by the key results for both the in-sample fitting stage, and out-of-sample validation in Section 5.4. Finally, Section 5.5 summarizes concluding remarks.

5.2 Data

5.2.1 Nature of Data and Source

The data used in this research have been provided by one of the major insurance companies operating in the Egyptian market. The company was selected based on its large market share in group health insurance during the period of the study. The original dataset supplied consisted of two separate files: the first one contained a table for the details related to the policies (e.g., variables related to policyholders and insureds, including coverage), and the second one contained a table of information related to paid claims.

The supplied data were very raw in nature. Therefore, considerable amounts of time and effort had to be spent in cleaning and preparing these data for the analysis. This included for example (among many other things) aligning discrepancies and inconsistencies between the two files in order to be able to link them together, cleaning odd values, cleaning duplicate records, and completing missing information. Finally, the data had to be reorganized in a suitable format for the analysis with statistical software. Overall, data preparation can be described as one of the most challenging tasks in the empirical work done in this research and indeed the most time consuming.

The original files were provided at very detailed level, that is, individual claims records for each insured within the group policies. However, as explained in more detail later (Section 5.2.3.1), during the modeling process, these data were aggregated to the level of *coverage per policy*. Accordingly, the dataset provided with this chapter represents the final dataset after aggregation and few other adjustments to protect the identity of the insurance company and policyholders. This dataset is sufficient to reproduce all the results for the models. However, some of the overall summary statistics and other figures and tables used later in the discussion of the variables may not be directly available from this dataset, as they require a more detailed level of data not supplied here for confidentiality. Yet, these figures and tables were kept here to help the readers to get an overall feeling of the original data and how it was adjusted to produce the supplied dataset. This is expected to be particularly beneficial to practitioners, as it can help them to relate the discussion to other real datasets encountered in practice.

It is also important to note that aggregation from original files was done using the *policy year* method, which is also known as the *underwriting year* method (Werner and Modlin, 2010, p. 43). As discussed in various sources (see, e.g., Anderson et al., 2007; Brown and Gottlieb, 2001; McClenahan, 2004; Werner and Modlin, 2010), this means that policy year X accounts for all transactions (e.g., claims, exposures, premiums) related to policies in force in calendar year X, regardless of the actual date for these transactions. This in turn implies that in case of annual policies, the total claims for policy year X will not be completed until the end of calendar year $X + 1$. This is because some policies may be issued as late as December 31 X. Therefore, under this aggregation method, each policy year of data actually requires 24 months of observation. This could represent a disadvantage in practical applications, especially if the number of complete years of data available is limited. However, this aggregation method offers several other advantages that justified its selection for this research. For example, compared to other aggregation methods, this method reduces the amount of records required to aggregate the data (which was very critical given the large volume of the dataset). It also provides a perfect match between the definitions of the various variables; . . . and so on.[4]

---

[4] For more detail, regarding the advantages of the policy year method and other possible aggregation methods, interested readers may refer to the previously cited references.

Therefore, although the final dataset used in this research covered policy years 2002 to 2006, the observation period actually extended to December 31, 2007, to account for all transactions related to policy year 2006. Moreover, consistent with previous studies, the final year in the dataset (policy year 2006) was reserved for out-of-sample validation.

5.2.2 Some Overall Statistics

Table 5.1 summarizes some of the key indicators for each of the policy years included in the analysis in order to get an overall feeling of the nature of the dataset. All these numbers are based on the final dataset after cleaning and aggregation, as explained before. It is also important to note that all claims figures reported here are net of all cost-sharing arrangements, as will be described in Section 5.2.3.2.3. As for exposures, they were first calculated on the insured level, based on the exact amount of time spent by each insured in coverage over the relevant policy year. Hence, the entry and exit dates for each insured as well as the start and end dates for each policy were taken into account in this calculation. These individual-level exposures were then aggregated as needed to the higher level required by the models considered later. This calculation method ensured accurate account of the exact coverage period of each insured in the sample taking into account the possibility of late entrance and/or early exit.

As expected, the dataset was unbalanced. Therefore, although the total sample contained 5 policy years, the average number of policy years of data available for each policy in the dataset amounted for about 2 years only. It is also interesting to note that although about 48% of the policies had only one year of data, the remaining ones had two or more years. In fact, about 13% of the policies in the sample were in force for the full 5 policy years. This in turn implies that there is a good chance that repeated/panel

Table 5.1. *Some Overall Statistics for the Final Dataset*

Policy Year	Total Number of Policies	Total Incurred Losse	Total Number of Insureds	Total Exposure
2002	65	LE11,893,151	27,444	26,625
2003	73	LE15,515,181	34,219	33,385
2004	78	LE19,975,868	47,123	43,846
2005	88	LE41,659,568	105,813	79,612
2006	89	LE68,979,625	110,249	107,104

Note: It should be also noted that the main reason for the sudden increase in the numbers in years 2005 and 2006 compared to earlier years is the addition of a large policy to the portfolio in the middle of year 2005, which covered about 50,000 insureds. Throughout this chapter, "LE" stands for Egyptian pound.

effect can have significant impact on the results. However, this will be confirmed later based on the model fitting results.

5.2.3 Introducing Key Variables

5.2.3.1 The Dependent/Outcome Variable

The dependent variable used in all the models considered in this research is the pure premium, as denoted by equation (5.1). This pure premium can be calculated at different level of aggregation, depending on the nature of the available data and the purpose of the analysis. Although, as mentioned earlier, the original database for this research was provided at a very granular level (per insured per transaction), it was important to aggregate it into a reasonable level. This was necessary not only to ensure the feasibility of the modeling process (both in terms of available computing power and running time) but also to ensure the data requirements for the proposed models are reasonable for practical purposes:

$$\text{Pure Premium} = \frac{\text{amount of incurred losses}}{\text{number of insured years}} \tag{5.1}$$

For instance, attempting to work using insured-level data (even after aggregating it on annual basis) was not feasible because of the huge amount of records of data, especially if we would like to allow for the differences in benefit packages between these insureds. This also would have implied that the resulting model would require such level of detailed data as inputs, which may be impractical for ratemaking purposes. On the other hand, too much aggregation (e.g., total annual data per policy regardless of benefits details) could have masked important information. Therefore, after some attempts, it was decided to consider data at the *coverage level per policy*. In other words, pure premium was calculated per *type service/degree/policy/policy year,* as benefit packages were defined per service/degree/policy/policy year (as explained in more detail later).

Another important aspect of the dependent variable relates to its statistical distribution. In general, it is not expected for the pure premium to be normally distributed. This is particularly true in case of health insurance data due to the presence of a large proportion of zero losses. Therefore, it is usually customary to use the natural log of this variable to reduce the effect of this problem. In fact, it is common to use log (1+dependent variable) to mitigate the problem of taking log of zeros (see, e.g., Frees et al., 2001). Therefore, in this research we use this convention in all the reported models.[5] Figure 5.1 shows the quantile-quantile (Q-Q) plot for the pure premium before and after taking the natural log based on the full sample. It is clear that the

---

[5] An alternative approach to handle these issues, not considered in this chapter, is using the Tweedie distribution.

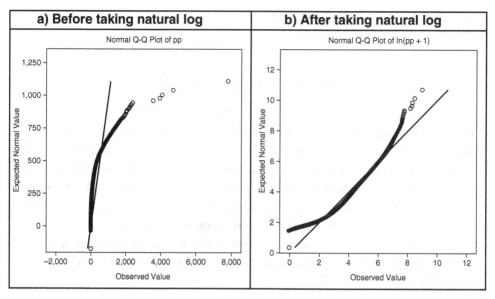

Fig. 5.1. Normal QQ plot of the pure premium (pp) before and after taking its natural log.

second graph is relatively closer to a normal distribution with points getting closer to the straight line.

One final point to note about the dependent variable used in this research relates to the effects of cost-sharing arrangements and inflation/time trends on the claims figures, which in turn affect the pure premium. These effects have been taken into consideration (as shown later) by using appropriate explanatory variables, rather than making direct adjustments to the values of the dependent variable prior to the analysis. This helps to show explicitly the impact of these factors. Moreover, it eliminated the need to find a suitable inflation index for adjustment, especially in the lack of a reliable published one for the Egyptian market.

5.2.3.2 *Benefit Package/Coverage*

As mentioned earlier, the data used in this research was very flexible in terms of coverage definition. In particular, the benefit package was defined by three main dimensions: (1) the type of health service covered; (2) its level of quality; and (3) cost-sharing arrangements, which in turn contained three main aspects: (a) maximum limits on the total annual amount of paid claims, (b) maximum limits on the number of claimants, and (c) co-insurance. Thus, overall, there were five dimensions to the problem.

It is also interesting to note that these dimensions could differ not only between policies but also for different insureds within the same policy. More specifically, for each group policy, the benefit package for each year of coverage was divided into one or more categories referred to as the *degree of service*. Within each degree of service category, the previously mentioned dimensions were defined. In the same time, each insured in the policy was assigned to a specific degree of service. Thus, different insureds within the same policy could have different details for the benefit package depending on their assigned degree of service (which acts as categorization factor).

Thus, overall we can think of the provided benefit package as the result of a multi-ways classification of these five aspects. Therefore, it was important to properly organize and categorize these variables to arrive at a suitable and manageable number of risk cells within the model. This was particularly important, as it affected the speed and feasibility of the model estimation process. It was also important in translating these factors into reasonable categories for quotation purposes. To clarify these issues, each of key dimensions for the benefit packages is discussed in more details in the following sub-sections, which also summarize relevant data adjustments (where applicable) prior to the modeling process.

5.2.3.2.1 Degree of Service As explained before, degree of service here acts as a proxy for defining different categories of benefit packages within the same group policy. The insurer database allowed for a maximum of 5 degrees of services per policy per year, as illustrated in Table 5.2.

As explained before, each insured in a particular group policy was assigned to a particular category of degree of service based on the policyholder preferences. Classification for each insured can change from one year to another. However, it is assumed to remain constant over the year (the file has been adjusted to ensure that). All other details related to the benefit package, including the main degrees of service, could also vary from year to another for the same group policy.

More than half of the policies in the sample (55.7%) contained only one degree of service. On the other hand, the other half of policies contained more than one degree of service, with two and three categories for degree of service being predominant (29.5%

Table 5.2. *Codes for the Degree of Service Categories and Corresponding Labels*

Degree_of_Service_Code	Degree_of_Servic
1	Suit
2	Excellent First Class
3	Regular First Class
4	Excellent Second Class
5	Regular Second Class

Table 5.3. *Summary Statistics for Limit on Amount per Degree for Inpatient Service*

		Limit on amount (LE)				
		Count	Min	Max	Mean	Median	Standard deviation
Inpatient	Suit	47	8,000	150,000	48,381	50,000	38,676
	Excellent First Clas	304	2,000	170,000	28,721	20,000	25,120
	Regular First Clas	217	2,500	100,000	13,070	10,000	12,451
	Excellent Second Class	36	2,000	20,000	8,174	7,000	5,234
	Regular Second Class	4	5,000	9,900	6,225	5,000	2,450

and 12%, respectively). It should be noted however that the definitions of these degrees differed between policies and services, and across time. This is clear for example from the way cost-sharing arrangements were defined. For instance, for a particular policy the definition of first degree can differ for each service leading to different limits on amounts, co-insurance, and so on. Even within the same policy/service, the definition can change from one year from another, in addition to possible changes in the distribution of insureds between these degrees. Similarly, the definition of the same service/degree varied from one policy to another due to differences in cost-sharing arrangements. Table 5.3 provides an example to illustrate the point.

This table shows the summary statistics for limit on amount for the inpatient service broken down by the degree of service. It is clear from that table that even for the same service the definition of limit on amount differs not only *between* degrees, but also *within* degrees. This is clear from the various summary statistics including standard deviation and the range of the values (summarized by min, max, mean, and median). For example, the mean of limit on amount for the "Suite" degree is almost double that for "Excellent First Class," which illustrates differences between degrees. Even within the same degree for example "Suite" degree (for the same service, i.e., inpatient), the limit on amount ranges from LE8,000 to LE150,000 with a median of LE50,000 and standard deviation of LE38,676. This illustrates the high variability in definitions of limit on amount even within the same degree/service.

In light of all the preceding, it was not possible to merge these degrees into a fewer number of categories. This was not also necessary, as their breakdown seemed logical with reasonable number of distinct levels. Thus, we benefited from the capabilities of multilevel modeling to be able to model this variable as it is, taking into account all these important differences.

5.2.3.2.2 Type of Service Within each degree per policy per year, the health services covered were defined using codes referred to here as "type of service." The original file contained about 82 such codes. However, it became clear from preliminary investigation of the data that there was a need to regroup these codes into a smaller number of categories. This was necessary for various reasons: the most important one is that it seemed that there were some inconsistencies in the way these codes were defined. More specifically, the same service label was sometimes given different codes in different policies without any clear distinction. For example, the original database contained about 5 different codes for optical services. Thus, it was important to recode them into a new single code to ensure a meaningful interpretation of results, especially within ratemaking context. This also helped to reduce the number of records and remove unnecessary cross-classification (in case of multilevel model). This in turn reduced computing requirements and significantly improved running times for the models especially multilevel ones.

After some investigations of the description of the provided codes as well as related amount of exposures, it was decided to recode this field into new 16 different codes only.[6] Figure 5.2 provides a summary of these new codes. It also shows the distribution of claims in the (full) sample based on these codes. It is clear from the graph that medicines' category had the highest percentage of incurred losses. The cumulative percentage line overlaid on the graph also shows the high concentration of claims within the top 5 types of service, which alone total for about 93% of all claims in the sample.

5.2.3.2.3 Cost-sharing Arrangements Cost-sharing arrangements for the policies under consideration were defined on the service level. In other words, for the same degree/policy/policy year, cost-sharing arrangements varied from one service to another. Accordingly, for the same service, cost-sharing details could differ depending on the corresponding degree of service, policy, or policy year. Three main types of cost sharing existed in the data, as follows:

a. *Limit on amount*. This refers to the limit on total annual amount of paid claims per insured for each service. All the records in the data file contained such limit. So, none of the benefits were uncapped. However, the amounts of these limits varied between degrees, services, policies, and/or policy years, as explained before. It was found better to take use the natural log of this variable in the models to achieve a reasonable interpretation of the coefficient in this case, as the dependent variable was also transformed to natural log, as explained before. In particular, the coefficient in this case would refer elasticity rather than semi-elasticity, which seems more reasonable. It is also important to note that as zero was not a permissible value for this variable. So, it was necessary to center it to ensure a meaningful interpretation of the intercept. This centering was

---

[6] It should be noted that cost-sharing arrangements within these new categories were calculated as the averages of old values for previous underlying categories.

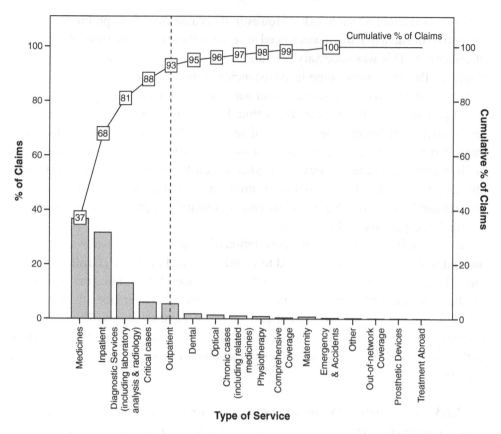

Fig. 5.2. Distribution of claims per type of service. This graph is based on data from the full sample and the new assigned codes for type of service.

done using the grand mean for this variable across the in-sample data, that is, 8.7963. Therefore, the final used variable was referred to as *ln_limit_Amount_8.7963*.

b. *Limit on number.* This refers to the limit on the number of claimants per coverage (i.e., degree/service) for each policy per policy year. This limit was not very common in the dataset. It existed for only some of the records related to certain types of services such as dental and optical. The dataset used the zero value to refer to a benefit record that did not have a limit on number, that is, uncapped benefits. However, using this value for modeling purposes would have led to the opposite interpretation with zero meaning that zero (i.e., no) insured were allowed to use this benefit. Therefore, it was necessary to find a more meaningful proxy/transformation for this variable. After some investigation, it was decided to convert this number to a percentage of the total number of insureds per coverage/policy/policy year. Thus, a 100% (instead of zero) would imply no limit on the number of claimants. Then, similar to limit on amount, values for this new variable were centered around the overall mean (88.58%) leading the final used variable *Perct_Limit_Number_88.58*.

c. *Co-insurance*. These were expressed in the original data as percentages. Therefore, there was no need to take their natural log. Similarly, there was no need to center it, as zero in this case is a meaningful permissible value. However, it is interesting to note that this type of cost-sharing (similar to limit on number) was used for only some of the records, which usually related to particular types of benefits, especially medications.

5.2.3.3 Industrial Classification

The nature of the policyholder's business can have an important impact on the health claims of affiliated insureds. This is due to its effect on the nature of risks the insureds are exposed to during work time. Moreover, it can acts as a proxy for other important factors related to the general profile of the insureds (e.g., level of education, social economic status age), which in turn do affect health claims. Therefore, it is usually one of the important rating factors for group health insurance (see, e.g., Comstock and Ford, 2000, p. 434). It is also possible to add an additional layer of information related to the split of employees between various categories of occupations such as managerial, clerical, and manual. However, this was not available in the supplied data.

In fact, the original dataset contained just a single field for policyholder industry for each policy. This field contained some general (in-house) categories used by the insurer to define the industry for each insured. The original dataset contained 33 different codes. These codes did not seem very distinctive and informative for ratemaking purpose. Therefore, it was important to regroup them into categories that are more meaningful for ratemaking purpose. This regrouping was also important to reduce the number of unnecessary distinct values for the variable, which in turn reduced the number of cross-classifications produced by multilevel models and hence significantly improved running time.

Another important aspect that induced this regrouping is the presence of some concerns regarding its reliability. In particular, the insurer supplying the data reserved the right to manipulate the industrial categories for some of the records to protect the identity of the policyholders. Despite this limitation, we decided to keep this variable in the analysis due to its importance, in order to provide guidance for further similar analysis, especially given that the main purpose of the empirical study in research is to illustrate the modeling technique discussed rather than to produce actual rates. Thus, although this regrouping may have reduced the effect of this problem, this is of course not guaranteed. Therefore, results related to this factor should be used with caution.

To select an appropriate coding system for industrial classification, a number of standard industrial classification systems were consulted to find a suitable one for the nature of the available data and the purpose of this research. This investigation was induced by examples of online health insurance quotation forms for international insurers, which used a standard industrial classification system. After some investigation, it was decided to reassign/recode the original 33 categories into only

Table 5.4. *Summary of Industrial Classification Codes and Related Descriptions*

Industrial Code	Description
1	Agriculture, forestry and fishing
2	Manufacturing, mining and quarrying and other industrial activities
3	Construction
4	Wholesale and retail trade, transportation and storage, accommodation and food service activities
5	Information and communication
6	Financial and insurance activities
7	Real estate activities
8	Professional, scientific, technical, administrative and support service activities
9	Public administration and defence, education, human health and social work activities
10	Other service activities

Source: United Nations (2008, 274 Table 4.1).

10 different categories using the *High-level SNA/ISIC aggregation (A*10)*, as summarized in Table 5.4. This is the high-level aggregated form of the *International Standard Industrial Classification of All Economic Activities (ISIC)* developed by the United Nations (for more detail, see United Nations, 2008).

5.2.3.4 Other Explanatory Variables/Covariates

In addition to the explanatory variables discussed earlier, there were other important explanatory variables considered in the models. These were based on previous studies, as well as common rating factors for group health insurance. These variables included the following:

a. Time-related variables (Time and Time_squared) to allow for trend in data. These were based on policy year values after recording into 0, 1, 2, and so on, in order to ensure correct interpretation of the intercepts;

b. Two variables related to the number of insureds both at the degree/service level and the policy level. These variables were transformed into natural log scale and centered around the overall mean for the same reasons explained before for the limit on amount; and

c. Another two variables for the percentage of female insureds both at the degree/service level and the policy level. Similar to the co-insurance variable, there was no need to take the natural log of these variables or to center them.

It is also interesting to note in that regard that it is acceptable in multilevel modeling to use the same variable with different levels of aggregation at the different levels of the model. This is similar to what was done here for the number of insureds and percentage of female insureds, where each one of them was considered at two different levels. In fact, this is an additional reason for the high flexibility of multilevel modeling.

5.3 Methods and Models

5.3.1 The Modeling Building Strategy

As explained by Frees (2004b, p. 4), "in most investigations, the process of developing a model is as informative as the resulting model." In fact, it can be described as "part of the art of statistics," where statistics itself can be described as "the art of reasoning with data" (Frees, 2004b, p. 5). This is particularly true in case of multilevel modeling, due to its very flexible specification, which can handle a wide variety of model designs. In other words, although this flexibility can provide the researcher with many opportunities to explore, it can also lead to some challenges in selecting the appropriate design; especially in case of an extensive dataset with various possibilities to look at it (similar to the dataset used in this research). Therefore, multilevel modeling is often described as more complicated than single-level modeling (Hox, 2010). It also requires careful planning prior to the analysis. This is often described as the *model building strategy* or the *analysis strategy* (see, e.g., Fielding, 2010, p. 22; Hox, 2010, p. 54).

Therefore, before going into the details of the fitted models, it is important to outline the model building strategy adopted. This strategy has been decided in light of three main aspects: (1) theoretical considerations, including recommended strategies; (2) key relevant previous studies; and (3) the nature of the available data. More specifically, overall, we use Hox's (2010) steps for the *bottom-up* model development approach, as summarized in Table 5.5. However, rather than starting directly with

Table 5.5. *Summary of Multilevel Modeling Steps Suggested by Hox (2010)*

Step	Description
Step 1	*"Analyze a model with no explanatory variables"* i.e. *"the intercept-only model"*
Step 2	*"Analyze a model with all lower-level explanatory variables fixed".*
Step 3	*"Add the higher level explanatory variables"* (fixed).
Step 4	*"Assess whether any of the slopes of any of the explanatory variables"* should be converted from fixed to random. i.e. *"the random slope/coefficient model"*
Step 5	*"Add cross-level interactions between explanatory group-level variables and those individual-level explanatory variables that had significant slope variation in step 4".*

Source: Table prepared based on direct quotes from Hox (2010, 56–59).

an intercept-only multilevel model, we start by single-level models, as suggested by Gelman and Hill (2007). This helps to illustrate the importance of multilevel modeling and its effect on improvement in results compared to single-level models. This comparison is also consistent with the work done in some of the relevant studies. Moreover, as the dataset used in the empirical work in this research has panel aspects, we follow Singer's (1998) recommendation and attempt different structures for the variance-covariance matrix for the repeated effects/residuals in the final stages of the model development process.

5.3.2 Estimation Method and Software

The fitted models have been estimated using maximum likelihood (ML) rather than restricted maximum (REML). This is because ML is usually easier to explain. It also facilitates the comparison of different models using likelihood-based tests. Yet, it should be noted that the estimates for fixed effects will be the same under both methods (Albright and Marinova, 2010). The difference is in the estimates for the covariance parameters, which are usually lower for ML (StataCorp, 2009).

Consistent with Volume I of this book, the computer codes and data for the fitted models will be available online. However, there are many other alternatives software that can handle multilevel modeling. These include both general-purpose statistical packages and specialized software.

5.3.3 Comparing the Models

Consistent with similar studies, *Akaike's information criterion (AIC)* is the measure used to compare the results of the proposed models. It represents an index to compare the relative goodness of fit of models. The index is built in a way such that smaller values indicate better fit of the models. It has several advantages over other possible alternatives including (a) its ability to compare between nonnested models, as opposed to other indexes that require the compared models to be nested;[7] Furthermore, (b) in case of ML estimation, it can compare models that differ in both the fixed parts and the random parts, as opposed to REML estimation, where it should be used to compare to models that differ only in the random parts, and (c) it includes a penalty for increasing the number of the parameters in the model, as illustrated in equation (5.2):

$$AIC = -2\ln(L) + 2k \qquad (5.2)$$

---

[7] *Nested models* here means that *"one model is a subset of the other"* (Frees, 2010, p. 341). In other words, *"two models are said to be nested if the more complex model can be built from the simpler model by addition of one or more parameters, e.g. regression coefficients"* (Steele, 2008, p. 8).

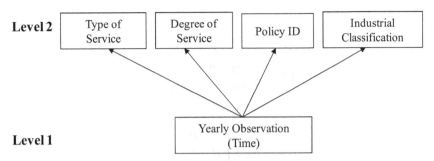

Fig. 5.3. Classification diagram for fitted multilevel models.

In this equation, L denotes the maximized value of the likelihood function for the model under consideration, while k is the number of parameters in that model. Therefore, increasing the number of the parameter will lead to a higher value of AIC (i.e., poorer fit of the model). Thus, this index takes into account the principle of parsimony.

5.3.4 The Fitted Models

As mentioned earlier, the dataset used in this research was divided into two samples: (1) *the in-sample*, which covers policy years 2002 to 2005 and is used for the preliminary fitting of the models, and (2) *the out-of-sample*, which covers policy years 2006 and is used for validating the models. Meanwhile, the attempted models can be broadly classified into two main categories: (1) single level models and (2) multilevel models.

Table 5.A.1 and Table 5.A.4 in the appendix provide a brief description of the fitted models, with the former table focusing on single level models and the latter one focusing on multilevel models.[8] The classification diagram in Figure 5.3 summarizes the cross-classified two level structure adopted in the fitted multilevel models.

The assumptions used for covariance matrix structures used while fitting these models (as explained in Table 5.A.4) included the *"unstructured"* form as illustrated by equation (5.3); and the *"compound symmetry-correlation metric"* form (referred to thereafter as *CS*) as illustrated by equation (5.4). It is clear from these two equations that under the first assumption, the covariance matrix is defined by 10 parameters, whereas under the second assumption, it is defined by only two parameters

---

[8] It should be noted that the results of the multilevel models reported here focus on the first three steps in Table 5.5. This because the attempts to apply steps 4 and 5 were not successful in achieving better results.

$(\sigma^2$ and $\rho)$:

$$\mathbf{R1} = \begin{bmatrix} \sigma_1^2 & \sigma_{21} & \sigma_{31} & \sigma_{41} \\ \sigma_{21} & \sigma_2^2 & \sigma_{32} & \sigma_{42} \\ \sigma_{31} & \sigma_{32} & \sigma_3^2 & \sigma_{43} \\ \sigma_{41} & \sigma_{42} & \sigma_{43} & \sigma_4^2 \end{bmatrix} \tag{5.3}$$

$$\mathbf{R2} = \sigma^2 \begin{bmatrix} 1 & \rho & \rho & \rho \\ \rho & 1 & \rho & \rho \\ \rho & \rho & 1 & \rho \\ \rho & \rho & \rho & 1 \end{bmatrix} \tag{5.4}$$

5.4 Results

5.4.1 Estimation Results (in-sample)

In this section, the focus is on in-sample results. These results are summarized in Table 5.A.2 for single level models and Table 5.A.5 for multilevel models. The key comments on these results are summarized in the following related tables, which are Table 5.A.3 and Table 5.A.6, respectively.

Based on the results and comments discussed in the previously mentioned tables, it is clear that multilevel models provide better results than single level models. Models 9 and 10 in particular provided the best fitting results in terms of smallest AIC. They also allowed for more features of the data structure than any of the others models and using less parameters than model 8. However, it is important to validate these results using another dataset (the out-of-sample dataset), which is considered in more details in the following section.

5.4.2 Model Validation (out-of-sample)

In the previous section (in-sample fitting), AIC was used to assess the goodness of fit of models. In this section, another important tool is used for validating the models. That is out-of-sample fitting. In particular, as mentioned before, data for policy year 2006 was withheld while fitting the previous models. Then, these estimated models together with the input fields from 2006 data were used to calculate the predicted pure premiums for 2006. These predicted values were then compared to the actual observed pure premiums figures for 2006.[9]

---

[9] It should be noted that consistent with Rosenberg et al. (2007), the out-of-sample dataset has been adjusted to remove records related to cross-classification values appearing for the first time in policy year 2006. This is because we don't have estimates for the random effects for these combinations. For example, policy IDs appearing for the first time in policy year 2006 were removed since the fitted models contains policy ID as one of the random effects.

Table 5.6. *In-Sample AIC versus Out-Of-Sample MAE*

		Brief Description	AIC (in-sample)	MAE (out-of-sample)
Single Level Models[a]	Model 1	Intercept only	18,997.44	LE110.82
	Model 2	Intercept + Time + Time^2	19,000.12	LE110.58
	Model 3	Intercept + Time	18,998.43	LE110.71
	Model 4	Model 3 + all other explanatory variables	18,799.17	LE109.34
Multilevel Models	Model 5	Intercepts only	15,328.18	LE84.83
	Model 6	Intercepts + Level 1 variable (Time)	15,325.47	LE85.17
	Model 7	Model 7 + Level 2 all other explanatory variables	15,269.55	LE84.00
	Model 8	Model 7 with UN matrix	14,657.92	LE83.65
	Model 9	Model 7 with CS matrix	14,653.87	LE83.49
	Model 10	Model 9 with two insignificant variables removed	14,650.05	LE83.49

Note: MAE figures in this table are based on pure premium (pp), and not ln(pp+1).
[a] An additional single level model suggested during the review process of this chapter (but not considered here), is to further expand model 4 to include the categorical variables such as type of service, degree of service, etc. This helped to improve results significantly. Yet, multilevel models continued to be better especially after adjusting for the panel aspects of the data.

To summarize the out-of-sample validation results for each model, we use the *mean absolute error (MAE)* statistic,[10] as illustrated in equation (5.5). This is based on relevant previous studies (see, e.g., Frees and Miller, 2004; Rosenberg et al., 2007):

$$MAE = \frac{\sum |observed\ pp - predicted\ pp|}{n} \tag{5.5}$$

Table 5.6 summarizes these MAE results for out-of-sample validation compared to the previous AIC figures for the in-sample fitting. As we can see from this table, in-sample results are consistent with out-of-sample validation results. For example, as more features of the nature of the data structure is recognized within the model, the fitting and prediction results improve. The most important changes occur when we moved from single-level models to multilevel models (starting from model 5). Another important but less notable change occurs when the panel aspects of the data are recognized by changing the assumption for the covariance matrix (starting from model 8). Overall, models 9 and 10 provided best results in terms of smallest AIC

---

[10] An alternative approach suggested for future work during the review process of this chapter is the use of a Gini index, as discussed in more in detail Frees et al. (2014).

and MAE. However, model 10 may be better for practical purposes since it requires less data and is more parsimonious in terms of number of parameters. Hence, it is the recommended model for this study.

5.5 Conclusions

This research illustrated the importance of multilevel modeling for actuarial applications, within the context of group health insurance ratemaking. Some of key findings and recommendations can be summarized as follows:

1. It is clear that the special nature of data has significant impact on the validity of the fitted models. This include in particular multilevel structures and panel aspects. Therefore, it is important to consider this issue in the design of future models based on similar data.
2. This research also highlighted the significant impact of differences in benefit packages between group health insurance policies. Moreover, it also illustrated how this can be modeled within a multilevel modeling framework. This represents an important point that was often overlooked in previous studies despite its significance (as shown by empirical results). Therefore, it should be taken into consideration in future researches. It is also important to note that the differences in coverage considered in this research contained more than one dimension. In particular, they were not limited to differences in cost sharing arrangements only, but also included differences in types of services covered, and differences in classes/levels of coverage (degrees).
3. Based on the empirical results for the final two models (models 9 and 10), it is clear that cost-sharing arrangements have a significant impact on the estimated pure premiums. Therefore, it is important to take them into consideration in future research and practical applications. In particular, in light of t-statistics and p-values, co-insurance seems to be the most significant element. This is then followed by limit on amount. Finally, there is the limit on number, which appears to be insignificant in the empirical results in this research. However, it should be noted that the impact of the factor may be masked in this case by its small presence in the dataset in hand, since it was limited to only particular types of services, as explained in the research.
4. It is also clear from the empirical results in this research the importance of attempting different variance-covariance structures for the residuals in case of panel models. Therefore, it is important to take care of this issue in future studies with panel aspect.
5. This research also illustrated out-of-sample validation as an important additional tool for assessing the suitability of a proposed model. In this research, the results of the empirical work showed conformity between in-sample fitting results and out-of-sample validation. However, this is not necessarily always true. Therefore, it remains important to consider out-of-sample validation in future empirical studies.
6. As illustrated throughout this research, it is also very important to spend the necessary time and efforts to explore the data under consideration before starting to fit models. This is necessary not only for validity checks and cleaning up, but also to do the

necessary adjustments to ensure meaningful interpretation of results. In this context, these adjustments included for example taking natural logarithm of some of the variables, centering and recoding them (where necessary). Therefore, it is important to take care of this critical phase in future relevant studies.

Meanwhile, there are various ways in which this research can be extended, which represent potential areas for further research. For example, it can be useful to repeat this research using different datasets to see if the same empirical results hold or not. These datasets may also contain additional explanatory variables that were not available for this research. It will be also interesting to consider additional multilevel designs. This may include for instance adding more layers to the multilevel model, for example a company level in a study that involves data collected from more than one insurance company. Similarly, a country or a region level can be added, depending on the available data and its consistency. In brief, multilevel modeling opens the door to a very wide range of possible research designs. These possibilities can differ significantly in their level of complexity. Therefore, it is important to assess this increasing complexity against possible gains. That why Goldstein (2011, p. 14), for example, emphasizes that *"multilevel models are tools to be used with care and understanding."*

Acknowledgments

This chapter is based on the primary author's PhD dissertation completed at Faculty of Commerce, Cairo University, Egypt. She gratefully acknowledges the encouragement and feedback provided by the dissertation supervisor Prof. Galal A. H. Harby and the rest of the examination committee.

An initial draft of this chapter (Hammad and Harby, 2013) was presented by the primary author as a research paper at the international workshop "Perspectives on Actuarial Risks in Talks of Young Researchers" (PARTY 2013). Another related paper (Hammad, 2014) was also presented at the International Congress of Actuaries (ICA2014) and was awarded second place for best paper in the nonlife track. Accordingly, the primary author would like to thank participants and organizers of these events for important and encouraging feedback.

Special thanks to Prof. Edward W. (Jed) Frees for his encouraging and valuable comments to improve this work and for his suggestions for possible future extensions.

Appendix

Table 5.A.1. Description of the Single Level Models Fitted to the Dataset

Model	Key Features	Description	Notation		
			Subscript(s) Definition	The Model	Key Assumptions for Random Terms
Model 1	– Single-level – intercept-only – cross-sectional	An intercept-only simple regression model.	$i = 1, 2\ldots, 4286 =$ an index of the number of observations/records in the in-sample dataset.	$y_i = \beta_0 + \varepsilon_i$	$\varepsilon_i \sim N(0, \sigma^2)$
Model 2	– Single-level – intercept + two trend variables [Time & Time_Squared] – (independently) pooled cross-sectional.	Compared to the previous model, two explanatory variables [Time and Time²] are now added to reflect time trend. Time is treated here as a continuous variable and recoded as 0, 1, 2 . . . etc.	Same as before	$y_i = \beta_0 + \beta_1 Time + \beta_2 Time^2 + \varepsilon_i$	$\varepsilon_i \sim N(0, \sigma^2)$
Model 3	– Single-level – intercept + one trend variable only [Time] – (independently) pooled cross-sectional	Compared to the previous model, Time_Squared variable has been removed.	Same as before	$y_i = \beta_0 + \beta_1 Time + \varepsilon_i$	$\varepsilon_i \sim N(0, \sigma^2)$
Model 4	– Single-level – intercept + all potential explanatory variables including Time – (independently) pooled cross-sectional	Compared to the previous model, 7 additional explanatory variables (in addition to Time) has been added.	Same as before	See equation (5.6)	$\varepsilon_i \sim N(0, \sigma^2)$

Note: As explained before, in all the models fitted in this research the dependent variable y was defined as $\ln(pp+1)$.

$$y_i = \beta_0 + \beta_1\ Time\ + \beta_2\ \text{ln\_limit\_Amount\_8.7963} + \beta_3\ \text{Perct\_Limit\_Number\_88.58} + \beta_4\ \text{Co-insurance} + \beta_5\ \text{ln\_noInsureds\_degree\_4.1975} + \beta_6\ \text{ln\_noInsureds\_policy\_5.1246} + \beta_7\ \text{Perct\_Females\_degree} + \beta_8\ \text{Perct\_females\_policy} + \varepsilon_i$$

(5.6)

Table 5.A.2. *Key Results for Fitted Singel-Level Models (in-sample)*

	Single Level Models											
	Model 1			Model 2			Model 3			Model 4		
Parameter	Estimate	t	Sig.	Estimate	t	Sig.	Estimate	t	Sig.	Estimate	t	Sig.
Intercept	2.523	74.452	0.000	2.495	35.090	.000	2.474	41.449	0.000	2.288	27.860	.000
Time				-0.028	-.255	.799	0.031	1.006	.314	0.012	.402	.688
ln_limit_Amount_8.7963										0.016	.758	.449
Perct_Limit_Number_88.58										0.006	5.185	.000
Co-insurance										0.094	12.842	.000
ln_noInsureds_degree_4.1975										0.091	3.492	.000
ln_noInsureds_policy_5.1246										-0.065	-2.287	.022
Perct_Females_degree										0.000	.041	.968
Perct_females_policy										0.004	1.080	.280
Time_squared				0.019	.558	.577						
Estimates of Covariance Parameters												
Residual	4.922			4.920			4.920			4.682		
AIC	18,997.44			19,000.12			18,998.43			18,799.17		

149

Table 5.A.3. *Interpretation of Results for the Fitted Single Level Models*

Model	Key Related Comments and Interpretation of Results
Model 1	This represents the simplest model that can be fit to the data. However, it totally ignores the nature of the dataset structure, as well as any correlations between observations and time-effects. In fact, the estimate for intercept coefficient in this case is simply the overall mean of the response variable. In other words, $\hat{\beta}_0 = \bar{y}$, which is expected based on formulas for simple regression. Based on the estimation results in Table 5.A.2, it is clear that this intercept is statistically significant with the high values of the t-test ($=74.452$) and zero p-value. However, the relatively high variance of the residuals [the estimate for $\sigma_\varepsilon^2 \approx 4.92$ is approximately double the estimate for the intercept coefficient] suggests that there is still high variability in the data that should be explained through further improvements of the model.
Model 2	Compared to the previous model, adding the two time variables [*Time* and *Time_Squared*] led to a slight deterioration in AIC value. The two variables also seem to be insignificant based on the low values for the t-statistic and high p-values. Therefore, in the following model *Time_Squared* is removed to check if this will improve results.
Model 3	Compared to the previous model, removing *Time_Squared* variable restored AIC to a slightly better level similar to original AIC estimate for model 1. It also improved the significance of *Time* variable, however it continues to be statistically insignificant (t-statistic $= 1.006 < t_{\infty,5\%} = 1.645$). In light of these results and based on expectations regarding the nature of data *Time_Squared* variable will be removed from the following models. However, the *Time* variable will be retained in the future models. This is because we expect its statistical significance to become clearer as the model's structure improves.
Model 4	Compared to previous model (model 3), adding the remaining covariates to the model improved the fitting of the model. This is clear from the smaller AIC. Some of the covariates appear to be relatively more significant. However, we defer judging these significance levels until the effect of the nature of data has been taken into account through multilevel modeling, as illustrated in the following models.

Table 5.A.4. *Description of the Multilevel Models Fitted to the Dataset*

Model	Key Features	Notation			Key Assumptions for Random Terms
		Description	Subscript(s) Definition	The Model	
Model 5	– 2-level – intercepts-only – cross-sectional	Consistent with step 1 in Table 5.5, we start multilevel modeling with an intercepts only model. Given the structure of the data, the model is a 2-level cross-classified model, where yearly observations are treated as cross-classified at level 2 by policy ID, degree of service, type of service, and industrial classification. This is graphically illustrated in Figure 5.3	$t =$ time $= 0, 1, 2, 3$ (for in-sample) $d =$ degree of service ID $= 1, 2, \ldots 5$ (for more details, see Table 5.2) $s =$ type of service ID $= 1, 2, \ldots 16$ (for more details, see Figure 5.2) $p =$ policy ID $c =$ industrial classification ID $= 1, 2, \ldots, 10$ (for more details, see Table 5.4)	Level 1: $y_{t(dspc)} = \pi_{0(dspc)} + e_{t(dspc)}$ Level 2: $\pi_{0(dspc)} = \beta_{00} + r_{0d} + r_{0s} + r_{0p} + r_{0c}$ $\rightarrow y_{t(dspc)} = \underbrace{\beta_{00}}_{Fixed}$ $\underbrace{+ r_{0d} + r_{0s} + r_{0p} + r_{0c} + e_{t(dspc)}}_{Random}$	All random terms are assumed to be distributed $N(0, \sigma^2 \mathbf{I})$, i.e. a scaled identity covariance matrix, with a different σ^2 for each of the random terms. This scaled identity assumption includes the random errors terms, which in turn implies no repeated measures/panel effect.
Model 6	– 2-level – intercepts + level 1 explanatory variables (Time) – cross-sectional	Consistent with step 2 in Table 5.5, in this model level 1 explanatory variables are added to the previous multilevel model as fixed effects. In this case, these variables are limited to the Time variable.	Same as above	Level 1: $y_{t(dspc)} = \pi_{0(dspc)} + \pi_1\, Time_{t(dspc)}$ $\quad + e_{t(dspc)}$ Level 2: $\pi_{0(dspc)} = \beta_{00} + r_{0d} + r_{0s} + r_{0p} + r_{0c}$ $\rightarrow y_{t(dspc)} = \underbrace{\beta_{00} + \pi_1\, Time_{t(dspc)}}_{Fixed}$ $\underbrace{+ r_{0d} + r_{0s} + r_{0p} + r_{0c} + e_{t(dspc)}}_{Random}$	Same as above

(continued)

151

Table 5.A.4. (continued)

Model	Key Features	Description	Notation		
			Subscript(s) Definition	The Model	Key Assumptions for Random Terms
Model 7	– 2-level – intercepts + all explanatory variables (at both levels) – cross-sectional	Consistent with step 3 in Table 5.5, in this model level 2 explanatory variables are added to the previous multilevel model as fixed effects. Thus, the total is 8 explanatory variables.	Same as above	See equation (5.7)	Same as above
Model 8	– 2-level – intercepts + all explanatory variables (at both levels) – panel, with "unstructured" variance-covariance matrix for the random errors.	This model is the same as the previous model. However, the assumption for the random errors (residuals) has been changed to allow for the repeated measures/panel effects. We start with the most unrestricted variance-covariance matrix structure. That is the "unstructured" option.	Same as above	Same as above	All random terms $\sim N(0, \sigma^2 \mathbf{I})$ as above except $\mathbf{e} \sim N(0, \mathbf{R1})$ where $\mathbf{R1} =$ unstructured covariance matrix as defined in equation (5.3)
Model 9	– 2-level – intercepts + all explanatory variables (at both levels) – panel, with CS variance-covariance matrix for the random errors.	This model is the same as the previous model. However, the assumption for the random errors (residuals) has been changed to a simpler variance-covariance matrix. That is a CS structure instead of "unstructured"	Same as above	Same as above	All random terms $\sim N(0, \sigma^2 \mathbf{I})$ as above except $\mathbf{e} \sim N(0, \mathbf{R2})$ where $\mathbf{R2} = $ CS covariance matrix as defined in equation (5.4)

| Model 10 | – 2-level
– intercepts + all explanatory variables (at both levels) except *Perct_Limit_Number_88.58*, and *Perct_Females_degree* – panel, with "compound symmetry" variance-covariance matrix for the random errors. | This model is the same as the previous model. However, the two most insignificant explanatory variables based on the results of the previous model have been removed. These are *Perct_Limit_Number_88.58*, and *Perct_Females_degree*. | Same as above | See equation (5.8) | Same as above |

Note: As explained before, in all the models fitted in this research the dependent variable *y* was defined as ln(pp+1).

$$
y_{t(dspc)} = \begin{aligned}[t] &\left.\begin{aligned}\beta_{00} + \pi_1\,\text{Time}_{t(dspc)} + \pi_2\,\text{ln\_limit\_Amount\_8.7963}_{t(dspc)}\\ + \pi_3\,\text{Perct\_Limit\_Number\_88.58}_{t(dspc)} + \pi_4\,\text{Co-insurance}_{t(dspc)}\\ + \pi_5\,\text{ln\_noInsureds\_degree\_4.1975}_{t(dspc)}\\ + \pi_6\,\text{ln\_noInsureds\_policy\_5.1246}_{t(dspc)}\\ + \pi_7\,\text{Perct\_Females\_degree}_{t(dspc)} + \pi_8\,\text{Perct\_females\_policy}_{t(dspc)}\end{aligned}\right\}\textbf{\textit{Fixed}}\\ &\left.+\ r_{0d} + r_{0s} + r_{0p} + r_{0c} + e_{t(dspc)}\right\}\textbf{\textit{Random}}\end{aligned}
\tag{5.7}
$$

$$
y_{t(dspc)} = \begin{aligned}[t] &\left.\begin{aligned}\beta_{00} + \pi_1\,\text{Time}_{t(dspc)} + \pi_2\,\text{ln\_limit\_Amount\_8.7963}_{t(dspc)}\\ + \pi_3\,\text{Co-insurance}_{t(dspc)} + \pi_4\,\text{ln\_noInsureds\_degree\_4.1975}_{t(dspc)}\\ + \pi_5\,\text{ln\_noInsureds\_policy\_5.1246}_{t(dspc)}\\ + \pi_6\,\text{Perct\_females\_policy}_{t(dspc)}\end{aligned}\right\}\textbf{\textit{Fixed}}\\ &\left.+\ r_{0d} + r_{0s} + r_{0p} + r_{0c} + e_{t(dspc)}\right\}\textbf{\textit{Random}}\end{aligned}
\tag{5.8}
$$

153

Table 5.A.5. *Key Results for Fitted Multilevel Models (in-sample)*

	Multilevel Models											
	Cross-sectional						Panel					
	Model 5		Model 6		Model 7		Model 8		Model 9		Model 10	
Parameter	Estimate	t	Estimate	t	Estimate	t	Estimate	t	Estimate	t	Estimate	t
Intercept	2.180	4.679	2.084	4.464	1.968	4.000	1.988	4.050	1.984	4.044	1.984	4.043
Time			0.056	2.186	0.051	2.017	0.053	2.814	0.053	2.765	0.053	2.769
ln_limit_Amount_8.7963					0.058	2.528	0.063	2.365	0.064	2.407	0.065	2.431
Perct_Limit_Number_88.58					0.000	.459	0.000	.261	0.000	.375		
Co-insurance					−0.028	−4.544	−0.028	−3.797	−0.028	−3.758	−0.028	−3.757
ln_noInsureds_degree_4.1975					0.141	5.764	0.160	5.871	0.161	5.873	0.159	5.878
ln_noInsureds_policy_5.1246					−0.068	−1.628	−0.093	−2.201	−0.093	−2.190	−0.091	−2.167
Perct_Females_degree					0.001	.426	−0.001	−.280	−0.001	−.215		
Perct_females_policy					0.005	1.229	0.005	1.407	0.005	1.377	0.005	1.609
Estimates of Covariance Parameters												
Residual	1.904		1.900		1.874		*see matrix 1 below*		*see matrix 2 below*		*see matrix 3 below*	
Intercept [subject = Type_of_Service_new_Code]	3.259		3.251		3.444		3.406		3.396		3.404	
Intercept [subject = Degree_of_Service_Code]	0.015		0.014		0.035		0.043		0.045		0.043	
Intercept [subject = Policy_ID]	0.479		0.495		0.431		0.411		0.408		0.407	
Intercept [subject = Industry_new_code]	0.038		0.035		0.036		0.034		0.035		0.035	
AIC	15,328.18		15,325.47		15,269.55		14,657.92		14,653.87		14,650.05	

Matrix 1: Residual Covariance (R) Matrix for Model 8

Policy_Year	2002	2003	2004	2005
2002	1.982	0.992	0.904	0.942
2003	0.992	2.045	1.030	0.912
2004	0.904	1.030	1.940	0.926
2005	0.942	0.912	0.926	1.741

Unstructured

Matrix 2: Residual Covariance (R) Matrix for Model 9

Policy_Year	2002	2003	2004	2005
2002	1.915	0.945	0.945	0.945
2003	0.945	1.915	0.945	0.945
2004	0.945	0.945	1.915	0.945
2005	0.945	0.945	0.945	1.915

Compound Symmetry (Correlation Metric)

Matrix 3: Residual Covariance (R) Matrix for Model 10

Policy_Year	2002	2003	2004	2005
2002	1.916	0.945	0.945	0.945
2003	0.945	1.916	0.945	0.945
2004	0.945	0.945	1.916	0.945
2005	0.945	0.945	0.945	1.916

Compound Symmetry (Correlation Metric)

Note: p-values have been omitted from this table to reduce its size.

Table 5.A.6. *Interpretation of Results for the Fitted Multilevel Models*

Model	Key Related Comments/Interpretation of Results
Model 5	This represents one of the simplest possible multilevel models in light of the nature of the structure of the data in the sample. In particular, the model contains only the fixed and random intercepts without any explanatory variables. It also assumes the simplest structure for the variance-covariance matrices for all random effects including residuals. That is the scaled identity structure, which in turn implies ignoring any repeated effects or correlations between observations. Despite these limitations, recognizing the multilevel structure of the data led to a significant improvement in the fitting results compared to the previous single level models. This is clear from the significant reduction in AIC results. For example, if we compare this model to model 4 (which represents the single-level model with the smallest AIC value), we will notice that AIC dropped from 18,799.17 to 15,328.18. We also look forward for more improvement in fitting results, as more features of the data recognized in the latter models.
Model 6	Compared to the previous model, AIC has slightly improved. More important, compared to the previous single level models, the statistical significance of the *Time* variable is also now clear with a t-statistic $= 2.186 > t_{\infty,5\%} = 1.645$.
Model 7	Again compared to the previous model, AIC is still improving. The statistical significance of the explanatory variables varies with number of insureds per benefit package (*ln_noInsureds_degree_4.1975*) and *co-insurance* appearing to be the most significant factors at this stage. However, it is better to defer making final decision regarding this issue until all other steps of the multilevel modeling process are completed.
Model 8	In this model, we moved from a cross-sectional structure to a panel/longitudinal structure by changing the assumption for the residuals' variance-covariance matrix structure. This helped to recognize an important new aspect of the nature of the data under consideration. That is the underlying correlation between observations for the same subject over time (i.e. the repeated effect). This in turn significantly improved fitting results as illustrated by the smaller AIC value (14,657.92). The significance of explanatory variables also changed. A closer look on the estimated variance-covariance matrix for the residuals (matrix 1) reveals a clear resemblance among the values for the off-diagonal terms. The diagonal terms also seem more or less similar. These observations suggest the possibility of using a simpler matrix structure, which can reduce the number of parameters in the model. Therefore, in the following model we attempt the simpler matrix structure. That is "Compound Symmetry."[a]
Model 9	Reducing the number of parameters by assuming a simpler variance-covariance matrix structure improved AIC results, since this goodness of fit measure penalizes for the number of parameters assumed in the model. It is also interesting to note that the resulting estimated matrix (matrix 2) is very close in its values for the unstructured matrix assumed in the previous model (matrix 1), although it is defined by only two parameters instead of 10 parameters. Only three variables in the model are statistically insignificant. These are *Perct_Limit_Number_88.58*, *Perct_Females_degree*, and *Perct_females_policy*, with the first two being the most insignificant. Therefore, in the following model we check the effect of removing them from the model.

Table 5.A.6. (continued)

Model	Key Related Comments/Interpretation of Results
Model 10	Again, reducing the number of parameters by removing the two most insignificant explanatory variables improved AIC results. It is also interesting to note the improvement in the statistical significance of the *Perct_females_policy* variable, with t-statistic now standing at 1.609 instead of 1.377 in the previous model. Although strictly speaking, this is still statistically insignificant (as it is $< t_{\infty,5\%} = 1.645$), we prefer to leave this variable in the final model. This is because (1) it is close of being statistically significant; (2) we also believe that it is important to leave at least one variable related to the gender of the insureds, as in general it is expected to be related to heath claims, especially that some benefit categories are applicable only to females such as maternity.

[a] It should be noted that some other structures for the variance-covariance matrix were also attempted. However, none of them outperformed the compound symmetry structure.

References

Albright, J. J., and D. M. Marinova. *Estimating Multilevel Models using SPSS, Stata, SAS, and R*. Working Paper, 2010.

Alexander, D., N. Hilary, and S. Shah. *Health Care Module: Private Medical Insurance*. Faculty & Institute of Actuaries, London, 2001.

Anderson, D., S. Feldblum, C. Modlin, D. Schirmacher, E. Schirmacher, and N. Thandi. *A Practitioner's Guide to Generalized Linear Models*. 3rd ed. Casualty Actuarial Society, 2007.

Beam, B. T. *Group Health Insurance*. 2nd ed. American College, Bryn Mawr, PA, 1997.

Brown, R. L., and L. R. Gottlieb. *Introduction to Ratemaking and Loss Reserving for Property and Casualty Insurance*. 2nd ed. ACTEX, Winsted, CT, 2001.

Comstock, S. J., and A. D. Ford. Estimating basic medical claim costs. In W. F. Bluhm, R. B. Cumming, and J. E. Lusk (Eds.), *Group Insurance*. 3rd ed. ACTEX, Winsted, CT, 2000.

Fielding, A. Module 8: Multilevel Modelling in Practice: Research Questions, Data Preparation and Analysis *LEMMA (Learning Environment for Multilevel Methodology and Applications)*. Centre for Multilevel Modelling, University of Bristol, 2010.

Foubister, T., S. Thomson, E. Mossialos, and A. McGuire. *Private Medical Insurance in the United Kingdom*. European Observatory on Health Systems and Policies, Copenhagen, 2006.

Frees, E. W. *Longitudinal and Panel Data: Analysis and Applications in the Social Sciences*. Cambridge University Press, New York, 2004a.

Frees, E. W. Regression models for data analysis. In J. L. Teugels and B. Sundt (Eds.), *Encyclopedia of Actuarial Science*. John Wiley, Hoboken, NJ, 2004b.

Frees, E. W. *Regression Modeling with Actuarial and Financial Applications*. Cambridge University Press, New York, 2010.

Frees, E. W., G. Meyers, and A. D. Cummings. Insurance ratemaking and a Gini index. *The Journal of Risk and Insurance, 81*(2): 335–366, 2014.

Frees, E. W., and T. W. Miller. Sales forecasting using longitudinal data models. *International Journal of Forecasting, 20*(1): 99–114, 2004.

Frees, E. W., V. R. Young, and Y. Luo. A longitudinal data analysis interpretation of credibility models. *Insurance: Mathematics and Economics, 24*(3): 229–247, 1999.

Frees, E. W., V. R. Young, and Y. Luo. Case studies using panel data models. *North American Actuarial Journal, 5*(4): 24–42, 2001.

Gelman, A., and J. Hill. *Data Analysis Using Regression and Multilevel/Hierarchical Models.* Cambridge University Press, New York, 2007.

Goldstein, H. *Multilevel Statistical Models.* 4th ed. John Wiley, West Sussex, UK, 2011.

Hammad, M. S. A. *A Primer in Multilevel Modeling for Actuarial Applications.* Paper presented at the 30th International Congress of Actuaries, Washington, DC, USA, 2014.

Hammad, M. S. A., and G. A. H. Harby. *Using Multilevel Modeling for Group Health Insurance Ratemaking: A Case Study from the Egyptian Market.* Paper presented at the Perspectives on Actuarial Risks in Talks of Young Researchers (PARTY), Ascona, Switzerland, 2013.

Hox, J. J. *Multilevel Analysis: Techniques and Applications.* 2nd ed. Routledge Academic, New York, 2010.

McClenahan, C. L. Ratemaking. In R. F. Lowe (Ed.), *Foundations of Casualty Actuarial Science.* 4th ed. Casualty Actuarial Society, Arlington, VA, 2001.

McClenahan, C. L. Ratemaking. In J. L. Teugels and B. Sundt (Eds.), *Encyclopedia of Actuarial Science.* John Wiley, Hoboken, NJ, 2004.

O'Grady, F. T. *Individual Health Insurance.* Society of Actuaries, 1988.

Orros, G. C., and J. M. Webber. Medical expenses insurance – An actuarial review. *Journal of the Institute of Actuaries, 115*: 169–269, 1988.

Rosenberg, M. A., E. W. Frees, J. Sun, P. H. Johnson, and J. M. Robinson. Predictive modeling with longitudinal data: A case study of Wisconsin nursing homes. *North American Actuarial Journal, 11*(3): 54–69, 2007.

Singer, J. D. Using SAS PROC MIXED to fit multilevel models, hierarchical models, and individual growth models. *Journal of Educational and Behavioral Statistics, 23*(4): 323–355, 1998.

Skipper, H. D. *Insurance in the General Agreement on Trade in Services.* Washington, DC: American Enterprise Institute (AEI) for Public Policy Research, 2001.

StataCorp. xtmixed: Multilevel mixed-effects linear regression. *Stata Longitudinal-data/Panel-data Reference Manual* (Release 11 ed.). Stata Press, Texas, 2009.

Steele, F. Module 5: Introduction to multilevel modelling concepts *LEMMA (Learning Environment for Multilevel Methodology and Applications).* Centre for Multilevel Modelling, University of Bristol, 2008.

Taylor, G. Non-life Insurance. In J. L. Teugels and B. Sundt (Eds.), *Encyclopedia of Actuarial Science.* John Wiley, Hoboken, NJ, 2004.

United Nations. *International Standard Industrial Classification of all Economic Activities: Revision 4.* Department of Economic and Social Affairs: Statistics Division, New York, 2008.

Werner, G., and C. Modlin. *Basic Ratemaking.* 4th ed. Casualty Actuarial Society, 2010.

6

Clustering in General Insurance Pricing

Ji Yao

6.1 Introduction

Clustering is the unsupervised classification of patterns into groups (Jain et al., 1999). It is widely studied and applied in many areas including computer science, biology, social science and statistics. A significant number of clustering methods have been proposed in Berkhin (2006), Filippone et al. (2008), Francis (2014), Han et al. (2001), Jain et al. (1999), Luxburg (2007), and Xu and Wunsch (2005). In the context of actuarial science, Guo (2003), Pelessoni and Picech (1998), and Sanche and Lonergan (2006) studied some possible applications of clustering methods in insurance. As to the territory ratemaking, Christopherson and Werland (1996) considered the use of geographical information systems. A thorough analysis of the application of clustering methods in insurance ratemaking is not known to the author.

The purpose of this chapter is twofold. The first part of the chapter will introduce the typical idea of clustering and state-of-the-art clustering methods with their application in insurance data. To facilitate the discussion, an insurance dataset is introduced before the discussion of clustering methods. Due to the large number of methods, it is not intended to give a detailed review of every clustering methods in the literature. Rather, the focus is on the key ideas of each methods, and more importantly their advantages and disadvantages when applied in insurance ratemaking.

In the second part, a clustering method called the exposure-adjusted hybrid (EAH) clustering method is proposed. The purpose of this section is not to advocate one certain clustering method but to illustrate the general approach that could be taken in territory clustering. Because clustering is subjective, it is well recognized that most details should be modified to accommodate the feature of the dataset and the purpose of the clustering.

The remainder of the chapter proceeds as follows. Section 6.2 introduces clustering and its application in insurance ratemaking. Section 6.3 introduces a typical insurance dataset that requires clustering analysis on geographic information.

Section 6.4 reviews clustering methods and their applicability in insurance ratemaking. Section 6.5 proposes the EAH clustering method and illustrates this method step by step using U.K. motor insurance data with the results presented in Section 6.8. Section 6.7 discusses some other considerations, and conclusions are drawn in Section 6.8. Some useful references are listed in Section 6.9.

6.2 Overview of Clustering

6.2.1 Introduction of Clustering

The definition of clustering is not unique. Generally, *clustering* is the process of grouping a set of data objects into cluster or clusters so that data objects within a cluster have high similarity in comparison to one another, but are dissimilar to objects in other clusters (Han et al., 2001). Usually a *similarity measure* is defined and the clustering procedure is to optimize this measure locally or globally.

It is important to understand the difference between clustering and discriminant analysis. In discriminant analysis, we have a set of preclassified samples, which could be used to train the algorithm to learn the description of each class. For example, we have a set of claims, some of which are fraud claims. These fraud cases are used to train the algorithm to find a rule that predicts the probability of fraud claims in future cases. However, in the case of clustering, these preclassified samples are not available. So all these rules have to be derived solely from data, indicating that clustering is subjective in nature.

With so many clustering methods available in the literature, it is a very difficult task to choose the appropriate method. Two considerations in selecting a clustering method would be the purpose of clustering and the feature of the specific dataset in hand.

6.2.2 Purpose of Clustering in Insurance

There are many reasons to use clustering in insurance ratemaking. First is for a better understanding of the data. After grouping data object into clusters, the feature of each cluster is clearer and more meaningful. For example, it is useful to cluster similar occupations and analyze their claim experience together.

Second is to reduce the volatility of data and to stable the rates over time. Because the amounts of data are usually limited over a certain period, historical data in each segment may show high volatility. In ratemaking, if analysis is only based on experience of each single segment, the resulting rates will be volatile. Appropriate clustering also alleviates this problem.

Third is to reduce the number of levels in rating factor. For example, in ratemaking for vehicles, it is possible to have rates for each individual vehicle type, probably because enough historical data have been collected over a long period. However, this may be difficult to implement and usually similar vehicles will be clustered together.

Fourth is to smooth the rates so as to make them more reasonable and interpretable. For example, in territory ratemaking, there may be marketing, regulative, or statute limitations, where adjacent territories should have similar rates. Some clustering methods may reduce the probability that the rate of one location is abruptly different to its neighbor area.

6.3 Dataset for Case Study

6.3.1 Description of the Dataset

In the case study we consider the territory clustering for ratemaking in motor insurance. The raw data we have are the geographical information in form of postcode, exposures, actual claim numbers, and other rating factors. All these postcodes are then translated into longitudes and latitudes. We focus this analysis on claim frequency.

In the United Kingdom, it is a normal practice to use postcode as a rating factor. The postcode is in a hierarchical structure, and there are in total about 2 million postcodes. This number is too large to analyze, so the data are first aggregated at the postcode district level, which has about 2,900 districts. However, this number is still too high for pricing, so the purpose of clustering analysis to group them into a relatively low number of postcode groups so that it is manageable in a pricing structure.

The difference between GLM (without postcode) predicted claim frequency and the actual claim frequency is the residual that will be clustered. More discussion of this approach is presented in Section 6.5. Samples of the residual are illustrated in Table 6.1. Columns highlighted in bold will be used in clustering analysis. These residuals are also plotted in Figure 6.1. The darker is the color, the worse (higher) is the actual claim frequency compared to the predicted claim frequency in the areas. Although overlapping, it is quite clear that there are clusters: London area and Midlands are worst in risk, while North and Wales are much better.

Table 6.1. *Sample of Data for Clustering*

Postcode	**Longitude**	**Latitude**	Exposure	Actual Claim Frequency	Predicted Claim Frequency	**Claim Frequency Difference**
AB10	**57.135**	**−2.117**	757	13.2%	19.0%	**−5.8%**
B1	**52.478**	**−1.907**	52	26.9%	17.3%	**9.6%**
SE2	**51.489**	**0.117**	539	18.5%	16.6%	**2.1%**

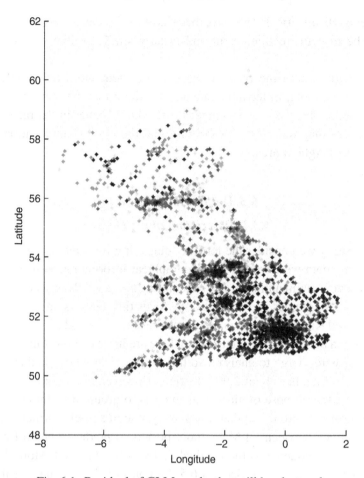

Fig. 6.1. Residual of GLM results that will be clustered.

6.3.2 *Nature of Insurance Dataset*

The nature of the data is also critical in choosing a clustering method. Usually the data type is numerical in the insurance context; claim frequency and severity would be good examples. Some information that is originally expressed in nonnumerical format, such as postcodes, can be translated into a numerical format. However, in some cases, such translations may not be possible; one example is occupations. In this chapter, the focus is on numerical data, or data that could be translated into a numerical format.

Second, insurance data usually are multidimensional; some are related to risk characteristics and some are related to the rating factors that need to be clustered. For example, in territory clustering, there may be one dimension of claim frequency and two dimensions of longitude and latitude. However, in most cases, the dimension would not be too high. It is well understood that high-dimensional clustering is very different to low-dimensional (Jain et al., 1999). The focus of this work is on low-dimensional clustering.

Third, the data would usually have a large amount of noise, because of the uncertain nature in insurance. Ideally, we should use expected claim frequency or expected loss in clustering. However, only the observed claim experience is available for analysis. This uncertainty should be considered in designing the similarity measure.

Finally, the insurance data may not be well separated, and the change between clusters could be gradual. For example, in territory clustering, the difference in risk characteristics between two adjacent areas usually is quite small. So the task is to find the boundaries where the difference is relatively large. This indicates that some methods that require the data to be well separated may not be suitable.

6.4 Clustering Methods

There are many clustering methods in the literature, and detailed reviews are briefed in Section 6.1. In this section, each method is briefly introduced, and the focus is on its applicability in insurance ratemaking.

6.4.1 Partitioning Methods

Broadly speaking, a partitioning method organizes the data objects into a required number of clusters that optimizes a certain similarity measure. In a narrower definition, partitioning is a method that is implemented by an iterative algorithm, along with a similarity measure, based on the distance between data objects. In the context of insurance ratemaking, the distance could be the difference in claim frequency/severity, difference in the numerical rating factors, or a combination of these two.

Generally, the algorithm of partitioning methods is to

1. randomly choose initial data objects as the center or representative points of the clusters;
2. calculate the membership of each data object according to the present center or representative points of the clusters;
3. update the center or representative points of the clusters, so that the total similarity measure is optimized;
4. if there is a change in center or representative points of the clusters, then go to step 2; otherwise, stop.

There are different methods depending on how the similarity measure is chosen and how the center or representative points of the clusters are defined.

6.4.1.1 k-Means Method

The center of cluster, m_i, is defined as the mean of each cluster C_i, that is,

$$m_i = \frac{1}{n_i} \sum_{\mathbf{x} \in C_i} \mathbf{x}$$

where $\mathbf{x}$ is data object and n_i is the number of data objects within cluster C_i. The total similarity measure is the squared-error function around the center of each cluster, that is,

$$f = \sum_{i=1}^{k} \sum_{\mathbf{x} \in C_i} |\mathbf{x} - m_i|^2$$

where k is the number of clusters.

This method is easy to understand and apply. The time complexity of this method is also lower than the k-medoids method. So generally, it is one of the most popular clustering methods. However, it is very sensitive to noise and outliers, because the mean of data objects in each cluster is used to represent each cluster. This is a big problem for insurance data, as outliers are always expected. It is also difficult to choose the appropriate number of clusters. This may not be critical though, because in insurance ratemaking, the number of clusters may be determined by other factors, such as IT limitation. The silhouette coefficient is also introduced to solve this problem by Berkhin (2006), Han et al. (2001), Jain et al. (1999), and Xu and Wunsch (2005). The results of k-means methods tend to be sphere shaped, as the squared-error function is used as similarity measure. This applies to most methods that use distance as similarity measure. This drawback is quite critical in territory clustering, as the natural clusters are not necessarily sphere shaped. Also, the k-means method doesn't work very well when the density of data changes. Finally, the efficiency of the k-means method is greatly affected by the initial setting, and sometimes it may only converge to a local optima. In practice, this may be solved by running the program several times with different initial settings.

6.4.1.2 k-Medoids Method

This is similar to the k-means method but defines the most centrally located data object of cluster C_i as center of cluster to calculate the squared-error function. Because of this, this method is less sensitive to noise and outliers. However, the procedure to find the most centrally located object requires much longer running times than the k-means method. This basic method is named the partition around medoids (PAM) method. Clustering Large Application (CLARA) and Clustering Large Application based upon RANdomized search (CLARANS) were later proposed to reduce the time complexity. However, these methods are subject to the same problems that the k-means method suffers from, as mentioned in the previous section.

6.4.1.3 Expectation Maximization (EM)

Rather than representing each cluster by a point, this method represents each cluster by a probability distribution. In step 1, each cluster is represented by a default probability distribution. In step 2, the probabilities of each data object belonging to every cluster C_i are calculated by the probability distribution representing cluster C_i. Then every data object is assigned to the cluster that gives highest probability. In step 3, the probability distribution is then recalculated for each cluster based on the new members of each cluster. If there is any change in the probability distribution that represents each cluster, then go to step 2; otherwise, the iteration stops.

The time complexity of EM is lower than k-medoids, but it experiences most of the problem the k-means suffers from. To make matters worse for the EM method, the choice of probability distribution gives rise to more complexity.

6.4.2 Hierarchical Methods

Hierarchical methods create a hierarchical decomposition of the given set of data objects to form a dendrogram, a tree, which splits the dataset recursively into smaller subsets. So the number of cluster is not chosen at the early stage of analysis in this method. The following are variations of hierarchical methods.

6.4.2.1 Agglomerative Nesting (AGNES) and Divisia Analysis (DIANA)

Both are earlier hierarchical clustering methods, where AGNES is bottom-up while the DIANA is top-down. In AGNES, clustering starts from subclusters that each include only one data object. Then the distances between any two subclusters are calculated and the two nearest subclusters are combined. This is done recursively until all subclusters are merged into one cluster that includes all data objects. In DIANA, clustering starts from one cluster that includes all data objects. Then it iteratively chooses the appropriate border to split one cluster into two smaller subclusters that are least similar to each other.

Slightly different from the object-to-object definition of similarity measures in partitioning methods, the similarity measure in hierarchical methods should be cluster-to-cluster. Different similarity measures of two clusters can be defined. Common similarity measures are as follows:

1. Min distance: $d_{\min}(C_i, C_j) = \min_{p_i \in C_i, p_j \in C_j} d(p_i, p_j)$, where $d(\cdot, \cdot)$ is the similarity measure of two data objects p_i, p_j and C_i, C_j are two clusters;
2. Max distance: $d_{\max}(C_i, C_j) = \max_{p_i \in C_i, p_j \in C_j} d(p_i, p_j)$;
3. Average distance: $d_{\text{avg}}(C_i, C_j) = \frac{1}{n_i n_j} \sum_{p_i \in C_i, p_j \in C_j} d(p_i, p_j)$, where n_i and n_j are size of clusters C_i and C_j, respectively.

The concept is easy to understand and apply. The resulting clusters are less sphere-shaped than partitioning methods but still have some tendency, because distance is used as the similarity measure. The number of clusters is also chosen at a later stage, which is better than partitioning methods. The performance regarding noise and out-lier depends on the similarity measure chosen. However, the most critical problem of the AGNES and DIANA methods is that the oversimplified similarity measure often gives erroneous clustering results, partly because hierarchical methods are irre-versible. Another problem is that the complexity of time, which depends on the num-ber of data objects, is much higher than that of the k-means method.

6.4.2.2 *Balanced Iterative Reducing and Clustering using Hierarchies (BIRTH)*

The key idea is to compress the data objects into small subclusters in the first stage and then perform clustering with these subclusters in the second stage. In the second stage, the AGNES or DIANA method could be used. In the literature, BIRTH is specifically named after the method that uses a tool called clustering feature (CF) tree (Han et al., 2001).

One advantage is that it greatly reduces the effective number of data objects that need to be clustered and reduces the time complexity.

However, it still tends to have spherical clusters because the similarity measure has the same definition as AGNES or DIANA.

6.4.2.3 *Clustering Using Representatives (CURE) and CHAMELEON*

The key idea of CURE is to use a fixed number of well-scattered data objects to rep-resent each cluster, and these selected data objects are shrunk toward their cluster centers at a specified rate. Then two clusters with closest "distance" will be merged. The "distance" can be defined in any way as in Section 6.4.2.1.

Compared with AGNES and DIANA, CURE is more robust to outliers and has a better performance when clusters have a nonspherical shape. However, all parameters, such as number of representative data points of a cluster and shrinking speed, have a significant impact on the results, which makes the CURE method difficult to interpret and to apply in practice.

In the CHAMELEON method, instead of distance, more sophisticated measures of similarity, namely, *interconnectivity* and *closeness*, are used. CHAMELEON also uses a special graph partitioning algorithm to recursively partition the whole set of data objects into many small, unconnected subclusters.

CHAMELEON is more efficient than CURE in discovering arbitrarily shaped clus-ters of varying densities. However, the time complexity, which is on the order of square of number of data objects, is quite high.

The ability to form arbitrarily shaped clusters makes these two methods quite attrac-tive in territory clustering. However, both methods are complicated to apply and there-fore not further developed in this chapter.

6.4.3 Density-based Methods

Most partitioning and hierarchical methods use the similarity measure based on distance. However, density could also be used as the similarity measure. An intuitive understanding of this method is that, for example, satellite towns around a big city can often be clustered with the big city, while rural areas are less clustered.

6.4.3.1 Density-Based Spatial Clustering of Application with Noise (DBSCAN)

This method defines the density of a data object as the number of data objects within a distance of each object. If the density of a data object is high, which means the data object is very similar to its neighbors, it should be clustered with those neighboring data objects. This is exactly the basic idea in DBSCAN method. After calculating the density of every data object, clusters are generated by several rules, where the basic idea is to expand every cluster as far as the density of the neighboring data object is higher than a threshold. Outliers will be discarded and not grouped to any clusters.

The advantage of this method is that it could find arbitrary shapes of clusters. However, the efficiency of this method largely depends on parameters chosen by the user, so it requires a high level of expertise to apply this method successfully. Also it does not work very well for large or high-dimensional datasets, because the time complexity is very high in finding all those neighboring data objects, and any intermediate results are not an approximation to final results.

6.4.3.2 Ordering Points to Identify the Clustering Structure (OPTICS)

Rather than producing a clustering of data objects for certain chosen parameters as in DBSCAN, the OPTICS method produces a cluster ordering for a wide range of parameter settings. The user then can perform clustering interactively by using the cluster ordering results.

In addition to the ability to form arbitrarily shaped clusters, this method solves the shortcoming of the DBSCAN method due to dependency on parameters. However, the OPTICS method still has all other problems that the DBSCAN does.

6.4.3.3 Density-Based Clustering (DENCLUE)

This method is efficient for large datasets and high-dimensional noisy datasets, and it can also find arbitrarily shaped clusters, which makes it suitable for insurance ratemaking. However, there are many parameters to set and that may be difficult to apply for nonexperts. Details of the algorithm are discussed in Berkhin (2006), Han et al. (2001), Jain et al. (1999), and Xu and Wunsch (2005).

6.4.4 Grid-Based Methods

These methods quantize the space into a finite number of cells, forming a grid structure, on which all of the operations for clustering are performed. The basic grid-based algorithm defines a set of grid cells, assigning data objects to the appropriate grid cell, and computes the density of each cell. After cells with density below a certain threshold are eliminated, clusters are generated by either combining adjacent groups of cells with similar density or by minimizing a given objective function.

The advantage is fast processing time, which is typically independent of the number of data objects and only dependent on the number of cells in each dimension of the quantized space. However, it usually has the disadvantage that the shape of the clusters is limited by the shape of the grids. Nevertheless, smaller grids can reasonably overcome this problem, which has become feasible nowadays because of rapid development of high-speed computers. So this is a promising clustering method for insurance ratemaking.

STING, WaveCluster, and CLIQUE are three advanced grid-based methods. Each of these methods differs in how information about data objects is stored in each grid and what clustering principle is used. STING explores statistical information; WaveCluster uses wavelet transform to store the information, while CLIQUE discovers subclusters using the apriori principle.

6.4.5 Kernel and Spectral Methods

Both the kernel method and the spectral method are relatively new methods. Although they are originated from different backgrounds, recently studies indicate that there is a possible connection between these two methods (Filippone et al., 2008; Luxburg, 2007).

The key idea of the kernel method is to map the data into a high-dimensional space, called the *feature space*, so that nonlinear features in the low-dimensional space become linear in the feature space. The conventional clustering methods introduced in previous sections are then applied in the feature space.

The main tools for spectral clustering methods are graph Laplacian matrices (Luxburg, 2007) and associated eigenvectors, which are widely studied in spectral graph theory. The original data are first transformed into a *similarity matrix*, which is defined as the matrix of similarity measures, and their eigenvectors. Then the conventional clustering methods, such as k-means methods, are applied on the similarity matrix or eigenvectors.

Kernel-based methods may be useful when clustering is based on textual information. Text kernels define a natural distance between different claim adjuster notes, for instance. However, although claimed easy to implement (Luxburg, 2007), it is actually not that easy to use for nonexperts. So these two methods are not further discussed.

6.5 Exposure-Adjusted Hybrid (EAH) Clusering Method

The choice of clustering method depends on the feature of the data and purpose of clustering. Most of the methods introduced in Section 6.4 could be used in appropriate situations. However, in insurance ratemaking, another consideration is that the method needs to be easy to understand and use. Based on this philosophy, this chapter is focused on how to modify the partitioning and hierarchical methods to accommodate the needs of insurance ratemaking.

The proposed EAH method is a combination of the partitioning and hierarchical methods. This method also adjusts the similarity measure by exposure to take account of the volatility of insurance data. The whole procedure, when customized to territory clustering, is as follows:

1. Use generalized linear model (GLM) technique to model the claim experience;
2. Calculate the residual of GLM results as the pure effect of territory;
3. Use partitioning methods to generate small subclusters that contain highly similar data points;
4. Use hierarchical methods to derive the dendrogram clustering tree;
5. Choose appropriate number of clusters and get corresponding clusters;
6. Repeat steps 3–5 with different initial settings to find relatively consistent patterns in the clusters;
7. Use the territory clustering result to rerun GLM and compare the results with that of step 1. If there is a large difference in the resulting relativities from GLM, then start again from step 1; otherwise, stop.

6.5.1 Comments on EAH Method

The purpose of steps 1 and 2 is to calculate the "pure" effect of the territory. Because of the correlation between rating factors, the effect of territory cannot be calculated by simple one-way analysis. A common approach is to use the GLM (Anderson et al., 2004). However, as the output from territory clustering usually will be fed into the GLM again to calculate the final relativities, there are two possible approaches:

1. Include all rating factors other than territory in the first GLM, and consider the residual as the pure effect of territory. Perform the clustering analysis and have the resulting clusters fed into the second GLM, including all rating factors.
2. Include all rating factors, including a high level group of territory in the first GLM, and consider the residual as the pure effect of territory. Perform the clustering analysis and have the resulting cluster fed into second GLM.

The problem with approach 1 is that the relativities of other rating factors will change between the first and the second GLM because the second GLM includes a new rating factor. Approach 2 has the same problem, although to a less extent. In both cases, it is necessary to compare the relativities of all the other rating factors between the two GLMs. If the relativity changes significantly, then the whole procedure should be repeated from step 1, and this iteration stops when the relativities don't change much between the first and the second GLM. Because in most cases approach 2 has a smaller number of iterations, it is better to take this approach, if possible.

Steps 3–6 are the clustering procedure. It could be replaced by any other methods in Section 6.4. However, whichever methods are used, the definition of similarity measure must be modified to accommodate the feature of insurance data. Usually, each data point has at least two types of data: one is the measure of geographical information and the other is the measure of claim potential/risk characteristics. The most common measure for geographical information is Euclidean distance:

$$g(x_i, y_i, x_j, y_j) = (x_i - x_j)^2 + (y_i - y_j)^2$$

where (x_i, y_i) is longitude and latitude of data object i and (x_j, y_j) is those of data object j. However, because of the curvature of the Earth's surface, some other definitions could be used. One such formula is the Haversine formula, which gives the shortest distance over the Earth's surface between two locations.

As for the claim potential/risk characteristics, claim frequency, severity, or burning cost can be used. However, since the claim severity can be quite volatile in most cases, claim frequency is commonly used. The similarity measure can be defined as Euclidean distance $(\mu_1 - \mu_2)^2$, where μ_1, μ_2 are claim frequencies. However, while Euclidean distance should be calculated by the expected claim frequency, only actual claim frequency is available for analysis. The uncertainty of the data must be considered in the definition of similarity measures. One solution is that, if it is assumed that every risk in both territories has the same variance σ^2, then the observed actual claim frequency μ_1 and μ_2 are approximately normally distributed with variance σ^2/E_1 and σ^2/E_2, where E_1 and E_2 are exposures in each territory, respectively. This assumption could be justified by the central limit theorem. So the variance of $\mu_1 - \mu_2$ is $\sigma^2/E_1 + \sigma^2/E_2$, which is used to adjust the Euclidean distance

$$f(\mu_1, E_1, \mu_2, E_2) = -\frac{(\mu_1 - \mu_2)^2}{(1/E_1 + 1/E_2)}$$

where σ^2 is dropped as it will be merged into the weight parameter introduced next.

Another question is how to combine the two measures. The solution proposed in this chapter is to use the weighed sum of two similarity measures:

$$g(\cdot) + w \cdot f(\cdot)$$

This weight w has to be chosen tentatively and subjectively.

In step 3, the number of small subclusters is chosen by the user. Because of the high time complexity of the hierarchical clustering method in step 4, this number cannot be too high. On the other hand, if the number of small subclusters is too low, the performance of the EAH method will deteriorate to the partitioning method. Some number around hundreds could be used, but the number should also depend on the clustering purpose and on features of the dataset.

The choice of the number of clusters in step 5 is also largely subjective and usually affected by other considerations, such as IT limitations or market practices. However, the general rule is to not put a threshold at the place, where there is only a small change in similarity measures. This will be illustrated later in the following case study.

6.6 Results of Case Study

6.6.1 Results of the k-Means Method

The k-means method is first applied. The results are plotted in Figures 6.2–6.5 for different settings. In all cases, 10 clusters are generated. Figure 6.2 plots the clustering results for weighting parameter $w = 1$, and Figure 6.3 gives the result for the same

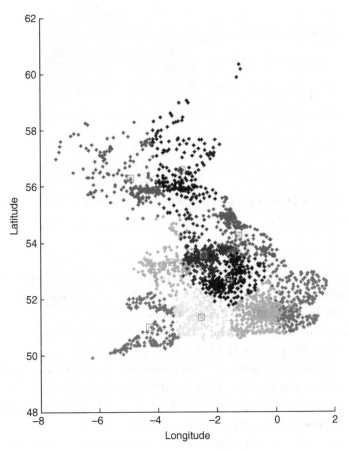

Fig. 6.2. Results of k-means clustering method with $w = 1$.

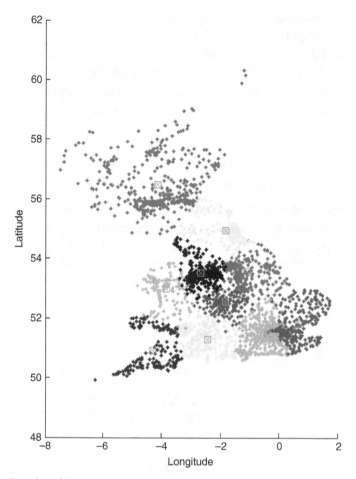

Fig. 6.3. Results of the k-means clustering method with $w = 1$ and different initial setting from Figure 6.2.

weighting parameter $w = 1$ but different initial settings. Although similar in the south, the results are significantly different in the north. It is very difficult to determine which one is better by looking at the initial dataset in Figure 6.1.

Result of $w = 0.1$ is plotted in Figure 6.4 and $w = 10$ is in Figure 6.5, and they have the same initial settings as Figure 6.2. The larger the parameter w, the more weight is put on the similarity measure in claim experience and the less weight is put on the geographical closeness. Figure 6.4 shows a much clearer border than Figure 6.2, while Figure 6.5 shows more overlapping. Probably the result in Figure 6.5 is not acceptable, but the choice between Figure 6.2 and Figure 6.4 is quite subjective.

These results highlight some features of k-means methods. The sensitivity to initial settings is a big problem, and the choice of parameters is also difficult. However, the

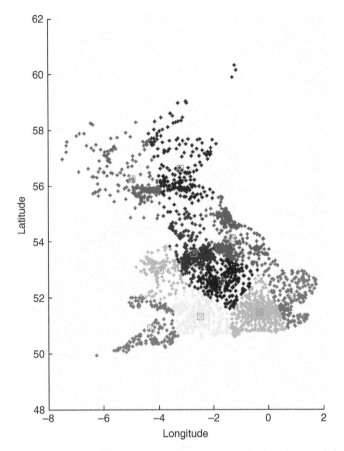

Fig. 6.4. Results of the k-means clustering method with $w = 0.1$.

dependence on parameters may not be a big problem, as Figure 6.2 looks very similar to Figure 6.4.

6.6.2 Results of the EAH Method

Here the results from each step of the EAH method are presented. In step 3, 200 small subclusters are generated. The output of center of each cluster is shown in Figure 6.6.

In step 4 of hierarchical clustering methods, AGNES, the average distance defined in Section 6.4.2 is used in the weighted similarity measure proposed in Section 6.5.1. The resulting dendrogram is shown in Figure 6.7, where the number of subclusters is not shown on the x-axis because there are too many to be shown in a readable format. The y-axis is the value of similarity measure at which two subclusters are merged, which is termed the *merging points*. The first 20 merging points are listed in Table 6.1. The first value is 29.0071, which means that if any two clusters with

Fig. 6.5. Results of the k-means clustering method with $w = 10$.

similarity measure less than 29.0071 can be merged, there will be only one cluster. Similarly, if any two clusters with similarity measure less than 4 can be merged, then there will be 8 clusters (because 4 is between 3.8875 and 4.7887).

In step 5, the number of clusters has to be chosen based on the dendrogram output. The general idea is not to put the threshold at the place where change in similarity measure is small. This is because, if the change in similarity measure is quite small, such as the gap between number 10 and number 11, 12 and 13, or 13 and 14 in Table 6.2, it is not very clear which two subclusters should be merged, making the results less reliable. Based on this rule, it is better to have 8 or 12 clusters in this case. The result of 12 clusters is plotted in Figure 6.8.

The whole procedure could be re-run from step 3 with different initial settings in the k-means method. Another possible result is plotted in Figure 6.9. There is still

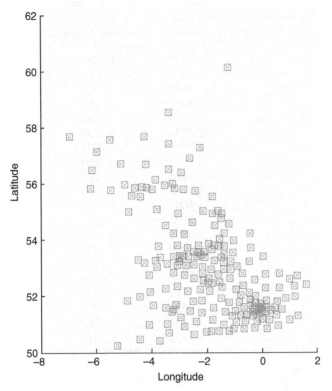

Fig. 6.6. Output from step 3 of 200 small clusters.

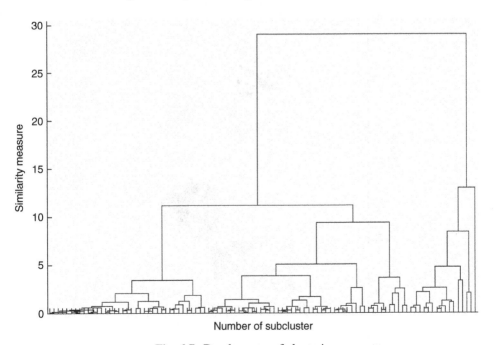

Fig. 6.7. Dendrogram of clustering.

Table 6.2. *First 20 Merging Points*

Number	Similarity Measure	Change in Similarity Measure
1	29.0071	16.0212
2	12.9859	1.805
3	11.1809	1.7825
4	9.3984	0.9691
5	8.4293	3.3747
6	5.0546	0.2659
7	4.7887	0.9012
8	3.8875	0.2687
9	3.6188	0.2026
10	3.4162	0.0561
11	3.3601	0.7895
12	2.5706	0.0205
13	2.5501	0.0402
14	2.5099	0.3665
15	2.1434	0.1108
16	2.0326	0.0013
17	2.0313	0.034
18	1.9973	0.177
19	1.8203	0.1282
20	1.6921	0.2814

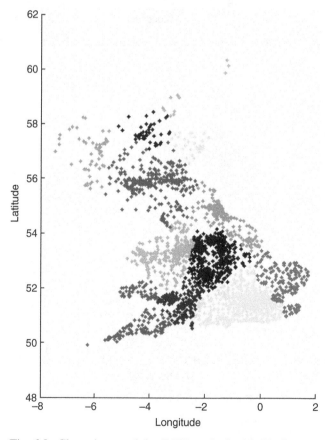

Fig. 6.8. Clustering result by EAH method with 12 clusters.

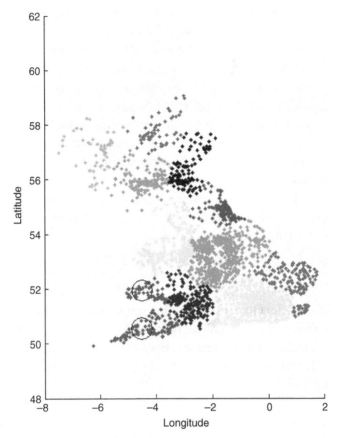

Fig. 6.9. Clustering result by EAH method with 12 clusters using different initial setting to Figure 6.8.

an apparent difference between Figures 6.8 and 6.9 which means that this method still converges to a local optimum. However, the difference is much smaller than that between Figures 6.2 and 6.3 in this case.

6.7 Other Considerations

In this section some other considerations in clustering are introduced and briefly explained. One common problem is the existence of obstacles and constraints in clustering. For example, in Figure 6.9, the two circled areas are not adjacent because of the gulf. However, when distance is used to define a similarity measure, they are very close. One solution is to introduce a distance function that includes this information, for example, the distance between any two points crossing the gulf doubles the normal Euclidean distance. There are other methods in Berkhin (2006), Han et al. (2001), Jain et al. (1999), and Xu and Wunsch (2005).

Whether to use claim frequency, severity, or burning cost is also an interesting problem. As explained in Section 6.4, there is a strong tendency to prefer using claim frequency. However, in cases when claim severity is different between territories, it may be more reasonable to use claim severity or burning cost. In such situations, the variance adjustment to the Euclidean distance could be different, and it could also affect the magnitude of weighting parameter w.

Finally, checking the effectiveness of clustering is also difficult. As illustrated in the case study, it is very difficult to compare the results from different clustering methods or from the same methods with different initial settings. One solution is to repeat the clustering procedure a large number of times and find a consistent pattern. Another is to check with external information, such as industry benchmarks. The third option is to split the data in half, using half of the data to do clustering analysis and the other half to test whether the same pattern appears.

6.8 Conclusions

Clustering is an important tool in data mining for insurance ratemaking. However, the choice of clustering methods is difficult because there are a large number of clustering methods in the literature and no conclusion which method is always best. The philosophy suggested in this chapter is to use as simple a method as possible, as far as there is no critical drawback.

Broad review of clustering methods shows that partitioning methods without proper modifications are not suitable for insurance ratemaking. Hierarchical methods have much better performance but are limited by high time complexity in calculation, so they struggle with large datasets. Advanced methods could improve the efficiency of clustering, but they may be difficult to understand and apply. So from a practical point of view, emphasis in this chapter is on modifying the partitioning and hierarchical methods to accommodate the needs of insurance ratemaking.

In the proposed EAH clustering method, the exposure-adjusted similarity measure is used to take account of the uncertainty of insurance data, and the k-means method is applied first to generate subclusters to reduce the time used in the hierarchical methods. Case study results show that this method could alleviate some problems of basic partitioning and hierarchical methods.

Because of the unsupervised nature of clustering, there is no definite best clustering method; other methods introduced in this chapter could give reasonable solutions in appropriate situations. Nevertheless, it is hoped that various considerations mentioned in this chapter could give some help to practical users of clustering in insurance ratemaking.

References

Anderson, D., S. Feldblum, C. Modlin, D. Schirmacher, E. Schirmacher, and N. Thandi. A practitioner's guide to generalized linear models. *Casualty Actuarial Society Discussion Paper Program*, 2004.

Berkhin, P. Survey of clustering data mining techniques. Technical Report, Accrue Software, 2006.

Christopherson, S., and D. L. Werland. Using a Geographic Information System to identify territory boundaries. *Casualty Actuarial Society Forum*, Winter 1996.

Filippone, M., F. Camastra, F. Masulli, and S. Rovetta. A survey of kernel and spectral methods for clustering. *Pattern Recognition*, 41(1): 176–190, 2008.

Francis, L. Unsupervised learning. In E. W. Frees, G. Meyers, and R. A. Derrig (eds.), *Predictive Modeling Applications in Actuarial Science: Volume 1, Predictive Modeling Techniques*, pp. 280–311. Cambridge University Press, Cambridge, 2014.

Guo, L. Appling data mining techniques in property/casualty insurance. *Casualty Actuarial Society Forum*, Winter 2003.

Han, J., M. Kamber, and A. K. H. Tung. Spatial clustering methods in data mining: A survey. In Miller, H., and J. Han (eds.), *Geographic Data Mining and Knowledge Discovery*. Taylor and Francis, London, 2001.

Jain, A. K., M. N. Murty, and P. J. Flynn. Data clustering: A review. *ACM Comput. Surveys*, 31: 264–323, 1999.

Luxburg, U. V. A tutorial on spectral clustering. *Statistics and Computing*, 17(4): 395–416, 2007.

Pelessoni, R., and L. Picech. Some applications of unsupervised neural networks in rate making procedure. *1998 General Insurance Convention & ASTIN Colloquium*, 1998.

Sanche, R., and K. Lonergan. Variable reduction for predictive modeling with clustering. *Casualty Actuarial Society Forum*, Winter 2006.

Xu, R., and D. Wunsch. Survey of clustering algorithms. *IEEE Trans. Neural Networks*, 16: 645–678, 2005.

7

Application of Two Unsupervised Learning Techniques to Questionable Claims

PRIDIT and Random Forest

Louise A. Francis

Chapter Preview. Predictive modeling can be divided into two major kinds of modeling, referred to as supervised and unsupervised learning, distinguished primarily by the presence or absence of dependent/target variable data in the data used for modeling. Supervised learning approaches probably account for the majority of modeling analyses. The topic of unsupervised learning was introduced in Chapter 12 of Volume I of this book. This chapter follows up with an introduction to two advanced unsupervised learning techniques PRIDIT (Principal Components of RIDITS) and Random Forest (a tree based data-mining method that is most commonly used in supervised learning applications). The methods will be applied to an automobile insurance database to model questionable[1] claims. A couple of additional unsupervised learning methods used for visualization, including multidimensional scaling, will also be briefly introduced.

Databases used for detecting questionable claims often do not contain a questionable claims indicator as a dependent variable. Unsupervised learning methods are often used to address this limitation. A simulated database containing features observed in actual questionable claims data was developed for this research based on actual data. The methods in this chapter will be applied to this data. The database is available online at the book's website.

7.1 Introduction

An introduction to unsupervised learning techniques as applied to insurance problems is provided by Francis (2014) as part of *Predictive Modeling Applications in Actuarial Science, Volume I*, a text intended to introduce actuaries and insurance

---

[1] The simulated data are based on a research database, originally constructed to investigate claims that were suspected to be illegitimate, such as staged accidents and inflated damages. The term *fraudulent* is generally not used in referring to such claims as claims that meet the definition of criminal fraud comprise a very small percentage of claims.

professionals to predictive modeling analytic techniques. As an introductory work, it focused on two classical approaches: principal components and clustering. Both are standard statistical methods that have been in use for many decades and are well known to statisticians. The classical approaches have been augmented by many other unsupervised learning methods such as neural networks, association rules and link analysis. While these are frequently cited methods for unsupervised learning, only the kohonen neural network method will be briefly discussed in this chapter. The two methods featured here, PRIDIT and Random Forest clustering are less well known and less widely used. Brockett et al. (2003) introduced the application of PRIDITs to the detection of questionable claims in insurance. Lieberthal (2008) has applied the PRIDIT method to hospital quality studies.

Breiman and Cutler incorporated unsupervised learning capability into their open source software for performing Random Forest. The current R implementation is the R library randomForest. Shi and Horvath (2006) provided an introduction to how the method works when applied to a tumor clustering problem, along with a tutorial for implementing Random Forest clustering. This chapter will apply the methods to questionable claims data.

7.2 Unsupervised Learning

"Unsupervised learning," a term coined by artificial intelligence professionals, does not involve dependent variables and predictors. Two common unsupervised learning methods, cluster analysis and principal components analysis, were introduced in Chapter 12 of Francis (2014) along with examples of implementation in R.

Why develop a model that does not have a dependent variable? To motivate an understanding of applying unsupervised learning in insurance, we use the questionable claims example. A common problem in claims is the absence of a dependent variable. That is, the claims data that are used to construct questionable claims models do not clearly label the records as to whether a questionable claim is suspected. Sometimes surrogates such as whether an independent medical exam was ordered or whether a referral was made to a special investigation unit (Derrig and Francis, 2008) can be used. Sometimes unsupervised learning is used to address this challenge. Two overall approaches are available:

- Use unsupervised learning methods to construct an index or score from the variables in the file that have been found related to questionable claims. Brockett et al. (2003) showed how the PRIDIT technique can be used to perform such a task. PRIDIT will be one of the methods used in this chapter.
- Use a clustering type of procedure to group like claim records together. Then examine the clusters for those that appear to be groups of suspected questionable claims. Francis (2014) showed a simple application of clustering to classify claims as into legitimate

vs. suspected questionable claims. Derrig and Ostaszewski (1995) showed how fuzzy clustering could be used to identify suspected questionable claims. The second method used in this chapter, Random Forest, will be compared to clustering.

If a variable related to questionable claims is in fact available in a dataset,[2] as is the case with the questionable claims data (both original data and simulated data), the unsupervised learning methods can be validated.

7.3 Simulated Automobile PIP Questionable Claims Data and the Fraud Issue

Francis (2003, 2006), Viaene (2002), and Brockett et al. (2003) utilized Massachusetts Automobiles Insurers Bureau research data collected in 1993. The data were from a closed personal automobile industry PIP dataset. The data contained information considered useful in the prediction of questionable claims. These data were the basis of the simulated data used in this chapter. We have used the description of the data as well as some of the published statistical features to simulate automobile PIP claims data. The use of simulated data enables us to make the data available to readers of this book.[3] Note that while we incorporate variables found to be predictive in prior research, our variables do not have the exact same correlations, importance rankings, or other patterns as those in the original data. The original data had more than 100 variables in it, but only a subset have been considered for inclusion in the simulated data.

In this chapter a distinction is made between questionable claims and fraud. Derrig (2013), in a presentation to the International Association of Special Investigative Units, went into some detail about the difference. Historically, fraud has often been characterized as "soft fraud" and "hard fraud." Soft fraud would include opportunistic activities, such things as claim buildup (perhaps in order to exceed the state's PIP tort threshold, allowing the claimant to sue for damages) and up-coding of medical procedures in order to receive higher reimbursement. Soft fraud has sometimes been referred to as "abuse." Hard fraud includes staged accidents on behalf of a fraud ring when no accident in fact occurred.[4] According to Derrig, from a legal perspective, for an activity to qualify as fraud, it must meet the following four requirements: (1) it is a clear and willful act; (2) it is proscribed by law, (3) in order to obtain money or value (4) under false pretense. Abuse or "soft fraud" fails to meet at least one of these principles. Thus, in many jurisdictions, activities that are highly problematic or abusive are not illegal and therefore do not meet this definition of fraud. Derrig believes that the word "fraud" is ambiguous and should be reserved for the category of criminal

---

[2] Note that the variables can be considered surrogate variables.

[3] A part of the research for this chapter was to develop a dataset that can be made publicly available for research on predictive modeling methods.

[4] See Wikipedia article on insurance fraud at http://www.wikipwdia.org/ and Coalition Against Insurance Fraud website, http://www.insurancefraud.org/.

fraud. Although a rule of thumb often cited is that 10% of insurance claims costs are from fraudulent[5] claims, Derrig asserts, based on statistics compiled by the Insurance Fraud Bureau of Massachusetts, that the percentage of criminal fraud is far lower, 1% or 2%. As a result of this, Derrig, and many other insurance professionals, use the term "questionable claims" rather than "fraud." Note that many of the references cited in this chapter (perhaps because they are older references) used the term "fraud" or "fraud and abuse" instead of "questionable claims."

Derrig advocated the use of predictive analytics to the questionable claims problem. Derrig and others (see Derrig and Weisberg, 1995) participated in assembling a sample of claims from the Automobile Insurers Bureau of Massachusetts (AIB) from the 1993 accident year in order to study the effectiveness of protocols for handling suspicious claims and to investigate the possible use of analytics as an aid to handling claims. The sample data contained two kinds of data: claims file variables and red flag variables. The claims file variables represent the typical data recorded on each claim by insurance companies. Thus, the claims data contains numeric (number of providers, number of treatments, report lag) as well as categorical variables (injury type, provider type, whether an attorney is involved, whether claimant was treated in the emergency room).

The "red flag" variables were particular to the study and are not variables typically contained in insurance claims data. These variables are subjective assessments of characteristics of the claim that are believed to be related to the likelihood it is or isn't a legitimate claim. The red flag variables had several categories such as variables related to the accident, variables related to the injury, variables related to the insured and variables related to the treatment. An example is the variable labeled "ACC09," an accident category variable denoting whether the claims adjustor felt there was no plausible explanation for the accident.

Based on concepts and relationships observed in the AIB data, a simulated database was created. The simulated data for this chapter has 1,500 records. The original AIB data has 1,400 records. The database contains simulated predictor variables similar (i.e., in variable name, and direction of the relationship to the target) to actual variables used in previous research from the original database, as well as a simulated target variable. The original data contained several potential dependent variables. The simulated data contain only one, an indicator variable that indicated whether the claim is believed to be questionable. An advantage of this simulated data is that it can be freely shared with others and can be used to do research on the methods in this chapter. Table 7.1 shows the red flag variables in the simulated data. Table 7.2 shows the claim file variables.

---

[5] See Wikipedia article on insurance fraud. The article cites the Insurance Information Institute, however, the Institute's website now refers to "questionable" claims rather than fraud and does not cite a particular percentage.

Table 7.1. *Red Flag Variables*

Variable	Label
Inj01	Injury consisted of strain or sprain only
Inj02	No objective evidence of injury
Inj06	Nonemergency treatment was delayed
Ins07	Was difficult to contact/uncooperative insured
Acc04	Single vehicle accident
Acc09	No plausible explanation for accident
Acc10	Claimant in old, low-valued vehicle
Acc15	Very minor impact collision
Acc19	Insured felt set up, denied fault
Clt07	Was one of three or more claimants in vehicle

The original AIB data contained two overall assessments from separate specialists as to whether the claim was legitimate or whether it was believed to have some degree of suspicion. The variables were in the form of scores, which ranged from 0 to 10 and 1 to 5, respectively. Note that these were subjective assessments, as the actual classification of the claims was unknown. For both variables, the lowest category (0 and 1 respectively) denoted a legitimate claim.[6] In the simulated data, a single binary variable "suspicion" indicates a questionable claim.[7] The variable is coded 1 for no

Table 7.2. *Claim File Variables*

Variable	Label
legalrep	Claimant represented by a lawyer
sprain	Back or neck sprain
chiropt	Chiropractor/physical therapist used
emtreat	Received emergency room treatment
police	Police report filed
prior	History of prior claims
NumProv	Number of health care providers
NumTreat	Number of treatments
RptLag	Lag from accident to date of report
TrtLag	Lag from accident to date of first treatment
PolLag	Lag from policy inception to accident
Thresh	Damages exceed threshold
Fault	Percentage policyholder fault
ambulcost	Cost of ambulance

---

[6] Thus both of these variables could be used to construct additional binary categorical variables indicating whether a claim was legitimate or had some level of suspicion of being questionable.

[7] In the original research, claims specialists created a multicategory variable indicating (1) probable legitimate or evidence of a questionable of the following kinds, (2) excessive treatment, (3) opportunistic fraud, no injury, (4) opportunistic fraud, injury, (5) planned fraud.

suspicion and 2 for suspicion of being questionable. Approximately one-third of the simulated records have a coding of 2, indicating some level of suspicion. This variable will be used in assessing the unsupervised learning methods but not in building the unsupervised models.

7.4 The Questionable Claims Dependent Variable Problem

Insurance claims data typically do not contain a variable indicating whether the claim is considered questionable. That is, even if the claims adjuster or other insurance professional considers the claim suspicious, there is no record in the claims data of that suspicion. Certain surrogate variables may capture information on some claims. For instance, many claims database contain a variable indicating that a referral is made to a special investigation unit (SIU). However, only a small percentage of claims receive an SIU referral (as these frequently represent claims suspected to be criminally fraudulent), so the absence of a referral does not mean that the claim was deemed legitimate. The absence of a target variable in most claims databases suggests that an unsupervised learning approach could be very helpful. For instance, if unsupervised learning could be applied to the features in the data to develop a score related to whether the claim is questionable, the score could be used to classify claims for further handling, such as referral to an SIU. The PRIDIT method is an approach to computing such a score from claim predictor variables, when a target variable is not present.

7.5 The PRIDIT Method

PRIDIT, an acronym for principal components of RIDITS, are a percentile-based statistic. The RIDIT transformation is generally applied to variables whose values can be considered in some sense to be ordered. These might be answers to a survey (i.e., disagree, neutral, agree, etc.), but the variables might also be binary categorical variables such as the red flag variables in our claims data, where one of the values on the variable is believed to be related to suspicion of a questionable claim and the other to a likely legitimate claim.

Bross in his paper introducing RIDITs states that in a number of his studies it could simplify complex data and make it possible to answer some of the investigator's questions (Bross, 1958, p. 19). The RIDIT statistic is considered distribution free. Bross states the term "RIDIT" was selected to have similarity to "probit" and "logit," two common transformations of categorical data, and the first three letters stand for *R*elative to an *I*dentified *D*istribution. It is a probability transformation based on the empirical distribution of data. He also views it as a way to assign a weight to the categories of ordered data and notes that the RIDIT may be assigned based on a "base group," say, healthy people in a study of a medical intervention. In the example in his paper, he used a 10% sample of his car accident dataset to calculate the RIDITS.

Table 7.3. *Calculation of a RIDIT*

Injury Severity	Count	Cumulative Count	Probability	Cumulative Probability	RIDIT
Low	300	300	0.3	0.3	0.15
Medium	600	900	0.6	0.9	0.6
High	100	1000	0.1	1	0.95
Total	1000		1		

For an ordered categorical variable X, where the values of X can be numbers (such as 1, 2) or qualitative values (such as low, medium, high), first compute the proportion of records in each category. Then compute the cumulative proportion for each value of X (going from low values of X to high values of X). The formula for the RIDIT based on these empirically based probabilities is

$$RIDIT(X_i) = P(X < X_{i-1}) + \frac{1}{2}P(X = X_i)$$

Table 7.3 presents an example of the calculation of a RIDIT for a theoretical injury severity variable following Bross's example.

A different version of the formula is given by Brockett et al. (2003):

$$RIDIT(X_i) = P(X < X_i) - P(X > X_i)$$

Note that Bross's RIDIT ranges from zero to one, while the Brockett et al. RIDIT can range from –1 to 1. Although these two definitions of the RIDIT score appear to be somewhat different, they actually behave similarly. The Brockett et al. RIDIT is a linear transformation of the RIDIT as defined by Bross. If one assumes that one-half of the category $P(X = X_i)$ belongs to $P(X < X_i)$ and one-half to $P(X > X_i)$, then the transformation $2 * RIDIT_{Bross} - 1$ produces the Brockett et al. RIDIT.

PRIDITs involve performing a principal components or factor analysis on the RID-ITS. This approach is distinguished from classical principal components in that the principal components procedure is applied to a transformation of the original data. Brockett and Derrig (2003) introduced this approach to insurance professionals and applied the technique to investigating questionable claims where it was found to be an effective approach to identify questionable claims. The data used in the Brockett et al. study were conceptually similar to the dataset we use in this chapter. However, the questionable claims data in this chapter are simulated, not actual data. As noted by Brockett et al. (2003), a useful feature of the PRIDIT method is that each variable in the PRIDIT score is weighted according to its importance. That is, when developing a score to classify claims, one wants to give greater weight to the variables most related to whether the claim is questionable.

7.6 Processing the Questionable Claims Data for PRIDIT Analysis

For the example in this chapter, all categorical variables were in binary form, where computing the RIDIT is straightforward. In general, for variables that originally have multiple categories that do not have any natural ordering, such as injury type, a method of creating ordered variables is needed. In this example the categorical variables were turned into one or more binary variables (such as sprain versus all other injuries). The numerical variables were binned into no more than 10 ordinal levels. In general, variables with no zero mass point, such as report lag, were split into even bins (in the case of report lag 5 bins) based on quantiles. Other variables with a zero mass point such as ambulance cost (many claimants did not use an ambulance and therefore had zero as an ambulance cost) were binned judgmentally, with the first bin (often with over 50% of the records) containing the zero records.

7.7 Computing RIDITS and PRIDITS

In general statistical software for computing the RIDIT transform of a variable is not widely available. According to Peter Flom of Statistic Analysis Consulting[8] SAS's Proc FREQ can do RIDIT. In addition, R has a RIDIT library. However, we were unable to adapt that function to our application requiring outputting individual RIDIT scores to claims records. Therefore we developed R code specifically for computing and assigning the RIDIT to each record.[9] The R code is available with this book on the book's website. The following is a snippet of R code that shows the computation of the RIDIT for one column of the original data (denoted mydata).

```
worksheet = data.frame(table(mydata[,i]))   # converts
results of frequency table to data frame
  temp = cumsum(worksheet$Freq)
  worksheet$CumSum = union(0,temp[-length(temp)])
# cumulative sum of all prior freq table entries
# compute the RIDIT
 worksheet$Ridit = (0.5*worksheet$Freq +
    worksheet$CumSum)/totalrows
  worksheet$Ridit_scaled = 2 * worksheet$Ridit - 1
```

Once the RIDITs have been calculated, principal components/factor analysis can be performed in virtually any statistical software package. We have used SPSS (factor

---

[8] http://www.statisticalanalysisconsulting.com/using-ridits-to-assign-scores-to-categories-of-ordinal-scales/.
[9] Some of the code used was supplied by Lee Yang.

analysis), the princomp, and the factanal function from Venables and Ripley (1999) show examples of the use of the R princomp function. Following is a snipet of code for computing the PRIDIT where the -RIDITs are in the dataset "riditsheet."

```
# use princomp to get the PRIDIT
# use data in data frame riditsheet
pca_out = princomp(riditsheet,
cor=TRUE,scores=TRUE)
# create scree plot
plot(pca_out, main="Scree Plot of PRIDITs")
# get loadings of variables on principal components
loadings<-as.matrix(pca_out2$loadings)
```

7.8 PRIDIT Results for Simulated PIP Questionable Claims Data

A PRIDIT analysis was performed on the 10 red flag variables and 14 claim file variables. A scree plot can be used to evaluate the importance of each factor or component from a factor or principal components analyis. The plot displays the amount of the variance of the data explained by each factor (component). Figure 7.1 shows that the first few factors explain a large percentage of the variability of the variables (i.e., of the RIDITs). The first component explains about 25% of the variability.

The loadings of each variable on each component can be output by the pca function. In this example, only loadings on the first component are shown. The magnitude of the loading of the RIDITs of the variables on the components informs us as to the relative importance of each variable. Table 7.4 displays the loadings on the first component for the top 10 (by absolute value) variables.

Fig. 7.1. Scree plot of principal components of RIDITs.

Table 7.4. *Component Loading*

Variable	Component 1 Loading
sprain	0.342
Inj01 (strain/sprain only)	(0.323)
Inj02 (No evidence inj)	(0.316)
legalrep	0.303
NumProv	(0.301)
NumTreat	(0.291)
chiro/pt	0.290
ambulcost	(0.219)
emtreat	0.212

From these loadings we can tell that injury (i.e., sprain) and treatment variables (number of providers, use of chiropractor) have a high loading (in absolute value terms) on the first component, along with whether the claimant has legal representation.

7.9 How Good Is the PRIDIT Score?

Brockett et al. (2003) used the suspicion scores assigned by experts in a confirmatory analysis of their PRIDIT results. In the original AIB data the scores were subjectively assigned. The PRIDIT method as presented by Brockett et al. (2003) used only the first component. Brockett et al. noted after regressing the scores on the claim file variables, that the apparent weights assigned by claims experts did not always agree with that assigned by PRIDIT. In their view the differences highlight a weakness of subjective scores. That is that there are inconsistencies between different experts making an evaluation with the same data, and the experts may under or overweight some variables when making a judgment involving many variables. They concluded that a value of the PRIDIT procedure is its ability to objectively determine the weights assigned to each variable based on the evidence in the data.

In the simulated data used in the PRIDIT example, the target variable has not been subjectively assigned but has been simulated from an underlying distribution, where on average about one-third of the claims are expected to be in some way questionable. For assessment purposes, the PRIDIT is taken to be the first principal component/factor[10] only. A quick analysis indicated that other components, especially the second, also had predictive value, though the value of second and higher components are not explored further in this chapter. Table 7.5 displays the means of the PRIDIT score for

[10] A factor analysis as well as a principal components procedure can be used to derive the PRIDITs.

Table 7.5. *Means of PRIDIT Score*

Report			
PRIDIT score			
Suspicion	Mean	N	Std. Deviation
0	.3255	1035	.91513
1	−.7245	465	.77588
Total	.0000	1500	1.00000

each of the fraud categories as measured by the suspicion variable. Note that there is a large difference in PRIDIT score for the legitimate group, denoted with a zero in the table, and the questionable claims, denoted 1 in the table,[11] as well as in Figure 7.2, which shows the mean of each group and 95% confidence interval for the means.

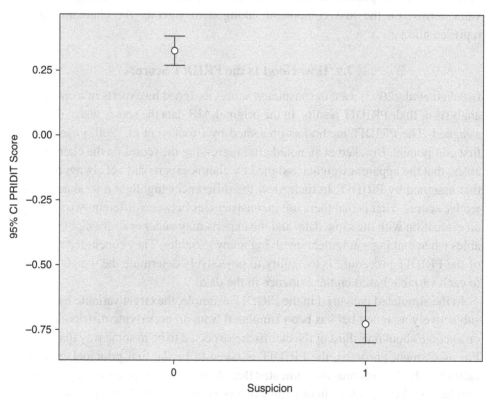

Fig. 7.2. PRIDIT score error bar graph.

---

[11] Note that the standard deviation shown is the sample standard deviation, not the standard deviation of the mean, which would be divided by the square root of the sample size minus 1.

The statistics indicates a strong relationship between the PRIDIT score and propensity for questionable claims. Note that the PRIDIT score appears to be negatively correlated with the probability of being a questionable claim. The nature of the relationship can be discerned by evaluating the relationship of the score to some of the variables. For instance, the average scores of positive records for the sprain injury

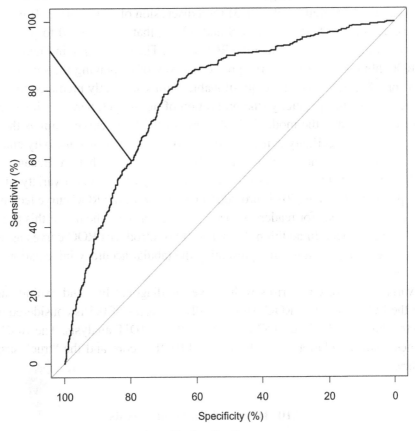

Area Under the Curve

Test Result Variabl(s): PRIDIT score

Area	Std. Error[a]	Asymptotic Sig.[b]	Asymptotic 95% Confidence Interval	
			Lower Bound	Upper Bound
.800	.012	.000	.777	.823

[a] Under the nonparametric assumption.
[b] Null hypothesis: true area = 0.5.

Fig. 7.3. ROC curve for suspicion category using PRIDIT as predictor.

category are negative as are the average scores for records that are positive for chiropractor/physical therapist use. Moreover ambulance cost is often negatively related to suspicion, as claimants truly injured in an accident are transported by ambulance to a hospital, but not questionable claimants. Both of these have been shown in other studies to be positively related to suspicious claims (Francis, 2003, 2012[12]).

A common tool in evaluating the effectiveness of a numeric predictor for accurately predicting a binary target variable is the Receiver Operating Characteristics (ROC) curve. See Gareth et al. (2013) for a discussion of ROC curves. R has several libraries, such as, ROCR, ROCwoGS and pROC, that can be used to plot an ROC curve and compute the area under the ROC curve. The ROC curve in Figure 7.3 used the pROC library. The ROC curve provides a way of displaying the sensitivity (the proportion of "true" target, here questionable claims, correctly predicted to be questionable) versus the specificity (the proportion of non-target, here legitimate claims, correctly predicted by the model.[13] In the case of the ROC curve 1 minus the specificity rather than specificity is used on the *x*-axis. Measures of sensitivity and specificity are sensitive to the threshold or cutoff point of the prediction. Because of this the ROC curves displays the sensitivity versus (1-sensitivity) at a variety of points for the predictor. Guillén (2014) provides an overview of the ROC curve technique in Volume I of this series for readers who are not familiar with the use of this procedure for assessing models. In addition, Francis (2003) introduces ROC curves as applied to insurance examples, after first presenting the tabular accuracy information and its limitations.

A variable whose curve rises well above the diagonal line and exhibits an area under the ROC curve (AUROC) substantially in excess of 0.5 is considered a good predictor. Figure 7.3 is the ROC curve from the PRIDIT analysis. The ROC curve indicates a strong relationship between the PRIDIT score and the "true" suspicion category.

7.10 Trees and Random Forests

Computationally intensive techniques collectively known as *data mining* have gained popularity for explanatory and predictive applications in business. Many of the techniques, such as neural network analysis, have their roots in the artificial intelligence discipline. One of the most popular of the data-mining tools, decision trees, originated in the statistics discipline, although an implementation of trees or classification and regression trees (C&RT) known as C4.5 was independently developed by artificial intelligence researchers. The classic book on trees by Breiman et al. (1984)

---

[12] The analysis in the 2012 study used real data, i.e., the original 1993 AIB data.

[13] Note that in predictive modeling, it is typical to use the ROC curve on hold-out data that were not used in building the model.

provided an introduction to decision trees that is still considered a standard resource on the topic. Trees use a recursive partitioning approach. DeVille (2006) provides an easy to understand introduction to a variety of decision tree methods, however, the illustrations do not use insurance data. Derrig and Francis (2008) provide an introduction to tree methods that use insurance data and are therefore appropriate for an actuarial audience. This reference is downloadable from the Casualty Actuarial Society's website at http://www.casact.org. Because tree methods are an important modeling tool, the reader is encouraged to read one or more of the references on trees. In addition, an excellent introduction to trees is provided in the chapter "Tree-Based Methods" of Gareth et al. (2013). This is also available for free: http://www-bcf.usc.edu/~gareth/ISL/. The book's website also provides examples of R code for the tree-based methods. Note that R code accompanying this chapter will also have examples of R code for trees used in this chapter.

Decision trees are run in two modes, classification or regression, depending on whether the dependent variable is categorical or numeric. A different loss function is optimized for each of the two modes. Derrig and Francis (2008) and Gareth et al. (2013) provide further information on the loss functions.

Many tree model software tools can output an importance ranking of the predictor variables in the model. We will be utilizing this feature later when we compare Random Forest (RF) clustering against classical clustering. Two reasons for the popularity of decision tree techniques are (1) the procedures are relatively straightforward to understand and explain and (2) the procedures address a number of data complexities, such as nonlinearities and interactions, that commonly occur in real data. In addition, software for implementing the technique, including both free open source as well as commercial implementations, has been available for many years. Another advantage claimed for tree methods is that the method is believed to be robust to outliers among predictor variables, as the cut point for the trees (for numeric variables) is based on ordinal relationships. Once a tree model has been fit, the relationships can be displayed graphically as an upside down tree. An example of the output of a tree used to model the dependent variable Suspicion (denoting a legitimate or suspicious claim) is shown in Figure 7.4.

Ensemble models are composite tree models.[14] A series of trees is fit and each tree improves the overall fit of the model. The ensemble model's prediction is a weighted average of the single tree predictions. In the data-mining literature, two common ensemble techniques are referred to as "boosting" (Hastie et al., 2003; Friedman, 1999) and Random Forests (Breiman, 2001). As boosting is not the focus of this chapter, it will not be discussed further. Random forest uses the ensemble method of

---

[14] Ensembles of other kinds of modeling methods can also be computed to improve performance over stand-alone methods.

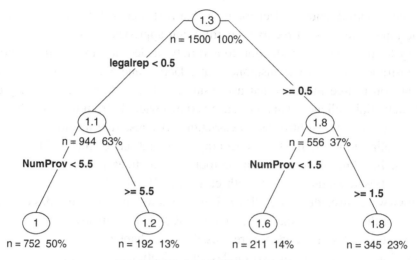

Fig. 7.4. Example of decision tree.

"bagging." Bagging is an ensemble approach based on resampling or bootstrapping. Bagging is an acronym for "bootstrap aggregation" (Hastie et al., 2003). Bagging uses many random samples of records in the data to fit many trees. For instance, an analyst may decide to take 50% of the data as a training set each time a model is fit. Under bagging, 100 or more models may be fit, each one to a different 50% sample. The trees fit are unpruned[15] and may be large trees with more than 100 terminal nodes. By averaging the predictions of a number of bootstrap samples, typically using a simple average of all the models fit, bagging reduces the prediction variance.[16] The implementation of bagging used in this chapter is known as Random Forest. Breiman (2001) points out that using different variables, as well as different records in the different trees in the Random Forest ensemble, seem to reduce the correlation between the different models fit, and improve the accuracy of the overall prediction. Derrig and Francis (2008) provide an additional discussion of the Random Forest ensemble method. Their research indicated that Random Forest, along with one other ensemble method (stochastic gradient boosting) outperformed the other tree-based methods tested on an insurance claims dataset. Note that Gareth et al. (2013) introduce Random Forest and supply examples of R code.

7.11 Unsupervised Learning with Random Forest

Random Forest can be run in two modes: supervised learning and unsupervised. The most common use of the Random Forest procedure is for supervised learning

---

[15] Pruning is used to reduce the size and complexity of trees and to prevent overfitting.
[16] Hastie et al. describe how the estimate resulting from bagging is similar to a posterior Bayesian estimate.

applications, which is not the focus of this chapter. Shi and Horvath (2006) provide an excellent overview of using Random Forest for unsupervised learning. When run in unsupervised learning mode, the Random Forest procedure can produce a proximity matrix. The proximity matrix is a measure of how similar one record is to another record. The measure is based on how often the records being compared are in the same terminal node of stand-alone trees. Keep in mind the Random Forest method produces an ensemble of single trees which are weighted together to produce a final prediction for each record. In computing a proximity measure each tree gets a vote. The total number of times each of two records being compared are in the same terminal node divided by the total number of tree is their proximity between the two records. This measure will vary between zero and one.

The proximity statistic just described can be computed whenever Random Forest is run as a supervised learning tool. To compute a proximity matrix in an unsupervised learning application a dependent variable is artificially created. This pseudo dependent variable is created as an artifact of creating a simulated or "synthetic" database that does not contain the structure, that is, the dependencies and interactions, of the original data. Shi and Horvath mention two methods of simulating the synthetic data. The most common approach referred to by Shi and Horvath (2006) as "Addcl1" in their paper is described as sampling from the product of marginal distributions. It is equivalent to independent sampling from each variable. This is as opposed to randomly sampling from each record where all values of all variables are used once the record is randomly selected. With independent sampling only one value for one variable of one record is selected with each draw. Thus the dependencies are broken and the "synthetic" data can be contrasted with the actual data in a supervised learning model. A binary variable is created that indicates which data the record is from (actual or synthetic), and a Random Forest is run as a supervised learning model with the binary variable as the dependent variable. From the Random Forest ensemble model a proximity matrix can be computed as described above. The proximity between any two records (i and j) can then be transformed into a dissimilarity using the following formula per Shi and Horvath:

$$d_{ij} = \sqrt{1 - p_{ij}}, d_{ij} = dissimilarity, p_{ij} = proximity$$

The dissimilarity matrix can then be used as input to a standard clustering procedure. In our examples, we use the pam (partition against medoids) function of the R cluster library, per the examples and tutorial of Shi and Horvath (2007).

7.12 Software for Random Forest Computation

For the analysis in this chapter, the R randomForest library was used. In addition to the randomForest procedure, a clustering procedure is needed. In this chapter, the R cluster library was used. An introduction to clustering and the R cluster library is provided in Volume I of this series by Francis (2014).

7.12.1 Application of Random Forest Clustering to Suspicious Claims Data

Random Forest clustering was applied to the simulated questionable claims data variables. When a dependent variable is not specified, the R random Forest function is run in unsupervised mode. The approach was as follows:

- The claim file variables and the red flag variables are input into the R randomForest function from the randomForest library.
- The number of trees was chosen to be 500 reflecting the recommendations of Shi and Horvath that many trees be fit.
- A proximity matrix was output.
- The procedure was repeated a second time to produce a second proximity matrix, per the recommendation of Shi and Horvath that multiple forests be run.
- The two proximity matrixes were averaged.
- The dissimilarity matrix was computed from the average proximity matrix.
- The dissimilarity matrix was supplied to the pam clustering procedure to perform k-means clustering.
- K = 2, 3, and 4 clusters were computed, and for each scenario the record was assigned to one of the clusters.
- For comparison, the pam function was used to run an ordinary k-means (i.e., not using RF) clustering on the predictor variables. The dissimilarities used in the classical clustering is the Euclidean distance measure.

The following snippet of code shows the computation of an unsupervised random forest using the dataset named datRF:

```
Suspicious<-
randomForest(datRF,ntree=500,proximity=T)
```

The "true" value for the suspicion variable was used in validating the clusters. An objective is to determine if one or more of the clusters created by the RF clustering and the Euclidean clustering seemed to have a high representation of suspicious claims. The two techniques of evaluation we will use are as follows:

- The chi squared statistic
  This classic statistic is used to evaluate when there is a statistically significant relationship between cross-classified variables. The higher the value of the statistic, the stronger the relationship between two categorical variables.

Table 7.6. *Chi Square Statistic for*
Random Forest and Euclidean Clusters

k	Random Forest	Euclidean
2	183	254
3	604	191
4	**715**	254

• The tree importance ranking of the different variables

Once clustering has been performed, the various clusters can be used as predictors in a tree model as seen in Figure 7.5, where suspicion is the dependent variable and the clusters are the predictors. The model will rank each variable in importance, assigning the highest statistic (and rank as first) to the variable which contributes the most to minimizing the loss function. Due to the small number of predictors in this test, a simple tree rather than a more complicated Random Forest model was used. The rpart function from R, which is a very common function from R used for tree modeling, was used.

The statistics were examined to determine which k (i.e., how many clusters) seemed to perform the best separation of records, and which clustering method (RF clustering or k-means clustering with Euclidean distance) performed best. Table 7.6 shows the chi square statistics.

The chi square statistic suggests that the Random Forest clusters for $k = 4$ groups do the best job of segmenting claims into groups based on the probability of suspicious claims. The table of the proportion of suspicious claims with each cluster is shown for the Random Forest and Euclidean clusters with $k = 4$ groups (see Figure 7.5).

The statistics for the Random Forest clusters indicate that a high suspicion cluster has 91% of claims that are suspicious and a low suspicion cluster has 2% of claims that are suspicious. Two other random forest clusters have somewhat modest mean percentages (17% and 24%). This compares to the Euclidean clustering where the high suspicion cluster has 54% suspicious claims and the low suspicion cluster has 5% suspicious claims and two moderate clusters have about 25% suspicious claims.

Table 7.7. *Proportion of Suspicious Claims by Cluster*

Group	Random Forest % Suspicious	N	Euclidean % Suspicious	N
1	24%	501	**54%**	536
2	2%	389	5%	365
3	**91%**	317	26%	390
4	17%	293	25%	209

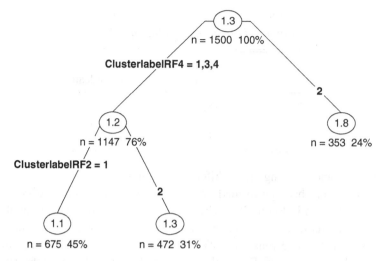

Fig. 7.5. Tree of suspicion of questionable claims and cluster. The value shown in each node is the average value of the Suspicion variable which takes on the value 1 for legitimate and 2 for suspected questionable claim.

In actual analyses using unsupervised learning, the data would not contain the independent variable so we would have to use the other variables in the data to subjectively label clusters as low, medium and high suspicion level groups. For instance, we could examine a table of some of the key statistics defining the clusters.

Table 7.8 indicates that the high suspicion (group 3) versus the low suspicion group (group 2) is characterized by a high proportion of claims involving sprains and the use of a chiropractor/physical therapist, a significantly longer treatment lag and lower proportion of claims meeting a tort threshold. Also the low suspicion group has higher average ambulance costs (presumably because the presence of an obvious significant injury leads to the use of an ambulance). The average number of treatments is higher for the low suspicion group, but these differences are not that large.

A simple Tree model was run separately for the RF clusters and the Euclidean clusters and then for both. The models were used to determine the importance ranking of

Table 7.8. *Descriptive Mean Statistics for Random Forest Clusters*

RF Four Group Cluster	Sprain	Chiro/pt	NumProv	NumTreat	TrtLag	Thresh	ambulcost
1	.83	.91	2.11	2.92	1.79	.84	62.81
2	.07	.31	3.32	4.52	1.61	.81	270.54
3	.88	.93	2.62	3.62	14.95	.31	203.58
4	.09	.30	5.98	8.72	4.55	.32	273.78
Total	.50	.64	3.29	4.62	5.06	.62	187.64

Table 7.9. *Ranking of Random Forest*
Clusters in Predicting Suspicion

Cluster	Rank	Statistic
RF 4 Group	1	88
RF 3 Group	2	8
RF 2 Group	3	4

each of the predictors. That is, if the cluster variable for $k = 2$ was ranked number 1 in importance, we have an indication that $k = 2$ is the best selection for classifying claims into legitimate/questionable classes. For the RF clustering, the 4-group cluster was ranked most important, while for Euclidean clustering the 2-group cluster was ranked most important. These ranking agree with those produced by the chi square statistic. When both the RF clusters and the Euclidean clusters were used as predictors in the tree model, the RF 4-group cluster was ranked first and the RF 2-group cluster was ranked second. The Euclidean 4-group cluster ranked fourth in importance, behind all of the RF clusters. See Tables 7.9 and 7.10.

The importance rankings were also used to compare the PRIDIT score to the clusters. The importance ranking is displayed in Figure 7.6. The tree ranked the RF4-group cluster as most important in predicting questionable claims, followed by the PRIDIT score. In general, these tests indicate that the two unsupervised techniques featured in this chapter outperform classical clustering in identifying questionable claims. Note that in a previous analysis (Francis, 2012) on actual questionable claims data, the PRIDIT score ranked higher than the RF clusters.

It should be noted that the Random Forest procedure can rank variables in importance to the (unsupervised) model. This ranking can be contrasted with the loadings from the principal components procedure used in the PRIDITs. The comparison, shown in Table 7.11, indicates significant differences between the two procedures in the importance of variables.

Table 7.10. *Ranking of Random Forest and*
Euclidean Clusters in Predicting Suspicion

Cluster	Rank	Statistic
RF 4 Group	1	115.0
RF 2 Group	2	5.3
RF 3 Group	3	3.7
Euclid 4 Group	4	2.9
Euclid 3 Group	5	2.7

Table 7.11. *Ranking of Top 10 Variables in Random Forest Clustering. Note this ranking is based on a single run of one of the two trees. Importance statistics can vary from one run of a random forest tree to another.*

Variable	Importance	Statistic
PolLag	1	90.1
Fault	2	76.6
ambulcost	3	68.9
RptLag	4	60.1
TrtLag	5	52.2
NumTreat	6	46.8
HospitalBill	7	37.5
NumProv	8	37.2
Acc10	9	18.6
Acc15	10	15.5

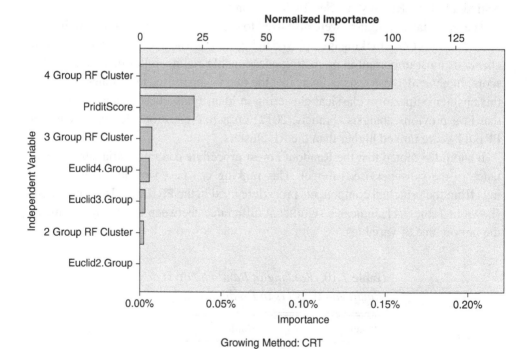

Fig. 7.6. Ranking of PRIDIT, RF clusters, and Euclidean clusters in predicting suspicion.

7.13 Some Findings from the Brockett et al. Study

Brockett et al. (2003) investigated a number of data and model characteristics in their 2005 study of the AIB research sample, including

- How consistent were insurance expert evaluations of claims; and
- How consistent was the PRIDIT score with adjuster evaluations.

The AIB data contained two different evaluations of the likelihood the claim was questionable (1) an assessment score (on a scale of 0–10) from a claims adjuster reflecting the likelihood the claim was questionable and (2) an assessment score from a fraud expert from the Insurers Fraud Bureau of Massachusetts.

Brockett et al. performed a regression analysis using each of the two assessment scores as a dependent variable. They found a relatively high spearman (nonparametric) correlation (0.78) between the PRIDIT score and the prediction from the regression on the adjuster's score, but a lower correlation (0.60) between the PRIDIT score and the actual adjuster's score. A similar pattern was observed between the PRIDIT score and the regression prediction from the investigator's score (0.64) and the actual investigator's score (0.49). Brockett et al. suggest that the adjuster and investigator regression scores are more objective evaluations as people have difficulty weighing together many factors at one time. The AIB data contained 65 red flag indicators that were used by the adjusters and investigators. Determining the weight to give to each red flag variable in an overall score can be a challenge, and different adjusters/investigators will assign different weights. Brockett et al. note that even though individuals may have difficulty weighing together individual variables the subjective assessments of insurance experts are needed to score the individual red flag variables. They also suggest that the lower correlation between the PRIDIT score and both the regression prediction and actual value from the investigators score is because the investigators focus more on criminal fraud as opposed to other kinds of abuse. They note some inconsistency between the adjusters' and the investigators' actual scores, that is, a correlation between 0.56 and 0.60. Brockett et al. also suggest that when assessing claims, the adjusters focus on information that will help them adjust the claim while the investigators focus on information related to legal fraud, thus their evaluation framework is different.

The Brockett et al. study findings appear to support (1) the value of analytic models for evaluating questionable claims, whether supervised or unsupervised, and (2) the PRIDIT method as applied to the AIB data appeared to produce a score that was consistent with scores obtained from supervised learning modes.

In this study the unsupervised learning methods have only been tested for consistency against a known (simulated) target variable. The data used for this chapter, because they are simulated, do not contain a variable capturing a subjective assessment of a claim, therefore comparisons like those of Brockett et al. cannot be performed.

Francis (2012) presented the results of applying PRIDIT and Random Forest clustering to the original AIB PIP claims data. That is, the methods were applied to actual as opposed to simulated data. The analysis indicated that the PRIDIT method outperformed Random Forest clustering and classical clustering, but that classical clustering outperformed Random Forest clustering.

The purpose of this chapter was to provide an instructional example of the application of advanced unsupervised learning methods. Therefore a dataset was used that can be shared with other researchers but does not contain all of the features of the original data upon which it is modeled.

7.14 Random Forest Visualization via Multidimensional Scaling

The randomForest package offers the user an option to use multidimensional scaling (MDS), which is a technique primarily used for data visualization. Typically, multidimensional data are reduced to two or three dimensions and then plotted on a graph. It is conceptually similar to principal components analysis, in that many dimensions can be reduced to the first two or three principal components and then plotted. However, unlike principal components, a distance matrix rather than a covariance or correlation matrix is typically used to reduce the dimensions of the data. The dimensions are estimated by the MDS procedure in such a way as to preserve as accurately as possible, the distances between records. Kruskal and Wish (1978, page 23) give the following formula:

$$\min \sum_i \sum_j (f(\delta_{ij}) - d_{ij})^2$$

That is, MDS attempts to minimize the difference between actual distances in many dimensions, and the distances in a smaller number, typically two- or three-dimensional representation of the original data. Once these dimensions have been fit, the data can be plotted. The function being optimized is often scaled, and a square root of the scaled function is taken:[17]

$$\min \sqrt{\frac{\sum_i \sum_j (f(\delta_{ij}) - d_{ij})^2}{scale}}$$

In R, classical MDS is implemented with the cmdscale function. The randomForest library contains a multidimensional scale plotting function MDSplot. Per the randomForest package description, the MDSplot function passes the compliment of the randomForest proximities (i.e., 1 − proximity) to the cmdscale function, to obtain the coordinates to plot. Figure 7.7 illustrates the application of multidimensional scaling to the questionable claims data. The shape of the points displayed on the plot depend

---

[17] See Kruskal and Wish (1978, p. 24).

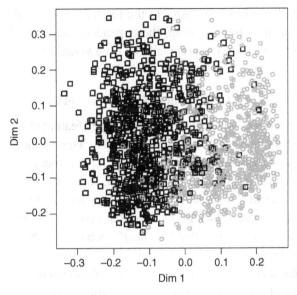

Fig. 7.7. Multidimensional scaling, symbol based on value of sprain.

on the value of the variable sprain (a circle = sprain, square = no sprain). It appears that more circles (sprains) appear on the right side of the graph.

For informational purposes, a graph with the symbol based on the value of Suspicion is also shown. This graph shown is in Figure 7.8, where a circular symbol denotes a legitimate claim and a triangle a questionable claim. The plot indicates that

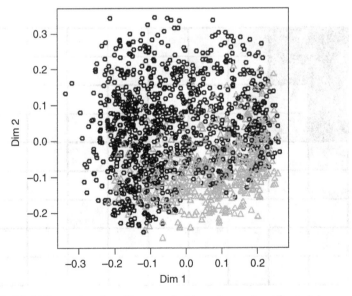

Fig. 7.8. Multidimensional scaling, symbol based on value of suspicion.

the questionable claims tend to cluster in the top left region of the graph. However, when applying unsupervised learning, the dependent variable will typically not be available and therefore would not typically be used visualizations.

7.15 Kohonen Neural Networks

Kohonen neural networks (also called self-organizing feature maps) are another unsupervised learning method used for visualizing data. This method is mentioned only briefly in this chapter to make readers aware of it. The method is typically used to create two dimensional graphs that, by inspection, can be used to find records that are "close" to each other in a statistical sense, and thus may be similar to each other in some characteristic of interest such as claims that may be questionable. An influence measure is used to allow records that are "near" each other to be moved close to each other on a two-dimensional grid. Any given claim can influence a number of units in a given region that it is "near" to. Like clustering, Kohonen networks use an iterative procedure. Unlike classical clustering it uses a nonlinear statistical measure to group process the data. The packages kohonen and SOM in R can be used to produce the Kohonen maps. Weherns and Buydens (2007) describe the kohonen package. Brockett et al. (1998) provide an introduction to Kohonen neural networks and show how Kohonen networks can be used to find questionable claims.

Figure 7.9 presents a conceptual example of a Kohonen network map that is not based on actual data. In the graph, each square is a "unit" of the network. The color of each unit is related to the value of one or more variables related to the target of interest.

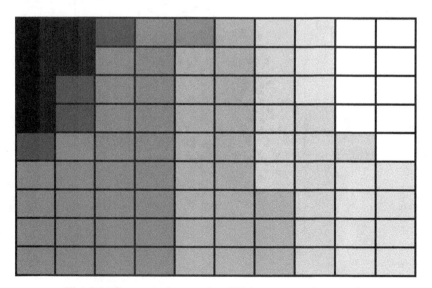

Fig. 7.9. Conceptual example of Kohonen neural network.

PIP Claims Data Feature Map Legal

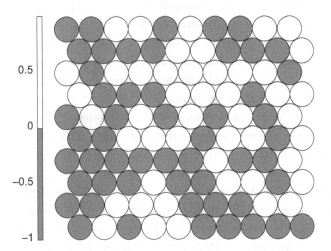

Fig. 7.10. Kohonen neural network map using questionable claims data.

For instance, in Brockett et al. (1998), the colors of the units were based on the sum of the weights[18] of binary red flag variables similar to those in Table 7.1. A value of 1 on each variable in the claims data was believed to be related to the likelihood of a suspicious claim. Each unit is assigned a value or weight for each of the red flag variables. Assuming a similar coloring scheme, the very dark region in the upper left of Figure 7.9 can be thought of as a region of claims likely to have a high likelihood of being questionable. The white region in the upper right can be thought of as a region where claims have a low probability of being questionable.

Figure 7.10 presents an example of a self-organizing feature map that used the data from this chapter and the R kohonen library. Each circle on the graph is considered a unit or "node" in a network. The graph is colored by whether or not the claims in the node involved legal representation, a feature related to whether the claim is questionable in this database.

7.16 Summary

Two unsupervised learning methods, PRIDIT and Random Forest clustering were applied to insurance data. One objective of unsupervised learning is to score records for characteristics of interest (such as suspicion of submitting questionable claims) in the absence of an identifiable dependent variable in the data. The illustration in this

---

[18] More precisely, it was based on the square root of the squared values of the difference between the unit's weights and the null vector.

chapter demonstrated the possible usefulness of PRIDIT, a principal components technique applied to the RIDIT transformation of variables and RF clustering, an ensemble tree based method that can be used for finding groups in the data. The PRIDIT score could be used to classify claims for further handling. Using RF clustering, one or more of the groups may be identified for follow-up action, such as request for an independent medical exam (to validate the claim) or referral to a special investigation unit (for investigation of abuse or fraud).

The "true" suspicion value was used in order to assess the unsupervised methods in this chapter. On the simulated questionable claims data, the R rpart library was used to build a tree model to predict questionable claims, with the PRIDIT score, the RF clusters and classical Euclidean clusters as predictors. One of the outputs of the tree model is a ranking of the variables in importance in predicting the target. Both RF clustering and the PRIDIT method performed well in the testing and both outperformed classical Euclidean clustering in identifying questionable claims. Similar results were found by Francis (2012) when applied to the actual 1993 AIB data rather than simulated data.

A useful feature of the PRIDIT method is that it produces a single score that can be used to sort claims on questionableness (or on some other feature of interest to a business). The Random Forest clustering method does not have this feature,[19] and further analysis using descriptive statistics from the variables used for clustering is required to identify the clusters that contain questionable claims.

References

Aldender, M., and R. Bscorelashfield. *Cluster Analysis*. Sage, Thousand Oaks, CA, 1984.

Breiman, L. Random Forests. *Machine Learning*, 45(1): 5–32, 2001. Also available at https://www.stat.berkeley.edu/~breiman/randomforest2001.pdf.

Breiman, L., A. Cutler, and W. Liaw. Package randomForest. http://www.r-project.org/.

Breiman, L., J. H. Friedman, R. Olshen, and C. Stone. *Classification and Regression Trees*, Chapman and Hall/CRC, Boca Raton, FL, 1984.

Brockett, P. L., R. A. Derrig, L. L. Golden, A. Levine, and M. Alpert. Fraud classification using principal component analysis of RIDITs. *Journal of Risk and Insurance*, 69(3): 341–371, 2003.

Brockett, P., and A. Levine. On a characterization of RIDITS. *Annals of Statistics*, 5(6): 1245–1248, 1977.

Brockett, P., X. Xia, and R. Derrig. Use of Kohonen's self organized feature maps to uncover automobiler bodily injury claims fraud. *Journal of Risk and Insurance*, 65(2): 245–274, 1998.

Bross, I. How to use Ridit analysis. *Biometrics*, 14(1): 18–38, 1958.

Coaley, K. *An Introduction to Psychological Assessment and Psychometrics*, Sage, Thousand Oaks, CA, 2010.

---

[19] The multidimensional scaling feature of randomForest could be used to compute "scales." This approach has not been investigated as a method for computing a "score" that might be used to predict which claims are questionable.

Derrig, R. Using predictive analytics to uncover questionable claims. Presentation to the International Association of Special Investigative Units, 2013.

Derrig, R. and L. Francis. Distinguishing the forest from the trees. *Variance*, 2: 184–208, 2008. Available at: http://www.casact.org/research/dare/index.cfm?fa=view&abstrID=6511.

Derrig, R. and K. Ostaszewski. Fuzzy techniques of pattern recognition in risk and claim classification. *Journal of Risk and Insurance*, 62(3): 447–482, 1995.

Derrig R., and H. Weisberg. A report on the AIB Study of 1993 PIP Claims, Part 1, Identification and investigation of suspicious claims. Automobile Insurers Bureau of Massachusetts, 1995.

DeVille, B. *Decision Trees for Business Intelligence and Data Mining*, SAS Institute, 2006.

Francis, L. Martian Chronicles: Is MARS better than neural networks. 2003 CAS Winter Forum, 2003. http://www.casact.org/research/dare/index.cfm?fa=view&abstrID=5293.

Francis, L. Review of PRIDIT. Presentation at CAS Ratemaking Seminar, 2006.

Francis, L. Unsupervised learning applied to insurance data, Salford Data Mining Conference, 2012.

Francis, L. Unsupervised learning. In E. W. Frees, G. Meyers, and R. A. Derrig (eds.), *Predictive Modeling Applications in Actuarial Science: Volume 1, Predictive Modeling Techniques*, pp. 280–311. Cambridge University Press, Cambridge, 2014.

Friedman, J. Stochastic gradient boosting. http://statweb.stanford.edu/~jhf/ftp/stobst.pdf, 1999.

Gareth, J., D. Witten, T. Hastie, and R. Tibshirini. *An Introduction to Statistical Learning*. Springer, New York, 2013.

Guillén, M. Regression with categorical dependent variables. In E. W. Frees, G. Meyers, and R. A. Derrig (eds.), *Predictive Modeling Applications in Actuarial Science: Volume I, Predictive Modeling Techniques*, pp. 65–86. Cambridge University Press, Cambridge, 2014.

Hastie, T., R. Tibshirani, and J. Friedman. *The Elements of Statistical Learning*. Springer, New York, 2003.

Insurance Information Institute. Information on fraud. http://www.iii.org/facts_statistics/fraud.html.

James, G., D. Witten, T. Hastie, and R. Tibshirani. *An Introduction to Statistical Learning with Applications in R*. Springer, New York, 2013.

Kaufman, L., and P. Rousseeuw. *Finding Groups in Data*. John Wiley, New York, 1990.

Kim, J., and C. W. Mueller. *Factor Analysis: Statistical Methods and Practical Issues*, Sage, Thousand Oaks, CA, 1978.

Kruskal, J. and M. Wish. Multidimensional Scaling. Sage University Press, 1978.

Lieberthal, D. R. Hospital quality: A PRIDIT approach. *Health Services Research*, 43(3): 988–1005, 2008.

Maechler, M. Package "cluster," 2012. www.r-project.org.

Shi, T., and S. Horvath. Unsupervised learning with Random Forest predictors. *Journal of Computational and Graphical Statistics*, 15(1): 118–138, 2006.

Shi, T., and S. Horvath. A Tutorial for RF Clustering, 2007. ftp://labs.genetics.ucla.edu/horvath/RFclustering/RFclustering.htm.

Smith, L. A tutorial on principal components. http://www.sccg.sk/~haladova/principal_components.pdf, 2002.

Venables, W., and B. Ripley. *Modern Applied Statistics with S-PLUS*, Springer, New York, 1999.

Viaene, S. Learning to detect fraud from enriched insurance claims data: Context, theory and application, PhD dissertation, KatholiekeUniversiteit Leuven, 2002.

Weherns, R., and L. Buydens. Self and supervised maps in R. *Journal of Statistical Software*, 21(5), 2007.

8

The Predictive Distribution of Loss Reserve Estimates over a Finite Time Horizon

Glenn Meyers

Chapter Preview. This chapter shows how to take the output of a Bayesian MCMC stochastic loss reserve model and calculate the predictive distribution of the estimates of the expected loss over a finite time horizon. Then given a 99.5% VaR regulatory capital requirement, it shows how to calculate the regulatory capital for a one-, two-, and three-year time horizon.

As an insurer gathers more data on its loss development in subsequent calendar years, this chapter finds that in most cases, it can release capital to its investors over time. But in other cases it will have to add capital in subsequent years. In keeping with the 99.5% VaR criterion, it finds that for many insurers, this additional capital can be substantial. As capital becomes more expensive to the stressed insurer, it might be prudent capital management for an insurer to voluntarily raise that capital in advance. This chapter shows one way to calculate the amount of voluntary capital that will be needed to satisfy the 99.5% VaR requirement for the next calendar year.

8.1 Introduction

In Meyers (2015) I applied Bayesian Markov chain Monte Carlo (MCMC) models to stochastic loss reserving problems. The goal there was to predict the distribution of outcomes after ten years of development. The focus of that monograph was to test how well those models predicted the distribution of outcomes on a large number of loss development triangles that are reported in Schedule P of the National Association of Insurance Commissioners (NAIC) annual statements. The monograph identifies two models, the correlated chain ladder (CCL) model and the changing settlement rate (CSR) models as the best performers on incurred loss triangles and paid loss triangles, respectively. This chapter will focus on the CCL model on incurred loss triangles.

While the time frame of 10 years of development is good for testing models, operationally it is of little use. Insurance executives and regulators have a much shorter time frame. We see evidence of that concern in the 99.5% value of risk (VaR) over a one-year time horizon specified by Solvency II for calculating the amount of capital to support the loss reserve liability.[1] One rationale for the one-year time frame that I heard was that insurers have the opportunity make adjustments as time passes.

What gets posted at the end of one year is not the ultimate loss. Instead one posts the estimate of the ultimate loss given one more year of data. As pointed out in Ohlssona and Lauzeningksb (2009), one needs to get the predictive distribution of the estimates to calculate the amount of capital to support the loss reserve. Merz and Wüthrich (2008) give a formula to calculate the range of estimates for the chain ladder model.

Given a loss triangle and the assumptions underlying the model, a Bayesian MCMC model produces (say) 10,000 equally likely scenarios consisting of the underlying parameters of the model. One can use one of the scenarios to simulate the possible future developments of the loss triangle. Using the simulated losses, one can then use the MCMC model to get one future estimate of the ultimate losses. Repeating this exercise 10,000 times gives the distribution of loss estimates. If it takes a minute to get a single estimate, getting 10,000 estimates would take about a week to run.

This chapter describes a much faster approach. This approach takes a simulated set of losses and using Bayes's theorem, it calculates the posterior probability of each of the 10,000 scenarios given those simulated losses. Using the parameters of each scenario, it then calculates ultimate loss estimate as the posterior probability weighted expected value of the ultimate losses for each of the 10,000 scenarios. Repeating this calculation 10,000 times, which runs in a matter of minutes in the current computing environment, gives a predictive distribution of ultimate loss estimates.

The simulated set of losses can consist of losses from the next calendar year or, for that matter, losses in the next n calendar years.

At the time the European Union was formulating Solvency II requirements in the mid-2000s, I heard a number of concerns voiced at the International Actuarial Association meetings about the one-year time horizon as applied to nonlife insurance. The argument given against the one-year time horizon was that nonlife reserves were too volatile to get reliable estimates after one year. If an upward development is indicated after one year, the cost of raising additional capital can become much higher for a stressed insurer. It can be significantly less expensive to raise the capital in advance a significant upward development. But as time progressed, the insurers' operational desire for a short time horizon seems to have won out. The internet searches

---

[1] The complete text of the Solvency II Framework Directive can be found at the EIOPA website at https://eiopa.europa.eu/en/activities/insurance/solvency-ii/index.html. The part of the directive that is relevant to this chapter is in Articles 77 and 104 of the Framework Directive.

I have done on the subject of Solvency II have yielded many conference presentations on how to implement Solvency II, and nothing that questions the one-year time horizon.

This chapter will use the model and revisit the one-year time horizon. Given an insurer's loss triangle, it will calculate how often and by how much capital will have to be raised under the Solvency II requirement. Here is a high-level summary of the findings:

- As new data come in over time, the amount of capital needed to support the liability under the Solvency II requirement usually decreases. In most of scenarios, the insurer need not add capital even if the ultimate loss estimate increases.
- In other scenarios the estimate of the liability and/or the capital needed to support it increase to the point where it is likely to need additional capital.
- The relative probabilities of the preceding two cases vary significantly by insurer, requiring minimal additions to capital for some insurers and significant additions for others.

Despite these results, I do not anticipate that the European Union will change the capital requirements for Solvency II. However, we should note that insurers often carry capital in excess of the regulatory capital. I expect the ideas put forth in this chapter will help insurers determine how much capital they need to have to avoid the costly process of obtaining additional capital in the upcoming years.

8.2 The CAS Loss Reserve Database

The calculations described in this chapter will be illustrated with cumulative incurred loss triangles taken from the CAS Loss Reserve Database. This database consists of a sample of 10×10 triangles taken from the 1997 NAIC Schedule P database. This database, along with a complete description of how it was constructed and how the insurers were selected, is available on the CAS website at http://www.casact.org/research/index.cfm?fa=loss_reserves_data.

The calculations described in this chapter will be illustrated with the loss triangles in Table 8.1. As can be seen in Figure 8.1, Triangle 1 exhibits the usual upward loss development pattern. Triangle 2 exhibits an unusual downward loss development pattern with a fairly high degree of volatility.

The following sections will also provide graphics of summary statistics for 200 insurers, 50 each from the commercial auto, personal auto, workers' compensation, and other liability lines of business. The criteria for selecting these insurers is based on stability of earned premium and stability of the net to direct premium ratio. These are the same 200 insurers I used in Meyers (2015). Appendix B of that monograph provides more detail on the criteria used for selecting the insurers.

Table 8.1. *Illustrative Triangles*

					Triangle 1					
AY\Lag	1	2	3	4	5	6	7	8	9	10
1988	1722	3830	3603	3835	3873	3895	3918	3918	3917	3917
1989	1581	2192	2528	2533	2528	2530	2534	2541	2538	
1990	1834	3009	3488	4000	4105	4087	4112	4170		
1991	2305	3473	3713	4018	4295	4334	4343			
1992	1832	2625	3086	3493	3521	3563				
1993	2289	3160	3154	3204	3190					
1994	2881	4254	4841	5176						
1995	2489	2956	3382							
1996	2541	3307								
1997	2203									

					Triangle 2					
AY\Lag	1	2	3	4	5	6	7	8	9	10
1988	44422	41170	40192	40318	39302	37681	35674	31972	30057	27491
1989	39041	40654	39745	39335	37406	35638	31998	30467	27548	
1990	43581	41868	40551	40625	38934	34364	31878	31849		
1991	49754	50523	50020	48611	43222	40609	39510			
1992	50468	52047	50620	47177	44698	43396				
1993	61520	60053	57803	56699	56883					
1994	72661	69873	68106	68518						
1995	80297	77550	74040							
1996	73544	75130								
1997	63309									

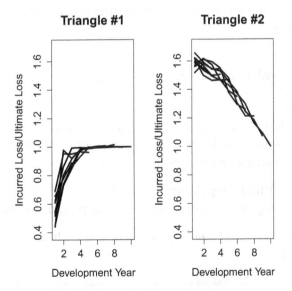

Fig. 8.1. Loss development patterns.

8.3 The Correlated Chain Ladder Model

Let $C_{w,d}$ denote the accumulated incurred loss amount for accident year, w, and development lag, d, for $1 \leq w \leq K$ and $1 \leq d \leq K$. $C_{w,d}$ is known for the "triangle" of data specified by $w + d \leq K + 1$. The goal of a loss reserve model is to estimate the loss amounts in the last column of data, $C_{w,K}$ for $w = 2, \ldots, K$.[2]

In this chapter $K = 10$ for our data. Let's also assume that $C_{w,10}$ is the ultimate loss for accident year w. While reserving actuaries are rightly concerned with loss development beyond the 10th year, very few Bayesian MCMC models deal with this since most publicly available loss triangles stop after 10 years. Is should be possible to do Bayesian MCMC analyses by making some tail factor assumptions. Researchers who want to develop such a model could start by reading Clark (2003).

One of the key findings reported in Meyers (2015) was that the currently popular Mack (1993, 1994) model underestimates the variability of the distribution of the outcomes. The observation that the Mack model underestimated the variability of the ultimate loss estimates, suggested a direction to go in order to fix it. Here are two ways to improve the recognition of the inherent variability of the predictive distribution:

1. The Mack model multiplies the age to age factors by the last observed loss, $C_{w,11-w}$. One can think of the last observed losses as fixed level parameters. A model that treats the level of the accident year as random will predict more variability.
2. The Mack model assumes that the loss amounts for different accident years are independent. A model that allows for correlation between accident years could increase the standard deviation of $\sum_{w=1}^{10} \widetilde{C}_{w,10}$.

I then proposed the CCL model and demonstrated that it validates on the holdout, lower triangle, data.

Let

1. Each $\alpha_w \sim$ normal $(\log(Premium_w) + logelr, \sqrt{10})$ where the parameter $logelr \sim$ uniform $(-1, 0.5)$;
2. $\mu_{1,d} = \alpha_1 + \beta_d$;
3. $\mu_{w,d} = \alpha_w + \beta_d + \rho \cdot (\log(C_{w-1,d}) - \mu_{w-1,d})$ for $w > 1$;
4. $\widetilde{C}_{w,d}$ has a lognormal distribution with log mean $\mu_{w,d}$ and log standard deviation σ_d subject to the constraint that $\sigma_1 > \sigma_2 > \ldots > \sigma_{10}$.

To prevent overdetermining the model, set $\beta_{10} = 0$. The parameters $\{\alpha_w\}$, $\{\sigma_d\}$, ρ and the remaining $\{\beta_d\}$ are assigned relatively wide prior distributions, as follows:

1. Each $\alpha_w \sim$ normal $(\log(Premium_w) + logelr, \sqrt{10})$ where the parameter $logelr \sim$ uniform$(-1, 0.5)$.

---

[2] To distinguish observations from simulated values and random variables, let $C_{w,d}$ be an observed loss, $\widetilde{C}_{w,d}$ denote a random variable, and $C_{w,d}^{(i)}$ denote a simulated value from a parameter set generated by the ith MCMC simulation. In situations where both observed and simulated values are in the expression, the "simulated" convention will apply.

2. Each $\beta_d \sim$ uniform $(-5, 5)$ for $d < 10$.
3. $\rho \sim$ uniform $(-1, 1)$.
4. Each $\sigma_d = \sum_{i=d}^{K} a_i$ where $a_i \sim$ uniform $(0, 1)$.

I then used a Bayesian MCMC model to produce a sample of 10,000, indexed by the superscript i, equally likely parameter sets $\{\alpha_w^{(i)}\}_{w=1}^{10}$, $\{\beta_d^{(i)}\}_{d=1}^{9}$, $\rho(i)$, $\{\sigma_d^{(i)}\}_{d=1}^{10}$ from the predictive distribution.

8.4 The Predictive Distribution of Future Estimates

Let's use this sample from the posterior distribution to represent all the possible futures for a given loss triangle. Let's now turn to translating the parameters in this sample into statistics of interest to an actuary. The first step is to simulate future outcomes for each parameter set, i. Then do the following:

1. Set $\mu_{1,d}^{(i)} = \alpha_1^{(i)} + \beta_d^{(i)}$.
2. Set $C_{1,d}^{(i)} = C_{1,d}$ from the top row of the observed loss triangle.
3. Set $\mu_{w,d}^{(i)} = \alpha_w^{(i)} + \beta_d^{(i)} + \rho^{(i)} \cdot (\log(C_{w-1,d}^{(i)}) - \mu_{w-1,d}^{(i)})$.
4. If (w, d) is in the lower triangle, simulate $C_{w,d}^{(i)}$ from a lognormal $(\mu_{w,d}^{(i)}, \sigma_d^{(i)})$ distribution.

The next step is to get the path of loss estimates corresponding to each outcome in our sample. Let $T_{CY}^{(k)}$ be a set of losses in the kth sample (observed in the upper triangle and simulated, separately for each k, in the lower triangle) incurred at the end of future calendar year $CY (= 1, \ldots, 9)$. Specifically,

$$T_{CY}^{(k)} = \left\{ \begin{array}{lll} C_{w,d} & : & w + d \leq 11 \\ C_{w,d}^{(k)} & : & 11 < w + d \leq 11 + CY \end{array} \right\}$$

Let $\phi_L(x|\mu, \sigma)$ be the probability density function for a lognormal distribution. Then

$$\Pr\{T_{CY}^{(k)}|i\} = \prod_{C_{w,d}^{(i)} \in T_{CY}^{(k)}} \phi_L\left(C_{w,d}^{(i)}|\mu_{w,d}^{(i)}, \sigma_d^{(i)}\right) \tag{8.1}$$

Using Bayes's theorem, along with the fact that initially, each i is equally likely, we have that the posterior probability for each i

$$\Pr\{i|T_{CY}^{(k)}\} = \frac{\Pr\{T_{CY}^{(k)}|i\} \cdot \Pr\{i\}}{\sum_{j=1}^{10,000} \Pr\{T_{CY}^{(k)}|j\} \cdot \Pr\{j\}} = \frac{\Pr\{T_{CY}^{(k)}|i\}}{\sum_{j=1}^{10,000} \Pr\{T_{CY}^{(k)}|j\}} \tag{8.2}$$

The expected ultimate loss given $T_{CY}^{(k)}$ is then given by

$$E_{CY}^{(k)} = \sum_{w=1}^{CY+1} C_{w,10} + \sum_{i=1}^{10,000} \sum_{w=CY+2}^{10} e^{\mu_{i,w,10} + \sigma_{i,10}^2/2} \cdot \Pr\{i|T_{CY}^{(k)}\} \tag{8.3}$$

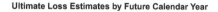

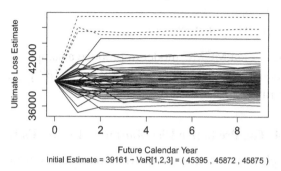

Fig. 8.2. Paths of loss estimates for Insurer 1.

The first sum in equation (8.3) accounts for the accident years that have already reached their ultimate value. The second sum is the expected value of the ultimate value for the accident years that have not yet reached their ultimate value.

An insurer starts with its initial estimate of losses, $E_0^{(k)}$, based on the original triangle, $T_0^{(k)}$. At the end of the first calendar year, it now has the trapezoid, $T_1^{(k)}$, which it uses to obtain its next estimate, $E_2^{(k)}$. It continues similarly until the losses reach their ultimate value, which in our case is $E_9^{(k)}$. Repeat this calculation for all 10,000 values of k.

Figures 8.2 and 8.3 show subsample paths for Insurers 1 and 2, respectively. I chose the subsample by first sorting the paths in order of their ultimate values and then choosing the 100th, 300th, ..., 9,900th paths for the solid paths. As we are interested in the extreme paths, I also chose the 9,925th, 9,950th, and 9,975th dashed paths. The ultimate for the 9,950th path represents the value-at-risk (VaR) at the 99.5% level.

The set $\{E_{CY}^{(j)}\}_{j=1}^{10,000}$ represents the possible values the distributions take for future calendar year CY. The probability one attaches to these values depends upon the data

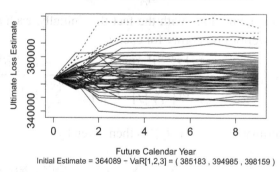

Fig. 8.3. Paths of loss estimates for Insurer 2.

available at the beginning of the calendar year under consideration. For example, at the initial valuation at $CY = 0$, all probabilities are equally likely and predictive distribution of future estimates for a n-year time horizon is given by the set of ordered pairs

$$\left\{\left(E_{n-1}^{(j)}, 0.0001\right)\right\}_{j=1}^{10,000} \tag{8.4}$$

More generally, at the beginning of calendar year CY, one has the data in trapezoid, $T_{CY}^{(k)}$. One can then use equation (8.2) to calculate $\{\Pr\{j|T_{CY}^{(k)}\}\}_{j=1}^{10,000}$. The predictive distribution of future estimates for a n-year time horizon, starting with calendar year CY is given by the set of ordered pairs.[3]

$$\left\{\left(E_{CY+n-1}^{(j)}, \Pr\{j|T_{CY}^{(k)}\}\right)\right\}_{j=1}^{10,000} \tag{8.5}$$

Given the predictive distribution of future estimates, one can then find 99.5% VaR by first sorting the set $\{\Pr\{i|T_{CY}^{(k)}\}\}_{j=1}^{10,000}$ in the increasing order of $E_{CY+n-1}^{(j)}$. Then one can find a J such that the cumulative probability of $E_{CY+n-1}^{(J)} \leq 0.995 \leq$ the cumulative probability of $E_{CY+n-1}^{(J+1)}$. One then calculates the 99.5% VaR, denoted by $A_{CY,n}^{(k)}$, from the "empirical" distribution by linear interpolation.

The subheadings for Figures 8.2 and 8.3 give the 99.5% VaRs for Triangles 1 and 2 for the one, two- and three-year time horizons. Notice that, for the most part, the paths level off after three calendar years. This leveling off of the 99.5% VaR is almost always the case for the 200 triangles and so I included the calculations for only the one-, two-, and three-year time horizons in this chapter.

The R Script to do the calculations described previously are on this book's website. Here is a high-level outline describing how it does the calculations:

1. Read in the loss triangle from the CAS Loss Reserve Database
2. Use the CCL model to obtain a sample of parameter sets $\{\alpha_w^{(i)}\}_{w=1}^{10}$, $\{\beta_d^{(i)}\}_{d=1}^{9}$, $\rho^{(i)}$, $\{\sigma_d^{(i)}\}_{d=1}^{10}$ for $i = 1, 2, \ldots, 10{,}000$.
3. Simulate one set of possible future losses $C_{w,d}^{(i)}$ for each (w, d) in the lower triangle and for each parameter set $\{\alpha_w^{(i)}\}_{w=1}^{10}$, $\{\beta_d^{(i)}\}_{d=1}^{9}$, $\rho^{(i)}$, $\{\sigma_d^{(i)}\}_{d=1}^{10}$.
4. Use equation (8.3) to calculate $E_{CY}^{(k)}$ for $CY = 0, 1, \ldots, 9$ and $k = 1, \ldots, 10{,}000$.
5. From step 4, we now have a list of conditional expected values $\{E_{CY}^{(i)}\}_{i=1}^{10,000}$ for $CY = 0, 1, \ldots, 9$. Recalculating[4] $\{\Pr\{j|T_{CY}^{(k)}\}\}_{j=1}^{10,000}$ we then form the two components of Equations (8.4) and (8.5) to gives the predictive distributions for time horizons $n = 1, 2,$ and 3, $CY = 0, 1, \ldots 9$, and $k = 1, \ldots, 10{,}000$.
6. From the distributions, $\{(E_{CY+n-1}^{(j)}, \Pr\{j|T_{CY}^{(k)}\}\}_{j=1}^{10000}$ calculate the 99.5% VaR, $A_{CY,n}^{(k)}$, for $n = 1, 2,$ and 3, $CY = 0, 1, \ldots 9$, and $k = 1, \ldots, 10{,}000$.

---

[3] Since this chapter uses 10×10 triangles, it caps $CY + n - 1$ at 9.
[4] Instead of storing $\{\Pr\{i|T_{CY}^{(k)}\}\}_{i=1}^{10,000}$ for each of the 10,000 ks from the step 4 calculation.

Until fairly recently, the total number of calculations needed to do the preceding was prohibitive. The calculations were run on a late-model laptop making use of the speedy matrix calculations and parallel processing that are available in the R programming language. The run time was about five minutes per triangle.

8.5 The Implications for Capital Management

For discussion purposes, let's define the regulatory capital standard based on the 99.5% VaR over an n-year time horizon, with n to be determined. For Solvency II, $n = 1$. This section will explore the consequences of the choice of n. Given the loss trapezoid, $T_{CY}^{(k)}$, the regulatory capital required to support the liability at the end of calendar year with a n-year time horizon is given by

$$R_{CY,n}^{(k)} = A_{CY,n}^{(k)} - E_{CY}^{(k)} \tag{8.6}$$

One can view the regulatory capital as being the the difference between the regulatory assets, $A_{CY,k}^{(k)}$, and the current estimate of the incurred loss, $E_{CY}^{(k)}$.

At the end of the calendar year, CY, one has an updated loss trapezoid, $T_{CY+1}^{(k)}$, from which one can calculate $A_{CY+1,n}^{(k)}$, $E_{CY+1}^{(k)}$ and then $R_{CY+1,n}^{(k)}$. Let's consider the difference in the regulatory capital, $R_{CY,n}^{(k)} - R_{CY+1,n}^{(k)}$. When it is positive, the difference can be refunded to the owners for use in other investments. When it is negative, the owners should be required to add capital to support the ongoing liabilities. Next let's consider the difference in the current estimate of the incurred loss, $E_{CY}^{(k)} - E_{CY+1}^{(k)}$. When it is positive, the difference can be similarly be refunded to the owners. When it is negative, the owners should similarly be required to add capital. Let's define the capital released at time $CY + 1$, $D_{CY+1,n}^{(k)}$, as the sum of the two refunds/additions:

$$
\begin{aligned}
D_{CY+1,n}^{(k)} &= R_{CY,n}^{(k)} - R_{CY+1,n}^{(k)} + E_{CY}^{(k)} - E_{CY+1}^{(k)} \\
&= A_{CY,n}^{(k)} - E_{CY}^{(k)} - \left(A_{CY+1,n}^{(k)} - E_{CY+1}^{(k)}\right) + E_{CY}^{(k)} - E_{CY+1}^{(k)} \\
&= A_{CY,k}^{(k)} - A_{CY+1,n}^{(k)}
\end{aligned}
\tag{8.7}
$$

In words, the amount of capital released at the end of the future calendar year CY is the difference between the required assets required at the beginning of the calendar year, CY, and then assets required at the end of the calendar year.

The set $\{D_{CY+1,n}^{(k)}\}_{CY=0}^{8}$ represents the path of the released regulatory capital over the range of calendar years for the kth sample. Figures 8.4 and 8.5 show the possible paths

Time Horizon = 1 Year

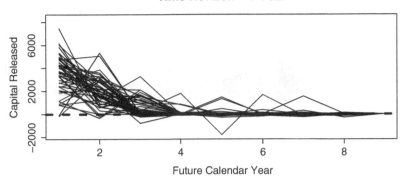

Time Horizon = 2 Years

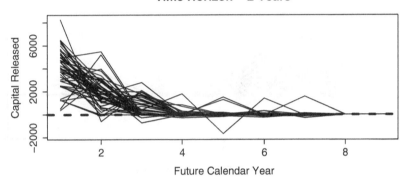

Time Horizon = 3 Years

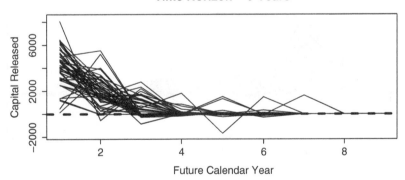

Fig. 8.4. Sample loss paths for Triangle 1.

of the released regulatory capital for the one-, two-, and three-year time horizons for a subsample of our 10,000 possible values of k. For Insurer 1, the overwhelming majority of the paths consisted entirely of positive releases, with only small differences obtained by increasing the time horizon. For Insurer 2, additions to the regulatory

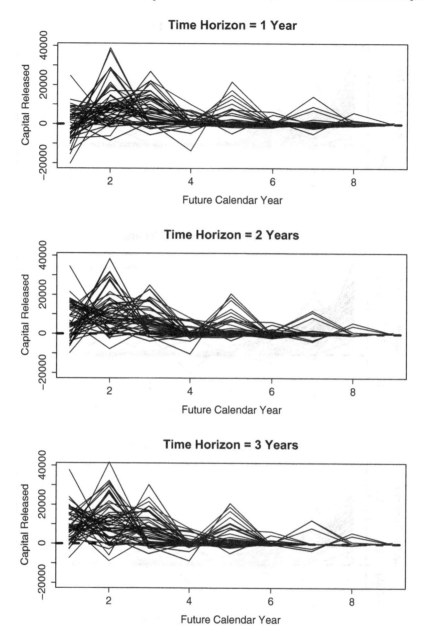

Fig. 8.5. Sample capital paths for Triangle 2.

capital were frequent occurrences, and noticeable difference obtained by increasing the time horizon.

I ran a similar analysis for all 200 loss triangles included in Meyers (2015). Figure 8.6 shows a histogram of the number of paths the resulted in a capital addition

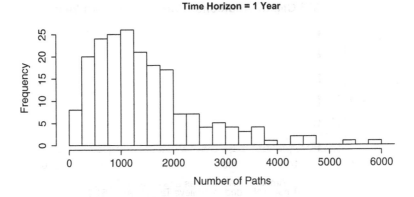

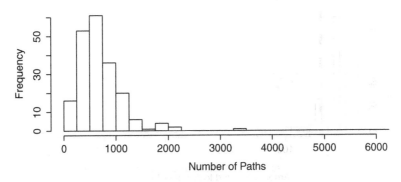

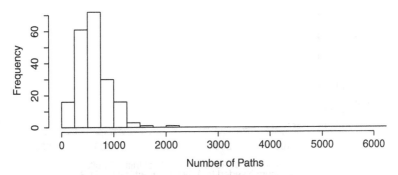

Fig. 8.6. Number of paths that indicate additional capital for 200 triangles.

at the end of the first ($CY = 0$) calendar year. All 200 triangles had at least some paths where it was necessary to add capital.

As mentioned above, the analysis of all 200 loss triangles indicated that there were at least paths that resulted in adding capital. In discussions with those whose

373 Capital Additions − Time Horizon = 1 Year

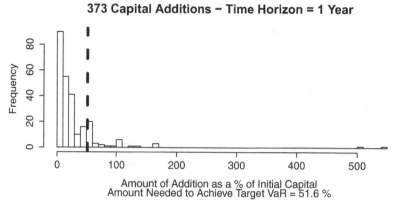

Amount of Addition as a % of Initial Capital
Amount Needed to Achieve Target VaR = 51.6 %

252 Capital Additions − Time Horizon = 2 Years

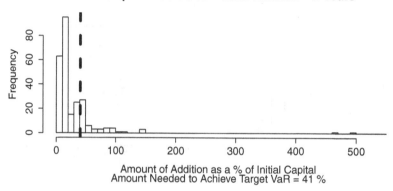

Amount of Addition as a % of Initial Capital
Amount Needed to Achieve Target VaR = 41 %

252 Capital Additions − Time Horizon = 3 Years

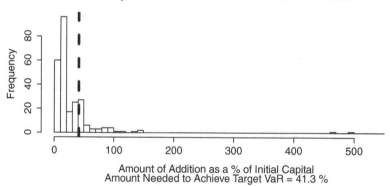

Amount of Addition as a % of Initial Capital
Amount Needed to Achieve Target VaR = 41.3 %

Fig. 8.7. Voluntary additional capital for Triangle 1.

responsibilities involve raising capital for insurers, I have heard that it is easier (and less expensive) to raise capital when there is no immediate need to use it.

An insurer might ask the the following question. "If we are likely to need regulatory capital next year and it is cheaper to add it now, how should we add?" In keeping with

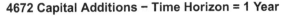

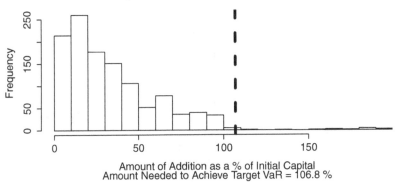

4672 Capital Additions – Time Horizon = 1 Year

Amount of Addition as a % of Initial Capital
Amount Needed to Achieve Target VaR = 106.8 %

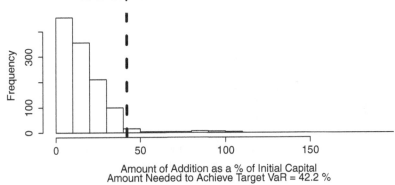

1848 Capital Additions – Time Horizon = 2 Years

Amount of Addition as a % of Initial Capital
Amount Needed to Achieve Target VaR = 42.2 %

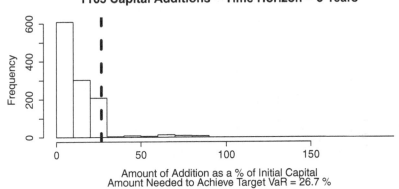

1165 Capital Additions – Time Horizon = 3 Years

Amount of Addition as a % of Initial Capital
Amount Needed to Achieve Target VaR = 26.7 %

Fig. 8.8. Voluntary additional capital for Triangle 2.

the 99.5% VaR requirement for required assets, let me suggest that an insurer should add the 9,951th highest required capital addition at the end of the first calendar year from our sample. Figures 8.7 and 8.8 show histograms of the sample capital additions for Insurers 1 and 2 with one-, two-, and three-year time horizons.

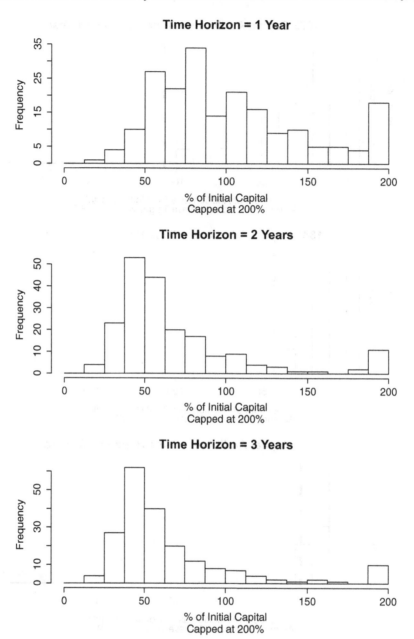

Fig. 8.9. Voluntary additional capital for the 200 triangles.

By the above criteria, Insurer 1 should add about 50% of its initial capital as voluntary capital for the one year time horizon. Insurer 2 should add over 100% of its initial capital as voluntary capital for the one-year time horizon. The voluntary capital additions are somewhat less for Insurer 1 and significantly less for Insurer 2 for the two- and three-year time horizons.

Figure 8.9 shows the indicated voluntary capital additions for all 200 triangles for the one-, two-, and three-year time horizon. These additions can be significant. For example, the voluntary addition is at or above the original regulatory requirement for 88, 31, and 27 for the one-, two-, and three-year time horizons, respectively.

8.6 Summary and Conclusions

This chapter shows how to take the output of a Bayesian MCMC stochastic loss reserve model and calculate the predictive distribution of the estimates of the expected loss over a finite time horizon. Then given a 99.5% VaR regulatory capital requirement it showed how to calculate the regulatory capital for a one-, two-, and three-year time horizon.

As an insurer gathers more data on its loss development in subsequent calendar years, this chapter finds that in most cases, it can release capital to its investors over time. But in other cases it will have add capital in subsequent years. In keeping with the 99.5% VaR criterion it finds that for many insurers, this additional capital can be substantial. As capital becomes more expensive to the stressed insurer, it might be prudent capital management for an insurer to voluntarily raise that capital in advance. This chapter shows one way to calculate the amount of voluntary capital that will be needed to satisfy the 99.5% VaR requirement for the next calendar year.

References

Clark, D. R. LDF curve fitting and stochastic loss reserving: A maximum likelihood approach. *Casualty Actuarial Society Forum*, Fall 2003.

Mack, T. Distribution-free calculation of the standard error of chain ladder reserve estimates. *ASTIN Bulletin*, 23(2): 213–225, 1993.

Mack, T. Measuring the variability of chain ladder reserve estimates. *Casualty Actuarial Society Forum*, Spring 1994.

Merz, M., and M. V. Wüthrich. Modelling the claims development result for solvency purposes. *CAS E-Forum*, Fall 2008.

Meyers, G. *Stochastic Loss Reserving Using Bayesian MCMC Models*. Casualty Actuarial Society Monograph 1, 2015. This monograph is available for download at http://www.casact.org/pubs/monographs/papers/01-Meyers.PDF.

Ohlssona, E., and J. Lauzeningksb. The one-year non-life insurance risk. *Insurance: Mathematics and Economics*, 45(2): 203–208, 2009.

9

Finite Mixture Model and Workers' Compensation Large-Loss Regression Analysis

Luyang Fu and Xianfang Liu

Chapter Preview. Actuaries have been studying loss distributions since the emergence of the profession. Numerous studies have found that the widely used distributions, such as lognormal, Pareto, and gamma, do not fit insurance data well. Mixture distributions have gained popularity in recent years because of their flexibility in representing insurance losses from various sizes of claims, especially on the right tail. To incorporate the mixture distributions into the framework of popular generalized linear models (GLMs), the authors propose to use finite mixture models (FMMs) to analyze insurance loss data. The regression approach enhances the traditional whole-book distribution analysis by capturing the impact of individual explanatory variables. FMM improves the standard GLM by addressing distribution-related problems, such as heteroskedasticity, over- and underdispersion, unobserved heterogeneity, and fat tails. A case study with applications on claims triage and on high-deductible pricing using workers' compensation data illustrates those benefits.

9.1 Introduction

9.1.1 Conventional Large Loss Distribution Analysis

Large loss distributions have been extensively studied because of their importance in actuarial applications such as increased limit factor and excess loss pricing (Miccolis, 1977), reinsurance retention and layer analysis (Clark, 1996), high deductible pricing (Teng, 1994), and enterprise risk management (Wang, 2002). Klugman et al. (1998) discussed the frequency, severity, and aggregate loss distributions in detail in their book, which has been on the Casualty Actuarial Society syllabus of exam Construction and Evaluation of Actuarial Models for many years. Keatinge (1999) demonstrated that popular single distributions, including those in Klugman et al. (1998), are not adequate to represent the insurance loss well and suggested using mixture exponential distributions to improve the goodness of fit. Beirlant et al. (2001) proposed a flexible generalized Burr-gamma distribution to address the heavy tail of loss and validated the effectiveness of this parametric distribution by comparing its implied excess-of-loss reinsurance premium with other nonparametric and semi-parametric distributions. Matthys et al. (2004) presented an extreme quantile estimator to deal with extreme insurance losses. Fleming (2008) showed that the sample average of any small data from a skewed population is most likely below the true mean and warned the danger of insurance pricing decisions without considering extreme events. Henry and Hsieh (2009) stressed the importance of understanding the heavy tail behavior of a loss distribution and developed a tail index estimator assuming that the insurance loss possess Pareto-type tails. Clark (2013) discussed the limitations of Pareto associated with infinite right tail and variance, and proposed a statistical upper truncation point to eliminate unreasonable large losses and to ensure the existence of first and second moments of the Pareto distribution.

Traditional actuarial distribution analysis investigates the loss distribution without considering the impact of covariates at the individual risk level. For example, in excess-of-loss reinsurance pricing, large loss distribution analysis is essential. A certain form of distribution (e.g., Pareto) is often fitted using historical observations of large claims. Only loss data are needed to fit the loss distribution. Once the parameters of the distribution are estimated, the expected losses by reinsurance layer can be easily derived. Reinsurers use the information for pricing while reinsureds use it to negotiate the price or make the decision on the layers. Similarly, in DFA (dynamic financial analysis) and ERM (enterprise risk management), large losses are randomly drawn from a predetermined single fat-tailed loss distribution or a mixture of distributions. The underlying risk characteristics at policy level are seldom used. The loss simulations are repeated for many simulation years and the one-year or multiyear financial impacts of large losses and various reinsurance options can be evaluated.

9.1.2 Conventional Regression Analysis on Severity

It is practically appealing in the loss distribution analysis to incorporate risk characteristics at individual policy or exposure level. Large losses vary significantly by the underlying characteristics of individual risks. In commercial property, many variables (such as industry group, territory, size of building, protection class) jointly impact large loss propensity: plastic manufacturers are more likely to be burned down by fire than dental offices; beach properties in Florida are more likely to suffer total losses from hurricane; only large buildings with high LOI (limit of insurance) can produce huge losses while small buildings cannot generate million-dollar property losses; the properties in ISO Protection Class 10 are far from fire stations and hydrants, and therefore are more likely to suffer total fire losses. The large loss distributions derived from the whole-book analysis cannot provide the insights of individual risk classifications. When business mix shifts, the loss distributions using historical large claims may provide misleading information. For example, suppose an insurance company enters the high-value home market and starts writing more homes at high coverage A limits. The large loss distribution derived solely using historical loss data will understate the large loss potential in the future. A regression analysis would provide more accurate estimation. The loss distribution parameters, such as mean and standard deviation, will be determined by explanatory covariates including coverage A limit, construction type, Protection Class, construction age, insureds' insurance score, and so on. Once the regression coefficients are parameterized using historical claims, actuaries can estimate the loss distributions of individual exposures in the inforce book or the expected future book. Although the regression parameters are calculated using the historical book, the loss distribution derived from regression analysis is driven by the explanatory variables of the inforce book, and therefore will reflect the business mix shift.

Regression analysis, especially the generalized linear model (GLM), has become more popular in property and casualty actuarial fields in the past twenty years. Dean (2014) in Chapter 5 of Volume I of this book provided a detailed introduction to GLM theory. Frees (2014) in Chapter 6 of Volume I discussed frequency and severity models, the most popular GLM applications in the classification ratemaking of property and casualty insurance. Mildenhall (1999), in his milestone study, investigated the systematic relationship between GLMs and traditional minimum bias methods, and demonstrated minimum bias models are specific cases of GLM. After Mildenhall (1999), the theoretical debate on GLMs within property and casualty actuaries was over. The actuarial practitioners moved forward and the GLM discussions focused on its applications. Holler et al. (1999) introduced two chi-square tests to validate GLMs. Gordon and Jørgensen (2002) proposed to use double GLM assuming a Tweedie distribution to address the dispersion of insurance loss cost. Anderson et al. (2004) documented many real-world application insights from the perspective of practitioners. Fu and Moncher (2004) compared the popular log-linear model assuming lognormal distribution against a GLM gamma model and concluded that a GLM gamma model is more robust. Guven (2004) used the polynomials of latitude and longitude to model territorial relativities and expanded the applications of GLMs into traditional territorial ratemaking. Mosley (2004) applied GLMs to estimate the ultimate claim settlement amounts and to evaluate claims trends. Although GLMs had been explored by academia in loss reserving studies earlier than in pricing (Kremer, 1982; Taylor and Ashe, 1983; Renshaw, 1989; Renshaw and Verrall, 1994), reserve actuaries did not use GLMs in practice until recent years. Several recent stochastic reserve investigations focused on testing exponential family distributions beyond over-dispersed Poisson and gamma. For example, Taylor (2009) and Boucher and Davidov (2011) used Tweedie distribution, the most popular distribution by pricing actuaries in modeling the loss cost, to improve the goodness of fit of GLMs on loss triangle data.

9.1.3 Regression Analysis with Fat-Tailed Distributions

Although actuarial studies on fat-tailed distributions and on regressions have progressed rapidly, there is significantly less effort on combining the two areas of research in actuarial practice. Fu and Wu (2007) generalized the conventional minimum bias method and allowed the variance of the loss to be any desirable power function of the mean. Klugman et al. (1998) discussed that GLM theory does not restrict the distribution to be from the exponential family. Venter (2007) expanded this idea by exploring various forms of distributions. Under the framework of Venter (2007), the relationship of variance to mean no longer uniquely defines the distribution, therefore giving GLMs more flexibility to model different tails properties including skewness and other higher moments. Frees et al. (2009) used the GB2 distribution (generalized beta of the second kind) within a hierarchical regression framework to model the long-tailed nature of auto insurance claims. Parsa and Klugman (2011) proposed to use copula regression as an alternative to GLM for modeling insurance loss, because of its ability to choose distributions for dependent variables that are not members of the exponential family. Shi (2014), in Chapter 10 of Volume I of this book, discussed a few regression methods to deal with fat tails of insurance losses. Heapplied a GB2 model with a logarithmic link function to medical care cost data and demonstrated that the GB2 distribution fits the heavy tail of the data better than gamma and inverse Gaussian GLMs under the same multiplicative model specification.

The research of generalizing GLMs by using fat-tailed distributions and removing the restriction of exponential family distributions is theoretically sound, but does not get much attraction in practice. Shi (2014) commented that although heavy-tailed parametric distributions have been extensively studied in modeling insurance data, the applications of regression models based on those parametric distributions (Pareto, GB2, etc.) are sparse. Two constraints may hinder the research development and its implementation toward this direction. First, popular statistical software does not provide easy-to-use packages for parametric regression models with non-exponential family distributions and therefore the numerical solution can become very cumbersome. One straightforward numerical algorithm of relaxing the exponential family distributions is the fixed-point iterative approach proposed by Fu and Wu (2007).[1] Mildenhall (2005) and Venter (2007) have specifically discussed this numerical scheme. Mildenhall (2005) commented that the numerical solution is not easy to apply and that it may not converge rapidly. Second, single distributions with fat-tailed properties, as showed in Keatinge (1999), usually do not fit insurance data well. One example is the Pareto distribution. Both practitioners and academia love Pareto because of its ability to fit extreme values. Consistent with Clark (2013), the

---

[1] Academics have investigated the numerical solutions of GLMs much earlier. For example, the quasi-likelihood method by Wedderburn (1974) allows the extension of distributions beyond the exponential family.

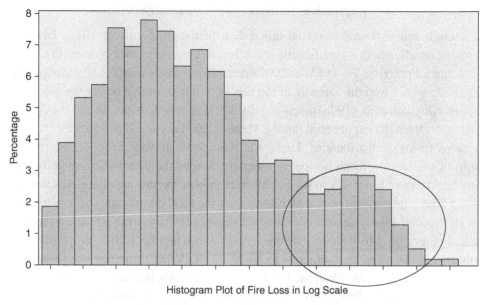

Histogram Plot of Fire Loss in Log Scale

Fig. 9.1. Histogram of homeowner fire loss.

authors' experience is that Pareto often underestimates "large but not extreme" loss while it overstates "extreme" loss. Figure 9.1 is a histogram of homeowner fire losses, and it illustrates Keatinge's argument well. The loss at log scale seems to be from two distributions. It is a natural observation in property and casualty insurance that the majority of fire claims are "normal" partial losses while a small percentage of claims are "severe" total losses. Single fat-tailed distributions such as Pareto, inverse Gaussian, or GB2 distributions cannot capture this specific phenomenon of loss density.

Whole-book distributional analysis assumes that insurance risks are homogenous, but insurance risks in the real world are heterogeneous. Some heterogeneities are observable. For example, industry group and protection class affect property large claim propensity and they are observable. To represent the observable heterogeneity inherent in the insurance loss, Shi (2014) discussed that actuaries often split the data into a few more homogenous subpopulations (such as male vs. female) and then fit separate distributions on each subset. The data splitting approach can only address the observed heterogeneity for a small number of subpopulations using one or two variables. If the data are sliced too thin using multiple variables, the fitted distributions are not credible. Regression analysis is a more appealing approach as it contemplates observable multivariate heterogeneities without compromising much of the credibility.

Heterogeneities are often not directly observable in insurance data. For example, injury severity intuitively influences the amount of loss payment in workers' compensation claims. Minor medical-only claims rarely penetrate $5,000, while the average "severe" claim with indemnity is over $50,000. The losses from the two subgroups clearly follow very different distributions. However, there is no direct objective measure of injury severity in the workers' compensation claims database (Johnson et al., 1999). Comorbidity is another example of unobserved heterogeneity. Claimants with certain health issues, such as diabetes and obesity, are more likely to stay out of work for a longer period of time than healthy claimants, and therefore produce larger workers' compensation losses. When pricing workers' compensation policies, few companies request the comorbidity information of the policyholders' employees. In the claims process, comorbidity can only be known on a small percentage of claims several months after the reporting date. Those unobservable latent classification variables can introduce underdispersion, overdispersion, or heteroskedasticity in a traditional regression model (Kessler and McDowell, 2012). To deal with unobservable heterogeneity, econometricians have developed various regression models such as two-stage least squares and finite mixture models.

In this study the authors attempt to combine two tracks of actuarial studies in regression and distribution analyses, and enhance the popular GLM regression by relaxing its reliance on single distributions from exponential family. To address heteroskedasticity, heterogeneity, and fat tails, we are specifically interested infinite mixture model (FMM), which expands GLM by allowing heterogeneous and mixture distributions. To facilitate the numerical computation, we only tested the mixture combinations of exponential family distributions.[2] FMM supplements the traditional mixture distribution analysis by contemplating individual risk characteristics at the policy level and capturing the business mix shift. It enhances the regressions assuming single distributions (standard GLM and GB2 models) as the mixture distribution can better represent the heterogeneous nature of insurance risks and improves the goodness of fit on the fat tails of insurance loss. The authors also tested the double generalized linear model (DGLM).

The regression approach illustrated in this study can be applied in various actuarial applications. In traditional loss distribution studies such as reinsurance and enterprise risk management, the interest of analysis is on the whole book, not necessarily on specific risks. Reinsurers are interested in how many large losses may penetrate the reinsurance retention and how much loss is recoverable in the layer. In DFA (dynamic financial analysis), the focus is the impact of large losses on the income statement and balance sheet. The analysts are not interested in knowing which policies will produce those large losses. The benefit of regression analysis is to provide a more accurate whole-book view by aggregating predictions from individual risks. In other actuarial

---

[2] Nonexponential family mixtures, such as a gamma-lognormal mixture, are easy to solve numerically in traditional distribution analysis. In a regression framework, numerical solution is a challenge for practitioners.

applications, the insights on individual policies or claims can be the key to success. To allocate claims resources efficiently, it is important to know which individual claims have high propensities to become large losses so that the best adjusters can be assigned to those complicated claims. Regression models are very helpful inidentifying which claims need managers' early attention. In pricing, actuaries may need to allocate the reinsurance cost to individual policies. Large fabric manufacturers and plastics makers would assume higher costs of XOL (excess of loss) reinsurance than small offices and institutions using the regression approach.

The remainder of the chapter is organized as follows:

- Section 9.2 briefly discusses DGLM and FMM.
- Section 9.3 describes the workers' compensation claims data for the case study. It illustrates the skewedness and fat-tailed nature of insurance data.
- Section 9.4 performs traditional distribution analysis. The results clearly shows that none of the popular single distributions fits the data well and mixture distribution can improve the goodness of fit significantly.
- Section 9.5 is the univariate and correlation analysis. The univariate analysis shows the relationship between ultimate claims cost and individual covariates. The correlation analysis checks the relationship among the covariates.
- Section 9.6 conducts regression analysis using workers' compensation claims data and discusses two potential applications: claims triage and high-deductible pricing. The results from DGLM and FMM are compared with those from GLM. It demonstrates the flexibility of FMM in addressing the distribution-related difficulties such as heteroskedasticity, heterogeneity, and fat tails. On the opposite side of the coin, we also discuss the parameter risks and potential problem associated with overfitting.
- Section 9.7 outlines our conclusions.

9.2 DGLM and FMM

9.2.1 DGLM

As Dean (2014) discussed in Chapter 5 of Volume I of this book, GLM substantially relaxes the requirements for ordinary linear regressions by providing a choice of non-normal distributions for the observations and by allowing additivity of the systematic effects to hold on a transformed scale with the choice of scale being made independently of the choice of distribution.

Standard GLMs assume that the scale or dispersion factor is a constant. Insurance claims data of ten display heterogeneous dispersions. If the density function and the variance formula vary by individual risk characteristics, the dispersion parameter ϕ will be ϕ_i. It now becomes necessary to model the dispersion ϕ_i along with the mean μ_i. The dispersion not only impacts the coefficient estimation for μ_i but, more importantly, it is essential in obtaining correct standard errors and confidence intervals. In many studies, modeling the dispersion will be of direct interest in its own right to identify the sources of variability in the observations. For example, the interest of reinsurance pricing is not the mean, but the expected amount of recovery, which is jointly determined by the likelihood of loss penetrating the retention the conditional expected value when loss is over the retention, and the volatility of loss over the retention. All three components are increasing functions of the dispersion factor. If the mean μ_i of loss is the same, the greater the dispersion ϕ_i, the higher the reinsurance price. Notice that with the mean μ_i and the weight ω_i given, modelling the dispersion is same as modelling the variance of the response.

Double generalized linear models are thus developed to allow the simultaneous modelling of both the mean and the dispersion by using a linked pair of generalized linear models. This idea was first put forward by Pregibon (1984) and described in detail in Chapter 10 of McCullagh and Nelder (1989). Further developments and applications in insurance claims data are given by Nelder and Pregibon (1987), Smyth (1989), Smyth and Verbyla (1999), and Smyth and Jørgensen (2002). For those readers interested in the dispersion submodel, please refer to Section 10.5 of McCullagh and Nelder (1989).

The mean and dispersion of a generalized linear model are orthogonal, which allows us to estimate the mean coefficients β and the dispersion coefficients λ through sequential iterations. Given any working value for λ, we can estimate β using an ordinary generalized model. Given any working value for β, we can estimate λ using a GLM with a gamma distribution. These estimation procedures alternate between one iteration for the mean submodel and one iteration for the dispersion submodel until reaching overall convergence.

9.2.2 FMM

Classical GLMs are a special case of the finite mixture models in which the distribution of the data has only a single component. Finite mixture models extend the distribution of the responses to be a finite mixture of distributions, that is, each observation is drawn with unknown probability from one of several distributions. Unlike nonparametric methods, such as kernel density estimation, a finite mixture model provides a parametric alternative that describes the unknown distribution in terms of mixtures of known distributions.

The density function of a finite mixture model can be expressed as

$$f(y) = \sum_{j=1}^{k} \pi_j(z_j, \alpha_j) p_j(y; x_j^T \beta_j, \phi_j) \tag{9.1}$$

with the mixture probabilities π_j satisfying $\pi_j \geq 0$, for all j; and $\sum_{j=1}^{k} \pi_j(z_j, \alpha_j) = 1$. Here the number of components in the mixture is denoted as k. The mixture probabilities π_j can depend on some regressor variables z_j[3] and regression parameters α_j. Each component has a density function p_j which can also depend on some regressor variables in x_j, regression parameters β_j, and possibly some scale parameters ϕ_j. The component density functions p_j might belong to different families. If they are of the same family, the model is called homogeneous.

Finite mixture models have been extensively developed in the literature of statistics. The development of these models dates back to the work of Newcomb (1886) and Pearson (1894). More recent literature includes Everitt and Hand (1981), Titterington et al. (1985), and McLachlan and Peel (2000). Finite mixture models of standard linear regression models as well as generalized linear models were developed in Wedel and DeSarbo (1995).

Finite mixture models with a fixed number of components are usually estimated using the expectation-maximization algorithm (Dempster et al., 1977) within a maximum likelihood framework, orusing MCMC algorithm within a Bayesian framework, as described in Diebolt and Robert (1994).

With the flexibility of components and mixing probability, Kessler and McDowell (2012) advocate that finite mixture models are very useful in many applications such as estimating multimodal or heavy-tailed densities, fitting zero-inflated or hurdle models to count data with excess zeros, modeling underlying heterogeneity, addressing overdispersion, fitting regression models with complex error distributions, classifying observations based on predicted component probabilities, accounting for unobservable or omitted variables, estimating switching regressions, and so on. The opposite side of flexibility is additional parameter risks. The model parameters increase linearly with the number of mixture distributions. In insurance practice, the authors seldom apply FMM with more than two distributions because those models are so flexible that they can be very sensitive to random noises.

9.3 Data

The study is based upon a simulated workers' compensation claim data by stratifying and bootstrapping the GLM residuals.[4] The covariates are five variables available at the first notice of loss (FNOL):[5] injury code 1, injury code 2, claimant age, class code group, and fatal indicator. Injury code 1 (IC1) is a severity measure of injuries ranking from "A" to "E"[6] created by claims adjusters using injury-related information such as body part and injury type.[7] "A" represents the most severe claims while "E" is the least

---

[3] If the number of mixture component is larger than 2, theoretically z can vary by j. In actuarial practice, it is common to use one set of variables for all js. SAS and R FMM packages do not provide options to allow z to vary by j.

[4] All major patterns discussed in this study can be observed in the real data, but the significance levels may vary.

[5] To obtain the residuals for bootstrapping, a few non-FNOL variables, such as comorbidity, are used in the regression.

[6] Five bins are arbitrary for the illusion purpose. The variable can be much more refined in practice.

[7] In claims database, body part is stored in AIA code 1 and injury type is stored in AIA code 2.

severe claim. For example, "ankle sprain" is in "E" while "skull crushing" is in "A." Injury code 2 (IC2) is another grouping of injury severity using the similar information but from a different perspective. The two variables have strong correlations, but do not always point to the same direction. For example, urine track infection might be "minor" from the perspective of health care professionals. In worker's compensation claims, it is often related to injured workers in wheel chairs, which can generate large losses. The claimant ages are binned into 3 groups from "01" to "03" as age increases. NCCI (National Council on Compensation Insurance) class codes are clustered into 2 groups "01" and "02." "01" is low-risk industries such as accountants and actuaries working within "four walls" and "02" represents more hazardous professions. Mid-risk classes (such as diary and farm workers) and high-risk classes (such as roofers and lumberjacks) are grouped together in "02" for illustration purpose. All the missing values are grouped into the bin with the most observations.[8] Losses are trended and developed to ultimate.[9] Several other FNOL variables may impact the workers' compensation loss, such as NCCI hazard grade, cause of injury, jurisdiction state, and territorial medical index. To simplify the illustration, those variables are not included in this study. The target or dependent variable is "loss payment plus allocated loss adjustment expense" (ALAE). Some claims are closed without any payment of loss and expense. For example, a policyholder may report a severe head injury that is not employment related. Although the injury may generate large medical treatment bills, the loss is not covered by workers' compensation insurance. The "closed without payment" claims are removed from the data.[10] Many claims are expense only without loss. The expense-only claims are included in the data. For example, adjusters may request certain information through fax from employers and pay for the fax cost on rejected claims. It is not uncommon to find expense-only claims under ten dollars.

There are total 110,461 simulated claims. All the losses are rescaled by dividing the sample average so that the mean of these claims is set to be 1; the standard deviation and the coefficient of variation are same and equal to 3.396; the skewness and the kurtosis are 9.420 and 186.280, respectively. The 25th, 50th, 90th, 95th, 99.5th, and 99.99th percentiles are 0.033, 0.088, 2.139, 5.635, 20.963, and 84.438, respectively.

---

[8] The missing treatment is outside of the scope of this study. "Missing" often implies that a claim is not serious so that claims adjusters or call center clerks did not bother to collect the data. If we use "missing" as separate categorical bins, the coefficients of "missing" are close to those of the largest bins.

[9] The development is relatively small on the case reserves excluding pure IBNR (incurred but not reported). Including IBNR in loss development factors, the ultimate loss at individual claims level is overstated.

[10] Most of closed without loss and expense payment claims are on minor non-compensable injuries. Adding those records in, there would be little changes in the flagged claims for the claims triage application. For the high-deductible application, zeros will lower the mean of the fitted distributions. To represent excessive zeros, the authors need to fit a three-component mixture: zero, a normal (small) loss distribution, and an abnormal large loss distribution. The model becomes more complicated; but the net results are very close to the model specifications of two gamma mixtures excluding the closed without payment claims.

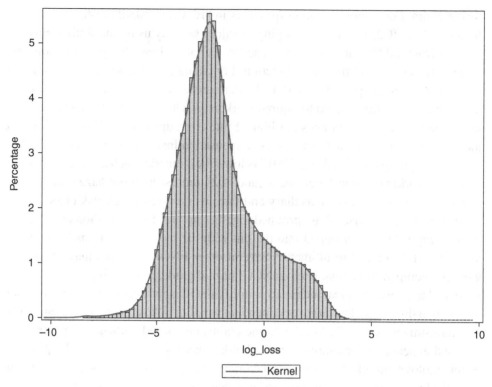

Fig. 9.2. Probability density of simulated WC loss.

Figure 9.2 exhibits the probability histogram of the simulated loss and the kernel probability density function at a log scale.[11] The density plot does not have two modes as in Figure 9.1, but it has a heavier right tail than lognormal (lognormal loss will produce a symmetrical pdf plot at log-scale). Because expense-only claims are included in this study, the density plot also has a relatively long left tail.

9.4 Traditional Distribution Analysis

For illustrative purposes we fit the distributions by traditional whole-book analysis using popular distributions including Pareto, lognormal, gamma, inverse Gaussian, and Weibull. Figure 9.3 reports the density plots of the fitted single distributions versus that of the data. From straightforward visualization, Pareto probably fits the data the best although none of the distributions offers a great fit. Gamma, the most widely used distributions by actuaries in fitting severity models in GLM, seems to provide the worst fit among all the tested distributions. Table 9.1 reports the counts

---

[11] The distribution analysis is done on the original scale. If we plot the fitted distributions on the original scale, all of them are very right-skewed and the visual effect is not as clear as on the log scale.

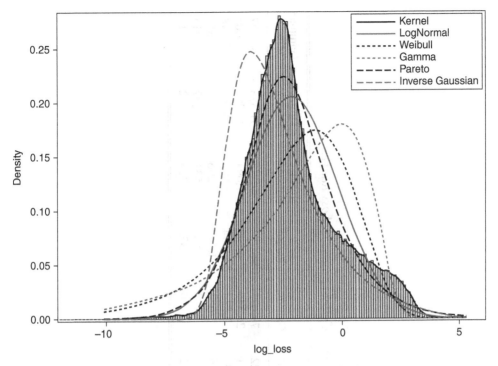

Fig. 9.3. Traditional analysis: Single distributions.

of actual observations with losses less than 1, between 1 and 5, 5–25, 25–50, 50–100, 100+, comparing them with the expected number of observations from the fitted distributions. The actual loss data is much skewed: 85.0% of claims are below the mean; 2.6% of claims are 10 times larger than average and those 2.6% claims produce 45% of overall loss; about 0.3% of claims are 25 times larger than average, and those 0.3% claims produce 10.7% of loss. Table 9.2 exhibits the percentage differences between the projected counts and actual counts for the tested distributions. From 0 to 1, lognormal fits the data the best, the expected claim count within the range is 95,456, 1.7% off the observed count of 93,854. From 1 to 5 (or 84.97 to 94.46 percentile), Pareto performs the best with a −8.5% error rate in the count projection. From 5 to 10 (or 94.46 to 97.41 percentile), gamma provides the best fit and the count error is 17.1%. Above 10, all the single distributions provide disappointing projections: no one has an error rate within 20% in any tested ranges. From 10 to 25 (97.41 to 99.71 percentile), the actual observed count is 2,541. All the single distributions are biased downward and significantly underestimate the count. The best fit is from Pareto, which projects 1,347 claims in the range and understates the count by 47%. From 25 to 50 (99.71 to 99.96 percentile), Pareto and inverse Gaussian overestimate the count by 101.8% and 89.0%, respectively; while lognormal, Weibull, gamma underestimate the counts by

Table 9.1. *Actual versus Expected Numbers of Observations by Loss Ranges*

Lower	Upper	Observed	% of Counts	Lognormal	Weibull	Gamma	Pareto	Inverse Gaussian	Gamma2 Mixture	Gamma3 Mixture
0	1	93,854	84.97%	95,456	90,222	79,673	96,283	99,574	91,373	94,027
1	5	10,490	9.50%	12,025	17,321	26,349	9,597	7,094	12,282	10,005
5	10	3,256	2.95%	1,744	2,205	3,814	1,794	1,603	4,362	3,548
10	25	2,541	2.30%	912	666	622	1,347	1,296	2,281	2,556
25	50	281	0.25%	221	44	3	567	531	157	315
50	∞	39	0.04%	103	2	0	873	363	2	11

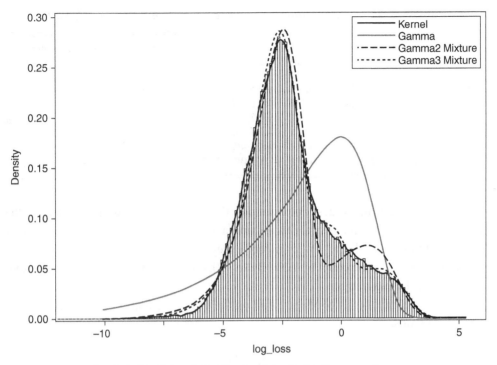

Fig. 9.4. Traditional distributional analysis: Gamma mixture.

21.4%, 84.3%, and 98.9%, respectively. On the extreme tail above 50, all the single distributions perform very poorly in predicting the counts. The actual observation is 39, while the expected counts by Pareto, inverse Gaussian, and lognormal are 873, 363, and 103, respectively. On the opposite side, Weibull and gamma go to the opposite extremes and the expected counts are 2 and 0, respectively.

To improve the goodness of fit, the authors test several mixture distributions. To simplify the illustrations, only gamma mixtures are reported. Figure 9.4 shows the density plots of single gamma, two-gamma mixture, and three-gamma mixture. From a simple visualization, two-gamma mixture improves the fit on both left and right tails significantly. In the right middle side of the distribution, the fit is off significantly: the density of actual loss is straightly decreasing while two-gamma mixture has two modes. The fit from three-gamma mixture is almost perfect.[12] By Table 9.2, the major improvement of two-gamma mixture is that it provides a superior fit on the large loss in the (10, 25) range. Pareto is the best fit of single distributions for this range, which understates the count by 47%. By comparison, two-gamma mixture only underestimates the count by 10.2%. Two-gamma mixture does not outperform single

---

[12] In the extreme right tail over 50 (99.96 percentile, or 1 in 2,500 claims), the fit is bad. The density is close to zero so that the readers cannot tell the difference visually.

Table 9.2. *Percentage Difference between Actual and Expected Counts*

Lower	Upper	Lognormal	Weibull	Gamma	Pareto	Inverse Gaussian	Gamma2 Mixture	Gamma3 Mixture
0	1	1.7%	−3.9%	−15.1%	2.6%	6.1%	−2.6%	0.2%
1	5	14.6%	65.1%	151.2%	−8.5%	−32.4%	17.1%	−4.6%
5	10	−46.4%	−32.3%	17.1%	−44.9%	−50.8%	34.0%	9.0%
10	25	−64.1%	−73.8%	−75.5%	−47.0%	−49.0%	−10.2%	0.6%
25	50	−21.4%	−84.3%	−98.9%	101.8%	89.0%	−44.1%	12.1%
50	∞	164.1%	−94.9%	−100.0%	2138.5%	828.2%	−94.9%	−71.8%

distributions in all the ranges. For example, Pareto beats two-gamma mixture in the (1, 5) range while gamma beats two-gamma mixture in the (5, 10) range. Three-gamma mixture fits all the ranges nicely except for the extreme right tail over 50, where it understates the count by 72%. Below 50, three-gamma mixture beats all other distributions by big margins.

To measure the overall goodness of fit on the fitted distributions, we calculate chi-square statistics,

$$\chi^2 = \sum_i^n \frac{(n_i - \hat{n}_i)^2}{\hat{n}_i} \tag{9.2}$$

where n_i is observed count in range i while $\hat{n}_i$ is the expected count from a fitted distribution for the same range. The smaller the χ^2, the better the goodness of fit. Table 9.3 shows the chi-square statistics for all tested distributions. Among single distributions, Pareto has the lowest χ^2 3,335, followed by lognormal 4,499. Property and casualty

Table 9.3. *Chi-Square Test of Goodness Fit*

Lower	Upper	Lognormal	Weibull	Gamma	Pareto	Inverse Gaussian	Gamma2 Mixture	Gamma3 Mixture
0	1	27	146	2,524	61	329	67	0
1	5	196	2,694	9,545	83	1,626	262	24
5	10	1,311	500	82	1,191	1,706	281	24
10	25	2,910	5,279	5,922	1,059	1,195	30	0
25	50	16	1,282	25,520	144	117	97	4
50	∞	40	600	1,444[a]	797	289	585	76
		4,499	10,501	45,037	3,335	5,261	1,321	128

[a] The expected count value 0.0007. Because the denominator is so small, chi-square statistic explodes to 2,286,079. The reported chi-square statistic 1,444 uses one as the expected count over 50 for gamma distribution.

actuaries in practice love Pareto and lognormal distributions. Their capability to represent insurance loss better than other single distributions is probably one of the major reasons. Single gamma has the worst fit with a χ^2 45,037. If the concern of an actuary is the full distribution, not just the mean, she/he should be careful in selecting gamma as it may significantly under-estimate the right tail. Two-gamma mixture clearly outperforms all single distributions as its chi-square statistic is 1,321, 60.4% below that of Pareto. Three-gamma mixture's χ^2 is 128, which is another big improvement[13] over the two-gamma mixture.

9.5 Univariate and Correlation Analyses

9.5.1 Univariate Analysis

In Section 9.4, we only investigate the dependent variable (loss) without reviewing the explanatory variables. Many variables impact workers' compensation claims losses. The most influential covariates are probably body part and injury type. In practice, these two variables have strong interactions. The combinations of two variables tell a more complete story than two separate variables. For example, "contusion" injuries are in general small claims. There is no significant cost difference between "ankle" and "lower back" contusions. Similarly, "sprain" injuries are also generally small claims. However, if the body part is "lower back," the "sprain" claim cost is no longer small. An average "lower back sprain" claim is multiple times bigger than an average "ankle sprain" claim. In this study we combine body part and injury type along with other injury information to create two interaction variables IC1 and IC2. The relationships between loss and these injury codes are displayed in Tables 9.4 and 9.5. Figures 9.5 and 9.6 visually show the average loss and coefficient of variation by those injury codes as the main interests of research are mean and variation of individual claims.[14] As expected, the data show strong skewedness. Table 9.4 shows that bins "D" and "E" of IC1 composes almost 73.3% claims but only produce 16.1% of ultimate loss. Table 9.5 shows that bins "A" and "B" of IC2 composes only 19.4% claims but produce 77.3% of ultimate loss. This is consistent with a common allegation in insurance industry that "20% claims produce 80% loss."

IC1 segments the claims very well from the perspective of the mean. The average claims size in "A" is 23.1 while the average size in "E" is 0.1. The injury in "A" is very severe and rare; and only 71 claims are in the classification. A few claims in

---

[13] The goodness of fit of three-gamma distribution below 25, or 99.7 percentile, is robust with little overfitting. Beyond the percentile, three-gamma may or may not over fit the data as there are not enough data points for the authors to conduct any reliable statistical tests on overfitting.

[14] The objective of claims triage model is to identify "large" and "volatile" claims in the early stage of claims handling. The objective of large deductible analysis is to understand the loss elimination ratio, which is sensitive to both mean and volatility of the underlying loss distribution.

Table 9.4. *Loss Statistics by IC1*

Injury Code1	N	Min	Max	Mean	Median	StdDev	CV	Skewness	Kurtosis	Count%	Loss%
A	71	0.0518	153.4	23.1	11.6	29.7	1.3	1.8	4.5	0.1%	1.5%
B	3,108	0.0019	143.8	5.3	1.8	9.7	1.8	5.3	44.4	2.8%	15.0%
C	26,328	0.0001	56.3	2.8	0.8	4.9	1.7	3.1	12.4	23.8%	67.5%
D	14,057	0.0001	29.5	0.8	0.2	1.7	2.1	4.2	26.9	12.7%	10.5%
E	66,897	0.0001	29.0	0.1	0.0	0.3	3.6	27.0	1294.5	60.6%	5.6%

Table 9.5. *Loss Statistics by IC2*

Injury Code2	N	Min	Max	Mean	Median	StdDev	CV	Skewness	Kurtosis	Count%	Loss%
A	332	0.0055	153.4	17.3	6.5	25.3	1.5	2.3	6.0	0.3%	5.2%
B	21,053	0.0001	84.4	3.8	1.1	5.8	1.5	2.6	9.7	19.1%	72.1%
C	20,939	0.0001	24.6	0.9	0.3	1.6	1.8	3.8	21.2	19.0%	17.5%
D	39,528	0.0001	5.2	0.1	0.1	0.2	2.1	9.3	120.6	35.8%	3.8%
E	28,609	0.0001	3.3	0.1	0.0	0.1	1.5	14.0	337.7	25.9%	1.4%

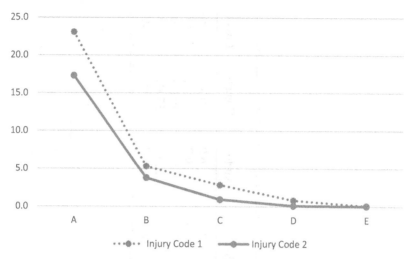

Fig. 9.5. Univariate analysis: Average loss by injury codes 1 and 2.

this group involve injuries that are not work-related and the expenses to handle those claims are significantly higher than the average expense in other groups. IC1 does not provide homogenous subgroups. In bin "E," a very small percentage claims could develop very large. This causes the coefficient of variation (CV, or standard deviation divided by mean) of bin "E" to be significantly higher than other groups. In regression analysis, gamma and lognormal assume constant CVs cross all the segments. IC1 clearly has heterogeneous CVs, which suggests that we may test DGLM or FMM if injury code is one of the major explanatory variables. IC2 does not separate the

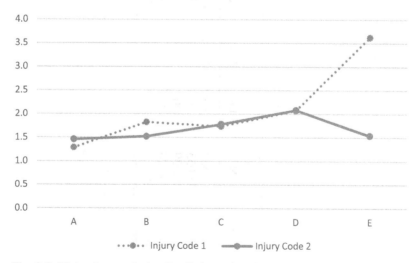

Fig. 9.6. Univariate analysis: Coefficient of variation by injury codes 1 and 2.

Table 9.6. *Loss Statistics by Fatal Indicator*

Fatal_Ind	N	Min	Max	Mean	Median	StdDev	CV	Skewness	Kurtosis	Count%	Loss%
1	118	0.0213	104.8	13.4	8.5	16.5	1.2	2.7	9.8	0.1%	1.4%
0	110,343	0.0001	153.4	1.0	0.1	3.3	3.4	9.3	186.7	99.9%	98.6%

mean as well as IC1 as shown in Figure 9.5. But its severe injury bins "A" and "B" include more observations than IC1. Bin "A" of IC2 have 332 claims versus 71 of IC1's "A." Figure 9.6 also demonstrates that IC2 has more homogenous CVs among the subgroups.

Table 9.6 shows the univariate analysis for fatal indicator. As expected, fatal claim is more expensive: the average fatal claim is 13.4 times the mean. Fatal claims are usually not very complicated to settle and rarely developed into extreme large losses. That is the reason that fatal claims are less volatile than nonfatal claims (fatal claims' CV is 1.2, significantly lower than nonfatal claims' 3.4). The CV difference between fatal and nonfatal claims is a good example of heterogeneous dispersion of insurance data.

9.5.2 Correlation Analysis

Correlation analysis is very important in modeling practice in multivariate regression, especially when there are many covariates. High correlation may cause the multicollinearity problem and the model may become unstable.[15] Table 9.7 reports the Pearson correlation[16] assuming all the variables are numerical (injury code A to E are treated as 5 to 1). It is clear that there is a correlation between injury codes 1 and 2. This is understandable since both variables are derived using body part and injury type along with other injury information. For example, all the parties (actuaries, claims adjusters, medical professionals, etc.) will categorize "skull crushing" as "severe." On the opposite side, "finger puncture" would be put into the "minor" category by most insurance professionals. The similar categorizations lead to a high correlation of 0.868 between IC1 and IC2. In practice, actuaries need to be very careful in putting two variables with such a strong correlation into one regression. If IC1 and IC2 provide redundant (or very similar) information, one of them should be removed from the regression. In this specific case, the correlation between IC1 and IC2 may not be as strong as Pearson correlation statistic indicates. Comparing Tables 9.4 and 9.5, IC1 has 71 claims in most severe bin "A," while IC2 has 332 observations in "A." Similarly, IC1 has 3,108 claims in the second most severe bin "B" versus IC2's 21,053. It is clear that the two variables provide correlated but different insights. Pearson correlation 0.868 may give a misleading perception that the correlation between IC1 and IC2 is very strong.

---

[15] In this specific study, there are only five explanatory variables. The correlations among variables do not cause much an instability problem in GLM and DGLM. If we add five more variables, the correlation issue has to be addressed as the standard deviations of the coefficients for certain categorical bins may become quite large, and sometimes the numerical solutions may not even converge. It is out of the scope of this study to deal with correlation-related problems.

[16] Not all the variables are ordinal. Otherwise, the statistic would be Spearman correlation.

Table 9.7. *Pearson Correlations of Explanatory Variables*

	injury_code1	injury_code2	age_group	class_group	fatal_ind
injury_code1	1.000	0.868	−0.013	0.006	0.061
injury_code2	0.868	1.000	−0.012	0.006	0.060
age_group	−0.013	−0.012	1.000	0.068	−0.003
class_group	0.006	0.006	0.068	1.000	−0.001
fatal_ind	0.061	0.060	−0.003	−0.001	1.000

The variables in the study are either ordinal or categorical variables.[17] Contingency coefficient or Cramer's V are more technically sound statistics to test correlations among categorical variables. Table 9.8 reports the contingency coefficients of the five tested variables. The contingency coefficient is defined as:

$$C = \sqrt{\frac{\chi^2}{n + \chi^2}} \tag{9.3}$$

where χ^2 follows a similar formula in equation (9.2) assuming variables i and j are independent.

$$\chi^2 = \sum_{i,j}^{n} \frac{(n_{i,j} - \hat{n}_{i,j})^2}{\hat{n}_{i,j}} \tag{9.4}$$

where $n_{i,j}$ is the observed count in cell (i, j) and $\hat{n}_{i,j}$ the expected count. The estimated probability of x_1 in bin i is $\frac{n_i}{n}$ and estimated probability of x_2 in bin j is $\frac{n_j}{n}$. If x_1 and x_2 are independent, the probability of "x_1 in i and x_2 in j" is $\frac{n_i*n_j}{n^2}$. The expected count of cell (i, j) is

$$\hat{n}_{i,j} = n * \frac{n_{i*}n_j}{n^2} = \frac{n_{i*}n_j}{n} \tag{9.5}$$

Table 9.8. *Contingency Coefficient of Explanatory Variables*

	injury_code1	injury_code2	age_group	class_group	fatal_ind
injury_code1	0.894	0.771	0.015	0.014	0.106
injury_code2	0.771	0.894	0.014	0.021	0.196
age_group	0.015	0.014	0.816	0.078	0.003
class_group	0.014	0.021	0.078	0.707	0.001
fatal_ind	0.106	0.196	0.003	0.001	0.707

[17] "Fatal indicator" is categorical. Fatal claims are usually large, but almost all the extreme large claims are from nonfatal injuries. "Age group" is often treated as categorical other than ordinal in property and casualty actuarial practice because the loss costs do not monotonically increase or decreases with the insureds' age.

Substituting equation (9.5) into equation (9.4), the chi-square statistic is

$$\chi^2 = \sum_{i,j}^{n} \frac{\left(n_{i,j} - \frac{n_{i*}n_j}{n}\right)^2}{\frac{n_{i*}n_j}{n}} \qquad (9.6)$$

Substituting (9.6) into equation (9.3), we get the contingency coefficient. The coefficient between injury codes 1 and 2 is 0.771, close to the maximum value of 0.894. The contingency coefficient C provides another evidence that the two codes are correlated.

9.6 Regression Analysis

9.6.1 GLM Results

We run a standard severity GLM with a log-link function using a gamma distribution. The fatal claims are taken out of the regression because (1) injury codes and other covariates do not matter once a claim is fatal and (2) fatal claims are not complicated from the perspective of claims handling and claims departments usually follow routine procedures to settle them. The objective of claims triage model is to identify complex nonfatal claims that may develop into catastrophic claims. Table 9.9 reports the regression coefficients and related statistics. If the coefficient is zero, it implies the base bin. By Table 9.9, the GLM coefficient of bin "A" of IC1 is 2.01. The base bin is "E." If everything else is equal, the expected bin "A" claim is 7.47 times of bin

Table 9.9. *Parameter Estimates of Standard Gamma GLM*

Parameter	Bin	Estimate	Standard Error
Intercept		−2.8219	0.0086
injury_code1	E	0	0
injury_code1	D	0.5358	0.0247
injury_code1	C	0.7748	0.025
injury_code1	B	0.9813	0.0344
injury_code1	A	2.0109	0.1645
injury_code2	E	0	0
injury_code2	D	0.6552	0.0099
injury_code2	C	2.2322	0.025
injury_code2	B	3.4397	0.0268
injury_code2	A	4.6718	0.0828
class_group	1	−0.2481	0.0101
class_group	2	0	0
age_group	1	−0.1992	0.0093
age_group	2	−0.0616	0.0097
age_group	3	0	0

Table 9.10. *GLM Projected Large Claim Counts versus Actual Observations*

Predicted Value		GLM			Whole-Book Gamma		
Low	High	Fitted	Actual	% off	Fitted	Actual	% off
0	1	89,919	93,835	−3.2%	79,588	93,835	−15.2%
1	5	14,629	10,466	31.6%	26,321	10,466	151.5%
5	10	3,672	3,234	8.1%	3,810	3,234	17.8%
10	25	1,908	2,508	−21.4%	621	2,508	−75.2%
25	50	184	266	−13.2%	3	266	−98.9%
50	∞	31	34	8.8%	0	34	−100.0%
≥5		5,795	6,042	−4.1%	4,434	6,042	−26.6%

"E" ($7.47 = e^{2.01}$). In the actual data, the average "A" claim size is over 200 times of "E" claims. The reason that fitted coefficient is far from actual univariate analysis is the correlation impact from IC2. The coefficient of "A" of IC2 is 4.67. This implies that everything else being equal, "A" claim by injury code 2 is 106.9 times of "E" claim. Because of injury codes 1 and 2 are correlated, the coefficients of IC2 contain most of the impact of IC1. After removing the effect from IC2 and other variables, bin "A" of IC1 is only 7.47 times of "E." Similarly, the GLM coefficient of class group 1 is −0.248, which implies that the average claim size of class group 1 is 22.0% ($= e^{-0.248} - 1$) below that of class group 2. In reality, class group 2 can have more severe injuries and much bigger severity. However, most of the difference between the class groups has been contemplated by injury codes 1 and 2. If a roofer falls down from a tall ladder and an accountant cuts a finger by paper, the severity difference is majorly driven by body part and injury type, not by the industry class. In other words, if an accountant falls from tall stairs and suffers a low-back injury, the claim can still be severe even though it is from a low-risk class.

To test the goodness of fit of regression models, we first compare the expected counts with the actual counts by ranges of loss. It is similar to the goodness of fit test in whole-book distribution analysis. In the standard GLM, the expected loss is $\hat{y}_i$ for claim i and the expected variance is $\hat{\varphi}\hat{y}_i^2$. The shape parameter is $1/\hat{\varphi}$ and the scale parameter is $\hat{\varphi}\hat{y}_i$. The expected probability that a claim falls in the range of (a, b) is $c_i = \int_a^b gamma(y_i, shape_i, scale_i)dy_i = \int_a^b gamma(y_i, 1/\hat{\varphi}, \hat{\varphi}\hat{y}_i)dy_i$. Adding up all the c_i, we can get the expected claims count in range (a, b). Table 9.10 reports the expected claims counts of selected loss ranges by GLM and whole-book distribution analysis. Comparing the fitted claims counts, it is clear that adding covariates drastically improves the goodness of fit. The other big benefit of GLM over the conventional distribution analysis is that it provides the insights for individual claims. Similar as whole-book distribution analysis, standard gamma GLM tends to underestimate the

Table 9.11. *GLM Residual Statistics by Predicted*
Value for Bias

Model	Fitted Group	Mean RawResidual	Mean PearsonRes
GLM	≤0.5	0.0013	0.0013
GLM	(.5, 1]	0.0017	0.0115
GLM	(1, 3]	−0.1558	−0.0648
GLM	(3, 7]	0.0421	0.0084
GLM	(7, 15]	0.5245	0.0438
GLM	>15	−1.2893	0.0252

large loss count. For large loss 5 times higher than the average, gamma GLM expects 5,795 claims count, versus the actual observation of 6,042. In the "10 to 25" and "25 to 50" ranges, GLM understates the count by more than 20%.

Secondly, we test the residuals. If the GLM is unbiased, the average of raw residuals should be close to zero by explanatory variables and by the predicted values. Raw residual is the difference between actual and predicted values. $\varepsilon_i = y_i - \hat{y}_i$. Pearson residual is defined as raw residual divided by the square root of predicted variance. $\varepsilon_{i,p} = \frac{y_i - \hat{y}_i}{\hat{\sigma}_i}$. In the standard GLM, $\hat{\sigma}_i = \sqrt{\hat{\varphi}}\hat{y}_i$, where $\hat{\varphi}$ is the constant dispersion factor. Table 9.11 shows the average values of raw and Pearson residuals by Predicted value. Table 9.12 exhibits the same statistics by injury code 2. By Table 9.11, GLM may have certain inherent biases: in "one to three" and "over 15" ranges, the GLM projection overstates the mean; in "3 to 15" ranges, the GLM projection understates the mean. By Table 9.12, GLM projections by injury code 2 are in line well with the actual observations. For the most severe injuries (IC2=A), GLM over projects the mean. Tables 9.11–9.12 show that GLM overestimates the mean for very large claims.

Table 9.12. *GLM Residual Statistics by Injury*
Code 2 for Bias

Model	Injury_ code2	Mean RawResidual	Mean PearsonRes
GLM	E	0.0006	0.0000
GLM	D	0.0006	0.0000
GLM	C	−0.0160	0.0000
GLM	B	0.0149	0.0000
GLM	A	−1.1881	0.0000

Table 9.13. *DGLM Parameter Estimation*

Model Component	Variable	Bin	Estimate	Standard Error
Mean	Intercept		−2.8187	0.0066
Mean	injury_code1	E	0	0.0000
Mean	injury_code1	D	0.5857	0.0222
Mean	injury_code1	C	0.8550	0.0225
Mean	injury_code1	B	1.0824	0.0336
Mean	injury_code1	A	2.0665	0.1818
Mean	injury_code2	E	0	0.0000
Mean	injury_code2	D	0.6543	0.0078
Mean	injury_code2	C	2.1747	0.0223
Mean	injury_code2	B	3.3606	0.0244
Mean	injury_code2	A	4.5744	0.0977
Mean	class_group	1	−0.2413	0.0088
Mean	class_group	2	0	0.0000
Mean	age_group	1	−0.2129	0.0081
Mean	age_group	2	−0.0729	0.0084
Mean	age_group	3	0	0.0000
Dispersion	Intercept		−0.1086	0.0074
Dispersion	injury_code2	E	0	0.0000
Dispersion	injury_code2	D	0.2445	0.0097
Dispersion	injury_code2	C	0.6831	0.0111
Dispersion	injury_code2	B	0.7475	0.0110
Dispersion	injury_code2	A	0.9962	0.0674

9.6.2 DGLM and FMM Results

Both count and residual tests suggest that standard GLM may not be adequate to handle heavy tails and heterogeneous variance. To improve the goodness of fit, DGLM and FMM are performed using the same data. DGLM coefficients are numerically calculated using the SAS procedure NLMIXED as described in Yan et al. (2009). The density function of loss is explicitly given with its mean μ_i specified by a transformed linear combination of the covariates X_i and its dispersion parameter φ_i specified by a second transformed linear combination of some (other) covariates[18] Z_i and then the two sets of coefficients (for mean and dispersion) are estimated by the maximal likelihood estimation method. The coefficients of finite mixture models are directly from SAS procedure FMM. Tables 9.13 and 9.14 display the model coefficients for DGLM and FMM, respectively. By Table 9.13, the coefficients of DGLM's mean component are very close to those of GLM. This is understandable because two models follow the exact same specification on the mean of loss. The difference of the two models is

---

[18] We only use one categorical variable, IC2, in the dispersion component of the DGLM model for illustration purposes.

Table 9.14. *FMM Parameters*

Model Component	Variable	Bin	Estimate	Standard Error
1st gamma	Intercept		−2.8628	0.0066
1st gamma	injury_code1	A	5.8999	0.2355
1st gamma	injury_code1	B	1.8920	0.0518
1st gamma	injury_code1	C	1.4485	0.0259
1st gamma	injury_code1	D	0.6256	0.0231
1st gamma	injury_code1	E	0	−
1st gamma	injury_code2	A	0.8470	0.0314
1st gamma	injury_code2[a]	B	0.8470	0.0314
1st gamma	injury_code2	C	0.7518	0.0250
1st gamma	injury_code2	D	0.4380	0.0076
1st gamma	injury_code2	E	0	−
1st gamma	class_group	1	−0.2537	0.0089
1st gamma	class_group	2	0	−
1st gamma	age_group	1	−0.2555	0.0083
1st gamma	age_group	2	−0.1101	0.0086
1st gamma	age_group	3	0	−
2nd gamma	Intercept		−0.1174	0.04267
2nd gamma	injury_code2	A	3.3418	0.09623
2nd gamma	injury_code2	B	1.9999	0.04099
2nd gamma	injury_code2	C	0.9709	0.04251
2nd gamma	injury_code2	D	0	−
2nd gamma	injury_code2[b]	E	0	−
2nd gamma	class_group	1	−0.2584	0.02271
2nd gamma	class_group	2	0	−
2nd gamma	age_group	1	−0.1317	0.01889
2nd gamma	age_group	2	0	−
2nd gamma	age_group[c]	3	0	−
Probability	Intercept		−5.4788	0.1261
Probability	injury_code2	A	6.1496	0.2008
Probability	injury_code2	B	5.7555	0.1274
Probability	injury_code2	C	4.7931	0.1273
Probability	injury_code2	D	2.1130	0.1291
Probability	injury_code2	E	0	−

[a] Injury code 2 "A" and "B" are binned together.
[b] Injury code 2 "D" and "E" are binned together.
[c] Age group 2 and 3 are binned together. Otherwise the numerical computation will not converge because of the multicolinearity problem.

that DGLM allows the dispersion factor in the variance term to vary by explanatory variables. The dispersion coefficient increases as the injury becomes more severe. Even though the fitted mean values are similar between GLM and DGLM, DGLM projects higher variances for more severe claims. The FMM coefficients have three components for the mean of first gamma distribution, the mean of the second gamma

Table 9.15. *Projected Means of Selected Segmentations by GLM, DGLM, and FMM*

IC1	IC2	Class Group	Age Group	GLM Mean	DGLM Mean	FMM 1st Gamma	FMM 2nd Gamma	1st Gamma Prob	FMM Mean
A	A	2	3	47.50	45.71	48.62	25.14	33.8%	33.09
A	B	2	3	13.86	13.58	48.62	6.57	43.1%	24.71
B	A	2	3	16.96	17.08	0.88	25.14	33.8%	16.93
B	B	2	3	4.95	5.08	0.88	6.57	43.1%	4.12
B	C	2	3	1.48	1.55	0.80	2.35	66.5%	1.32
C	C	2	3	1.20	1.23	0.52	2.35	66.5%	1.13
D	C	2	3	0.95	0.94	0.23	2.35	66.5%	0.94
D	D	2	3	0.20	0.21	0.17	0.89	96.7%	0.19
E	E	2	3	0.06	0.06	0.06	0.89	99.6%	0.06

distribution, and the probabilities of the claim being in these two distributions, respectively. Table 9.15 shows model-projected values for a small group of claims with selected values of covariates. For minor injuries, FMM project means close to GLM and DGLM. If both IC1 and IC2 are "D," GLM and DGLM expects single distributions with means of 0.20 and 0.21, respectively. FMM assumes that the claims will have 96.7% chance to be in a distribution with a smaller mean of 0.17 and 3.3% chance to be in another distribution with a large mean of 0.89. The mean values of mixture distributions are very close to GLM or DGLM mean. When there are a lot of observations for minor claims, all three models provide robust and accurate projections on the mean. On high-severity injuries, some claims can become very large; some claims might be settled at low amounts because the original codes of injuries at the first notice of loss were wrong; and other claims may become expense-only because they are not compensable by the insurance policies and rejected by the adjustors. The larger distributions from FMM will represent the huge claims better than GLM and DGLM while the smaller distributions reflect the latter two cases. For example, GLM and DGLM have fitted means 16.96 and 17.08 for the claims with IC1="B" and IC2="A," respectively. FMM shows that those claims have a 33.8% probability to be small with a mean 0.88 and 66.2% probability to be large with a mean of 25.14. The overall mean is 16.93, which is close with those of GLM and DGLM. It is a coincidence that three models project similar mean values for this group of severe injuries. For IC1="A" and IC2="A," FMM mean is 33.09, significantly lower than GLM and DGLM, whereas for IC1="A" and IC2="B," FMM mean is 24.71, significantly higher than GLM and DGLM.

To test DGLM and FMM, we perform the same large-loss count and residual tests. The calculations of expected counts from DGLM and FMM are similar with that of GLM. In DGLM, the shape parameter is $1/\hat{\varphi}_i$ and the scale parameter is $\hat{\varphi}_i\hat{y}_i$. The probability of claim i in range (a, b) is $c_i =$

Table 9.16. *DGLM and FMM Projected Large Claim Counts versus Actual Observations*

Predicted Value		DGLM			FMM		
Low	High	Fitted	Actual	% off	Fitted	Actual	% off
0	1	90,832	93,835	−3.2%	93,971	93,835	0.1%
1	5	13,776	10,466	31.6%	10,407	10,466	−0.6%
5	10	3,495	3,234	8.1%	3,351	3,234	3.6%
10	25	1,972	2,508	−21.4%	2,252	2,508	−10.2%
25	50	231	266	−13.2%	320	266	20.3%
50	∞	37	34	8.8%	42	34	23.5%
≥5		5,735	6,042	−5.1%	5,965	6,042	−1.3%

$\int_a^b gamma(y_i, 1/\hat{\varphi}_i, \hat{\varphi}_i \hat{y}_i) dy_i$. In FMM, let $\hat{\varphi}_1$ and $\hat{\varphi}_2$ denote the dispersion factors of gamma GLM 1 and 2, respectively; $\hat{y}_{i,1}$ and $\hat{y}_{i,2}$ are the predicted values of gamma GLM 1 and 2, respectively. The expected count of claim i is in range (a, b) is $\int_a^b (\hat{p}_i gamma_1(y_i, 1/\hat{\varphi}_1, \hat{\varphi}_1 \hat{y}_{i,1}) + (1 - \hat{p}_i) gamma_2(y_i, 1/\hat{\varphi}_2, \hat{\varphi}_2 \hat{y}_{i,2})) dy_i$.

Table 9.16 reports the goodness of fit tests on large claims counts. For large claims over 5 times of the mean, GLM underestimates the count by 4.1%. Table 9.16 shows that DGLM also understates the count, and the magnitude of underestimation is similar at 5.1%. FMM significantly outperforms GLM and DGLM and the projected count of large claims (over 5) is only 1.3% below the actual observation. By individual ranges, FMM provides the best projections in "5–10" and "10–25" claims. For the extreme large ranges over 25, FMM somehow overstates the count of losses: the expected count of claims is 362, 20.7% higher than the observed count of 300. Both DGLM and GLM understate the count for this range. DGLM's projection is 10.7% below the actual while GLM is 28.3% below.

The calculation of Pearson residual in DGLM is straightforward; $\varepsilon_{i,p} = \frac{y_i - \hat{y}_i}{\hat{\sigma}_i} = \frac{y_i - \hat{y}_i}{\sqrt{\hat{\varphi}_i \hat{y}_i}}$, where the dispersion factor $\hat{\varphi}_i$ is the predicted dispersion factor from the second GLM. In FMM, the estimation of variance is more complicated; y_i may follow two distributions: $\hat{p}_i$ is the estimated probability of the first distribution $f_1(y)$ and $\hat{\sigma}_{i,1}^2$ is the variance of the first distribution: $\hat{\sigma}_{i,1}^2 = \hat{\varphi}_1 \hat{y}_{i,1}^2$, and $1 - \hat{p}_i$ is the probability of the second distribution $f_2(y)$ and $\hat{\sigma}_{i,2}^2$ is the variance of the second distribution: $\hat{\sigma}_{i,2}^2 = \hat{\varphi}_1 \hat{y}_{i,2}^2$. The variance of mixture distribution from FMM is

$$\hat{\sigma}_i^2 = \int_0^\infty (y_i - E(y_i))^2 f(y_i) dy_i$$

$$= \hat{p}_i^3 \hat{\sigma}_{i,1}^2 + \hat{p}_i^2 (1 - \hat{p}_i) \hat{\sigma}_{i,2}^2 + \hat{p}_i^2 (1 - \hat{p}_i)(\hat{y}_{i,2} - \hat{y}_{i,1})^2 + 2\hat{p}_i^2 (1 - \hat{p}_i) \hat{\sigma}_{i,1}^2$$

$$+ 2\hat{p}_i (1 - \hat{p}_i)^2 \hat{\sigma}_{i,2}^2 + \hat{p}_i (1 - \hat{p}_i) \hat{\sigma}_{i,1}^2 + \hat{p}_i (1 - \hat{p}_i)^2 (\hat{y}_{i,2} - \hat{y}_{i,1})^2 + (1 - \hat{p}_i)^3 \hat{\sigma}_{i,2}^2$$

$$= \hat{p}_i \hat{\sigma}_{i,1}^2 + (1 - \hat{p}_i) \hat{\sigma}_{i,2}^2 + \hat{p}_i (1 - \hat{p}_i)(\hat{y}_{i,2} - \hat{y}_{i,1})^2 \qquad (9.7)$$

Table 9.17. *DGLM and FMM Residual Statistics
by Predicted Value for Bias*

Model	Fitted Group	Mean RawResidual	Mean PearsonRes
DGLM	≤0.5	0.0015	0.0018
DGLM	(.5, 1]	0.0037	0.0135
DGLM	(1, 3]	−0.1689	−0.0695
DGLM	(3, 7]	0.0306	0.0066
DGLM	(7, 15]	0.6444	0.0522
DGLM	>15	−0.9849	0.0223
FMM	≤0.5	−0.0001	−0.0005
FMM	(.5, 1]	−0.0016	0.0029
FMM	(1, 3]	−0.1004	−0.0292
FMM	(3, 7]	0.0513	0.0061
FMM	(7, 15]	−1.4078	−0.0554
FMM	>15	0.0722	0.0133

Tables 9.17 and 9.18 exhibit the tests for unbiasedness by fitted value and by IC2. Comparing Tables 9.11 and 9.12 with Tables 9.17 and 9.18, the mean values of raw residuals are very similar between GLM and DGLM. This is expected because GLM and DGLM have the same model specification for mean. FMM does not outperform GLM or DGLM in the unbiasedness test. FMM biases (measured by the absolute values of mean residuals) are significantly better than GLM in the ranges of "1–3" and "15 above" but significantly worse in the ranges of "3–7" and "7–15." By IC2, the biases from FMM, DGLM, and GLM are close to zero for "B," "C," "D," and "E." For the most severe injury code "A," the average fitted value from FMM is slightly

Table 9.18. *DGLM and FMM Residual Statistics
by Injury Code 2 for Bias*

Model	Injury_ code2	Mean RawResidual	Mean PearsonRes
DGLM	E	0.0005	−0.0001
DGLM	D	0.0004	0.0000
DGLM	C	−0.0197	0.0003
DGLM	B	0.0069	−0.0001
DGLM	A	−0.9607	0.0017
FMM	E	−0.0003	−0.0023
FMM	D	0.0001	0.0008
FMM	C	−0.0062	−0.0005
FMM	B	0.0196	0.0000
FMM	A	−0.0307	0.0034

higher (0.031) than the actual average. It contrasts with GLM and DGLM, which on average overstate those claims by 1.188 and 0.961. This is because GLM and DGLM are not flexible enough to represent the extreme values on the right tail. The numerical results might be a compromise between the mean and extreme values: to improve the fits on large claims, the models sacrifice slightly the fits of mean.

FMM provides additional flexibility in modeling the right tails of loss distributions, but also introduces more parameters and therefore additional parameter risk. When a claim can be in two distributions and the probabilities of distributions vary by covariates, the model is so flexible that it will not only captures "true" underlying signal but also is very responsive to random noises. By varying seeds in the simulations, GLM and DGLM coefficients are relatively stable, whereas the coefficients for FMM can swing significantly. To use FMM in practice, actuaries need to test the overfitting problem thoroughly in both in-sample and out-of-sample validations, especially when there are correlations among certain covariates, when the data in certain segments are thin, or when various interaction terms of multiple variables are tested in the model. Business reasonability check is also important.

9.6.3 Actuarial Applications

The end results of large loss regression analysis are the fitted distributions for individual claims by the underlying injury characteristics. Many actuarial applications can benefit from those results. We will illustrate two practical applications: claims triage and high-deductible pricing.

In the claims triage model, the goal is to identify the claims that may become very large without proper handling. For example, if an injured worker is taking unnecessarily strong opioid drugs, he may become addicted and never return to work. An effective nurse case management may intervene the medical process early, avoid the drug addiction, and help the worker return to work. It would be a win-win solution. The injured worker will have a better life and the insurance company can reduce the claims cost. In pricing models, the focus is on the mean of frequency, severity, or loss cost. In the claims triage models, the focus is both mean and volatility. For small standard claims, the claims can be handled by STP (straight through processes). For large stable claims, such as fatal claims, no matter who is handling the claim, the results may not change much. For large volatile claims with a wide range of possible outcomes, proper claim intervention from experienced adjusters may significantly reduce the ultimate claim payment. To compare three models, we rank the claims by the expected mean from each model and flag about 10% claims,[19] and monitor the performance of

---

[19] The claims departments in insurance industry generally have the resources constraints to review potential large claims. The capacities vary by companies. Actuaries should consider claims departments' capacity when choosing

Table 9.19. *Percentages of True Positive Flags*

Model	Number of Flagged Claims	Actual Count of Large Claims	Percentage of Actual Large
FMM	9,641	2,718	28.19%
GLM	10,212	2,870	28.10%
DGLM	10,212	2,870	28.10%

those flagged claims. Table 9.19 reports the actual number and percentage of flagged claims that are actual large claims (defined as loss >5). Because the DGLM mean coefficients are very close to those of GLM, DGLM actually flags the same claims as GLM. FMM projects slightly fewer claims to be over 5. This result may look inconsistent with Table 9.16, which shows that FMM projects more counts of large claims. The number of claims with mean over 5 and the expected number of claims over 5 are two different concepts. Loss is a random variable: a claim with a mean over 5 may not become a large loss over 5 and another claim with a mean less than 5 can turn into a large loss. For the claims with expected values less than 5, the larger distributions from FMM will make them more likely to become large claims. The expected count of large losses from those un-flagged claims are significantly higher by FMM. For example, for claims with IC1=D, IC2=C, class=2, age=3, the expected values of GLM and FMM are 0.95 and 0.94, close to the whole-book average. The loss by FMM has a 33.5% of chance to be in a larger distribution with a mean of 2.35. The probabilities of the loss over 5 are 4.28% and 1.56% by FMM and GLM, respectively. The count of claims with the characteristics above is 5,299. FMM expects 227 claims to be over 5, significantly higher than the projection of 83 by GLM. The actual count of large claims is 224, and FMM performs better in predicting large loss from this type of claims. However, we will not flag those "average" claims in the triage model because the likelihoods of generating large losses are small by both GLM and FMM models. The advantage of FMM to accurately fit the right tail of this group of nonsevere injuries does not help from the perspective of the claims triage application: the percentages of accurate flagging in Table 9.19 are very close between GLM, DGLM, and FMM. The next actuarial application, high-deductible pricing, will benefit from this advantage of FMM as the interest of study is to measure the magnitude of the claim size on the right tail.

Workers' compensation insurance is an expensive product for most employers (Teng, 1994). High-deductible plans are a popular alternative for employers, especially mid- to large-sized companies, to meet their legal obligation because it gives the

---

the cutoff points of flagging claims. The flagged counts vary by model because the projected means are discrete. If the projected means are continuous, we can choose the cutoff points to flag the same count from all three models.

Table 9.20. *Whole-Book Loss Elimination Ratios from GLM, DGLM, and FMM*

Statistics	Actual	GLM	DGLM	FMM
Deducted Loss	88,642	94,420	92,277	87,814
Total Loss	108,879	109,213	109,400	108,613
Loss Elimination Ratio	81.4%	86.5%	84.3%	80.9%
Price as a % to Standard Policy	18.6%	13.5%	15.7%	19.1%

employers more control of their losses and significant expense saving on the insurance premium. To price a high-deductible plan, the key is to estimate the loss eliminated by the large dollar deductible and the credit risk associated with insured paying back the deductibles. Table 9.20 displays the total loss elimination for all the nonfatal claims by a deductible 10 (which is 10 times of average claim, or close to $100,000 if translating to a flat dollar amount). For each individual claim, we calculate the mean, loss distribution, and the expected deduction under the retention using GLM, DGLM, and FMM, respectively. Aggregating the expected losses and deductions of all the claims, we are able to derive the whole-book loss elimination ratio. By GLM, a deductible will eliminate 86.5% of loss from all the claims. Using actual data, it only eliminates 81.4% of loss. GLM underestimates the volatility of large loss and the likelihoods of the claims penetrating the retention level and therefore overstates the loss eliminated by the deductible. DGLM increases the volatility of large claims through the dispersion factor, and the loss elimination ratio reduces to 84.3%. FMM has a loss elimination ratio 80.9%, very close to the actual observation. Using GLM, the model-indicated high deductible credit is artificially high and the implied price would be 27.1% (=13.5%/18.6% − 1) lower than using actual data. Using DGLM, the price of high-deductible policies would be 15.6% inadequate. FMM clearly outperforms GLM and DGLM in predicting the loss eliminated by the deductible and the excess loss over the deductible.

The whole-book loss elimination ratios by actual data and FMM are very close; what are the advantages of using complicated regressions? The answer is that whole-book analysis only provide one average loss elimination ratio for all the policies. In reality, some low-risk policies, such as clerical and sales business, may have very small likelihoods to generate losses greater than the deductible and should receive bigger deductible credits, whereas high-risk policies, such as roofers and lumberjacks, are more likely to produce large claims, and should receive smaller high-deductible credits. The 81.4% credit from the whole-book analysis cannot help individual policies. If we apply the same type of analysis by segmentation, the data volume of any specific segment is too thin to be credible for high-deductible analysis. As Shi (2014) states, that regression method is a more appealing solution to address the problem. Suppose that a policy from a class group 2 has a 20% of chance to generate a claim in IC1=B,

Table 9.21. *Loss Elimination Ratios for a Hypothetical Policy*

Statistics	GLM	DGLM	FMM
Deducted Loss	1.398	1.231	1.194
Total Loss	3.474	3.502	3.475
Loss Elimination Ratio	40.2%	35.2%	34.4%
Price as a % to Standard Policy	59.8%	64.8%	65.6%

IC2=A, age=3, and an 80% of chance to have a claim in IC1=D, and IC2=E, and age=3. Table 9.21 shows the loss elimination ratios by GLM, DGLM, and FMM. Even though the whole-book loss elimination ratio is on average at 81.4%, this specific policy has a much lower percentage of loss that will be deducted by the retention. The example demonstrates the advantage of the regression method over whole-book distribution analysis: it could provide more insight on individual policies based upon their own risk characteristics.

The calculations are trivial, and we will only show the details on FMM. For the claim in IC1=D and IC2=E, the smaller gamma has a mean of 0.107, the larger gamma has a mean of 0.889, and the mean of mixture is 0.110. The probability of penetrating 10 is extremely small.

For the claim in IC1=B and IC2=A, it has a 33.8% probability to be in the smaller gamma distribution with a mean of 0.884 and almost all the loss will be deducted. The larger distribution has a mean of 25.140. Conditional on that the claim is the larger distribution, the expected loss under 10 is 7.908. For the mixture distribution, the expected loss elimination is 5.531 (=7.908*66.2%+0.884*33.8%) and the expected loss is 16.934 (=25.140*66.2%+0.884*33.8%).

On the policy, the expected loss on claim with IC1=D and IC2=E is 0.110; the expected loss on claim with IC1=B and IC2=A is 16.934. The overall expected loss is 3.475 (=0.110*80%+16.934*20%). The overall loss elimination is 1.194 (=0.110*80%+5.531*20%).

9.7 Conclusions

It is well known that insurance losses are skewed and fat-tailed. The authors use workers' compensation data to illustrate that popular single distributions such as lognormal, Pareto, and gamma do not fit insurance data well and that mixture distributions can improve the goodness of fit significantly. To incorporate the mixture distributions in the regression analysis of the modern predictive modeling era, the authors explore finite mixture model, which marries two well-studied actuarial fields of regression analysis (GLM) and fat-tailed distribution analysis (mixture distribution). The case study demonstrates that FMM can project the large-loss count and the loss elimination ratio by the high deductible significantly better than GLM. Because of its flexibility of fitting both small "normal" and large "abnormal" losses, FMM provides an additional technique to actuaries' toolbox as a useful supplement and complement of standard GLM. The potential applications may include increased limit factor, excess and high-deductible pricing, claim triage, and enterprise risk management, and so on.

References

Anderson D., S. Feldblum, C. Modlin, D. Schirmacher, E. Schirmacher, and N. Thandi. A practitioner's guide to generalized linear models. *Casualty Actuarial Society Discussion Paper Program*, 2004.

Beirlant, J., G. Matthys, and G. Dierckx. Heavy tailed distributions and rating. *ASTIN Bulletin*, 31:37–58, 2001.

Boucher, J., and D. Davidov. On the importance of dispersion modeling for claims reserving: An application with the Tweedie distribution. *Variance*, 5(2):158–172, 2011.

Clark, D. Basics of reinsurance pricing. *CAS Exam Study Note*, Casualty Actuarial Society, 1996.

Clark, D. A note on the upper-truncated Pareto distribution. *ERM Symposium*, 2013.

Dean, C. G. Generalized linear models. In E. W. Frees, G. Meyers, and R. A. Derrig (eds.), *Predictive Modeling Applications in Actuarial Science: Volume 1, Predictive Modeling Techniques*, pp. 107–137. Cambridge University Press, Cambridge, 2014.

Dempster, A. P., N. M. Laird, and D. B. Rubin. Maximum likelihood from incomplete data via the EM algorithm. *Journal of the Royal Statistical Society, Series B*, 39(1):1–38, 1977.

Diebolt, J., and C. P. Robert. Estimation of finite mixture distributions through Bayesian sampling. *Journal of the Royal Statistical Society, Series B*, 56:363–375, 1994.

Everitt, B. S., and D. J. Hand. *Finite Mixture Distributions*. Chapman and Hall, London, 1981.

Fleming, K. G. Yep, we're skewed. *Variance*, 2(2):179–183, 2008.

Frees, E. W. Frequency and severity models. In E. W. Frees, G. Meyers, and R. A. Derrig (eds.), *Predictive Modeling Applications in Actuarial Science: Volume 1, Predictive Modeling Techniques*, pp. 138–164. Cambridge University Press, Cambridge, 2014.

Frees, E., P. Shi, and E. Valdez. Actuarial applications of a hierarchical claims model. *ASTIN Bulletin*, 39(1):165–197, 2009.

Fu, L., and R. Moncher. Severity distributions for GLMs: Gamma or lognormal? Evidence from Monte Carlo simulations. *Casualty Actuarial Society Discussion Paper Program*, 2004.

Fu, L., and C. P. Wu. General iteration algorithms for classification ratemaking. *Variance*, 1(2):193–213, 2007.

Gordon, S. K., and B. Jørgensen. Fitting Tweedie's compound Poisson model to insurance claims data: Dispersion modelling. *ASTIN Bulletin*, 32:143–157, 2002.

Guven, S. Multivariate spatial analysis of the territory rating variable. *Casualty Actuarial Society Discussion Paper Program*, 2004.

Henry, J. B., and P. Hsieh. Extreme value analysis for partitioned insurance losses. *Variance*, 3(2):214–238, 2009.

Holler, K., D. Sommer, and G. Trahair. Something old, something new in classification ratemaking with a novel use of generalized linear models for credit insurance. *CAS Forum*, Winter 1999.

Johnson, W. G., M. L. Baldwin, and R. J. Butler. The costs and outcomes of chiropractic and physician care for workers' compensation back claims. *The Journal of Risk and Insurance*, 66(2):185–205, 1999.

Keatinge, C. Modeling losses with the mixed exponential distribution. *Proceedings of the Casualty Actuarial Society*, LXXXVI:654–698, 1999.

Kessler, D., and A. McDowell. Introducing the FMM procedure for finite mixture models. *SAS Global Forum*, 2012.

Klugman, S. A., H. E. Panjer, and G. E. Willmot. *Loss Models: From Data to Decisions*. John Wiley, New York, 1998.

Kremer, E. IBNR claims and the two way model of ANOVA. *Scandinavian Actuarial Journal*, 1982:47–55, 1982.

Matthys, G., E. Delafosse, A. Guillou, and J. Beirlant. Estimating catastrophic quantile levels for heavy-tailed distributions. *Insurance: Mathematics and Economics*, 34:517–537, 2004.

McCullagh, P., and J. Nelder. *Generalized Linear Models*. 2nd ed. Chapman and Hall/CRC, Boca Raton, FL, 1989.

McLachlan, G. J., and D. Peel. *Finite Mixture Models*. New York: John Wiley, 2000.

Miccolis, R. S. On the theory of increased limits and excess of loss pricing. *Proceedings of Casualty Actuarial Society*, LXIV:27–59, 1977.

Mildenhall, S. J. A systematic relationship between minimum bias and generalized linear models. *Proceedings of the Casualty Actuarial Society*, LXXXVI:393–487, 1999.

Mildenhall, S. J. Discussion of "general minimum bias models." *Casualty Actuarial Society Forum*, Winter 2005.

Mosley, R. Estimating claim settlement values using GLM. *Casualty Actuarial Society Discussion Paper Program*, 2004.

Nelder, J. A., and O. Pregibon. An extended quasi-likelihood function. *Biometrik*, 74:221–231, 1987.

Newcomb, S. A generalized theory of the combination of observations so as to obtain the best result. *American Journal of Mathematics*, 8:343–366, 1886.

Parsa, R. A., and S. A. Klugman. Copula regression. *Variance*, 5(1):45–54, 2011.

Pearson, K. Contributions to mathematical theory of evolution. *Philosophical Transactions, Series A*, 185:71–110, 1894.

Pregibon, O. Review of generalized linear models. *Ann. Statistics*, 12:1589–1596, 1984.

Renshaw, A. E. Chain ladder and interactive modelling (claims reserving and GLIM). *Journal of the Institute of Actuaries*, 116(3):559–587, 1989.

Renshaw, A. E., and R. J. Verrall. A stochastic model underlying the chain ladder technique. *Proceedings XXV ASTIN Colloquium*, 1994.

Shi, P. Fat-tailed regression models. In E. W. Frees, G. Meyers, and R. A. Derrig (eds.), *Predictive Modeling Applications in Actuarial Science: Volume 1, Predictive Modeling Techniques*, pp. 236–259. Cambridge University Press, Cambridge, 2014.

Smyth, G. K. Generalized linear models with varying dispersion. *J. R. Statist. Soc., Series B*: 51:57–60, 1989.

Smyth, G. K., and B. Jørgensen. Fitting Tweedie's compound Poisson model to insurance claims data: Dispersion modelling. *ASTIN Bulletin*, 32:143–157, 2002.

Smyth, G. K., and A. P. Verbyla. Adjusted likelihood methods for modelling dispersion ingeneralized linear models. *Environmetrics*, 10:696–709, 1999.

Taylor, G. C. The chain ladder and Tweedie distributed claims data. *Variance*, 3(1):96–104, 2009.

Taylor, G. C., and F. R. Ashe. Second moments of estimates of outstanding claims. *Journal of Econometrics*, 23:37–61, 1983.

Teng, M. S. Pricing workers' compensation large deductible and excess insurance. *Casualty Actuarial Society Forum*, Winter 1994.

Titterington, D., A. Smith, and U. Makov. *Statistical Analysis of Finite Mixture Distributions*. John Wiley, New York, 1985.

Venter, G. Generalized linear models beyond the exponential family with loss reserve applications. *Casualty Actuarial Society E-Forum*, Summer 2007.

Verbyla, A. P., and G. K. Smyth. Double generalized linear models: Approximate residualmaximum likelihood and diagnostics. Research Report, Department of Statistics, University of Adelaide, 1998.

Wang, S. A set of new methods and tools for enterprise risk capital management and portfolio optimization. *Casualty Actuarial Society Forum*, Spring 2002.

Wedderburn, R. W. M. Quasi-likelihood functions, generalized linear models, and the Gauss-Newton method. *Biometrika*, 61(3):439–447, 1974.

Wedel, M., and W. S. DeSarbo. A mixture likelihood approach for generalized linear models. *Journal of Classification*, 12:21–55, 1995.

Yan, J., J. Guszcza, M. Flynn, and C. P. Wu. Applications of the offset in property-casualty predictive modeling. *Casualty Actuarial Society Forum*, Winter 2009.

10

A Framework for Managing Claim Escalation Using Predictive Modeling

Mohamad A. Hindawi and Claudine H. Modlin

10.1 Introduction

Claims represent the biggest cost within a property and casualty insurance company. Managing the claims process is fundamental to the company's profitability; moreover, an effective claims operation drives customer satisfaction and policyholder retention. Given the importance of the claims management function and the vast amount of information collected on each claim, it is no surprise that analytics have provided substantial return on investment for insurers. Of course, the analytics have to be coupled with a technology platform that can provide seamless delivery to the claims function personnel.

Claims analytics often take two general forms: descriptive and predictive. Descriptive analytics involve robust reporting of trends in key performance indicators. This includes lagging indicators (e.g., payments closure patterns) and leading indicators (e.g., return to work, network penetration). Predictive analytics involve analyzing historical data at each stage in the claims cycle to influence decisions on future claims. Applications of predictive analytics in claims can address any stage of the claims life cycle – from first notice of loss through settlement and recovery.

This chapter discusses a type of predictive modeling application commonly referred to as claims triage. The broad objective of claims triage is to use the characteristics of each individual claim at a specific point in time to predict some future outcome, which then dictates how the claim will be handled. In practice, claims triage might identify simpler claims for fast-track processing or alternatively identify complex claims that require expert handling or intervention. Claims triage models can help assign claims to the right adjuster or inform the adjuster of what actions to take (e.g., when to dispatch an engineer to a claim site or when to assign a nurse case manager to a workers' compensation claim).

In this chapter, we discuss a specific application that seeks to identify those claims that have a higher likelihood to settle far in excess of early reported loss estimates. This early identification of likely claim escalation should enable the claims department to better manage and potentially mitigate the escalation. Much of our discussion is based on application to workers' compensation claims, but the methods and issues discussed can be relevant to other long-tailed lines with sufficient claims volume such as general liability.

Our approach to claims triage involves two stages of modeling. The stages are inter-related as the output of the first stage is used in the response variable of the second. The first stage, which we discuss in Section 10.2, involves modeling incremental paid losses of individual claims to forecast the future incremental payments. This projection, along with a tail factor adjustment, allows the modeler to estimate ultimate losses for each claim.

In the second stage of modeling, we estimate the likelihood that the difference between the estimated ultimate (as estimated in the first modeling stage) and the reported loss at a given age of the claim will pierce a certain monetary threshold. We discuss these models in Section 10.5.

The first stage of modeling, the claim development stage, is restricted to using claim attributes that will not change over the life of the claim. The second stage, the triage models, does not have this constraint. Consequently, we will address the addition of some novel data, text mined from claim adjuster notes and medical and billing data, in Section 10.3. Also, the addition of so many predictors requires variable reduction techniques to generate a more manageable number of variables prior to modeling. We will briefly discuss in Section 10.4 the use of a penalized regression model called the elastic net to identify the most predictive variables for modeling while leaving all technical detail of the elastic net to the appendix. Finally, we summarize the main conclusions and further research opportunities in Sections 10.6 and 10.7, respectively.

10.2 Loss Development Models

Building predictive models for a long-tailed line of insurance, where a large portion of historical reported claims remain open, begins with developing individual claims to ultimate. Applying aggregate development techniques such as traditional triangle-based methods are generally unsuitable for claims analytics applications because such methods ignore the difference in development rate based on individual claims characteristics. Capturing such differences in development patterns is critical for any claim analytics application and something a modeler needs to perform with care.

This section focuses on one particular method, the incremental paid development method. Generalized linear models are fitted to historical incremental paid loss amounts and used to generate ultimate loss forecasts for the inventory of claims.

10.2.1 Data Structure

A statistical model is as good as the data underlying it. This is true in particular for claims triage models. Claims triage models are typically built on the output of another set of predictive models, namely, loss development models. As a result, any bias in the data produces biased model outputs, which get compounded over successive iterations of modeling.

Most insurance companies' databases are transactional databases; that is, they contain a list of all transactions that affected each policy or claim. Typically, this format is too detailed and not suitable for predictive modeling projects addressing claim development. Instead, we care more about the sum total of payments made on an individual claim between successive points in time (referred to as snapshots or development lags).

The data table for claim development models typically contain three types of fields:

1. **Key** is a field or combination of fields to uniquely identify each claim record. For example, this could be a combination of a claim number and snapshot date or lag (defined here as the time from report date to valuation date).
2. **Metrics** are variables that describe the response and weights for the statistical analysis. For the incremental paid development method, the response (also known as the dependent variable) is the incremental amount paid between two development lags. The weights are discussed in Section 10.2.4.
3. **Explanatory variables** are variables that will be tested for statistical relationships to the response. As with any predictive model, a robust list of explanatory variables allows the modeler to capture the signal in the data. Explanatory variables are also known as predictors, independent variables, factors, and so forth. For claim development models, the predictors typically fall into a number of categories, including
   a. claim attributes, such as claim type, age of claim, and type of injury;
   b. claimant attributes, such as age, gender, and marital status;
   c. policy attributes, such as policy tenure, and policy type;
   d. external attributes, such as geodemographic data.

Table 10.1 provides a general example of the data format.

10.2.2 Practical Considerations

Development patterns can vary widely based on the type of claim and type of payment. Building one development model will not be satisfactory for most practical applications. For example, for workers' compensation, the development patterns vary based on whether the claim was classified as medical only or involved lost time and whether the payment consisted of medical payments, indemnity, or loss adjustment expense. Depending on the number of claims and the development patterns, more than one

Table 10.1. *Illustration of Data Format for Loss Development Models*

Claim Number	Quarterly Lag	Incremental Medical Payment	Incremental Expense Payment	State	Claimant Age	Claimant Gender	Policy Tenure	Policy Type
101	1	$0.00	$130.00	CA	35	Male	8	A
101	2	$395.85	$50.00	CA	35	Male	9	A
101	3	$0.00	$0.00	CA	36	Male	9	A
102	1	$500.00	$1000.00	PA	69	Female	2	B
102	2	$250.00	$100.00	PA	69	Female	3	B
103	1	$0.00	$500.00	PA	44	Female	6	A

development model may be recommended or even required. Provided that the data are available, the modeler may choose to build up to five different models to capture the different payment patterns. Table 10.2 shows the five different models. Additionally, statutory benefit changes for workers' compensation may require adjustments to historical data. Those adjustments are beyond the scope of this chapter.

Claims generally develop faster in the beginning and slow down over time. Moreover, there is no theoretical reason to choose snapshots of a claim equidistant from each other. As a result, choosing more frequent snapshots of each claim in the beginning and less frequent snapshots later on may produce more accurate development patterns. For example, the modeler may choose to have monthly (or even more frequent) snapshots of each claim in the first year, followed by a quarterly snapshot for the remaining life of the claim. However, unequal distances of time present a challenge with regard to the appropriate weight in the models.

While building claim development models, we need to restrict ourselves to claim attributes that are deterministic. This denotes attributes that do not change over time, such as a claimant's gender, or attributes that can be determined with certainty over time, such as a claimant's age. Attributes that change over time can be used for triage modeling but cannot be used for forecasting since their future value will not be known. This restriction excludes many important attributes, such as claim status (open versus closed) and attorney involvement. Some attributes do change over time but infrequently, such as marital status or number of dependents. Whether to use such

Table 10.2. *Five Possible Loss Development Models*

Claim Type	Payment Type		
	Medical	Indemnity	Expenses
Medical only	1	X	2
Lost time	3	4	5

attributes is a trade-off between their potential predictive power and the bias introduced by assuming that their values are constant over time.

10.2.3 Model Assumptions

Generalized linear models (GLMs) consist of a wide range of models and are well suited for modeling incremental paid loss amounts. The exponential family of distributions contains many familiar distributions including normal, Poisson, gamma, and Tweedie. Since there may be no payment between two consecutive snapshots, the distribution of the incremental paid amounts has a point mass at zero. This eliminates many familiar distributions such as normal and gamma.

The Poisson distribution is a reasonable distribution to use for such models, and given its wide commercial availability and ease of interpretation, it has an obvious appeal. If the data exhibit evidence of overdispersion, then the data can be modeled using a compound Poisson distribution. Stated loosely, overdispersion means there is greater variability than what is consistent with a Poisson formulation. For further information, we refer the reader to the paper by Noriszura Ismail and Abdul Aziz Jemain (2007).

Another familiar distribution that can be used is the Tweedie distribution. Similar to the Poisson distribution, the Tweedie distribution has a point mass at zero but is otherwise a continuous distribution. The Tweedie distribution has a variance function proportional to μ^p, where $p < 0$, $1 < p < 2$, or $p > 2$. The Tweedie distribution (where $1 < p < 2$) is typically used to model insurance loss costs and can be used in this context.

The log-link function is an appropriate choice for the GLM since it produces a multiplicative model, which is easy to interpret and more representative of the data. Moreover, the log-link function is also the canonical link function if the modeler chooses to use the Poisson distribution.

10.2.4 Prior Weights

Prior weights are used to incorporate assumed credibility of each observation into the model. While building incremental paid loss development models, there are at least four reasonable choices of prior weights to use:

1. Every observation has an equal weight of one.
2. Every observation has a weight proportional to the time period it represents.
3. Every observation has a weight of $1/n$ where n is the number of observations associated with that claim.
4. Every observation has a weight proportional to the time period it represents, and the sum of weights associated with every claim is one.

Table 10.3. *Forecasting of a Hyothetical Claim*

Quarterly Lag	Actual Payment	Predicted Payment	Mix of Actual and Predicted Payments
1	$0.00	$3.40	$0.00
2	$200.00	$15.43	$200.00
3	$40.00	$85.23	$40.00
4	$0.00	$98.54	$0.00
5		$67.50	$67.50
6		$54.53	$54.53
7		$40.40	$40.40
8		$32.01	$32.01
9		$20.11	$20.11
10		$15.32	$15.32
11		$12.04	$12.04
12		$7.04	$7.04
Total	$240.00	$451.55	$488.95

If the snapshots of each claim are equidistant from each other, the first and second options of the preceding list of prior weights are equivalent, and the third and fourth options are also equivalent. In practice, equal weight for every observation is the common method that many modelers use in this context.

10.2.5 Forecasting

Once models have been built and validated, the next step is to forecast the ultimate value of each claim. Each model prediction is a series of expected incremental payments for each claim at different points in time. For example, if the snapshots are quarterly, then the model predictions are a series of payments expected to be paid each quarter based on the claim characteristics. For a one-year old claim, four payment periods have already occurred. For example, consider the situation shown in Table 10.3.

There are two different choices to forecast the ultimate value of such a claim:

1. Ignore the actual known payment of the claim and use predictions from the model for each time period. In this case, the ultimate value of the claim would be $451.55.
2. Combine the actual known payments of the claim and the future predicted payments. In this case, the ultimate value of the claim would be $488.95.

Unfortunately both methods have shortcomings. The first method ignores the actual payments made on the claims, while the second method may introduce bias in the data as the more recent years, with more open claims, might be underestimated while the older years might be overestimated.

The choice of method depends on how the estimate of the ultimate value of individual claims will be used. On one hand, if the claim ultimate value is used to build claim severity models, then the first method of forecasting might be appropriate. On the other hand, if the claim ultimate value is used to build claims triage models, then the second forecasting method is more appropriate.

Regardless of which forecasting method is chosen, the estimated ultimate claim values in the aggregate should be close to the estimates obtained from traditional development techniques such as triangle-based methods.

10.2.6 Tail Forecasting

The loss development models provide a prediction for only the same number of years as the oldest claim in the dataset. For example, if the oldest claim is 10 years, then we can only use models to predict 10 years of payments for each claim. For most long-tailed lines of business, like workers' compensation, this may not be long enough. A reasonable approach to accommodate tail development is to adjust each claim by a constant factor equal to one plus this ratio: the sum of payments made after 10 years divided by the percentage of the cumulative paid amount in the first 10 years. This factor is generally calculated and applied separately for each development model.

10.3 Additional Data for Triage Models

While building the loss development models, we were restricted to using only deterministic claim attributes. As we proceed to the claims triage models, there is no such restriction. Therefore, it is important to consider every variable that may explain the signal in the data. In this section, we discuss additional data sources that may be considered for modeling. In particular, we will address the use of claim adjuster notes and certain types of medical and billing data though many sources of additional data may be considered in practice.

10.3.1 Text Mining Claim Adjuster Notes

It is estimated that more than 80% of business-relevant information originates in unstructured form, primarily text. Few would disagree that claim adjuster notes are the most important source of detailed information about individual claims. The adjuster notes typically have a wealth of information about the claim throughout its life cycle. Despite the wide agreement of the usefulness of this information, the use of claim adjuster notes is fraught with difficulty when applied in practice. To consider information from the claim adjuster notes in modeling, the information has to be converted into a structured format.

Table 10.4. *Illustration of Data Output from Text Mining*

Claim ID	MRI	Surgical	DME	Injection	Hernia	Pain
101	0	0	0	0	0	0
102	0	0	1	0	0	1
103	1	0	0	1	0	0
104	0	0	0	0	0	1
105	0	0	0	0	0	0

Text mining is a collection of techniques that extracts useful information from natural language text. Text mining techniques started in the 1980s but were primitive and labor intensive. Increases in computing power have enabled more applications of text mining. Text mining software is widely available from both commercial and open source companies. The interested reader may wish to consult Weiss et al. (2004) for a comprehensive introduction and overview of the field.

There are different ways to perform text mining. For our purpose, we only focus on identifying "key phrases," defined as one or more words that are connected to the phenomenon of interest (the claim). One approach to identify key phrases is to extract all (or at least many) of the phrases that occur in the text and then use one or more statistical techniques to select those phrases that seem to be most relevant to the phenomenon under study. This approach works in our situation because typically there are a large number of claim adjuster notes, but each note is small. Statistical analysis techniques work in this situation due to the large number of observations (notes) and the relatively small number of variables (phrases).

In its simplest form, each variable is an indicator of whether the phrase appears in the claim adjuster note at this point in the claim life cycle. This narrow focus excludes many interesting applications of text mining, such as considering the number of times the phrase appeared in the claim adjuster notes or a measure of the relative importance of the phrase; however, this is sufficient for our purpose.

Table 10.4 provides a general example of the data format of the text mining process output.

Extracting phrases from the text is a manageable process; however, a number of different issues may surface, which may be remedied by

1. Excluding certain characters, short words, numbers, and so forth, which are not relevant;
2. Correcting for misspelled words, which many text mining programs do automatically. However, we need to pay special attention to specific technical words that are unique to this field;
3. Grouping words with their shorthand equivalent, including acronyms, for example, durable medical equipment should be grouped with DME;

4. Grouping phrases with their synonyms – we should combine words such as *sick* and *ill*, which describe the same concept.

10.3.2 Medical and Billing Data

The second category of data, medical and billing data, consists of a number of data sources, including the International Classification of Diseases (ICD) codes, the Current Procedural Terminology (CPT) codes, and a list of prescription drugs prescribed to the claimant. The availability of this data to the insurance company depends to a large degree on the line of business. Workers' compensation insurance offers perhaps the greatest access to this information due to the first-party nature of the claim and the utilization of case management. For the remainder of this section, we provide a brief description of each one of these data sources and how to use them for modeling.

10.3.2.1 International Classification of Diseases (ICD) Codes

The International Classification of Diseases (ICD) is the international standard diagnostic tool for epidemiology and health management. The ICD is maintained by the World Health Organization and is designed as a health care classification system to provide a system of diagnostic codes for classifying diseases and external causes of injury.

The current edition of ICD codes used in the United States is ICD-9, which has been in use since 1979. Much of the rest of the world is using the 10th edition of ICD codes, namely, ICD-10. The ICD-9 contains more than 17,000 codes for procedures and diagnoses. Due to the nature of injuries and diseases that appear in casualty lines of business such as workers' compensation or auto bodily injury, only a subset of ICD-9 codes appears in a typical claims dataset. Nevertheless, we should expect to see at least several thousand different codes. Fortunately, the ICD-9 system is designed to map health conditions to corresponding generic categories together with specific variations. Major categories are designed to group together a set of similar diseases. As a result, it is possible to group different ICD-9 codes into a few hundred categories and subcategories, which would be more suitable to use in predictive modeling.

Using ICD-9 codes directly in a predictive model is challenging for two reasons. First, ICD-9 codes contain several thousand different codes. Using industry standard grouping of codes into a few hundred homogeneous categories and subcategories is useful to overcome the high dimensionality challenge. Second, claims may have multiple ICD-9 codes associated with them. Moreover, the list of ICD-9 codes may change over time as the diagnosis of the disease or the injury evolves. As a result, each claim may have multiple ICD-9 code categories associated with it. One possible approach to overcome this one-to-many relationship is to translate transactional ICD-9 codes into claim attributes suitable for modeling by creating a series of variables that indicate whether a category or subcategory of ICD-9 codes was used for the claim under consideration.

In general, there is high correlation between some of these ICD-9 indicators since certain diagnoses and procedures tend to appear together. This creates many challenges in identifying ICD-9 indicators that are most predictive. There are several techniques to identify the most significant variables including a relatively new technique called the elastic net which is discussed in more detail in Section 10.4.

ICD-9 codes represent some of the most difficult variables for modeling. To add insult to injury, the latest version of ICD codes (ICD-10) is much more comprehensive and contains more than 140,000 codes for procedures and diagnoses. ICD-10 is scheduled to be implemented in the United States by October 1, 2015. Once ICD-10 codes are implemented, a host of new challenges will be created, including the need for mapping between ICD-9 and ICD-10 codes since the modeling dataset will contain both ICD-9 codes for older claims and ICD-10 codes for more recent claims. Such mappings exist but are not perfect.

10.3.2.2 Current Procedural Terminology (CPT) Codes

The Current Procedural Terminology (CPT) codes are medical codes maintained by the American Medical Association. The CPT codes describe medical and diagnostic services and are designed to communicate uniform information about medical services and procedures among physicians, coders, patients, and payers. CPT codes are similar to ICD-9, except that they identify the services rendered rather than the diagnoses on the claim. One of the main uses of CPT codes is medical billing. There are approximately 7,800 CPT codes. Fortunately, similar to ICD-9 codes, the CPT codes are designed to map similar services into categories and subcategories. As a result, it is possible to group different CPT codes into a few hundred categories and subcategories, which are more suitable to use in predictive models.

Similar to ICD-9 codes, many claims have multiple CPT codes associated with them. The list of CPT codes will change over time as new services are rendered. The approach used for ICD-9 codes can also be used to translate those transactional CPT codes into claim attributes suitable for use in modeling.

Another similarity to ICD-9 codes is that, in general, there is high correlation between some of these new CPT indicators since certain services tend to be rendered together. Moreover, there is high correlation between CPT codes and ICD-9 codes. These correlations create the potential for model instability and issues with aliasing. Aliasing occurs when there is a linear dependency among variables. This dependency may be inherent in the definition of a variable (e.g., if the claimant gender is not female, it must be male) or it may occur from the nature of the data (e.g., there may be a perfect correlation such that if one variable is unknown in the data, another variable is unknown as well). Near-aliasing occurs when two or more variables contain levels that are almost, but not quite perfectly, correlated. This condition may lead to convergence issues or, at the very least, issues with interpretation of model results.

10.3.2.3 Prescription Drugs

In general, the insurance company may have access to the list of drugs prescribed to the claimant. Information available varies but typically includes drug name, strength, dose, and cost. Similar to the ICD-9 codes and CPT codes, some claims may have multiple drugs prescribed to the claimant and the list may change over time. Translating the transactional drug data into claim attributes suitable for use in modeling is required.

In a typical database, there are thousands of different drugs prescribed to patients. Adding different strength and doses, it is easy to reach tens of thousands of unique combinations. It should be immediately clear that some sort of grouping will be required to use this information. Unfortunately, unlike ICD-9 codes and CPT codes, there is no uniform system for naming prescription drugs. Multiple generic drug names may appear in the database, even though they are copies of a brand-name drug and have exactly the same dosage, intended use, and risks as the original drug. Moreover, different drugs may be treating the same condition.

A sensible approach is to try to map each drug in the database into one of several general categories such as narcotics, steroids, and antibiotics. In our experience, the number of categories could range from 30 to 100 categories. The number of categories will depend on the number of drugs to be mapped, the number of claims available, the level of granularity desired, and, more importantly, the time and resources available to do the mapping. This process is typically done manually and is time consuming. However, given the importance of prescription drugs in projecting costs, it should be completed with care.

10.4 Factor Selection

As discussed in the last section, the introduction of ICD-9 codes, CPT codes, pharmaceutical, and text mining variables exacerbates the modeling challenge of dealing with an extremely large number of highly correlated variables. This produces multicollinearity and near-aliasing and makes factor selection for modeling a difficult and unstable process.

The classical approach to dealing with a large number of variables has been to use some statistical technique to choose a short list of the most important variables to include in the modeling dataset and then build the desired model on such dataset. Many variable selection search approaches have been proposed to deal with these challenges, including greedy forward/backward regression, CART, AIC improvement rank on response, and principal components analysis ordering, to name just a few.

In this section we explore a novel use of a penalized regression method called the elastic net to address the challenge of having an extremely large number of highly correlated variables. We will give a brief introduction to the elastic net and demonstrate how it can be used as a powerful variable selection method that in many cases outperforms many other well-known methods (Williams et al., to appear). In Section 10.7, we will propose using the full power of the elastic net by allowing many variables to be in the model but with parameters that have been dampened, or shrunk, which would provide a stronger predictive power in most cases. Finally, we discuss all the technical detail of the elastic net in the appendix for the benefits of the interested reader.

First we discuss the elastic net for linear models and then extend later to generalized linear models. Given a variable y and a number of variables $x_1, \ldots, x_p$ that may be related to y, linear regression models are often fitted using ordinary least squares, where the parameter estimates $\widehat{\beta}$ are given by minimizing the sum of squared errors:

$$\widehat{\beta} = \arg\min_{\beta} \left\{ \sum_{i=1}^{N} \left(y_i - \alpha - \sum_{j=1}^{p} \beta_j x_{ij} \right)^2 \right\}$$

A penalized regression can be described as adding a penalty function (of the parameters) to the sum of squared errors which constrains the magnitude of coefficients in the regression model. In particular, the elastic net uses a sum of the L^1 (sum of absolute value) and L^2 (sum of squares) penalty functions:

$$\widehat{\beta}_{ENet} = (1 + \lambda_2) \cdot \arg\min_{\beta} \left\{ \sum_{i=1}^{N} \left(y_i - \alpha - \sum_{j=1}^{p} \beta_j x_{ij} \right)^2 + \lambda_1 \cdot \sum_{j=1}^{p} |\beta_j| + \lambda_2 \cdot \sum_{j=1}^{p} \beta_j^2 \right\}$$

We refer the reader to the appendix for the motivation of this definition of the elastic net. There are two tuning parameters in the penalty function, λ_1 and λ_2, and they can take any nonnegative value. Since our intent is to use the elastic net as a variable selection tool, it is convenient to ignore λ_2 (i.e., assume its value is equal to zero) and concentrate on λ_1. Later in this chapter, we will talk about the benefits of utilizing both tuning parameters in a full elastic net solution.

We focus on the main tuning parameter λ_1. When λ_1 is large enough, the penalty function is too large and all parameters are forced to be zero (i.e., we start with the mean model with no variables). As the value of λ_1 starts to decrease, the penalty decreases and variables enter the model (i.e., their coefficients start to be nonzero, one variable at a time). Variables that are most important in explaining the signal enter the model first followed by less important variables. As λ_1 approaches 0, the penalty

Table 10.5. *Elastic Net Variable Ranking Output*

```
Elastic net sequence
Computing X'X ...
Step 1:     Variable 37     added
Step 2:     Variable 12     added
Step 3:     Variable 49     added
Step 4:     Variable 82     added
Step 5:     Variable 42     added
Step 6:     Variable 19     added
Step 7:     Variable 1      added
......
```

function will be too small, and all variables will be included in the model. Hence, we obtain a complete list of variables ranked by their importance. In our application, we use this process to identify the top text mining, ICD-9, CPT, and pharmaceutical variables to include in the next step of modeling.

Table 10.5 illustrates a typical output of the list of variables as they enter the model one at a time. As mentioned earlier, variables enter the model based on their relative importance. Therefore, in this example, variable 37 is the most important variable because it entered the model first, followed by variable 12, variable 49, and so forth.

It is possible that a variable enters the model and then drops from the model, before entering again. This produces some ambiguity about the importance of that variable. In practice, we experienced this phenomenon in less than one percent of the variables that we considered.

The extension from the elastic net for linear models to the elastic net for GLMs is straightforward. For GLMs, the parameters are obtained by solving the following equation:

$$\widehat{\beta}_{ENet} = (1 + \lambda_2) \cdot \arg\min_{\beta} \left\{ -\log\{L(y; \beta)\} + \lambda_1 \cdot \sum_{j=1}^{p} |\beta_j| + \lambda_2 \cdot \sum_{j=1}^{p} \beta_j^2 \right\}$$

where $L(y; \beta)$ is the likelihood function corresponding to the generalized linear model under consideration. The main difference between the elastic net for the linear regression case and the more general case of generalized linear models is that the optimization problem is harder and slower to solve. However, many algorithms have been developed to solve this problem including linear regression, logistic and multinomial regression models, Poisson regression, and the Cox model.

For the purpose of the claim triage models application, readers may wish to use their favorite method to choose a short list of the most important variables to include in the modeling database. However, it is our experience that the elastic net method typically outperforms many of the more commonly used methods.

10.5 Modeling Method

Once the most predictive and relevant variables from the list of text mining, ICD-9, CPT, and pharmaceutical variables are identified, we can drop the rest of these variables from the data. We are finally ready to build the main claims triage models. As we described in Section 10.1, our goal is to identify claims with the largest likelihood of escalation. We define the claim incurred deficiency at a given point in time to be the difference between the ultimate value of the claim, which is previously estimated from the development models, and the reported (paid plus case reserve) amount of the claim at that point in time. The value of each claim incurred deficiency could be either a positive or negative amount and will change during the life cycle of the claim.

Instead of trying to directly model the claim incurred deficiency, we build a series of propensity models to identify those claims most likely to escalate above certain monetary thresholds. We use logistic regression to build those models.

The monetary threshold of each model built could be different. For example, we may choose a smaller threshold for a first notice of loss (FNOL) model since we know limited information about the claim at that time. However, we may choose a larger threshold for later models since the claim adjuster presumably knows much more about the claim by then and is only interested in larger monetary escalation. In any case, when choosing the monetary threshold to use, we need to balance choosing a high enough threshold to make the result relevant but not too high that we have a small number of claims that pierce the threshold.

For the rest of this section, we focus on only one of the models, the FNOL, to simplify the discussion. However, the discussion applies equally to models built at other points in time.

10.5.1 Data Format

Table 10.6 provides an illustration of the data format for the FNOL propensity model. For illustration purposes, we include in Table 10.6 a handful of claims characteristics that would be tested.

The escalation indicator is the target variable for the model. The remaining variables are the explanatory variables and should be defined to reflect what we know about the claim at that point in time, that is, at the first notice of loss. These claim characteristics will have different values as we consider models at different points in time.

Table 10.6. *Illustration of Data Format for Propensity Models*

		Claim Characteristics				
Claim ID	Escalation Indicator[a]	State	Gender	CPT Medical Imaging Indicator	Adjuster Notes–Pain Indicator	Narcotic Medication Indicator
101	0	PA	Male	0	0	0
102	0	CA	Female	1	0	0
103	1	CA	Female	0	1	1
104	0	PA	Female	1	0	0
105	0	PA	Male	0	0	1

[a] The escalation indicator is the indicator of whether the claim incurred deficiency exceeds some specified threshold.

10.5.2 Logistic Regression

Logistic regression is a probabilistic model. It is a special case of generalized linear models with a binomial response distribution and a logit link function. For a detailed discussion of logistic regression, we refer the interested reader to Guillén (2014) for further information. In our case, the logistic regression model predicts the probability that a claim incurred deficiency pierces the chosen monetary threshold.

The logistic model prediction provides ranking of all claims based on their probability of escalation. Typically, a model output is used to develop a more simplified score card for claim adjusters to use. The design of the scorecard depends on the needs of the business. For example, the goal may be to stratify all claims into three groups: high-, medium-, and low-risk groups. The percentage of claims targeted for each group should be decided by the claim department. For example, the target for the high-, medium-, and low-risk groups could be 10%, 20%, and 70%, respectively. To achieve that, two thresholds A and B should be chosen and the output of the model would identify which stratum the claim belongs to, as shown in Figure 10.1.

10.5.3 Practical Considerations

The selection of thresholds to stratify claims into high-, medium-, and low-risk strata is done based on historical claims. After implementation, the models will be used to score new, not historical, claims. It is unlikely that the initial choice of the thresholds will produce the same distribution of high-, medium-, and low-strata claims on the new claims or on an ongoing basis as the mix of claims may be changing over time. After

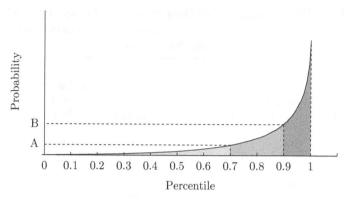

Fig. 10.1. Propensity model prediction.

implementing the models, we recommend recalculating and calibrating the thresholds to ensure the desired percentage of claims in each stratum.

The discussion has focused on FNOL models, but it is important to build models at different points of time to reevaluate the riskiness of the claim over time or to incorporate new information known about the claim. It is common to build four to six models to evaluate the claim from the FNOL and every month thereafter. Typically the points in time are selected based on the line of business and more importantly the existing processes within the claim department. In the initial phase, models may be built independently of each other; however, it is possible that predictions from those models contradict each other. Harmonization of all models is a critical step before implementation.

We focused on identifying claims with the biggest likelihood of escalation; however, the same technique can be used to identify large claims instead. The only difference is in the definition of the target variable. In our experience, identifying claims with high probability of escalation is more important to the claim adjuster than identifying large claims. Large claims that pierce the threshold would be typically considered catastrophic claims, especially if the threshold is high enough. Many of the catastrophic claims are actually known to the claim adjusters early on because of the severe nature of the injury or even the death of the claimant. Training a model to identify catastrophic claims may in fact severely limit its usefulness to the claim adjuster since it would not provide new information to the adjuster.

Instead of trying to model the claim incurred deficiency directly, we model whether the claim incurred deficiency pierces a certain threshold. Modeling claim incurred deficiency directly may seem to provide more information to the claim adjuster; however, it is more difficult. Depending on the circumstances, the value of the additional information provided might not be justified by the decrease in the model performance.

10.6 Conclusions

There are a variety of ways to measure the success of a predictive analytics project. These include immediate indicators such as statistical validation and understanding/ acceptance by the stakeholders. The true litmus test, however, lies in operationalizing the results and monitoring the outcome.

Claims triage models typically outperform expert judgment in identifying claims with a high propensity to escalate. This does not mean they are perfect (no model ever is). In our experience with workers' compensation, the identification of claims with the highest likelihood to escalate may be considered accurate 60%–80% of the time. The level of accuracy depends on the line of business and the volume and quality of claims data. Additionally, it is rather intuitive that propensity models targeted at a later valuation date (e.g., 90 days after report date) are in general more accurate than at FNOL. It is also not surprising that certain types of claims contributed the most to model error, for example, those claims that switch from medical only to medical plus lost time.

It is also important to emphasize that these types of models require monitoring and ongoing maintenance. First, the claims environment is not static. Second, claims triage models are designed to change behavior, which if successful means future experience will not look just like the past.

Our experience also suggests that claims triage models are well received by claims management. Some may argue that the models often confirm what the claims managers had already been thinking with respect to which predictors matter. That may be true to some extent, but the real value is the model's quantification of the effect of each predictor and how they combine together into a likelihood estimate.

Achieving buy-in from the claims department is not merely a function of building a good model. The process of socializing the model results is critically important. This requires clear, business-relevant communication on a regular basis so that education occurs and issues are addressed throughout the model building process.

Buy-in also needs to translate to implementable action. Claims triage models are about changing behavior – of the claims adjuster and, ideally by extension, the claimant. Designing an implementable action requires careful consideration of the various behaviors present in the claim settlement process. Also, it is advised to prototype a solution, learn from it, and iterate. This is a core principle in introducing innovation.

10.7 Further Research Opportunities

The previous sections alluded to several areas of potential further research in the area of claims triage or the components of claims triage discussed in this chapter. We summarize them here.

10.7.1 Developing Individual Claims to Ultimate

This chapter outlines an approach to identify claims that are likely to close at a value far in excess of an early estimate. We have discussed an approach that utilizes both open and closed claim data; consequently, the open claims need to be projected to ultimate. One alternative is to produce triage models on an inventory of closed claims only. That has the appeal of not having to project claims to ultimate. However, we have concerns about this approach because more recent closed claims are presumably biased toward simpler claims (as the more complex ones would still be open). If the modeler chose an older inventory of claims to address this issue, the data would be considered quite old. Nonetheless, we encourage practitioners to experiment with different claims inventories.

The approach described in Section 10.2 to develop claims to ultimate involves fitting models to incremental paid loss amounts at various points in time, which may or may not be equidistant. We presented options for defining the prior weights of each observation (equal weight of one, weight proportional to time period, weight divided equally between observations associated with that claim, and weight proportional to the time period it represents for each claim). We commented that the most common approach is to employ equal weights for each observation. We encourage readers to experiment with other approaches to identify the approach that provides the highest predictive power given the data used.

Also in Section 10.2 we discussed using a Poisson distribution to model incremental paid loss amounts. We encourage readers to test whether an overdispersed Poisson would provide better goodness of fit.

In addition to the approach described in Section 10.2 to develop claims to ultimate, there are several other methods for forecasting individual claim amounts. In fact, the area of individual claim loss reserving modeling has attracted a lot of researchers' attention in the last decade. For example, John B. Mahon (2005) applied a Markov transition matrix to model the ultimate claim sizes on the individual claim level. Christian R. Larsen (2007) proposed a set of stochastic models based on individual claims development. More recently Pietro Parodi (2014) proposed an approach similar to the approach used in pricing, where a separate frequency and severity model are developed and then combined by a simulation to produce the aggregate loss distribution.

10.7.2 Text Mining

In our discussion of text mining claim adjuster notes, we acknowledge that developing indicator variables that detect the presence of a phrase in the text at a point in time is suitable for mining claim adjuster notes (as they are large in number but the text is small in each). Readers may wish to investigate applications of text mining that consider the number of times a phrase appears in the text or a measure of relative importance of the phrase.

10.7.3 Triage Models

Section 10.5 of this chapter outlined an approach to triage claims based on models that predict the propensity for the projected ultimate amount of the claim to far exceed an early estimate. This is not the only approach to rank claims. Practitioners may consider these options:

1. **Rank claims based on models fit to the projected ultimate claim amount:** in our experience this approach to rank claims did not yield positive results given the data we used. We believe that it is easier to accurately predict the likelihood of a claim to escalate than it is to model the dollar amount of the claim.
2. **Rank claims based on the likelihood to be large:** this approach is a likelihood model so should produce results with reasonably good fit. In our experience, however, the claims department already has a good sense of many claims that are expected to be large (and are reserved as such). The key area of interest in claims triage is to identify those that at first notice of loss are not expected to be large.

We acknowledge there may be other approaches as well. A potential enhancement to the claims triage method we discussed is to better address claims that switch categories. Earlier in the chapter we mentioned that claims that changed category (e.g., from medical only to medical and lost time) did not validate as well in the claims triage models. One area of further research is to experiment with fitting models that predict the propensity of a claim to switch categories and use the results to recategorize claims into their appropriate claim type.

10.7.4 Elastic Net

Section 10.4 of this chapter discusses factor selection for application within a GLM. The primary technique discussed, the elastic net, has wider application than factor selection. In fact, one may conclude that we simply observed the order in which variables entered the penalized regression model in order to choose the top p factors to proceed to the GLM, but we ignored the contribution to predictive power of variables that did not make the cut. The elastic net by its very nature allows some factors to enter the model with parameters that have been dampened, or shrunk. This allows building very complex models with a very large number of variables with superior predictive power while guarding against overfitting. Another advantage of the elastic net is the ability to include highly correlated variables without creating unstable models. We encourage readers to experiment more with the elastic net to better understand the predictive power and materiality of the longer list of variables. Even if the intended modeling application is a GLM, consider amalgamating various "shrunk" variables into a single score that can be inserted into the GLM.

Appendix: Penalized Regression

This appendix complements Section 10.4 in the chapter. It is a primer in penalized regression methods, focusing on two particular types: ridge regression and lasso. This motivates the choice of the penalty function for the elastic net, which is essentially a combination of the aforementioned methods and consequently provides the advantages of both. We will also discuss in some detail the basic properties of the elastic net. Most of the material related to the elastic net is based on the original 2005 paper by Hui Zou and Trevor Hastie. We refer the reader to that paper for further detail.

Penalized regression is not a new concept. It has been in the literature for at least four decades. However, it continues to be an active area of research to this day.

For simplicity, we focus our discussion on linear models first and discuss extensions to generalized linear models (GLMs) later on.

In a generic sense, a penalized regression can be described as adding a constraint to ordinary least squares (OLS) that constrains the magnitude of coefficients in the regression model. This constraint is generally called a regularization term, and the technique is referred to as shrinkage because it typically, but not always, shrinks the otherwise applicable OLS coefficients toward zero.

Given a variable y and a number of variables $x_1, \ldots, x_p$ that may be related to y, linear regression models are often fitted using the least squares approach, where the parameter estimates $\widehat{\beta}_{\text{OLS}}$ are given by minimizing the sum of squared errors:

$$\widehat{\beta}_{\text{OLS}} = \arg \min_{\beta} \left\{ \sum_{i=1}^{N} \left(y_i - \alpha - \sum_{j=1}^{p} \beta_j x_{ij} \right)^2 \right\}$$

Without loss of generality, it is customary to assume that all predictors have been normalized to have a mean equal to zero and a standard deviation equal to one while the target variable is normalized to have a mean equal to zero. The penalized (or constrained) regression problem can be described as

$$\widehat{\beta}_{\text{Penalized}} = \arg \min_{\beta} \left\{ \sum_{i=1}^{N} \left(y_i - \alpha - \sum_{j=1}^{p} \beta_j x_{ij} \right)^2 + \lambda \cdot J(\beta_1, \ldots, \beta_p) \right\}$$

where $J(\beta_1, \ldots, \beta_p)$ is a nonnegative valued penalty function. Moreover, we assume that the penalty is zero if and only if $(\beta_1, \ldots, \beta_p) = (0, \ldots, 0)$; λ is a tuning parameter and can take any nonnegative value. For a fixed value of λ, the solution for the penalized regression is obtained by finding the parameter estimates $\widehat{\beta}_{\text{Penalized}}$ which minimizes the sum of squared errors plus the penalty term.

For different values of λ, we may obtain different parameter estimates. This is referred to as the regularization (solution) path which can be thought of as a function from the nonnegative numbers to R^p where

$$\widehat{\beta}_{\text{Penalized}} : \lambda \longmapsto (\beta_1, \ldots, \beta_p)$$

The result of using a penalty function is typically, but not always, shrinkage of parameter estimates compared with the nonpenalized model, that is, OLS.

By setting $\lambda = 0$, the penalty is zero and the penalized model reduces to the OLS model. As λ increases to ∞, the penalty becomes too large and in the limit all parameters in the model will be zero. Notice that the intercept will be zero because of the normalization assumption we made on the variables.

Unlike the OLS estimators, the penalized regression produces estimates of coefficients that are biased. Penalized regression deliberately introduces bias into the estimation of β to reduce the variability of the estimate. In many cases, this may lower the mean squared error compared to the OLS estimates, particularly when multicolinearity is present. Recall that

$$\mathrm{MSE} = \mathrm{Var}(\widehat{\beta}) + \mathrm{Bias}(\widehat{\beta})^2$$

Penalized regression is typically more suitable when the goal is predictive power instead of inference, which is typically the case in most insurance applications.

Depending on the form of the penalty function, the penalized regression model may have very different properties. The elastic net is built on two of the well-known penalized regression methods, namely, ridge regression and lasso, which we briefly introduce here.

Ridge Regression

Ridge regression is one of the oldest penalized regression techniques and was introduced by Arthur E. Hoerl and Robert W. Kennard (1970). Ridge regression uses an L^2 penalty function, that is, "sum of squares." The ridge regression optimization problem can be described as

$$\widehat{\beta}_{\text{Ridge}} = \arg\min_{\beta} \left\{ \sum_{i=1}^{N} \left(y_i - \alpha - \sum_{j=1}^{p} \beta_j x_{ij} \right)^2 + \lambda \cdot \sum_{j=1}^{p} \beta_j^2 \right\}$$

For a fixed value of λ, the solution for the ridge regression is obtained by finding the parameter estimates $\widehat{\beta}_{\text{Ridge}}$ which minimize the sum of squared errors plus the penalty term.

The impact of the ridge regression penalty function is typically dampening, or shrinking, all parameters. However, it can be shown that it never forces any parameter to be zero unless the parameter was already zero in the OLS solution. One of the interesting features of the ridge regression is a grouping effect and its ability to control well for multicollinearity.

Hui Zou and Trevor Hastie (2005, 306) defined the grouping effect as follows: "Qualitatively speaking, a regression method exhibits the grouping effect if the regression coefficients of a group of highly correlated variables tend to be equal (up to a sign change if negatively correlated). In particular, in the extreme situation where some variables are exactly identical, the regression method should assign identical coefficients to the identical variables."

The value of the grouping effect should be self-evident as it overcomes many problems created by multicollinearity including near-aliasing and model instability. Ridge regression exhibits the grouping effect as illustrated in Example 10.1.

Example 10.1. We assume that the true model is

$$y = 2 + x_1$$

We assume x_2 is another variable such that x_2 is almost equal to x_1. The OLS solution will be unstable and not even defined when $x_1 = x_2$. When $x_1 = x_2$, most software will eliminate one of the variables in this case.

In the extreme case where $x_1 = x_2$, an equivalent linear model is $y = 2 + \beta_1 \cdot x_1 + (1 - \beta_1) \cdot x_2$, where $\beta_2 = (1 - \beta_1)$. Ridge regression tries to fit the data such that it minimizes $\beta_1^2 + \beta_2^2$. This results in splitting the coefficients as equally as possible between the two variables. The ridge solution is

$$y = 2 + \frac{1}{2}x_1 + \frac{1}{2}x_2$$

The next example illustrates the shrinking of the parameters estimated from the ridge problem as the tuning parameter increases.

Example 10.2. We simulated 500 observations with five independent variables with the following assumptions:

1. $\text{Corr}(x_i, x_j) = 0$, for every $i \neq j$.
2. Each x_i is normalized to have a mean equal to zero and standard deviation equal to one.
3. The true model is $y = 10 \cdot x_1 - 8 \cdot x_2 + 6 \cdot x_3 - 4 \cdot x_4 + 2 \cdot x_5$.

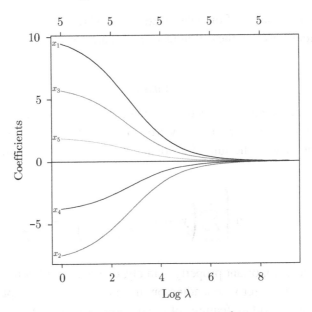

Fig. 10.2. Ridge regression output from R.

We fitted the model using the `glmnet` package in R. Following is the code and related output:

```
# Generate data
library(MASS)
set.seed(42)
n <- 500    # Number of observations
p <- 5   # Number of predictors
CovMatrix <- outer(1:p, 1:p, function(x,y) {ifelse(x == y,1,0)})
x <- mvrnorm(n, rep(0,p), CovMatrix)
y <- 10*x[,1] - 8*x[,2] + 6*x[,3] - 4*x[,4] + 2*x[,5] + rnorm(n)

# Fit models
library(glmnet)
fit.Ridge <- glmnet(x, y, family="gaussian", alpha=0)
plot(fit.Ridge, xvar="lambda",label=TRUE)
abline(a=0,b=0)
```

Figure 10.2 shows the ridge estimates of each coefficient as a function of log λ. The five curves labeled $x_1, \ldots, x_5$ are the parameter estimates for the variables $x_1, \ldots, x_5$, respectively. Notice that as λ approaches 0, we obtain the OLS solution, whereas as λ approaches ∞, all parameters shrink to nearly 0.

As shown in Example 10.2, the parameters of the ridge solution typically shrink as λ increases. However, that is not always true, especially when there is a high correlation between different variables. Some parameters may shrink while others may increase as the interactions between the different variables are more complex.

Lasso

Least absolute shrinkage and selecting operator (lasso) is another example of penalized regression and was introduced by Robert Tibshirani (1996). Lasso uses an L^1 penalty function, that is, the sum of absolute values. The lasso optimization problem can be described as

$$\widehat{\beta}_{\text{Lasso}} = \arg\min_{\beta} \left\{ \sum_{i=1}^{N} \left(y_i - \alpha - \sum_{j=1}^{p} \beta_j x_{ij} \right)^2 + \lambda \cdot \sum_{j=1}^{p} |\beta_j| \right\}$$

Lasso has one very important property, namely, coefficients of certain variables may be forced to be exactly zero, depending on the value of the tuning parameter λ. This is one of the most important features of lasso because it facilitates variable selection. It can be shown that, as the tuning parameter λ decrease from ∞ to 0, we start with the constant model with no variables, and then variables start entering the model one at a time based on their importance.

An important difference between lasso and ridge regression is that lasso leads to sparse solutions, potentially driving many coefficients to zero, whereas ridge regression leads to dense solutions, in which all coefficients are nonzero, unless they were zero in the OLS solution.

Example 10.3 illustrates the variable selection properties of lasso.

Example 10.3. We use the same simulated data used in the first ridge regression example (Example 10.1):

```
# Generate data
library(MASS)
set.seed(42)
n <- 500    # Number of observations
p <- 5    # Number of predictors
CovMatrix <- outer(1:p, 1:p, function(x,y) {ifelse(x == y,1,0)})
x <- mvrnorm(n, rep(0,p), CovMatrix)
y <- 10*x[,1] - 8*x[,2] + 6*x[,3] - 4*x[,4] + 2*x[,5] + rnorm(n)

# Fit models
library(glmnet)
fit.LASSO <- glmnet(x, y, family="gaussian", alpha=1)
plot(fit.LASSO, xvar="lambda",label=TRUE)
abline(a=0,b=0)
```

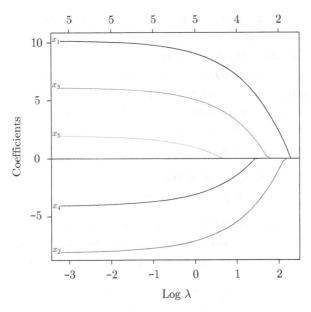

Fig. 10.3. Lasso output from R.

Figure 10.3 shows the lasso estimates of each coefficient as a function of log λ. The five curves labeled $x_1, \ldots, x_5$ are the parameter estimates for the variables $x_1, \ldots, x_5$, respectively. Since all predictors are normalized to have mean zero and standard deviation equal to one, the coefficient of each predictor is a good indicator of the relative importance of the predictor in explaining the signal. Notice that, for large values of λ, namely, $\log(\lambda) > 2.2$, the penalty is too large and the lasso solution is obtained by putting all parameters equal to zero; that is, the lasso solution is the mean model. As λ decreases, parameters enter the model one at a time in the order of importance, namely, x_1, x_2, x_3, x_4, x_5, when $\log(\lambda)$ approximately equals 2.2, 2, 1.9, 1.4, and 0.9, respectively.

Elastic Net

Hui Zou and Trevor Hastie combined both the penalty functions of ridge and lasso to define the elastic net to allow for both the grouping effect of ridge regression and the ability to generate a sparse model (variable selection) of lasso (Zou and Hastie, 2005). As a first attempt, they described the naïve elastic net as

$$\widehat{\beta}_{\text{Naïve ENet}} = \arg\min_{\beta} \left\{ \sum_{i=1}^{N} \left(y_i - \alpha - \sum_{j=1}^{p} \beta_j x_{ij} \right)^2 + \lambda_1 \cdot \sum_{j=1}^{p} |\beta_j| + \lambda_2 \cdot \sum_{j=1}^{p} \beta_j^2 \right\}$$

The linear term (L^1) of the penalty forces certain variables to be zero, allowing variable selection similar to lasso and generating a sparse model. While the quadratic term (L^2) of the penalty encourages the grouping effect similar to ridge regression as well as stabilizing the (L^1) regularization path and hence improving the prediction.

Even though the naive elastic net overcomes the limitations of lasso and ridge regression, Zou and Hastie indicated that empirical evidence shows it does not perform satisfactorily unless it is close to ridge or lasso. The naive elastic net can be viewed as a two-stage procedure:

Step 1: for each fixed λ_2, we first find the ridge regression coefficients.
Step 2: we do the lasso type shrinkage along the lasso coefficients solution paths.

Zou and Hastie showed that this amounts to incurring double shrinkage, which does not help to reduce variance and introduces extra bias. They corrected this extra bias by scaling the naive elastic net parameters. They defined the elastic net solution as

$$\widehat{\beta}_{\text{ENet}} = (1 + \lambda_2) \cdot \widehat{\beta}_{\text{Naïve ENet}}$$

In Example 10.4, we illustrate the ability of the elastic net to generate sparse models, whereas in Example 10.5, we illustrate the grouping effect of the elastic net.

Example 10.4. In this example, we simulated 2,000 observations with 1,000 uncorrelated predictors. The true model is $y = 4 \cdot x_1 - 3 \cdot x_2 + 2 \cdot x_3 - x_4$.

```
# Generate data
library(MASS)
set.seed(42)   # Set seed for reproducibility
n <- 2000   # Number of observations
p <- 1000   # Number of predictors
x <- matrix(rnorm(n*p), nrow=n, ncol=p)
y <- 4*x[,1] - 3* x[,2] + 2*x[,3] - x[,4] + rnorm(n)

# Fit models
library(glmnet)
fit.enet <- glmnet(x, y, family="gaussian", alpha=.95)
plot(fit.enet, xvar="lambda",label=TRUE)
abline(a=0,b=0)
```

Figure 10.4 depicts the changes in the coefficients of each of the 1,000 predictors as the tuning parameter λ_1 changes. As usual, it is best to view the graph from right to left. Since all predictors are normalized to have mean zero and standard deviation equal to one, the coefficient of each predictor is a good indicator of the relative importance of the predictor in explaining the signal. Notice that the first predictor to enter the model is x_1 followed by x_2, x_3, and x_4, respectively, which is consistent with their

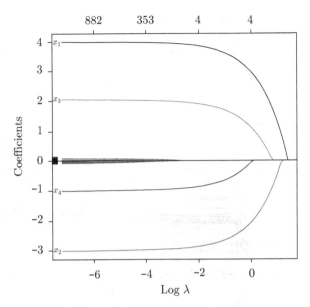

Fig. 10.4. Elastic net output from R.

relative importance. Much later, other predictors start entering the model with very small coefficients.

Example 10.5. This example illustrates the grouping effect of the elastic net (Figure 10.5). We simulated 500 observations and 50 predictors. All predictors are independent except x_1 and x_2 which have a high correlation of 0.9. The true model is $y = 3 \cdot x_1$. To obtain a strong grouping effect, we need to drop the alpha parameter from 0.95 to 0.20.

```
# Generate data
library(MASS)
set.seed(42)
n <- 500   # Number of observations
p <- 50    # Number of predictors
CovMatrix <- outer(1:p, 1:p, function(x,y) {ifelse(x == y,1,0)})
CovMatrix[1,2] <- .9
CovMatrix[2,1] <- .9
x <- mvrnorm(n, rep(0,p), CovMatrix)
y <- 3*x[,1] + 5*rnorm(n)

# Fit models
library(glmnet)
fit.enet <- glmnet(x, y, family="gaussian", alpha=.2)
plot(fit.enet, xvar="lambda",label=TRUE)
abline(a=0,b=0)
```

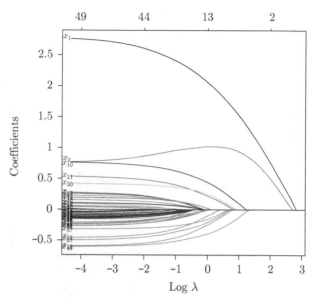

Fig. 10.5. Another elastic net output from R.

Notice how x_1 entered the model first, as expected, followed quickly by x_2 because of the high correlation between x_1 and x_2. For large values of the tuning parameter, the signal of x_1 is almost equally divided between x_1 and x_2.

Extension to GLMs

The extension from penalized linear regression to penalized GLMs is straightforward. For penalized GLMs, the coefficients are obtained by solving the following equation:

$$\widehat{\beta}_{\text{Penalized}} = \arg \min_{\beta} [-\log\{L(y;\beta)\} + \lambda \cdot J(\beta)]$$

where $L(y;\beta)$ is the likelihood function corresponding to the generalized linear model under consideration. One of the main differences between the linear regression case and the more general case of generalized linear models is that the optimization problem is harder and slower to solve in the general case. However, many algorithms have been developed to solve this problem.

Fitting the Elastic Net in R

There are several packages available in R to obtain the solution for the elastic net problem, including `glmnet`, `elasticnet`, and `penalized`, to name a few. Glmnet is written by Jerome Friedman, Trevor Hastie, Noah Simon, and Rob Tibshirani. The package includes efficient procedures for fitting the entire elastic net regularization path for linear, logistic, multinomial, and Poisson regression models as well as the Cox model. `Glmnet` is used in all examples in this chapter.

References

Guillén, M. Regression with categorical dependent variables. In E. W. Frees, G. Meyers, and R. A. Derrig (eds.), *Predictive Modeling Applications in Actuarial Science: Volume 1, Predictive Modeling Techniques*, pp. 65–86. Cambridge University Press, Cambridge, 2014.

Hoerl, A. Application of ridge analysis to regression problems. *Chemical Engineering Progress*, 58: 54–59, 1962.

Hoerl, A., and R. Kennard. Ridge regression: An application to nonorthogonal problems. *Technometrics*, 12: 69–82, 1970.

Ismail, N., and A. A. Jemain. Handling overdispersion with negative binomial and generalized Poisson regression models. *Casualty Actuarial Society Forum*, Winter 2007.

Larsen, C. R. An individual claims reserving model. *Astin Bulletin*, 37(1): 113–132, 2007.

Mahon, J. B. Transition matrix theory and individual claim loss development. *Casualty Actuarial Society Forum*, Spring 2005.

Parodi, P. Triangle-free reserving: A non-traditional framework for estimating reserves and reserve uncertainty. *British Actuarial Journal*, 19(01): 168–218, 2014.

Tibshirani, R. Regression shrinkage and selection via the lasso. *Journal of the Royal Statistical Society, Series B*, 58(1): 267–288, 1996.

Weiss, S. M., N. Indurkhya, T. Zhang, and F. Damerau. *Text Mining: Predictive Methods for Analyzing Unstructured Information*. Springer, New York, 2004.

Williams, B., G. Hansen, A. Baraban, and A. Santoni. A practical approach to variable selection – a comparison of various techniques. *Casualty Actuarial Society E-Forum*, to appear.

Zou, H., and T. Hastie, T. Regularization and variable selection via the elastic net. *Journal of the Royal Statistical Society, Series B*, 67: 301–320, 2005.

11

Predictive Modeling for Usage-Based Auto Insurance

Udi Makov and Jim Weiss

Chapter Preview. Usage-based auto insurance, also known as UBI, involves analyzing data collected from policyholders' vehicles via telematics to help determine premium rates. Behavioral information considered includes vehicles' speeds, maneuvers, routes, mileage, and times of day of operation. UBI has been described as a potentially significant advancement over traditional techniques that rely on information such as policyholders' ages as proxies for how riskily they drive. However, because data collected via telematics are volatile and voluminous, particular care must be taken by actuaries and data scientists when applying predictive modeling techniques to avoid overfitting or nonconvergence and to improve predictive power. In this chapter, we use a case study to evaluate how modeling techniques perform in a UBI environment and how various challenges may be addressed.

11.1 Introduction to Usage-Based Auto Insurance

11.1.1 Background

Usage-based auto insurance, more commonly known as UBI, represents a significant evolution in automobile insurance pricing. The mathematical approaches underlying UBI rating plans do not differ significantly from those used historically, but the information utilized is much more granular, presenting unique challenges. Traditionally, automobile rating plans have considered data elements such as a vehicle operator's age, the type of vehicle, and the region in which the vehicle is garaged in a multivariate context to estimate expected losses. Those variables are generally considered as rough proxies for how responsibly the vehicle is operated or the types of traffic conditions to which it may be subject. Since the number of such proxies is typically relatively small (e.g., dozens), the ability to differentiate between high- and low-risk policyholders is limited, and cross-subsidies are to some extent unavoidable. In contrast, advanced UBI assesses risk factors more precisely using a large number of variables produced by in-vehicle technology called telematics.

Policyholders participating in UBI authorize their insurers to use telemetrically collected information such as (vehicles')speeds, maneuvers, times of day of operation, and routes to help determine premium rates in future policy periods. This information essentially allows for the extraction of a dynamic "safe driving resume" for each policyholder vehicle. Whereas a vehicle operator's age or the region where he garages his vehicle is fairly static, and may change once or not at all each policy period, the quantities associated with UBI are collected at intervals as frequent as dozens of times per second for advanced implementations. The resulting dataset for actuaries to consider has clear "big data" characteristics – a large volume of rows, a wide variety of columns, and observations occurring at high velocity. In this chapter we discuss how techniques such as variable selection and generalized linear modeling (GLM) may be employed in a manner that deals with the unique challenges presented by UBI data, and where supervised machine learning techniques such as decision trees may be deployed alongside GLMs to arrive at more parsimonious models.

11.1.2 Data Collectible via Telematics

Table 11.1 represents a single, sample driving record collected from a vehicle using telematics. Many UBI programs collect such information once or more per second for periods of 90 or more days per vehicle to determine an appropriate discount to be applied during subsequent policy period(s).

These data present several challenges, many of which are outside the scope of this volume. For instance, accelerometer readings occur along three axes, which are generally regarded as up-down ("bumps"), forward-backward ("acceleration and braking"), and left-right ("cornering"). However, not all data collection devices are oriented such that their accelerometers' z-axes are "up-down" (as indicated by the -1.00 g-force), and expressing readings homogeneously between vehicles is an exercise in

Table 11.1. *Sample Data Record Collected from Vehicle Using Telematics*

Data Element	Data Value
Vehicle identification number	1234567890ABCDEFG
Date	11/01/2015
Time (UTC)	02:06:34
Global Positioning System latitude	41.773312800000000000
Global Positioning System longitude	-87.715253500000020000
Avg. speed (MPH, since prior obs.)	21.30
Accelerometer axis x readings (g-force)	$\{0.00, 0.11, 0.21, 0.11, 0.05\}$
Accelerometer axis y readings (g-force)	$\{-0.21, -0.23, -0.26, -0.14, -0.01\}$
Accelerometer axis z readings (g-force)	$\{-1.00, -1.00, -0.99, -0.98, -0.99\}$
Odometer reading (miles)	18,246

linear algebra. For the purposes of this volume we will limit our discussion of such issues to advising the reader that significant homogenization is necessary to make telematics data "model ready,"including synchronizing information collected using different enabling technologies.

From here, the following are among the greatest challenges with respect to predictive modeling itself.

Depth. For the average vehicle, 90 or more days of data collection will result in well over 100,000 rows of data with observations taken more than once per second. In contrast the models we build will predict quantities such as the number of claims per policy period (i.e., claims frequency). This will require compressing the thousands of rows into essentially one row per vehicle, while sacrificing as little of the predictive value associated with each second-by-second observation as possible.

Complexity. From the preceding data, it is tempting to rely on the number of times a threshold is exceeded to make a prediction, which approach was characteristic of early UBI implementations. For instance, a "harsh braking" event may be defined as a backward g-force sufficient to inflict mild disturbance on passengers, or an "excessive speed" event may be defined as an instance of traveling more than 10 MPH above the legal speed limit. In fact there may be circumstances where such behaviors present minimal accident risk (e.g., on an open road in broad daylight), and less obvious behaviors such as "moderate braking" while traveling the legal speed limit- may present greater accident risk (e.g., coming to a stop alongside a narrow, poorly lit road at night). Therefore, to obtain the best models, one must enrich the threshold-based approach with a larger number of variables than is obvious in the raw telematics data and apply robust variable selection techniques.

Overlap. Many of the quantities from the preceding observation may be investigated effectively albeit less precisely using traditional auto insurance rating variables. For instance, an individual who garages her vehicle in an area with many traffic lights may experience a larger number of higher g-force braking events, or an individual aged over 75 may operate his vehicle more during midday than during standard rush hours or late night. Because of these overlaps, naively including telematics-based variables in one's models – either alone, or in a model where traditional rating effects are also included as predictors or offsets– is unlikely to yield markedly better results. Instead we should define modeling variables in a manner that reflects the full informational value of how each behavioral incident occurred.

An additional modeling challenge, *dimensionality*, will be described in the next subsection.

11.1.3 Modeling Objectives and Data Preparation

For the purposes of this chapter we define four types of driving events which are reasonably consistent with those most often considered in UBI practice: acceleration, braking, turning left, and turning right. We assume here that vehicle mileage, which is included in many UBI rating plans, is ascertainable by means other than telematics (e.g., vehicle inspection reports), and therefore build models that investigate solely the care with which the vehicle is operated in order to predict claim frequency. Because one desirable property of UBI is that it incentivizes safe driving behavior, we attempt to identify relationships with expected loss that reflect whether optimal decisions were made in each scenario, as opposed to the sheer riskiness of the circumstances to which the vehicle was exposed – which we assume is reflected elsewhere in an insurer's rating plan. Finally, we attempt to build models in a manner that avoids imposition of any a priori notions of safe driving behavior upon variable selection.

To accomplish these objectives, we define variables in the following manner:

- Each telematics-based observation is associated with external ("static") databases to provide greater context (e.g., the type of location, weather conditions). Data elements such as Global Positioning System (GPS) coordinates are used to establish the connections to the external databases.
- We define ranges of values for each of the external and telemetrically collected variables which reflect the context in which each maneuver occurred. For example, we may create ranges for time of day (e.g., the morning rush of 6:00 to 10:00) or number of lanes on the road being travelled (e.g., up to two, three or four, greater than four). These ranges are derived using a "reverse engineering" approach, in a manner aimed at increasing predictive power.
- For each driving behavior, binary bins are defined (e.g., whether a particular magnitude of maneuver occurred at each observation point) to allow for discrete classification.
- Multidimensional variables called *driving data variables* (DDV) are created out of the binary variables. For example, a DDV may correspond to the frequency of the following: tailgating in snowy weather, lane changing when the number of lane exceeds four, or wide variations in vehicle velocity while driving during rush hour.
- The DDVs, as well as exposure, are summed over all observations for each risk and then expressed as incidence rates (i.e., per mile of driving or per hour of driving).
- The range of values of each DDV incidence rate across all vehicles is considered, and scale factors are applied so that the ranges for each DDV are similar. This normalization improves the interpretability of coefficients deriving from our models, allowing them to be compared to determine the relative importance of model variables.

Such an approach generates an enormous number of candidate variables (on the order of 10,000) for each vehicle from which to consider when constructing predictive models, which is an additional challenge – of our own making, but in the authors' opiniona necessary one – to adequately represent behavioral patterns using telematics data. We have thus essentially solved the "longitudinal problems" inherent in our dataset by reducing each vehicle to a single row, but in the process we have created nearly infeasible number of columns for modeling. In the sections that follow we debate the appropriate model form to apply to these DDVs, as well as the pros and cons of different approaches for reducing them to a manageable number that offers best prediction. In this chapter we focus on claims frequency, but the methodological insights may also extend to severity.

11.2 Poisson Model for Usage-Based Auto Insurance

11.2.1 Data and Model Form

The quantity we will predict using the DDVs described in the previous section is the number of claims. For each vehicle in our data sample (of approximately 800 private passenger vehicles) we have access to up to five years of claims experience predating the telematics observation period, to accompany between 90 and 365 days of driving behavior data. Table 11.2 summarizes these data.

To train the models, we will use the first 90 days of driving for each vehicle; subsequent 90-day periods will be "held out" and used to validate our models. Not all vehicles in the data sample have five full years of claims experience, so we are inclined to select a dependent variable related to the number of claims (i.e. claims frequency) rather than the sheer absence or presence of a claim. This leads us toward using a generalized linear model (GLM) with Poisson error structure to describe the data. Poisson regression is a widely used form for frequency modeling, and employing it in a UBI setting has the benefit of comfort and familiarity for stakeholders such as insurance regulators with whom the resulting rating plans must often be filed and reviewed. ISO models based on techniques such as those described in this section have been acknowledged or approved by regulators in more than 40 states in the United States.

The Poisson approach represents a practical but imperfect error structure for modeling claim frequency in UBI and auto insurance in general. As discussed in Chapter 4 of Volume I, a tenuous assumption of the Poisson is that the "the mean and variance of the responses are the same, that is $E(y_i) = Var(y_i) = \mu_i$. In practice, this assumption is not always satisfied by the data, due to an effect of over-dispersion $(Var(y_i) > E(y_i))$." Ismail and Jemain (2007) note that one consequence of imposing the Poisson error structure in the presence of overdispersion may be an underestimate

Table 11.2. *Summary of Claims Experience Used to Develop Models*

Data Element	Data Value
Vehicles included	825
Vehicle years	3,030 (3.673 vehicle years per included vehicle)
Incurred claims	78 (2.574 per hundred vehicle years)
Vehicles with multiple claims associated	7 (10% of vehicles with claims)

of standard errors and, as a result, overstated significance of regression parameters. Using several case studies, they show that negative binomial and generalized Poisson models produce similar estimates for regression parameters but larger standard errors, which may impel the Poisson modeler to include an excessive number of parameters.

Basic empirical statistics suggest that overdispersion may be a problem in our dataset, as the sample variance for claim frequency is more than 10 times the sample mean. On the other hand, lower dispersion, if not underdispersion, may be more consistent with conventional wisdom regarding UBI, which is that – because insurance rates are more directly related to driving behavior than under a traditional approach – it tends to attract a more homogenous group of policyholders who are less accident prone. The negative binomial regression is not equipped to handle underdispersion.

While cognizant of its limitations, we have elected to utilize the Poisson error structure because it produces similar estimates to alternative approaches with relatively simpler mathematical formulae than those alternative approaches. We also found that the Poisson regression outperformed other approaches that utilized relatively simple mathematical formulae, such as logistic regression. In subsequent sections we investigate the possibility of applying machine learning techniques to supplement or replace the methods described here and arrive at a leaner set of parameters.

Given the selected approach, our claim frequency formula is represented in Formula 11.2.1.

Formula 11.2.1 Representation of formula resulting from Poisson regression

$$E(\text{claims}) = \exp \left\{ \sum_{j=1}^{J} \alpha\{j\} DDV1\{j\} + \sum_{k=1}^{K} \beta\{k\} DDV2\{k\} \right. $$
$$\left. + \sum_{m=1}^{M} \vartheta\{m\} DDV3\{m\} + \sum_{n=1}^{N} \varphi\{n\} DDV4\{n\} \right\}$$

In this equation, which is a regression function of the logarithm of E (claims), θ represents the model's intercept term. J, K, M, and N represent the respective number of subclassifications within each family of DDVs of type 1, 2, 3, and 4, respectively, and α, β, ϑ, and φ are the modeled coefficients for these families of DDVs. The estimated quantity is the number of *Claims* occurring over a fixed period.

11.2.2 Variable Selection

Standard stepwise variable selection approaches associated with Poisson regression are often incapable of effectively handling as many variables as are generated by our

```
4257   proc hpgenselect data=week1;
4266      model NORM_CLAIM_5=      DDV_1_1 DDV_1_10 DDV_1_11 DDV_1_12 DDV_1_13 DDV_1_14 DDV_1_2
4266! DDV_1_3 DDV_1_4 DDV_1_5
4267   DDV_1_6 DDV_1_7 DDV_1_8 DDV_1_9 DDV_2_1 DDV_2_10 DDV_2_11 DDV_2_12 DDV_2_13 DDV_2_14
4267! DDV_2_2
4268   DDV_2_3 DDV_2_4 DDV_2_5
4271
4272          / Distribution=Poisson;
4273      selection method=stepwise /Choose p-value for stepwise/ details=Steps;
4274   run;
NOTE: The HPGENSELECT procedure is executing in single-machine mode.
NOTE: Convergence criterion (ABSGCONV=1E-7) satisfied.
NOTE: There were N observations read from the data set WORK.UBIDATA.
NOTE: PROCEDURE HPGENSELECT used (Total process time):
      real time            1:01:17.28
```

Fig. 11.1. Sample successful SAS run on single machine for sample of 24 acceleration DDVs.

method. For instance, in our case, the SAS procedure HPGENSELECT produces an unacceptably large number of variables which validate poorly.[1] On the other hand, functions such as "step" in R lack the benefit of considering significance at the individual variable level, instead optimizing the set of selected variables based on relative informational statistics such as the Akaike information criteria (AIC). (One advantage of AIC is that it reflects a "parameterization penalty" that helps prevent overfitting.) While stepwise and similar procedures have received criticism for overreliance on standard errors that may be biased toward variable significance, such metrics, when taken with the appropriate degree of circumspection, provide strong understandability benefits when later presenting a list of arrived variables to stakeholders such as insurance regulators. Meanwhile, Famoye and Rothe (2001) have found that stepwise-like techniques function acceptably in practice despite being computationally rigorous for the software packages that execute them. Therefore, in selecting variables, we seek to utilize stepwise selection to the extent possible.

To circumvent the limitations of our software, a relatively small number of variables (less than a hundred) are initially sampled thematically from the thousands of candidates. These variables are then run through a traditional (backward) stepwise procedure to detect the optimal subset (see Figure 11.1 for sample code in SAS). The procedure is repeated for another selected set of variables, and another, and so on. The plurality of 535 selected variables across the samples are then assembled and run together through a final stepwise procedure. The 57 "surviving" most significant variables form the basis for our Poisson regression.

---

[1] For instance, using the AUC approach described in the next subsection, our resulting models achieved an unacceptable "area under the curve" statistic of 59% using approximately 35 more variables than the approach we ultimately utilized.

11.2.3 Validation

After arriving at a model we evaluate the posited relationships with expected claim frequency for reasonability. The DDVs with the largest positive and negative coefficients are considered for whether they represent poor and excellent operation of the vehicle. Werner and Guven (2007) note that a "major mistake companies make . . . is is blindly implementing results without applying appropriate judgment. A quick review of the rating pages of various companies will often uncover patterns in relativities that often make no sense." In our case the DDVs that indicate the exercise of caution (e.g., mild to moderate lane changing) in congested traffic tend to decrease the prediction, while DDVs reflecting harsh maneuvering in situations where more control of the vehicle is necessary, or tailgating in times and places where other vehicle operators may not be expecting such maneuvers, tend to increase the prediction. This qualitative validation, which relates to our modeling objective of inputting a rating structure that incentivizes safer driving behavior, is supplemented with a number of quantitative validations.

Statistical significance. By dividing the coefficient by the standard error, we are able to calculate a "z-score" for each DDV. We then evaluate the probability of a having an experimental result equal to the one observed, or of greater magnitude, on a standard normal distribution. One interpretation is that, if our null hypothesis is that the variable is not significant (i.e., its coefficient should have been zero, implying the corresponding variable has negligible impact on the number of claims), then this "p-value" is the support to the null hypothesis. Almost all the DDVs we select have associated p-values less than 1%, at which level we can safely reject the null hypothesis, which is assumed correct, and the few DDVs having slightly greater p-values are qualitatively investigated for the reasonability of the indicated relationship with loss as described above. Although p-values have a reputation as a preferred method of validation for stakeholders such as regulators, they have been criticized for a bias toward variable significance. Further research presented in Section 11.3 lends credence to this theory. Therefore, for the purposes of the model in question, we perform additional validations to gain greater confidence in the predictions.

11.2.4 Holdout Driving Period

The remaining validation is this chapter is performed on a holdout driving period. That is, for the same set of vehicle operators whose data are used to train our model, we execute the models based on a different period of ninety days of driving (than was used for training). Given the enormous number of DDVs tested, this type of validation is critical to obtaining a comfort level that the models are not overfit to include nonrecurring, vehicle-specific events whose presence is limited to the original 90 days (of driving) used to train the model. An ideal validation would also consider how the model performs on vehicles not used in training the model. However, given the relatively small data sample discussed in this chapter, we elected to train the models using all available vehicles' data.[2]

ROC curves. ROC curves are useful tools for validating the performance of a predictive model. We calculate an ROC curve as follows. First, for any given threshold in a range of thresholds, we define the following:

- Risks with claims that have predictions exceeding the threshold are "true positives";
- Risks without claims that have predictions exceeding the threshold are "false positives";
- Risks with claims that have predictions below the threshold are "false negatives"; and
- Risks without claims that have predictions below the threshold are "true negatives."

The use of thresholds allows for a binary interpretation of the Poisson regression's predictions, even though the Poisson distribution itself predicts claim frequencies.

We next calculate the false positive rate and the true positive rate for the data. For instance, if the threshold is very large (approaches infinity), then the false positive rate (FPR = false positives divided by the sum of false positives and true negatives) will be zero, because there are no positives. For that same reason the true positive rate (TPR = true positives divided by the sum of true positives and false negatives) will also be zero. In contrast, if the threshold is very small (approaches zero), then both the TPR and FPR will be 100% (since there are no negatives). By plotting all possible TPR and FPR combinations as a curve, one can estimate the improvement over a naive approach where TPR and FPR increase at an equivalent rate. (If our model is effective, we expect TPR to increase at a faster rate than FPR as the positive threshold decreases.) The area under the ROC curve ("AUC") is used to validate model lift in the rest of this chapter. Figure 11.2 displays the ROC curve for our model.

AUCs' primary value are often thought to be in comparative analyses (e.g., does incorporating new information into the prediction result in a higher AUC index than before doing so?), and they will indeed be used for this purpose in Sections 11.3 and 11.4. There is no consensus in property and casualty insurance for what in and of itself constitutes an "acceptable" AUC. In the medical sector, there are general guidelines for acceptability whereby an AUC above 60% is required to justify a particular test.[3] Our Poisson model's AUC of 62% survives this standard, but – as will be shown in Section 11.4 – so does a model based solely on traditional rating variables. Particularly in instances like this, where one is devoid of a "clear win" on AUC, one should consider a range of other qualitative and quantitative metrics including but not limited to the ones in this chapter. Moreover, because AUCs have limited interpretability, they

---

[2] In a sense, we applied a random selection procedure on the predictor variables, but the dependent variables remaining unchanged in the validation setting.

[3] Tape (undated), http://gim.unmc.edu/dxtests/ROC3.htm.

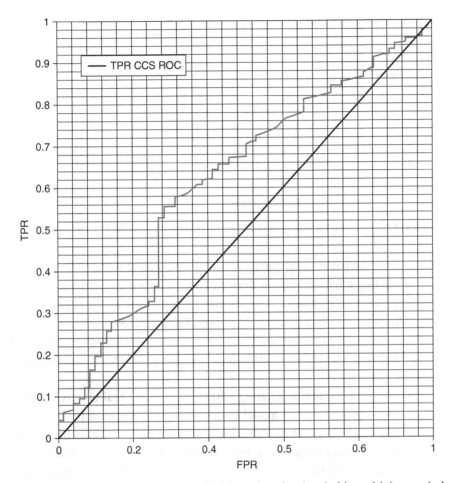

Fig. 11.2. ROC curve for Poisson GLM produced using holdout driving period (AUC = 62%).

are a less than ideal validation tool when presenting a model to stakeholders, particularly ones lacking strong technical background (as may be the case for regulators) and who may be more accustomed to conversing in quantities such as loss ratio.[4]

Loss ratio charts. In Section 11.1 we note overlap as a challenge of modeling for UBI. That is, many of the risk factors described by telematics data are already accounted for by proxy – albeit not as precisely – in a traditional rating plan. When we construct our models, we wish to investigate the "pure" relationships between driving safety with expected claim frequency and therefore do not include variables such as operators' age or gender in the models, either as direct effects or as offsets. We

---

[4] The difference between *p*-value and AUC validation is emblematic of the differences between explanatory and predictive modeling. For more information, see Shmueli (2010), http://arxiv.org/pdf/1101.0891.pdf.

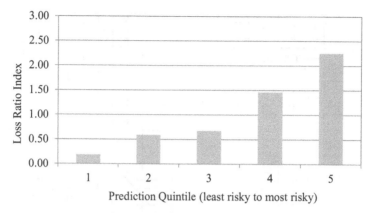

Fig. 11.3. Loss ratio quintile plot for Poisson model using holdout driving period.

hypothesize that the variation of claims frequency is so great within, say, a given operator age group that minimal value is derived from adding the traditional effects. (We test this hypothesis in Section 11.4.) This may be supported by the apparent overdispersion of our dataset in the aggregate. However, Sellers and Shmueli (2013) comment that the observed level of dispersion is not always reliable and may be the result of a mixture of dispersion levels in the data, and in future research we will further investigate this possibility.

Whether or not the traditional rating variables capture "real effects," a desirable property of the claim frequency model is that the results are multiplicative with the present rating plan. Our model runs the risk of this not being the case because it only predicts claim frequency (essentially assuming that the safety of vehicle operation is not predictive of severity) and is fit using only DDVs. Loss ratio charts are one method of addressing such concerns because they investigate not only the model's ability to predict claim frequency but also the additional predictive benefit provided on top of a traditional rating plan. Such charts are prepared as follows. As with the AIC method, all of the vehicles in the sample are "scored" using a different 90 days of driving than was used to train the model. The vehicles are then sorted from lowest to highest predicted claim frequency and divided into five equally sized groups or "quintiles." Within each quintile we calculate the loss ratio as the five-year losses for the period preceding the telematics observation period are divided by the corresponding five-year premiums (which consider the effects traditional factors). These results are plotted in Figure 11.3.[5]

Figure 11.3 shows that loss ratios increase steadily as our model predicts higher frequencies, with the models essentially identifying the riskiest 20% of vehicles

---

[5] Loss ratios are expressed relative to the average loss ratio for all vehicles combined to mask the loss characteristics of the underlying modeling dataset, which is proprietary.

(rightmost column) whose loss ratios are more than ten times that of the least risky 20% (leftmost column), even after traditional rating plan effects are considered by the denominator of the loss ratio.

11.3 Classification Trees

11.3.1 Introduction to Machine Learning for UBI

Section 11.1 of this chapter identifies dimensionality as a key challengein predictive modeling UBI using the DDV approach we expose. Section 11.2 then describes iterative stepwise selection techniques we developed to help deal with the large number of candidate variables. In contrast, Chapter 11 of the first volume suggests unsupervised learning techniques such as principal components analysis (PCA) can play a powerful role to reduce the number of input parameters in a supervised analysis. Such approaches ostensibly serve the principle of parsimony, that is, that the simplest possible solution that explains the data is preferred. However, whereas PCA can be effective in expressing large numbers of candidate variables in orthogonal linear combinations, reducing the number of candidate variables to a GLM, by so doing, it detracts from the understandability sought by our creating DDVs.[6] In this section we evaluate decision classification and regression trees (CART) as an alternative method of dimension reduction, and also (as an alternative) for the GLM itself. The CART approach has the benefit of maintaining more of the appearance and interpretability of the original DDVs when reducing dimensions.

There are a variety of algorithms that produce classification trees, but for the most part they are similar and may be classified as inductive learning techniques. To begin, a statistical test is specified, which is used how to determine which decision is optimal at each step of the process (e.g., minimize chi-squared error). The algorithm then identifies the one candidate variable, known as "the root," which is most significant in the specified regard, and partitions or "branches" the dataset into two homogenous groups according to the values of that variable. The exercise is then repeated for the two homogenous groups, known as "nodes," and then for the resulting four "nodes," and so on, until constraints specified by the user are achieved (e.g., maximum number of terminal nodes or "leaves"). The approach is classified as "greedy" in that it is stepwise optimal. "Pruning" algorithms are available that "look back" and eliminate nonsignificant leaves.

The data collected via telematics are ostensibly well suited for tree-type analysis. Mitchell (2007) posits several characteristics of problems that are appropriate for "decision tree" learning. First is that instances may be described by a fixed set of

---

[6] Trees are also advantageous over PCA for variable selection because they are supervised and hence take into account the input-output relationship.

attributes and their values, which is certainly the case with our DDVs. Second is that the target function has a discrete set of values, which is true for our dataset. Neither of the first two conditions renders trees any better suited for our analysis than a Poisson regression. However, the third condition is that "disjunctive descriptions" may be required, for example, a vehicle that both pulls over in unexpected places and exercises appropriate caution whenever pulling over may not be as high or low risk as either of the two conditions in isolation may suggest. Such interactive relationships are challenging to build into GLMs. Mitchell's final conditions relate to "noisy" training data (sparse or variant), which accurately describes many of our DDVs. Credit risk is often identified as a solid candidate for decision tree learning, and all the different types of transactional information which could impact a credit decision are mathematically similar to DDVs.For a more detailed treatment of tree methods, see Hastie et al. (2009). In the next subsection we test the effectiveness of tree techniques on the telematics data.

11.3.2 Tree Construction and Outcomes

For our UBI machine learning exercise we utilize the function "*rpart*," which is contained in the RPART package in R. Based on limited testing, we were unable to achieve as strong results on holdout using analogous utilities in SAS Enterprise Miner, which presents a visual interface with which to conduct the exercise.[7] The default for *rpart* is to make decisions that optimize with respect to Gini impurity.[8] The minimum possible complexity parameter of 0.01 is specified to minimize constraints on the algorithm and allow an elaborate tree. Using these inputs, we perform several tests to evaluate the extent to which machine learning can improve our predictive power.

Test 1: Tree applied to large set of DDVs. We begin by applying *rpart* to the same vehicles and 90 days of driving used to train our Poisson model. All 535 DDVs entered into our final stepwise selection procedure described in Section 11.2.2 are considered. A sample of the code used to produce the "tree" is represented in Figure 11.4, and the

```
tot <- rpart(NORM_CLAIM_5~DDV_1_14+DDV_1_25+... ... ... +DDV_6_4+DDV_6_11, UBIDATA, method
= "poisson" ,control=rpart.control(cp=0.01))
```

Fig. 11.4. Sample R code to perform decision tree analysis.

---

[7] To simplify the algorithm's decision-making criteria, we use *rpart*'s classification rather than its regression tree option, which is possible since our target variable of claim frequency over a fixed period is a discrete rather than a continuous one. The regression tree is intended for a continuous numeric outcome variable, but is computationally heavier.

[8] Gini impurity is a measure used in decision tree learning, which describes the extent to which the observations in a given tree node do not fall into a single target category.

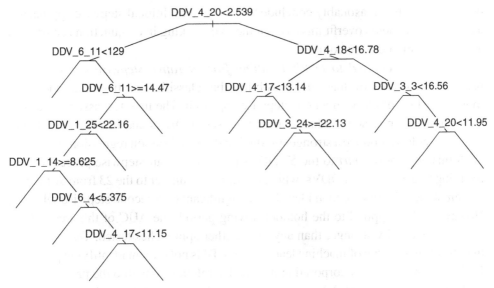

Fig. 11.5. Representation of tree construct produced using code in Figure 11.4 (illustrative only).

resulting construct is represented in Figure 11.5. Bramer (2002) and others have singled out tree algorithms for a predilection to overfit the datasets to which they are applied, for example, they may produce an excessive number of branches or generalize poorly to holdout datasets. Our tree does not appear to suffer from the former, as it contains only 23 DDVs (a relatively few 5 of which are identified by our stepwise procedure), compared to the 57 that survive the stepwise algorithm from above. However, when applied to the holdout driving period, the tree approach yields an inferior AUC of 58%, which is four points lower than our Poisson regression ("Test 0"). Therefore classification trees in and of themselves do not appear to be a viable alternative to our original model.

Tests 2 and 3: Poisson regression applied to DDVs identified by tree. We now consider the possibility that the tree from test 1 is in fact overfit. Using the 23 DDVs that emerge from the tree analysis, we refit our Poisson GLM, and the resulting prediction achieves an AUC of 62% when applied to the holdout driving data. This meets the acceptability threshold and demonstrates deterioration of only 1% compared to the full Poisson, which may also have been overfit or, at minimum, included an excessive number of marginal predictors. In fact, only 11 of the 23 DDVs were significant at the 5% level using our p-value criteria from Section 11.2.3. Since our tree appears to have identified several marginal variables, we perform a backward selection on the 23 DDVs identified in the decision tree and train our Poisson GLM for a third time on the reduced set of candidates. Eight DDVs are identified, and an AUC of 62% is again obtained on the holdout dataset, which is equal to that of the original model. Based on areas, one may reasonably conclude that either a traditional stepwise approach or a decision tree yields overfit models, but the two working in conjunction can produce a more parsimonious outcome.

Test 4: Tree applied to DDVs resulting from iterative stepwise approach. The previous three tests evaluate the possibility that classification trees may identify a more robust set of DDVs than our stepwise approach. The final test assumes our iterative stepwise approach produces an optimal set of DDVs and investigates whether the tree is able to produce a stronger prediction than the Poisson regression. To accomplish this, we apply *rpart* to the 57 DDVs that survive our stepwise procedure. The resulting tree contains 24 DDVs, which is similar in number to the 23 from test 1. Seventeen of these DDVs are then identified as significant by a second stepwise selection. However, when applied to the holdout driving period, the AUC of this tree is 66%, which is materially stronger than any of the other approaches tested. Test 4 suggests that the primary value of machine learning for UBI is not only in identifying predictive DDVs, but more so in incorporating disjunctive relationships into the prediction.

As noted in Section 11.2.3, while areas under the curve are a useful metric for comparative analyses, they may be more difficult to explain to stakeholders than more traditional metrics. Therefore, in addition, we ranked vehicles from lowest to highest prediction on the holdout driving period, divided them into three equally sized groups, and calculated claim frequencies (the predicted quantity). Here we consider claim frequency rather than loss ratio, which is considered in Section 11.2.3, because we are strictly evaluating the predictive power of each approach rather than how it may function in practice alongside other traditional rating variables. (The latter issue is further considered in Section 11.4.) Table 11.3 summarizes the results of all the different tests using both this and the area metric.[9]

Table 11.3. *AUCs and Tertile Claim Frequency using Holdout Driving Period (Machine Learning)*

Test	Variable Selection	Model Form	Index	Low 1/3	Mid 1/3	High 1/3	High to Low
0	Stepwise	Poisson Regression	62%	0.490	0.865	1.644	3.353
1	Tree	Tree	58%	0.577	1.038	1.385	2.400
2	Tree	Poisson Regression	62%	0.317	0.923	1.760	5.545
3	Tree then Stepwise	Poisson Regression	62%	0.721	0.808	1.413	1.960
4	Stepwise, Tree, Stepwise	Tree	66%	0.317	0.433	2.250	7.091

---

[9] Claim frequencies are expressed relative to the all vehicle average to mask the underlying loss characteristics of the underlying modeling dataset, which is proprietary. Note that further insight into the reliability of the various tools could be gained by bootstrapping the tests.

The approach of applying a classification tree to the outputs of our iterative stepwise procedure shows the strongest ability to differentiate high claim frequency versus low claim frequency vehicle operators.

11.4 Implementing UBI Models with a Traditional Rating Plan

All of the models described in this chapter predict claim frequency using DDVs alone. However, it is virtually unheard of for any UBI predictive model to be implemented as a standalone rating plan. UBI is typically offered to policyholders on an optional basis, and insurers thus far have shown minimal inclination to support categorically different rating plans for one segment of their overall auto business. Instead, UBI is typically implemented in the form of a multiplicative rating factor that is used alongside traditional ones such as age and gender. This is rational in the sense that such variables have proven over time to have predictive value. For instance, when we fit a Poisson regression on our dataset using different pluralities of traditional rating variables only, the model produces a maximum area under the curve of 62%, which is competitive with the DDV-based models we test in Section 11.3.2.[10] However, the traditional variables differentiate much less between the highest and lowest risk tertiles (maximum "high-low" quotient of 1.222) than the UBI models. Nevertheless, there seems to be enough value in (the traditional variables) that we wish to evaluate the most useful method to incorporate them into our predictions alongside DDVs.

Recall from Section 11.2.3 that our Poisson model based on DDVs alone identifies risk differences of up to 10 times on a loss ratio basis, that is, between risks otherwise deemed "identical" in a traditional rating plan. In this way the model's predictions may conceivably be used directly in a company's rating formula, for example, by discounting less risky operators within a specific vehicle operator classification by the amount indicated by the models. This is a very rudimentary example of "ensemble modeling" – a generic term for methods of combining the insights of multiple, independent predictive models into a single estimate for each risk. In the remainder of this section we will test other methods of combining the predictions to see if they produce superior results based on the metrics exposed in the previous section.

Had actuaries always had DDVs available to them, they may not necessarily have arrived at the same set of traditional variables or estimated effects as are in use as of the inception of UBI. Therefore one option to produce an ensemble estimate may be to reestimate the effects of each traditional variable in the presence of DDVs. For

---

[10] Note that since our holdout dataset consists of a different period of driving, as opposed to a different period of insurance coverage, there is not a true holdout dataset available for the traditional variables. Therefore, the area is not directly comparable to Table 11.3

Table 11.4. *AUCs and Tertile Claim Frequency using Holdout Driving Period (Ensemble Methods)*

Test	Approach	Area Under Curve	Claim Frequency			High Low
			Low 1/3	Mid 1/3	High 1/3	
5	Traditional Variables	62%	1.038	0.663	1.269	1.222
6	Traditional Variables + DDVs	67%	0.404	0.635	2.538	6.286

instance, the number of prior accidents of a vehicle operator may still be predictive of claims in the presence of DDVs, but the impact of this lagging indicator may be increased or decreased in the presence of leading indicators such as DDVs. That is, DDVs may detect some of the same underlying risk dynamics as accidents, reducing accidents' modeled effects, or they may render other proxies insignificant (e.g., age, gender), leaving an even stronger modeled effect for accidents. Meanwhile, a traditional variable such as insurance score (which reflects credit history) is often portrayed negatively due to its ambiguous causal connection to losses and is generally thought to be a proxy for responsibility. Its use is not even permitted for rating in a handful of jurisdictions. But insurance score may no longer be significant in the presence of DDVs. In this way, fitting traditional variables in the presence of DDVs is likely to result in the most interpretable combined implementation.

When we attempted to fit a model using the 57 DDVs resulting from our stepwise approach alongside traditional variables in the same Poisson regression, many of both types of variables (DDV and traditional) become insignificant. This is a desirable property because it improves the parsimony of the modeled solution. We were able to obtain an area under the curve of 67% and a high-low coefficient of 6.286, which is competitive with the strongest performing models displayed in Table 11.3. Table 11.4 summarizes the model evaluation metrics for the ensemble methods considered in this section.

11.5 Summary and Areas for Future Research

Telematics data collection provides auto actuaries with powerful new tools to differentiate between high and low risk policyholders, helping to address some of the realities of "cross-subsidy" which are present in traditional rating plans. UBI accomplishes this in a way that is intuitively appealing because of the perceived causal relationship between one's driving habits and his or her claims. However, newcomers to the UBI space should be mindful that the "Big Data" qualities of the telematics data present new challenges such as depth, complexity, redundancy, and dimensionality. These must be addressed through sensible data organization (such as our DDV approach) and deft variable selection in order for commonly used functions in statistical software packages to produce meaningful results. While common model constructs such as Poisson regression have interpretability benefits for presentation to stakeholders such as insurance regulators, techniques such as machine learning can also provide valuable insight, particularly as relates to the variable selection process.

Once a proposed model is arrived at, validation techniques should utilize independent holdout datasets to the extent possible (different driving and experience periods) and combine more theoretical metrics such as AUC with implementation-oriented analyses such as loss ratio charts. The ideal holdout would be an independent set of vehicles not used in model development at all. "Commonsense" evaluations of individual variables versus their coefficients are particularly useful for UBI to live up to its reputation as a tool that relates safe driving to reduce premiums when implemented in the form of a rating plan. Our initial research suggests that considering traditional variables alongside DDVs can produce an even stronger estimate than either approach in isolation.

The authors and their colleagues continue to explore advanced approaches to UBI modeling. Claim frequency models were considered in this chapter for illustration, but there is no reason to believe that the DDV approach proposed would not produce equally compelling insights when applied to claim severity. Also, UBI implementations take many approaches of which this chapter describes only one. While we sought to evaluate responsibility of vehicle operation by expressing DDVs as an incidence rate per unit of driving, "pay as you drive" (PAYD) UBI varies rates (either constantly or based on risk conditions) according to vehicle mileage. For such an implementation we may wish to alter the dependent variable to be claims per mile. Finally, we continue to explore which methods and models best describe the data. Mixed effects models may help address dispersion issues related to nonuniformity of UBI risks, while Lasso variable selection techniques hold strong potential for highly dimensional data such as ours.

Figure 11.3 suggests that differentiation on the order of 10 times ("all other things being equal") is possible with an advanced UBI approach such as the one described in this chapter. As increasing numbers of insurers embark on their UBI journeys, actuaries will be challenged to explore innovative techniques, including and beyond those considered in this chapter, to accurately differentiate risk and protect their companies from adverse selection.

Acknowledgments

The authors conducted this research as part of their employment with Verisk Analytics, which holds pending and issued patents related to UBI. While we have attempted to inform readers of essentials of predictive modeling for UBI, and the examples discussed in this chapter are illustrative, we have necessarily withheld key details or our approach where it may compromise Verisk's intellectual property.

The authors also wish to acknowledge Galit Shmueli for her valuable input and suggestions.

References

Bramer, M. Pre-pruning classification trees to reduce overfitting in noisy domains. *Intelligent Data Engineering and Automated Learning – IDEAL 2002 Lecture Notes in Computer Science*, 2002.

Famoye, F., and D. E. Rothe. Variable selection for Poission regression model. *Proceedings of the Annual Meeting of the American Statistical Association*, 2001.

Frees, E. W., G. Meyers, and A. D. Cummings. Insurance ratemaking and a Gini index. *Journal of Risk and Insurance*, 81(2): 335–366, 2010.

Hastie, T., R. Tibshirani, and J. Friedman. Additive models, trees, and related methods. In *The Elements of Statistical Learning*, pp. 295–334. Springer, Stanford, 2009.

Ismail, N., and A. A. Jemain. Handling overdispersion with negative binomial and generalized Poisson regression models. *CAS E-Forum*, Winter 2007.

Mitchell, T. M. Decision tree learning. In *Machine Learning*. McGraw-Hill, New York, 2007.

Schafer, J. The negative binomial model. In *Analysis of Discrete Data*. Pennsylvania State University, State College, PA, Spring 2003.

Shmueli, G. To explain or predict? *Statistical Science*, 25(3): 289–310, 2010.

Sellers, K. F., and G. Shmueli. Data dispersion: Now you see it . . . now you don't. *Communications in Statistics: Theories and Methods*, 42(17): 3143–3147, 2013.

Sellers, K. F., and G. Shmueli. A flexible regression model for count data. *The Annals of Applied Statistics*, 4(2): 943–961, 2014.

Tape, T. G. The area under an ROC curve. In *Interpreting Diagnostic Tests*. University of Nebraska Medical Center, Omaha, NE, n.d.

Werner, G., and S. Guven. GLM basic modeling: Avoiding common pitfalls. *CAS E-Forum*, Winter 2007.

Index